Tourism Governance

The role of governance has only recently begun to be researched and discussed in order to better understand tourism policy making and planning, and tourism development. Governance encompasses the many ways in which societies and industries are governed, given permission or assistance, or steered by government and numerous other actors, including the private sector, NGOs and communities.

This book explains and evaluates critical perspectives on the governance of tourism, examining these in the context of tourism and sustainable development. Governance processes fundamentally affect whether – and how – progress is made toward securing the economic, socio-cultural and environmental goals of sustainable development. The critical perspectives on tourism governance, examined here, challenge and re-conceptualise established ideas in tourism policy and planning, as well as engage with theoretical frameworks from other social science fields. The contributors assess theoretical frameworks that help explain the governance of tourism and sustainability. They also explore tourism governance at national, regional and local scales, and the relations between them. They assess issues of power and politics in policy making and planning, and they consider changing governance relationships over time and the associated potential for social learning. The collection brings insights from leading researchers, and examines important new theoretical frameworks for tourism research.

This book was originally published as a special issue of *Journal of Sustainable Tourism*.

Bill Bramwell is Professor of International Tourism Studies at Sheffield Hallam University, UK. He is co-founder and co-editor of the *Journal of Sustainable Tourism*, and he has published widely on tourism policy and planning, tourism development in differing economic and political contexts, and sustainable tourism.

Bernard Lane is Visiting Research Fellow at Sheffield Hallam University, UK, and co-founder and co-editor of the *Journal of Sustainable Tourism*. He is a consultant on sustainable tourism development and management with extensive experience in Europe, Asia and Australia at national, regional and local levels.

Tourism Governance

Critical Perspectives on Governance and Sustainability

Edited by
Bill Bramwell and Bernard Lane

LONDON AND NEW YORK

First published 2012
by Routledge
2 Park Square, Milton Park, Abingdon, Oxon, OX14 4RN

Simultaneously published in the USA and Canada
by Routledge
711 Third Avenue, New York, NY 10017

Routledge is an imprint of the Taylor & Francis Group, an informa business

This book is a reproduction of the *Journal of Sustainable Tourism*, vol. 19, issue 4-5. The Publisher requests to those authors who may be citing this book to state, also, the bibliographical details of the special issue on which the book was based.

British Library Cataloguing in Publication Data
A catalogue record for this book is available from the British Library

ISBN13: 978-0-415-58771-6

Typeset in Times New Roman
by Taylor & Francis Books

Disclaimer
The publisher would like to make readers aware that the chapters in this book are referred to as articles as they had been in the special issue. The publisher accepts responsibility for any inconsistencies that may have arisen in the course of preparing this volume for print.

Contents

CONTENTS

Notes on Contributors

Bill Bramwell is Professor of International Tourism Studies at Sheffield Hallam University, UK. He is co-founder and co-editor of the *Journal of Sustainable Tourism*, and he has edited books on tourism's relationships with partnerships, sustainability in Europe, rural development, and coastal areas in Southern Europe. His research interests include tourism policy and planning, tourism development in differing economic and political contexts, tourism and environmental politics, governance processes in tourism, and the application of political economy approaches to tourism development.

Dianne Dredge is Associate Professor in the School of Tourism and Hospitality Management at Southern Cross University, Australia. She combines work as an environmental planner, tourism academic and practitioner. She researches and publishes in the areas of tourism policy and planning, regional development, place-based planning, management of tourism places and tourism organisations.

Rosaleen Duffy is a Professor of International Politics at the University of Manchester, UK, following earlier work at the Universities of Lancaster and Edinburgh. She is primarily interested in political ecology, the global politics of conservation, the environmental impact of criminalisation and the politics of tourism. She has written extensively on those subjects and their links to eco-tourism, community-based tourism, neo-liberalism, conservation and protected areas.

Alison M. Gill is a Professor with a joint appointment in the Department of Geography and the School of Resource and Environmental Management, Simon Fraser University, Vancouver, Canada. Her research interests lie in tourism planning and the transformation of place, especially in mountain resort destinations.

C. Michael Hall is a Professor in the Department of Management, University of Canterbury, New Zealand; Docent in the Department of Geography, University of Oulu, Finland; and Visiting Professor in the School of Business and Economics, Linnaeus University, Kalmar, Sweden. He also holds positions at the Sheffield Business School, Sheffield Hallam University, UK, and the School of Tourism and Hospitality Management at Southern Cross University, Australia. He has wide-ranging interests in tourism, regional development, environmental history and change, and gastronomy. Michael is the author or editor of over 55 books as well as author of over 350 journal articles and book chapters.

Freya Higgins-Desbiolles is a Lecturer in Tourism in the School of Management of the University of South Australia. She holds degrees in politics and international relations, and she has worked for various development-related NGOs. Her research examines the concerns of "host" communities, tourism impacts, indigenous tourism and justice through tourism. She recently worked with indigenous Australian communities and Palestinians on projects fostering the use of tourism for community benefit. She has advised the Ecumenical Coalition on Tourism, and she is an executive committee member of the Responsible Tourism Network and the International Institute for Peace Through Tourism (Australian chapter).

Tazim Jamal is an Associate Professor in the Department of Recreation, Park and Tourism Sciences, Texas A&M University, USA. Her main research areas are community-based tourism planning, collaborative processes for sustainable development, and theoretical as well as methodological issues related to tourism and sustainability.

Bernard Lane is Visiting Research Fellow at Sheffield Hallam University, UK, and co-founder and co-editor of the *Journal of Sustainable Tourism*. As well as undertaking sustainable tourism research, he is a consultant on sustainable tourism development and management. He has extensive experience in Europe, Asia and Australia at national, regional and local levels. Clients have included the OECD, the EU, government agencies in the UK, Australia, Canada, Ireland and Japan, along with numerous local government organisations, communities and NGOs.

Sarah Li, formerly a Research Associate at the University of Tasmania, Australia, is an independent consultant specializing in China tourism development, policy and planning. Dr. Li has participated in more than 30 policy, planning and research assignments in China in the past 10 years and has compiled more than 50 refereed journal articles, book chapters, conference papers and reports on China.

Lorraine Moore was a Post-doctoral Researcher at the University of Manchester, UK. She is now an independent researcher affiliated with Manchester University; she has written on conservation and elephant management in Namibia, Thailand and Botswana.

Gianna Moscardo is a Professor in the Faculty of Law, Business and Creative Arts at James Cook University, Australia. She was previously the Project Coordinator with the CRC Reef Research, managing research and extension activities enhancing tourism's sustainability in northern Australia. Her qualifications in applied psychology and sociology support her research interests in understanding how tourists make decisions, evaluate their travel experiences and respond to interpretation. She has authored or co-authored over 130 internationally refereed academic publications, including two books on interpretation. She is a Fellow of the UNWTO's International Academy for the Study of Tourism.

Trevor Sofield is Professor of Tourism at the University of Tasmania, Australia, and is also a Research Professor with the Center for Tourism Planning and Research, Sun Yat Sen University, Guangzhou, China. Dr. Trevor Sofield has participated in more than 30 policy, planning and research assignments in China in the past 10 years and has compiled more than 50 refereed journal articles, book chapters, conference papers and reports on China.

E. Melanie Watt is the Executive Director of the Biosphere Institute of the Bow Valley in Canmore, Canada. She is also a Lecturer in the Department of Biological Sciences at the University of Calgary in Alberta, Canada. Her work focuses on community sustainability and ecological integrity.

Michelle Whitford is a Lecturer in the School of Tourism and Hospitality Management at Southern Cross University, Australia. She has research interests in the development, implementation and evaluation of tourism and events, public policy and indigenous tourism and events. Other research interests include sponsorship and events, indigenous events as vehicles for regional development, capacity building and indigenous events, indigenous event tourism attendance and public and private funding of indigenous event tourism.

Peter W. Williams is a Professor in the School of Resource and Environmental Management at Simon Fraser University in Vancouver, Canada, where he is the Director of the Centre for Tourism Policy and Research. His research interests are tourism policy, planning and management issues, especially strategies that lead to more sustainable use of natural and cultural resources.

Meredith Wray is a Senior Lecturer in the School of Tourism and Hospitality Management at Southern Cross University, Australia, and is actively engaged in tourism research. Her research work focuses primarily on tourism policy, planning, sustainable destination management, marketing and development. Meredith completed a Sustainable Tourism Cooperative Research Centre (STCRC) PhD scholarship in 2006 and was awarded the STCRC Award for Excellence in PhD research in 2007. She is actively involved in tourism planning and has led a major STCRC research project entitled "Sustainable Regional Tourism Destinations Project", examining best practice principles for destination development, marketing and management involving 21 regional tourism destinations across Australia. She recently completed a 10-year strategic tourism plan for Broken Hill, in Outback New South Wales.

Anne Louise Zahra lectures in both tourism and hospitality at the University of Waikato, New Zealand. Her current research areas include tourism and hospitality education, tourism policy, tourism organisations, destination management, volunteer tourism, human resource management issues in hospitality, multi-paradigmatic research methodologies and the ontological and epistemological foundations of tourism and hospitality research.

INTRODUCTION

Critical research on the governance of tourism and sustainability

Bill Bramwell and Bernard Lane

Sheffield Business School, Sheffield Hallam University, Howard Street, Sheffield S1 1WB, UK

Tailored and effective governance is a key requirement for implementing sustainable tourism: it can enhance democratic processes, provide direction and offer the means to make practical progress. This introduction explains how the papers in this collection provide critical assessments of the theory and practice of tourism governance and sustainability. It argues that theoretical frameworks are crucial to research on the subject as they affect the issues examined and the policy recommendations made. Several papers in the collection focus on relevant theoretical frameworks and concepts, while others consider governance at different geographical scales and the interconnections between those scales. The temporal dimensions of governance are also explored because sustainable development relates to long time horizons. Governance is also considered in relation to trade-offs, policy failures, learning processes, adaptive management, the public sphere and the principle of subsidiarity.

Introduction

This collection of papers examines the governance of tourism and sustainability. In the tourism literature, the term governance is used less frequently than the related terms of tourism politics, policy, policy-making and planning, and destination management (Dredge & Jenkins, 2007; Hall, 1994, 2008; Hall & Jenkins, 1995). While there seem to be differences between each of these terms and their tourism-related activities, they also overlap to varying degrees. For example, both planning and policy in tourism involve political debate about what the agenda is, what the issues are, who is involved or affected and the alternative courses of action that are available. The idea of governance includes within its compass all of these more established terms and activities. An understanding of these tourism activities can be enhanced by drawing on ideas from the rapidly expanding social science literature on governance (Kooiman, 2003; Rhodes, 1997). This literature often emphasises how governance cannot be understood in isolation from its relationships with society, including the societal groups that seek to influence the governance processes.

There are many potential uses of the concept of governance, and this diversity of uses exceeds any attempt to offer a short yet comprehensive account (Ruhanen, Scott, Ritchie, & Tkaczynski, 2010). Governance implies a focus on "systems of governing" and on the ways that societies are governed, ruled or "steered" (Bulkeley, 2005; Stoker, 1998). Governing systems provide means for "allocating resources and exercising control and co-ordination" (Rhodes, 1996, p. 653). Governance involves the processes for the regulation and mobilization of social action and for producing social order. According to Atkinson (2003, p. 103), governance involves processes "whereby some degree of societal order is achieved, goals decided on, policies elaborated and services delivered". The concept of governance is seen as broader than that of government, in recognition that often it is not just the formal agencies of government that are involved in governance tasks (Goodwin & Painter, 1996). Non-state actors that can be involved in governance include actors in the business, community and voluntary sectors.

The processes of tourism governance are likely to involve various mechanisms for governing, "steering", regulating and mobilizing action, such as institutions, decision-making rules and established practices. The forms of tourism governance can include hierarchical tiers of formal government, networks of actors beyond government, communities and also markets (Hall, 2011a). There are important power relations around tourism governance, with some groups in society, for example, having relatively more influence than others on the governance processes affecting tourism (Dredge & Jenkins, 2007; Hill, 1997). There can be significant conflicts around tourism governance as groups seek to secure their favoured policy decisions.

Tailored and effective governance is a key requirement for furthering the objectives of sustainable tourism in at least two senses. First, participation by a diverse range of actors in tourism decision-making potentially can enhance the democratic processes and ownership widely associated with sustainable development. At the local scale, for example, Mowforth and Munt (2009, p. 114) argue that "In the field of tourism, those who speak of sustainable development almost always include participation of the destination communities as one essential element or principle of that sustainability". Sustainable tourism also usually requires effective governance processes, adjusted to specific purposes and contexts, if it is to make progress towards securing the economic, socio-cultural and environmental goals of sustainable development. Such effective governance usually entails a need for appropriate institutions, decision-making rules and established practices. Subsequently, there is also a need to develop and apply suitable instruments to implement sustainable tourism. But governance guided by sustainable tourism objectives is likely to face major obstacles. These obstacles can arise, for example, because the concerns of sustainable tourism span numerous policy domains, many relevant policies are made in other policy domains and the relevant actors are diverse and have varied interests and priorities (Bramwell, 2011).

The papers in this collection assess aspects of the governance of tourism and sustainability. They show that a focus on governance can provide helpful insights into the issues related to tourism and sustainability. The contributions explore, first, some theoretical and conceptual frameworks that can assist in understanding the governance of tourism and sustainability. Second, some papers consider tourism governance at national, regional and local scales; one explores an example of how governance at the global scale can interact with local tourism practices. The third group of papers focuses on explaining temporal change in the governance of tourism and sustainability, and on social learning within such governance processes.

Two approaches to governance

It is helpful to recognise two distinctive approaches to conducting research on governance. The first approach considers the processes for governing, "steering", regulating and mobilizing social action that apply for the cases being studied (Bevir, 2009; Healey, 2006). The pattern of governing that arises may be led by government, but equally the state may play little or no role. In this approach, governance processes are likely to vary from case to case, but governance processes of some form will always be found. This general use of the governance concept enables researchers to explore the construction of social order, social coordination or social practices irrespective of their specific content and context.

The second approach considers that governance relates to specific trends in the roles and activities of the state in some countries following neo-liberal public sector reforms begun in the 1980s and 1990s (Bevir, 2009; Dredge & Jenkins, 2007; Shone & Memon, 2008). Typically, these reforms are said to have led to a shift from a hierarchical bureaucracy based on the state towards a greater use of networks beyond the state, as well as markets and quasi-markets. This use of the governance concept is firmly related to specific trends in the state's activities that are said to have occurred since the late twentieth century and particularly in certain countries.

Sustainable tourism

The papers here focus on the governance of sustainable tourism. The ideas behind sustainable tourism emerged earlier, but the term became popular following the release of the Brundtland Report (World Commission on Environment and Development, 1987). In that context, it is often defined as tourism that meets the needs of present generations without compromising the ability of future generations to meet their own needs. Sustainable tourism may be regarded most basically as the application of the sustainable development idea to the tourism sector. The paper by Hall (2011b) outlines key organising ideas behind the sustainable tourism policies of the United Nations' Environment Programme (UNEP) and World Tourism Organisation (UNWTO). Their policies focus on three dimensions or "pillars" of sustainable development, namely economic, social-cultural and environmental sustainability, and sustainable tourism is considered to involve striking a balance between these three dimensions. For Hall, the cornerstone of their sustainable tourism policy paradigm is the notion of so-called "balance".

There are varying views about sustainable tourism, however, as it is a socially constructed and contested concept that reflects economic interests, the ethical beliefs of different actors and the strength and effectiveness of various lobbies. Differing sustainable tourism concepts can be used by actors to achieve their socio-economic and political objectives. Weaver and Oppermann (2000, p. 353) suggest that "sustainable tourism is ... susceptible to appropriation by those wishing to pursue a particular political agenda". The varied viewpoints and continuing debates mean that it is becoming more widely accepted that the quest for a universally applicable definition of sustainable tourism will not be successful. There are critics, for example, of the UNEP and UNWTO view of sustainable tourism based on the notion of "balance" between economic, social and environmental issues. Cater (1995) argues that the language of "balance" can be misleading as economic growth through tourism will often conflict with environmental protection, with difficult "trade-offs" needing to be made between economic, social and environmental dimensions. Hunter (2002, pp. 10–11) also asserts that the idea of "balance" may be "used to mask the reality that economic growth is generally the primary concern". Hall (2011b) contends that in practice the so-called "balanced" approach results in continued economic growth. This may reflect a widespread pro-growth presumption within the present political–economic system. Thus, Harvey (2010, p. 27) indicates that "The current consensus among economists and within the financial press is that a 'healthy' capitalist economy, in which most capitalists make a reasonable profit, expands at 3 per cent per annum".

The sustainable tourism concept has become a key discourse through which tourism industry owners and managers, environmentalists, host communities, developers, politicians and academics frame certain tourism issues (Macnaghten & Urry, 1998). In liberal democracies, debates around disputed ideas such as sustainable tourism form an essential component of the political struggle over the direction of political and socio-economic development. Sustainable tourism has been useful in encouraging dialogue between individuals with different perspectives about tourism and its economic, social and environmental dimensions (Wall, 1997). The growing societal awareness of sustainable development issues has also helped to give prominence to the economic, environmental and socio-cultural problems connected with the tourism industry, although the evidence of continued growth in tourism's environmental impacts suggests that at best the practical achievements of sustainable tourism policies have been limited (Hall, 2011b). The burgeoning issues surrounding tourism's role in global warming and climate change have given new urgency to the sustainable tourism dialogue (Scott, 2011).

Critical perspectives

There is no single way to undertake "critical" research on tourism. The papers assembled here offer critical perspectives on the governance of tourism and sustainability, as suggested by the title of this collection. They challenge and re-conceptualise established ideas in the field, and thus they seek to advance conceptual thinking. In a discussion about innovation in sustainable tourism research, Liburd and Edwards (2010, p. 226) assert that "Critical thinking calls for an unrelenting examination of any form of knowledge . . . and underlying dogmas". Second, the contributions engage with theoretical frameworks from other social science fields, and this "permeability" across research domains provides new insights into tourism governance (Tribe, 2007).

Third, the papers provide assessments of the importance of interests, economic forces, power, institutional arrangements and governance processes; these are key aspects of society which interest researchers in many disciplines (Bianchi, 2009; Wilson, Harris, & Small, 2008). Finally, the authors present policy-relevant research, especially in relation to sustainable tourism policies, which potentially can help to improve society and reduce adverse environmental impacts. This policy relevance can also help to inform calls for social and political change and related action (Bramwell & Lane, 2006). Here, it should be noted that the collection provides numerous assessments of the practice of tourism governance. While there is discussion of prescriptive or normative approaches, these are grounded in assessments of what has actually happened and what has been more or less valuable in practice.

The organisation of the papers

Theoretical frameworks

The first four papers in the collection focus on identifying and assessing theoretical frameworks that explore and explain the governance of tourism and sustainability. Theoretical frameworks are crucial to research on tourism governance because they influence what is studied, how it is studied, the conclusions reached, the recommendations proposed as well as the political implications of the research.

Moscardo's (2011) paper examines the theoretical underpinnings behind the tourism policy and planning models found in the academic literature and in government and NGO guidelines. The diagrams used in these sources that visually summarise tourism policy and planning processes were subject to content analysis in order to assess their construction of knowledge. The diagrams are potentially important as they may indicate the social representations held by researchers and practitioners about how tourism should be managed and about whether and how destination residents should be involved in governance. Moscardo finds that the diagrams convey a hegemonic social representation that has altered little over the past two decades or more. She suggests that this social representation is rooted in business theory, that it encourages a reactive rather than proactive concern for sustainability and that it suggests that the core actors in tourism development processes are tourists, followed by external agents, tourism businesses and government actors. It also indicates that residents have at best a limited role in destination tourism policy and planning processes. It is argued that it is necessary to recognise this dominant social representation of tourism governance, to critically assess it in relation to potential alternative frameworks and to change it.

The importance of understanding the conceptual frameworks behind approaches to tourism governance is emphasised in the first of two papers by Hall (2011a). By creating a tourism governance typology, he shows how the tourism literature has not focused sufficiently on understanding how governance is conceptualised. He advocates a broad view of tourism governance that embraces a diversity of types of governance. A typology of frameworks of governance in western liberal democratic countries is presented. These models are based on the extent to which governance uses hierarchical forms of regulation and on the relative balance of power between the state and other policy actors. The paper discusses the resulting four modes of coordination: hierarchies, markets, networks and communities. Hall asserts that this typology can help researchers to understand key aspects of tourism governance in different contexts and can provide them with consistency in the concepts they use. The typology can also facilitate comparisons between policy choices and governance systems that affect tourism, as well as comparisons between governance in tourism and in non-tourism fields.

The potential benefits of using social theory in research on tourism governance are discussed by Bramwell (2011). The use of social theory from other fields of study can enrich research on tourism governance, and in turn the resulting research can contribute to debates about governance across the social sciences. Bramwell examines how one social theory, a strategic-relational political economy approach, offers insights into governance by the state that affects tourism and sustainability in destinations. This approach is examined through a literature review and through case studies taken from Germany, China, Malta, Turkey and the UK. There is discussion of how this political economy approach offers distinctive research perspectives on the governance of tourism and sustainability. These perspectives include the approach's holistic, relational and dialectical perspective, its focus on the state's roles in regulating the economic and political system and its concern to understand interactions between agency and structures in specific conjunctures. Other distinctive perspectives relate to the importance of spatial and temporal variations, the adaptation of state activities at different spatial scales and at different times, and the interpretation of path dependence and path creation.

Governance involves matters of collective concern and associated actions in the public sphere. Dredge and Whitford (2011) explore the multiple spaces in the public sphere where individuals and organisations discuss and debate public matters. They contend that assessments of tourism governance should consider how these spaces in the public sphere are constituted, by whom and for what purposes and interests. They use the case of the 2009 Australian World Rally Championship, held in the Northern Rivers region of New South Wales, to assess whether or not the different public spaces associated with this event facilitated discussions about sustainable tourism and whether or not these discussions informed the event's governance. They found that the instant creation of the institutional public sphere associated with this event, and the practices of the event organiser and state government, restricted both how and by whom key issues could be raised, and how they could be dealt with. The rapid speed of the process also inhibited actors from developing an awareness of the event's environmental and social impacts. While alternative public spheres emerged in opposition to the event that were characterised by activism and political protest, the actors involved in these alternative spheres generally lacked the resources to share their views.

National and regional governance

According to Williams (2009, p. 164), "The use of geographical scale is a particularly valuable device for drawing out key differences in emphasis and application within tourism planning", and this also applies for tourism governance. Governance occurs at different geographical scales, which may be transnational, national, regional or local. Because of widely differing situations in different places, the functions and activities of governance often vary within and also between the spatial scales. Although various geographic scales of tourism governance can be distinguished, these scales are interconnected rather than separate spheres (Hall, 2008). Geographical scale also has complex connections with sustainable tourism. Hall (2011b) notes, for example, how sustainability and environmental problems often cross geographical boundaries, with problems like climate change being global in scale. The issues around mobilising interest and action in response to sustainability problems may also vary between global and local scales. Included in this collection are papers that focus on tourism governance at national, regional and local scales, and one paper explores an example of how governance at the global scale can interact with local tourism practices.

The paper by Sofield and Li (2011) explores an evolving regime of governance and planning for tourism and sustainable development at a national scale. Their study of China adopts a holistic and multidisciplinary political economy perspective. They believe that this macro-level perspective enables them to appreciate how the governance of tourism and sustainability in China reflects the complex interactions between the nation's socio-political environment, economic structures, political institutions and cultural and philosophical heritage. Using this approach, Sofield and Li examine government interventions since the beginning of the "Open Door" policies of 1978 that allowed tourism development in China. Tourism has grown to become a major and multi-purpose "pillar industry" that includes economic, social, political and environmental contributions to national development. They consider how tourism policies have been affected in the last decade by government grappling with sustainability and structural issues. This has been influenced by the anthropocentrism and anthropomorphism inherent in the Chinese value systems derived from Confucian philosophy and Daoism. There have also been notable tensions between national policies encouraging sustainability and the problems that occur because economic development priorities are still dominant, particularly at the local scale.

Zahra (2011) examines regional-scale tourism governance in relation to subsidiarity as a normative principle of authority allocation. The principle of subsidiarity indicates that tasks should be accomplished by the lowest and most subordinate organisations that can do them, and that only in the case of failure is a larger or higher organisation justified in taking over these tasks. This principle is assessed in relation to Tourism Waikato, a regional tourism organisation (RTO) in New Zealand that before 2006 was supported by several local authorities. In 2006, a higher organisation, Hamilton City Council, withdrew its funding for this subordinate RTO because the RTO's branding conflicted with its own new image. Hamilton City Council took over tasks previously conducted by the subordinate RTO, and the RTO was disbanded. Zahra argues that the Council's actions contradict the principles of subsidiarity. She asserts that among RTO participants there should be a shift from interest based on self to an ethos of service to others, including to the wider community. Of course, the subsidiarity concept is contestable and affected by interests. Lafferty and Coenen (2001, p. 296), for example, suggest that in the case of subsidiarity in the European Union "What at first appears to be a clear-cut norm in favour of decentralisation emerges on closer investigation as a very elastic norm in favour of integrated, multi-level pragmatic governance".

Local and global–local governance

Higgins-Desbiolles (2011) evaluates government decisions concerning a development application to construct a tourist lodge at a pristine coastal site on Kangaroo Island in South Australia. The scheme was promoted as an "ecolodge" and as an ecotourism facility. She contends that, while ecotourism is credited with being a win–win option as it can create both development and conservation benefits, in practice trade-offs between development and the environment are often involved. It is argued that for the Kangaroo Island site government agencies allowed environmental protection to be traded-off in the pursuit of tourism development, income and employment. The agencies that focused on environmental protection at the site had much less influence on policymaking and policy outcomes than the government's more development-oriented organisations. Higgins-Desbiolles highlights the important point that decision makers in governance systems are likely often to focus on individual development proposals, potentially neglecting the bigger picture where impacts accrue incrementally and cumulatively. She urges a research agenda and also governance practices that fully recognise the cumulative macro-effects of numerous micro-level decisions; micro-level decisions can entail "death by a thousand cuts".

The potential roles of destination managers in taking educational and practical actions to engage residents and tourists in the management of sustainability within destinations are examined by Jamal and Watt (2011). They argue that destination organisations, including local government, national park authorities and destination marketing organisations, are often slow to inform citizens and tourists about conservation, managing resource use and climate change. There is an assessment of two NGO-facilitated initiatives to address sustainability and climate change through community-based social marketing and participatory local action in the mountain resort of Canmore in Canada. These initiatives directly involved local residents, short- and long-term visitors and also taxi drivers as key tourism-related actors. Jamal and Watt assess these initiatives in relation to Hannah Arendt's political theory of action. This theory indicates that the governance of tourism and sustainability in destinations should involve multiple participants and not just lie in the hands of a few. It should be a "performative" endeavour based on a flourishing public sphere of informed actors that are active creators of knowledge, understanding and action. Arendt also regards both contestation and consensus as potentially positive features of local democratic politics.

The paper by Duffy and Moore (2011) explores an example of how governance at the global scale can interact with local tourism practices. This is evaluated from a political economy perspective which asks who governs and who is governed, how are they governed and in whose interests and what are the implications for power and other relationships between the global and local scales? These questions are considered for the case of global NGOs concerned about the welfare of elephants used for trekking and safaris in tourist destinations within Thailand and Botswana. The NGOs have produced "expert" knowledge on good practices in elephant welfare and they seek to apply global standards across diverse locations. Duffy and Moore argue that attempts to establish global standards and regulation need to engage closely with local contexts and practices if the standards are to be acceptable and workable for actors in specific destinations. The NGOs often see elephants as "wild" animals, while local practices, especially in Thailand, value elephants as working animals. The NGOs can also fail to appreciate the genuine barriers to moving elephants out of tourism and into the wild, which are especially significant in Thailand. There are potential implications here for the governance of various environmental issues where global NGOs seek to have global standards applied in different localities.

Evolving and adaptive governance

Tourism governance often alters over time due to changing political contexts and other circumstances and as lessons are learnt from previous approaches and policies. Temporal trends in governance are especially important for sustainable development because its objectives relate to long time horizons. A significant trend in tourism governance is its growing emphasis on social learning, where actors share their knowledge, ideas and aspirations, and co-construct new visions and plans for action (Koutsouris, 2009). Social learning in governance has a temporal dimension when it is a continuing process that allows participants to react to changing circumstances and to learn lessons from evolving experience. Temporal changes in social and natural systems are often complex and unpredictable, and thus sustainable tourism planning is likely to be improved if it is flexible and adaptive (Bramwell & Pomfret, 2007; Liburd & Edwards, 2010). Miller and Twining-Ward (2005, p. 285) note that "adaptive management has been found to be a valuable technique allowing managers progressively to learn more about the systems they manage through trial and error, close stakeholder involvement and continuous monitoring". The last three papers in the collection focus on change in sustainable tourism governance and learning within governance processes.

Wray (2011) assesses whether the application of a planning approach based on interactions and shared learning among actors was successful in two destinations within New South Wales and Victoria in Australia. The approach involved a research team with expertise in sustainable tourism and participative planning working for a period of 2 years with local actors from government, business and the community. The research team sought to build a "transactive relationship" with the other participants, which brought together information, knowledge and skills from various actor perspectives, and developed mutual learning, a sense of ownership of the resulting policies and support for implementing those policies. Wray shows that the outcomes of the planning approach were different in the two destinations. The transactive planning process was largely successful where it had been assisted by a key state tourism organisation, and where local government had worked hard on relationship building. In the other destination, however, local government had been much less helpful, the actors were distrustful of local government and the final adopted plan did not fully represent the actors' views. Wray's findings suggest that efforts to foster learning and dialogue may be ineffectual if the main destination agencies are not committed to this approach.

The evolution of governance in the Canadian ski resort of Whistler is examined by Gill and Williams (2011). They use political economy and path dependence ideas to assess changes in the resort's development goals and governance system. Whistler's early pro-growth goals and management benefitted most actors because "development bonuses" from real estate projects provided residents with social and environmental benefits, creating a positive feedback that reinforced the established development path. Continued growth was allowed up to an agreed limit linked to an ambiguously defined environmental quality standard. Gill and Williams conclude that the resort's early regulatory system had "locked" development into a controlled growth path. Power remained with the same decision-makers who were still committed to growth up to an agreed capacity limit. When Whistler approached this capacity, however, a broad range of actors were included in developing an alternative governance model based on a fairly comprehensive and integrated sustainability strategy. Yet Gill and Williams suggest that Whistler has not abandoned its earlier pro-growth governance in favour of a more community-driven approach guided by sustainability principles. Instead, they identify a hybrid combination of these governance forms.

Hall (2011b) contends that among policy-makers there has been a failure to recognise that the claimed adoption of sustainable tourism objectives has not halted continued growth in tourism's contribution to environmental change. He suggests that sustainable tourism governance will be improved by considering the potential reasons for this "policy failure" and also how failures may be reduced. This requires "policy learning" based on previous and new experiences. Hall suggests that in practice much sustainable tourism policy learning has only been technical in nature, connected with adjustments to existing policy instruments, and he labels this as first-order governance change. At least some policy learning around sustainable tourism has concerned strategic changes, but within the existing policy paradigm of "balanced" sustainable development, and he labels this as second-order governance change. He argues, however, that there has been little progress among policy-makers in adopting third-order governance change, which is depicted as involving more profound shifts in the policy paradigm and goals, and which depends on conceptual learning. Thus, among policy-makers there is little sign of acceptance of a developing alternative sustainability paradigm based on ideas such as "degrowth", "steady state tourism" and "slow tourism".

References

Atkinson, R. (2003). Addressing urban social exclusion through community involvement in urban regeneration. In R. Imrie, & M. Raco (Eds.), *Urban renaissance? New Labour, community and urban policy* (pp. 101–119). Bristol: Policy Press.
Bevir, M. (2009). *Key concepts in governance*. London: Sage.
Bianchi, R. (2009). The "critical turn" in tourism studies: A radical critique. *Tourism Geographies, 11*(4), 484–504.
Bramwell, B. (2011). Governance, the state and sustainable tourism: A political economy approach. *Journal of Sustainable Tourism, 19*(4–5), 459–477.
Bramwell, B., & Lane, B. (2006). Policy relevance and sustainable tourism research: Liberal, radical and post-structuralist perspectives. *Journal of Sustainable Tourism, 14*(1), 1–5.
Bramwell, B., & Pomfret, G. (2007). Planning for lake and lake shore tourism: Complexity, coordination and adaptation. *Anatolia: An International Journal of Tourism and Hospitality Research, 18*(1), 43–66.
Bulkeley, H. (2005). Reconfiguring environmental governance: Towards a politics of scales and networks. *Political Geography, 24*(8), 875–902.
Cater, E. (1995). Environmental contradictions in sustainable tourism. *The Geographical Journal, 161*(1), 21–28.
Dredge, D., & Jenkins, J. (2007). *Tourism planning and policy*. Milton: Wiley.
Dredge, D., & Whitford, M. (2011). Event tourism governance and the public sphere. *Journal of Sustainable Tourism, 19*(4–5), 479–499.
Duffy, R., & Moore, L. (2011). Global regulations and local practices. The politics and governance of animal welfare in elephant tourism. *Journal of Sustainable Tourism, 19*(4–5), 589–604.
Gill, A., & Williams, P. (2011). Rethinking resort growth: Understanding evolving governance strategies in Whistler, British Columbia. *Journal of Sustainable Tourism, 19*(4–5), 629–648.
Goodwin, M., & Painter, J. (1996). Local governance, the crisis of Fordism and the changing geographies of regulation. *Transactions of the Institute of British Geographers, 21*, 635–648.

Hall, M. (1994). *Tourism and politics: Policy, power and place*. Chichester: Wiley.

Hall, M. (2008). *Tourism planning: Policies, processes and relationships*. Harlow: Pearson.

Hall, M. (2011a). A typology of governance and its implications for tourism policy analysis. *Journal of Sustainable Tourism, 19*(4–5), 437–457.

Hall, M. (2011b). Policy learning and policy failure in sustainable tourism governance. From first- and second-order to third-order change. *Journal of Sustainable Tourism, 19*(4–5), 649–671.

Hall, M., & Jenkins, J. (1995). *Tourism and public policy*. London: Routledge.

Harvey, D. (2010). *The enigma of capital and the crises of capitalism*. London: Profile.

Healey, P. (2006). Transforming governance: Challenges of institutional adaptation and a new politics of space. *European Planning Studies, 14*(3), 299–320.

Higgins-Desbiolles, F. (2011). Death by a thousand cuts: Governance and environmental trade-offs in ecotourism development at Kangaroo Island, South Australia. *Journal of Sustainable Tourism, 19*(4–5), 553–570.

Hill, M. (1997). *The policy process in the modern state*. Harlow: Pearson.

Hunter, C. (2002). Aspects of the sustainable tourism debate from a natural resources perspective. In R. Harris, T. Griffin, & P. Williams (Eds.), *Sustainable tourism: A global perspective* (pp. 3–23). Oxford: Butterworth-Heinemann.

Jamal, T., & Watt, M. (2011). Climate change pedagogy and performative action: Towards community-based destination governance. *Journal of Sustainable Tourism, 19*(4–5), 571–588.

Kooiman, J. (2003). *Governing as governance*. London: Sage.

Koutsouris, A. (2009). Social learning and sustainable tourism development; local quality conventions in tourism: A Greek case study. *Journal of Sustainable Tourism, 17*(5), 567–581.

Lafferty, W., & Coenen, F. (2001). Conclusions and perspectives. In W. Lafferty (Ed.), *Sustainable communities in Europe* (pp. 266–304). London: Earthscan.

Liburd, J., & Edwards, D. (2010). The future of sustainability. In J. Liburd, & D. Edwards (Eds.), *Understanding the sustainable development of tourism* (pp. 225–237). Oxford: Goodfellow.

Macnaghten, P., & Urry, J. (1998). *Contested natures*. London: Sage.

Miller, G., & Twining-Ward, L. (2005). *Monitoring for a sustainable tourism transition: The challenge of developing and using indicators*. Wallingford: CABI.

Moscardo, G. (2011). Exploring social representations of tourism planning: Issues for governance. *Journal of Sustainable Tourism, 19*(4–5), 423–436.

Mowforth, M., & Munt, I. (2009). *Tourism and sustainability: Development, globalisation and new tourism in the third world*. London: Routledge.

Rhodes, R. (1996). The new governance: Governing without government. *Political Studies, 44*, 652–667.

Rhodes, R. (1997). *Understanding governance: Policy networks, governance, reflexivity and accountability*. Buckingham: Open University Press.

Ruhanen, L., Scott, N., Ritchie, B., & Tkaczynski, A. (2010). Governance: A review and synthesis of the literature. *Tourism Review, 65*(4), 4–16.

Scott, D. (2011). Why sustainable tourism must address climate change. *Journal of Sustainable Tourism, 19*(1), 17–34.

Shone, M., & Memon, A. (2008). Tourism, public policy and regional development: A turn from neo-liberalism to the new regionalism. *Local Economy, 23*(4), 290–304.

Sofield, T., & Li, S. (2011). Tourism governance and sustainable national development in China: A macro-level synthesis. *Journal of Sustainable Tourism, 19*(4–5), 501–534.

Stoker, G. (1998). Governance as theory: Five propositions. *International Social Science Journal, 50*(155), 17–28.

Tribe, J. (2007). Critical tourism: Rules and resistance. In I. Ateljevic, N. Morgan, & A. Pritchard (Eds.), *The critical turn in tourism studies: Innovative research methodologies* (pp. 29–40). Oxford: Elsevier.

Wall, G. (1997). Sustainable tourism – Unsustainable development. In S. Wahab, & J. Pigram (Eds.), *Tourism, development and growth* (pp. 33–49). London: Routledge.

Weaver, D., & Oppermann, M. (2000). *Tourism management*. Milton: Wiley.

Williams, S. (2009). *Tourism geography. A new synthesis*. London: Routledge.

Wilson, E., Harris, C., & Small, J. (2008). Furthering critical approaches in tourism and hospitality studies: Perspectives from Australia and New Zealand. *Journal of Hospitality and Tourism Management, 15*, 15–18.

World Commission on Environment and Development (1987). *Our common future: The Brundtland report.* Oxford: Oxford University Press.

Wray, M. (2011). Adopting and implementing a transactive approach to sustainable tourism planning: Translating theory into practice. *Journal of Sustainable Tourism, 19*(4–5), 605–627.

Zahra, A. (2011). Rethinking regional tourism governance: The principle of subsidiarity. *Journal of Sustainable Tourism, 19*(4–5), 535–552.

Exploring social representations of tourism planning: issues for governance

Gianna Moscardo

School of Business, James Cook University, Douglas Campus, Townsville, Queensland, Australia

A major challenge for tourism as a social and economic activity and as an academic study is the integration of multiple perspectives into coherent frameworks. This paper explores this challenge and argues that a social representations approach allows for the critical analysis of formal approaches to tourism planning. Special attention is given to tourism development and governance in Africa and other emerging destinations. A content/semiotic analysis was conducted to examine figures summarising tourism planning models presented in the academic and government planning literature. This revealed a dominant social representation of tourism planning in which destination residents play only a minor role and are typically excluded from tourism governance and external agents, from both the private and public sectors, and their views of tourist needs are dominant. Most planning models were narrowly focused, had limited evaluation of all tourism benefits and costs, paid little attention to non-economic factors and did not integrate into wider development processes. The paper argues that this social representation assumes the core objective of tourism planning is to enhance outcomes for tourists and tourism businesses rather than for destination residents. Measures to enhance local governance capacity are suggested, with examples from the health, education and tourism sectors.

Introduction

Tourism has often been promoted as a promising solution to the various social and economic challenges faced by rural, remote and less developed regions. Unfortunately, the reality of tourism for many of these peripheral destinations is that it rarely lives up to what is promised and is often marked by community conflict and concern. This paper examines the potential of social representations theory (discussed below) to assist in understanding how communities in emerging tourism destinations can create and use knowledge about tourism to enhance their power to make decisions concerning tourism development in their regions. In particular, the paper describes a social representations model of tourism that links community understanding of tourism and its potential impacts to the social representations of tourism held by different actors in the development process. The paper argues that a social representations approach directs our attention to the social construction of knowledge about tourism and its impacts. It proposes that giving more power to resident communities to develop and present their own social representations of tourism itself is a necessary prerequisite for the governance of more sustainable approaches to tourism.

The central argument of this paper is made up of two parts. The first part of the argument proposes that differences in purported knowledge of tourism and tourists are often the basis of power imbalances in the relationships between peripheral destination communities and external agents. This proposal is supported by several existing analyses of tourism development. The second part of the argument is, however, novel in that it is proposed that this power imbalance is a consequence of the social representations of tourism and its planning held by the various actors in the tourism development process. More specifically, it is argued that there are two levels at which social representations can support the disempowerment of destination residents. Firstly, there are the social representations of the tourism development process held by tourism planners and the organisations that employ them. It will be argued, based on a content/semiotic analysis of publicly available tourism planning models, that destination residents are typically given very limited or no roles at all in the tourism planning and governance process and their lack of tourism knowledge and experience is used to support arguments that effective tourism development needs to be directed by external agents such as foreign tour operators, domestic but often distant government departments or foreign/domestic tourism destination marketing organisations. Secondly, there are the social representations of tourism itself held by both these planners and destination residents. Social representations theory argues that, where there is limited knowledge of tourism, a destination community must either develop its own social representation of tourism or adopt an existing one. The problem for many emerging destination communities is that where the planning process is directed by an external agent, then the social representation of the external agent may be imposed upon the community. The paper concludes by suggesting some ways to address this issue and improve governance for tourism planning.

Knowledge and power in tourism development and governance

Power in the tourism development context has been defined as "the capacity of individuals to make decisions that affect their lives" (Johnson & Wilson, 2000, p. 1892). Moscardo's (2005) analysis of more than 200 cases of tourism development in peripheral regions consistently identified the issue of who had the power to make decisions about the nature of the tourism development as a key determinant of the impacts of that development on the destination. That analysis also highlighted the importance of knowledge as a basis for that power. In the area of marketing, for example, a lack of local knowledge of markets and marketing resources is often cited as limiting the effectiveness of tourism development (Dieke, 2003; Sirakaya, Teye, & Sonmez, 2002; Victurine, 2000). In many cases, this lack of market and marketing knowledge results in a loss of control over tourism decisions to external tour companies and operations, undermining the power of communities to influence the tourism development (Briedenhann & Wickens, 2004; Wearing & McDonald, 2002).

There are a number of other ways in which destination residents can lose control over tourism development. Two ways that are commonly recognised in the tourism literature are relinquishing ownership of resources such as land and infrastructure to external businesses (Sulaiman, 1996), and a lack of democratic government procedures (Li, 2004). Two other paths to communities losing power over tourism development have been recognised but given much less academic consideration. These are a reliance on external consultants and organisations to develop tourism plans (Augustyn, 1998), and a lack of community understanding of tourism and its consequences (Chakravarty, 2003; Pearce, Moscardo, & Ross, 1996; Reid, Mair, & George, 2004; Timothy, 1999).

A review of the literature on tourism development and governance in Africa demonstrates the operation of these pathways and highlights the role of the social representations of tourism development held by the actors. Three important and related themes recur in various critical analyses of tourism development in African nations – the use of tourism as an argument for the imposition of western wildlife conservation practices on local residents, the limited benefits of tourism for local residents and the dominance of external agents in African tourism. The first theme is perhaps the most common one and is supported by numerous historical and contemporary analyses of the establishment of various protected areas (Akama, 1996; Brooks, 2005; Eastman, 1995; McGregor, 2005; Sindiga, 1999; van Beck, 2003). The typical pattern described is one in which local residents are displaced and excluded from areas deemed by European colonial powers or contemporary western environmental non-governmental organisations (NGOs) as important for wildlife conservation (Akama, 1996; Brooks, 2005; McGregor, 2005; van Beck, 2003). These forced removals are driven by western social representations of African landscapes as dangerous, endangered and wild. In these social representations, local people are excluded, except as guides, and this exclusion is typically associated with a loss of rights, disruptions to traditional agriculture and the generation of poverty and starvation (Akama, 1996; Ashley & Jones, 2001; Brooks, 2005; Ferreira, 2004; McGregor, 2005). This phenomenon is not restricted to Africa (Schmidt-Soltau & Brockington, 2007), with similar processes and results reported in a number of countries including China (Wang & Wall, 2007), Brazil (Ferreira & Freire, 2009) and Nepal (McLean & Straede, 2003).

Tourism is typically presented as an argument to support these processes and it is proposed that tourists will pay to see the natural landscapes that have been presented to them in both the popular and tourism media (Briedenhann & Wickens, 2004; Brooks, 2005; Eastman, 1995; Ferreira, 2004; van Beck, 2003). Unfortunately, the argument that tourism will provide economic benefits that will outweigh the costs imposed upon local residents is rarely evident in practice (Akama, 1996; Kirsten & Rogerson, 2002; Thompson & Homewood, 2002). High levels of economic leakage are associated with African tourism and result from the dominance of external agents in tourism provision – in particular, foreign tour operators and western NGOs (Dieke, 2003; Kirsten & Rogerson, 2002; Sindiga, 1999; Sirakaya et al., 2002). Although many African tourism developments are presented as eco-tourism and thus promoted to locals and tourists as sustainable and bringing benefits to locals (Eastman, 1995; Witz, Rassool, & Minkley, 2001), in most cases, existing tourism developments offer only token benefits to a limited few (Johnson & Wilson, 2000) and often result in unsustainable agricultural practices that directly contribute to environmental degradation (McGregor, 2005).

In summary, tourism governance in many African destinations appears to be driven by a social representation of tourism development or planning that assumes that African communities have little or no experience of tourism or tourists. This assumption is used to support arguments that effective tourism development needs to be directed by external agents such as foreign tour operators, national government tourism agencies or NGOs. These external agents offer a social representation of tourism development, which defines tourists as affluent, western and interested only in wildlife and which puts forward luxury enclave style tourism as the only viable option (Rogerson, 2004). Further, this social representation of tourism planning sees local residents as limited in their capacity to understand these tourists and contribute to this form of tourism and as having little ability to effectively conserve their natural environments. This social representation not only supports the removal of decision-making power from residents but also perpetuates tourism representations of African landscapes as a dangerous wilderness devoid of a meaningful human presence and, through these images, supports the continuing displacement of locals and disruptions to their livelihoods. As noted previously, this process is not peculiar to African destinations. Moscardo's (2005) examination of cases of tourism development in peripheral regions across a number of countries found evidence that destination residents are often excluded from the planning process and tourism governance in favour of external agents.

This brief review of analyses of tourism governance in Africa suggests that a social representation of tourism planning may exist, which is not conducive to improving tourism governance at the destination level. This paper seeks to explore and describe social representations of tourism planning.

Social representations

There is a need in tourism as a general field of research to find concepts and theoretical frameworks that can provide a way to link and integrate various and often divergent areas of tourism research (Aramberri, 2001; Cohen, 2004; Pearce, 2005). In the case of understanding tourism development processes, especially in peripheral destinations, it could be argued that such a framework would be most useful if it incorporated:

- a way to link individuals and their attitudes to the social context in which they live and operate (Jenkins, 2003);
- a recognition of the importance of power (Ryan, 2002); and
- an understanding of the link between knowledge and understanding of tourism, and control over tourism decisions (Moscardo, 2008a).

One theoretical approach that offers these features is that of social representations theory. Halfacree summarises Moscovici's (1984) description of social representations when he defines them as:

> mental constructs which guide us [and] define reality. The world is organized, understood and mediated through these basic cognitive units. Social representations consist of both concrete images and abstract concepts, organized around figurative nuclei which are a complex of images. (1993, p. 29)

Social representations are critical elements of social interaction and communication. Social representations theory provides a link between the concept of attitudes central to social psychology and the concept of representations used in sociology and anthropology (Moscovici, 2001). They allow groups to construct and share a common social reality (Andriotis & Vaughan, 2003) and provide guidelines to individuals for how to react to the phenomenon (Fredline & Faulkner, 2000).

According to Moscovici (2001), social representations are distinct from both attitudes and representations in that visual imagery is the central component of any social representation. Further, social representations theory explicitly addresses the link between the individual cognition and group social interaction. Philogene and Deaux (2001) note that social representations are created from social interactions within groups as members share their experiences. Once created though, these social representations then take on a life of their own, presented and repeated in the media and spread through further social interactions.

It is this link to group identity that highlights the importance of power and control. Social groups vary in their cohesion and power, and so Moscovici (2001) suggests that there are three levels or types of social representations.

- Hegemonic representations are those that emerge from groups with power and dominate social reality. They are often endorsed by scientific or professional groups and are widely presented in the media.
- Emancipated representations are not widespread but are popular within specific groups, such as professional societies, political parties and lobby groups.
- Polemical representations arise from conflict between social groups or divisions and are often associated with the rejection of a hegemonic representation.

According to Moscovici (2001), these social representations are developed through an iterative cycle of two related processes – anchoring and objectification. When social groups encounter new social issues or phenomena, they seek to find an existing example or information from elsewhere (De Paolis, 1990). This process is anchoring. In the case of tourism, for example, a community may look at the styles of tourism offered in neighbouring places as an example to either adopt or avoid. As a social representation evolves, the key concepts become associated with a specific visual image that simplifies the issue. This process is objectification (Moscovici, 2001). Both processes make a new concept or issue simple and familiar.

A number of authors have used social representations theory in tourism to analyse community attitudes towards, and responses to, tourism development (Andriotis & Vaughan, 2003; Fredline & Faulkner, 2000; Pearce et al., 1996; Yuksel, Bramwell, & Yuksel, 1999). But it is argued in the present paper that the theory could be used in a broader, more integrative fashion. Figure 1 presents a preliminary social representations model that highlights the interaction between three key groups in tourism development – destination residents, tourists and those who develop and plan for tourism. The model includes three key areas of intersection at which different social representations could operate. The first intersection is between planners/marketers and tourists and this is where destination images exist. The second intersection is between tourists and communities and this is where the research into tourism representations of destination and hosts focuses. The final intersection is between communities and planners and it is this one that offers a new area of focus on social representations of tourism.

At the centre of this model are the visual images that are used to portray the various social representations held by different groups within the model. It is proposed in this paper that social representations of tourism planning and development are linked to community understanding of tourism and control over tourism development. When communities have very limited understanding of tourism, social representations theory suggests that they can either develop their own social representation or adopt an existing one. It is further argued that residents in peripheral destinations are often given little choice but to accept the social representation of tourism held by tourism development agents, as these are the only options recognised and presented for discussion.

Alternatively, communities with limited experience of tourism may seek inappropriate examples from elsewhere to anchor their developing social representations. This adoption of tourism development styles from other places has been recognised in a number of destinations and is described by Richards and Wilson (2006) in urban tourism development as serial reproduction. While Hall (2007) critically analyses this process in the general context of regional tourism development, Pearce et al. (1996) provide some specific examples in

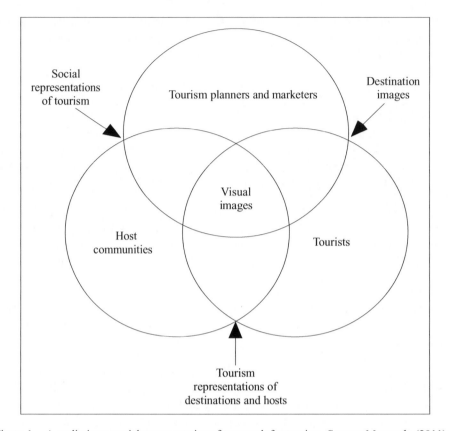

Figure 1.   A preliminary social representations framework for tourism. Source: Moscardo (2011).

rural regions of northern Australia. In this case, residents of peripheral regions often reported the style of coastal resort development, already in existence along the eastern Australian coast, as reference points for their evaluations of tourism. In other words, discussion of tourism development was typically limited to the styles of tourism already in existence and known about in comparable or nearby regions. Arguably, in Africa and in parts of South America, a similar pattern can be seen in which discussions of tourism development in emerging destinations are often limited to considerations of luxury eco-tourism options.

Also incorporated within these social representations of tourism planning held by those in the tourism development sphere are beliefs about how tourist destinations should be managed and the role that destination residents can play in tourism governance. Thus, destination communities can lose control over tourism development by accepting a social representation of tourism held by external agents that limits their role in tourism. Social representations of tourism are what communities and other stakeholders, such as development agencies and tourism marketers, believe about tourism, its operation and its likely consequences.

There has been almost no academic attention paid to the social representations of tourism held by those who work in tourism development organisations or by the academics and others who train these tourism planners. Arguably, these are the most important social representations of all, as they incorporate key beliefs about the role of residents, the type of tourism development and the way in which tourism is regulated and managed. The following sections of this paper will concentrate on analysing the social representations of tourism planning held by tourism professionals, academics and government agencies responsible for, or involved in, destination development.

Social representations of tourism development and planning

Very few tourism researchers have considered the social representations of tourism development evident in the tourism planning literature. Two reviews of tourism planning models or approaches do suggest some elements of what these social representations might look like. The review by Getz (1986) of more than 150 tourism planning models concluded with a list of problems associated with the approach to tourism planning that these models reflected. These included:

- A narrow focus on project or specific development planning;
- Limited analysis and evaluation of all tourism benefits and costs;
- A lack of attention paid to non-economic factors; and
- The need to integrate tourism into other development processes.

Twenty years later, Hall's (2005) description of different tourism planning traditions provides a framework for placing Getz's (1986) review in context. Hall (2005) identified five traditions of tourism planning.

- Boosterism – tourism is a good use of cultural and physical resources.
- Economic – tourism can be used like other industries to generate revenue and employment.
- Physical/spatial – tourism can be controlled through a consideration of its spatial and environmental features.
- Community – need for local control and balanced development.
- Sustainability – integration of social, economic and environmental aspects into planning systems.

Getz's models clearly fell within the first two traditions and his suggestions for moving forward highlighted the need to integrate aspects from the third and fourth traditions into tourism planning models (Getz, 1986). A more detailed reading of Hall's (2005) descriptions suggests that in the first tradition, residents are most likely to be seen as an element of destination attractiveness, while in the second they are a labour pool or resource to be exploited for tourism. No overt role for residents is explicated in the third tradition which is not surprising, given its focus on the physical aspects of destination settings. It is only in the last two traditions that residents are seen as part of the planning and control process.

It is worth noting that even 20 years on from Getz's (1986) review, Hall's (2005) work suggests that little has changed in practice, with many tourism plans still embedded in the boosterism or economic approaches. According to social representations theory, this is likely to be the case where there exists a dominant or hegemonic social representation of tourism development that supports the power of external agents or planning specialists as central to the tourism planning process, and central to its "success".

Finding and describing social representations

Studies into social representations have used a wide variety of methods, but generally, there is tendency towards more qualitative approaches and a focus on archival data such as news media reports, popular media and texts (Pearce et al., 1996). This paper sought to analyse the social representations of tourism planning through an examination of the figures and models used in tourism texts, and planning guidelines prepared by tourism academics, government and non-government agencies involved in tourism development and policymaking. These are the texts that are used to organise and structure tourism planning processes both in practice and in the education of new tourism managers and planners. The analysis focused on the figures and models as these form the visual imagery that is at the core of a social representation. The study used content and semiotic analyses to examine these figures. Mehmetoglu and Dann (2003) and Bell and Milic (2002) note the close links between content and semiotic analysis. Content analysis provides a quantitative description of the features of archival material (Bell & Milic, 2002). Semiotic analysis is a complementary process that looks at what is implied or signified by the objects used in the material being analysed and the relationships between them (Bell & Milic, 2002; Mehmetoglu & Dann, 2003).

The analysis was conducted on 36 tourism planning figures or models. These were selected by searching academic texts and papers using several different electronic academic databases and by using *Google* to search government and non-government agency websites. These searches were not restricted to any geographical location but were limited to sources in English. The search focused on those texts, papers or reports that included a visual diagram to summarise the planning process and it specifically sought models or steps in tourism planning for destinations. It did not include tourism systems models, texts on the development of specific forms of tourism or frameworks related to specific elements of tourism such as tourist motivation or decision-making. The search for the models continued until no new examples were found. It was originally planned to analyse changes in the models over time, and so, the models selected were not limited by their original date of publication, with models included from publications ranging from the early 1970s to 2008. It was found, however, that many models are recycled into other texts and planning guidelines, and so, there is no clear historical progression. A full list of texts can be supplied by the author on request.

Nearly half (16) of the models were found in academic texts, with the next most common source being NGO websites and documents (12) and the remaining eight found in government planning texts. The small numbers preclude any further analysis of the differences between these sources. It should be noted, however, that the pattern of recycling of models already identified was one in which models from academic texts were most commonly found to be repeated in NGO documents. This is consistent with the processes proposed for the dissemination and reinforcement of social representations (Philogene & Deaux, 2001).

There were three main types of model presentation. The first and most common (20 out of the 36 models) type was linear flow charts with steps summarised in boxes. Some of these included feedback loops between the boxes (eight), but generally, the process was presented as unidirectional. There were 10 models that used some sort of circular or cyclical presentation and three of these placed tourism development in the centre, with several processes or forces acting upon it. Six of the models were essentially a set of text statements setting the steps in the planning process as a series of separate points. The complexity of the models varied greatly with a range of 3–36 steps or elements included. The majority of the models, however, had between five and 11 elements and there was a substantial commonality in these elements.

Establishing goals/vision/objectives/problems	
Situation appraisal/analysis/research/inventory	
Stakeholder input/consultation	Development of strategies/plans/policies
Implementation/action	
Evaluation/monitoring/refinement	

Figure 2.   Summary of common steps in tourism planning models.

The set of points listed in Figure 2 is a summary of the most common elements or steps in the models, presented in the most commonly occurring sequence or order. The middle two steps (stakeholder input/consultation and development of strategies/plans/policies) are placed together because in some models (seven) stakeholder input comes before plans are developed, while in others (eight) it comes after the development of plans. In most cases, the additional elements were more details about the actions and requirements of these steps. For example, in the implementation step, a number of models divided this section into specific areas such as a marketing strategy, an infrastructure plan, a training strategy and a funding plan. Similarly, the situation appraisal/analysis step was broken into more specific areas such as an analysis of existing resources for tourism and a market assessment. Tribe (2004) has suggested that the field of tourism is characterised by a tension between tourism business studies and other approaches. The basic tourism planning approach outlined in Figure 2 can be clearly placed within this tourism business studies area, as it is essentially a simple traditional, business planning model. If the tourism planning models are derived from business studies, then we might expect to find that the range of stakeholders considered is likely to be limited to owners/shareholders, employees and customers or markets with a dominant focus on the last group. We might also expect that little attention is paid to the goal-setting step, as the goals for most businesses are based on some variation of growth and profit.

These two expectations were supported by the content analysis. The next steps in the analysis examined the type and role of stakeholders included in these models and the details provided about goal setting. A significant proportion (13) of the models did not mention stakeholders at all, a further 10 mentioned stakeholders as a general group with no specific description provided, two listed various sorts of stakeholders such as government agencies, unions, professional organisations and business, without including residents or community groups, while three included residents/public in an extensive list of stakeholders. The remaining eight specifically discussed residents/communities as the major or only stakeholders. Further examination of those models that included residents specifically or listed stakeholders in general found three distinctive patterns; in 12 models, stakeholders are mentioned once, usually in the first or second step or stage; in eight cases, stakeholders are mentioned once but typically towards the end of the process; and in the remaining five cases, stakeholders are mentioned more than once. In the first of these three patterns, stakeholders are seen as having legitimate input into the setting of the goals or objectives of the tourism plan (four cases), the development of the strategies (six cases) or were discussed in terms of assessing their willingness to participate in specific strategies (two cases). In the second of the three patterns, the inclusion of stakeholders is concerned with explaining the strategies to win support. In three of the five cases in which residents are mentioned more than once, they are included both in the development of goals and then again in the context of winning support for the proposed strategies. The residents of destination communities are given extensive input into the tourism planning process in only two models.

Given that each of the figures analysed were embedded in documents with accompanying text, it was decided to examine the possibility that stakeholders, especially destination residents, have a greater importance than what appears in the summary figures. This examination found no evidence to contradict the pattern established in the figures. Where goals were discussed in detail, all but three models focused on goals related to visitor numbers, income or specific business development opportunities. In summary, destination residents have only a limited role, with some recognition of their input into the setting of goals for a tourism plan and the need to have resident support for the proposed tourism strategies.

By way of contrast, tourists play a central role in the majority of the models, with 28 of the figures having at least one place in which tourists are explicitly discussed (only 11 have an explicit role for destination residents). Ten of the models include studies to determine and predict tourist demand, 13 include a step specifically on market analysis, six discuss determining and meeting tourist needs in detail, and 13 have marketing as their core strategy or activity. The four most common words used in conjunction with tourists were demand, needs, satisfaction and support, while the four most common words used in conjunction with destination residents were engagement, consultation, willingness and goals.

It is also worth noting that nine of the models include roles for external agents such as consultants, international investors and international tourism businesses, mostly in the appraisal/analysis and strategy development stages or both. In all cases, this gives these external agents considerable power in that they can control the information that is presented and used to develop plans and they can influence the options considered. This influence over the options considered is where external agents have the power to impose their perspectives on what appropriate forms of tourism might be for the destination.

Only one model discusses the integration of tourism into other regional or development plans. Nearly half of the models (17) do not specify who is responsible for the tourism planning process. For the rest, the responsibility is allocated to governments in general, some sort of planning or steering committee, a tourism office or marketing organisation, local government, and the private sector. In those cases that described a steering committee, the majority (four out of five) have representatives of destination residents or communities as one participant listed along with tourism businesses, tourism marketing organisations, NGOs, government agencies and tourism professional bodies. In only one case are destination residents given a central role in the governance of the planning process.

The final step explored the models for inclusion of strategies related to tourism impacts – both in terms of actions to minimise negative impacts and plans to maximise positive impacts. The majority of the figures (22) mention some aspect of impacts, although in six of these cases, impacts are simply mentioned but not discussed. The most common focus of those 16 models, where impacts are described, is on ways to prevent and minimise negative impacts, with the majority of these (13) being concerned with environmental impacts – only eight models include social/cultural impacts. In three models, social/cultural issues are discussed as constraints to tourism development rather than impacts of tourism. Three models discuss ways to maximise economic benefits, but these are all discussed in terms of returns for investors. Only three models included steps or elements concerned with enhancing destination residents/community benefits from tourism and only one explicitly discusses improvements to destination community capacity.

A hegemonic social representation of tourism planning

This content/semiotic analysis provides evidence that there exists a persistent, dominant or hegemonic social representation of the tourism planning/development process. The evidence suggests that little has changed since Getz's (1986) summary and the same problems that he reported are still apparent, with almost no integration of tourism into larger development plans or frameworks and very limited attention to the consideration of tourism benefits and costs. This hegemonic social representation exists and is repeated across the academic literature, in government and NGO guidelines for tourism planning and as part of the approach taken by tourism planning consultants. Core features of this social representation include:

- That tourism development is necessary and desirable (no model includes an option for making a choice about whether or not to proceed with tourism or an option in which tourism is evaluated against other development options);
- That tourism development is essentially a variation of business planning and the primary concern is to determine and meet customer/tourist needs;
- That the major issues to be managed are economic and environmental;
- That the core actors in the tourism development process, after the tourist, are external agents, tourism businesses and government agencies (other than local government); and
- That the destination residents have at best a limited role in the tourism planning and governance process.

Moscardo's (2005) analysis suggested that when tourism development was associated with these features, the process was much more likely to result in undesirable or unsustainable outcomes for destinations and their residents. Moscardo (2005) concluded that these features came from a lack of use of formal tourism planning models. The evidence here suggests that the opposite is true – these are the outcomes that would be expected if the dominant approach to tourism planning is used.

Implications for planning and governance

Despite widespread discussion of sustainability in the tourism literature and growing interest in governance issues, this analysis of tourism planning models suggests the existence of a dominant social representation embedded in a business approach that has little – if any – connection to sustainability issues or approaches. Dunphy and Benveniste (2000) describe six phases of corporate or business approaches to sustainability, ranging from total rejection of any sustainability agenda, through non-responsiveness, compliance, eco-efficiency and strategic sustainability, to ideological commitment. At each phase, the organisation takes on a broader and more committed approach to sustainability. Using this scheme, it could be argued that most of the tourism planning models analysed are in the non-responsive or compliance phases in which environmental issues are recognised, but responses are reactive rather than proactive.

This social representation of tourism planning is also an example of what Aras and Crowther (2009) would call an Anglo-Saxon model of governance characterised by a rule-bound, top-down approach to decision-making where power and control are invested in a small number of people who are supposedly working for the best interests of the larger group. In the social representation of tourism planning described in this study, it appears that the people with the power in tourism planning typically work for the best interests of tourism as an economic activity rather than for the destination residents. Aras and Crowther (2009) note that this is typical of some of the problems associated with an Anglo-Saxon model of governance. They go on to describe several alternative models of governance. Alternative development planning models also exist that pay significantly more attention to the wellbeing of those who have to live with the proposed development. In education, for example, there exist models in which the first step is to assess the needs of stakeholders directly with the stakeholders before establishing the vision or goals of the planning process, followed by activities to build community capacity to direct and benefit from the development (Siemens, 2009). Campbell, Kissoon, Syed, and Fraser (2008) provide an example of a similar approach in health planning. Alternatives also exist in tourism itself, presented in the work of Hall (2005), Moscardo (2008b), Pinel (1999), Reid (2003) and Scheyvens (2002) in which destination communities have a more direct role in tourism governance and in which the planning process includes steps in which communities get to decide whether or not to proceed with tourism as a development option, and are offered actions and strategies to build community capacity to manage and be involved in tourism development decisions. A critical element in these capacity-building processes is the enhancement of the knowledge that destination residents have of tourism, its forms and its impacts, both positive and negative. Enhancing resident knowledge of tourism is critical in empowering them to develop new and more appropriate social representations of what tourism might be for their destination. To achieve this end, it is, however, necessary to acknowledge, critically analyse and change the social representation of tourism planning that currently dominates the academic and government perspectives.

References

Akama, J. (1996). Western environmental values and nature-based tourism in Kenya. *Tourism Management, 17*(1), 567–574.

Andriotis, K., & Vaughan, R. (2003). Urban residents' attitudes toward tourism development: The case of Crete. *Journal of Travel Research, 42*, 172–185.

Aramberri, J. (2001). The host should get lost: Paradigms in tourism theory. *Annals of Tourism Research, 28*(3), 738–761.

Aras, G., & Crowther, D. (2009). Corporate governance and corporate social responsibility in context. In G. Aras & D. Crowther (Eds.), *Global perspectives on corporate governance and CSR* (pp. 1–42). Farnham: Gower.

Ashley, C., & Jones, B. (2001). Joint ventures between communities and tourism investors: Experiences in Southern Africa. *International Journal of Tourism Research, 3*, 407–423.

Augustyn, M. (1998). National strategies for rural tourism development and sustainability: The Polish experience. *Journal of Sustainable Tourism, 6*(3), 191–209.

Bell, P., & Milic, M. (2002). Goffman's gender advertisements revisited: Combining content analysis with semiotic analysis. *Visual Communication, 1*(2), 203–222.

Briedenhann, J., & Wickens, E. (2004). Tourism routes as a tool for the economic development of rural areas – Vibrant hope or impossible dream? *Tourism Management, 25*, 71–79.

Brooks, S. (2005). Images of "Wild Africa": Nature tourism and the (re)creation of Hluhluwe game reserve, 1930–1945. *Journal of Historical Geography, 31*, 220–240.

Campbell, B.J., Kissoon, N., Syed, N., & Fraser, H.S. (2008). Health human resource planning in Barbados and the Eastern Caribbean States: A matter of sustainability. *West Indian Medical Journal, 57*(6), 542–548.

Chakravarty, I. (2003). Marine ecotourism and regional development: A case study of the proposed Marine Park at Malvan, Maharashtra, India. In B. Garrod & J. Wilson (Eds.), *Marine ecotourism: Issues and experiences* (pp. 177–197). Clevedon: Channel View Publications.

Cohen, E. (2004). Backpacking: Diversity and changes. In G. Richards & J. Wilson (Eds.), *The global nomad* (pp. 43–50). Clevedon: Channel View Publications.

De Paolis, P. (1990). Prototypes of the psychologist and professionalisation: Diverging social representations of a developmental process. In G. Duveen & B. Lloyd (Eds.), *Social representations and the development of knowledge* (pp. 144–163). Cambridge: Cambridge University Press.

Dieke, P. (2003). Tourism in Africa's economic development: Policy implications. *Management Decision, 41*(3), 287–295.

Dunphy, D., & Benveniste, J. (2000). An introduction to the sustainable corporation. In D. Dunphy, J. Benveniste, A. Griffiths, & P. Simon (Eds.), *Sustainability: The corporate challenge of the 21st century* (pp. 3–18). Sydney: Allen & Unwin.

Eastman, C. (1995). Tourism in Kenya and the marginalization of Swahili. *Annals of Tourism Research, 22*(1), 172–185.

Ferreira, M.N., & Freire, N.C. (2009). Community perceptions of four protected areas in the Northern portion of the Corrado hotspot, Brazil. *Environmental Conservation, 36*(2), 129–138.

Ferreira, S. (2004). Problems associated with tourism development in Southern Africa: The case of the transfrontier conservation areas. *GeoJournal, 60*, 301–310.

Fredline, E., & Faulkner, B. (2000). Host community reactions: A cluster analysis. *Annals of Tourism Research, 27*(3), 763–784.

Getz, D. (1986). Models in tourism planning: Towards integration of theory and practice. *Tourism Management, 7*, 21–32.

Halfacree, K. (1993). Locality and social representation: Space, discourse and alternative definitions of the rural. *Journal of Rural Studies, 9*(1), 23–37.

Hall, C. (2005). *Tourism: Rethinking the social science of mobility*. Harlow: Prentice Hall.

Hall, C. (2007). Tourism and regional competitiveness. In J. Tribe & D. Airey (Eds.), *Developments in tourism research* (pp. 217–231). Kidlington: Elsevier.

Jenkins, O. (2003). Photography and travel brochures: The circle of representation. *Tourism Geographies, 5*(3), 305–328.

Johnson, H., & Wilson, G. (2000). Biting the bullet: Civil society, social learning and the transformation of local governance. *World Development, 28*(11), 1891–1906.

Kirsten, M., & Rogerson, C. (2002). Tourism, business linkages and small enterprise development in South Africa. *Development South Africa, 19*(1), 29–59.

Li, Y. (2004). Exploring community tourism in China: The case of Nanshan Cultural Tourism Zone. *Journal of Sustainable Tourism, 12*(3), 175–193.

McGregor, J. (2005). Crocodile crimes: People versus wildlife and the politics of postcolonial conservation on Lake Kariba, Zimbabwe. *Geoforum, 36*, 353–369.

McLean, J., & Straede, S. (2003). Conservation, relocation, and the paradigms of park and people management – A case study of Padampur Villages and the Royal Chitwan National Park, Nepal. *Society & Natural Resources, 16*, 509–526.

Mehmetoglu, M., & Dann, G.M.S. (2003). Atlas/ti and content/semiotic analysis in tourism research. *Tourism Analysis, 8*, 1–13.

Moscardo, G. (2005). Peripheral tourism development: Challenges, issues and success factors. *Tourism Recreation Research, 30*(1), 27–43.

Moscardo, G. (2008a). Building community capacity for tourism development: Conclusions. In G. Moscardo (Ed.), *Building community capacity for tourism development* (pp. 172–180). Wallingford: CABI.

Moscardo, G. (2008b). Community capacity building: An emerging challenge for tourism development. In G. Moscardo (Ed.), *Building community capacity for tourism development* (pp. 1–15). Wallingford: CABI.

Moscardo, G. (2011). Exploring social representations of tourism: Analysing drawings of tourism. In W. Gartner & C.H.C. Hsu (Eds.), *Handbook of tourism research*. Abingdon: Taylor & Francis.

Moscovici, S. (1984). The phenomenon of social representations. In R. Farr & S. Moscovici (Eds.), *Social representations* (pp. 3–70). Cambridge: Cambridge University Press.

Moscovici, S. (2001). Why a theory of social representations? In K. Deaux & G. Philogene (Eds.), *Representations* (pp. 8–35). Oxford: Blackwell.

Pearce, P. (2005). *Tourist behaviour: Themes and conceptual schemes*. Clevedon: Channel View Publications.

Pearce, P., Moscardo, G., & Ross, G. (1996). *Tourism community relationships*. Oxford: Pergamon.

Philogene, G., & Deaux, K. (2001). *Introduction*. In K. Deaux & G. Philogene (Eds.), *Representations of the social: Bridging theoretical traditions* (pp. 1–7). Oxford: Blackwell.

Pinel, D.P. (1999, April). Create a good fit: A community-based tourism planning model. In M.L. Miller, J. Auyong, & N.P. Hadley (Eds.), *Proceedings of the 1999 International Symposium on Coastal and Marine Tourism*. Vancouver. Retrieved March, 2011, from http://nsgl.gso.uri.edu/washu/washuw99003/28-Pinel.pdf

Reid, D. (2003). *Tourism, globalization and development: Responsible tourism planning*. London: Pluto Press.

Reid, D., Mair, H., & George, W. (2004). Community tourism planning: A self-assessment instrument. *Annals of Tourism Research, 31*(3), 623–639.

Richards, G., & Wilson, J. (2006). Developing creativity in tourist experiences: A solution to the serial reproduction of culture? *Tourism Management, 27*(6), 1209–1223.

Rogerson, C. (2004). Regional tourism in South Africa: A case of "mass tourism of the South". *GeoJournal, 60*, 229–237.

Ryan, C. (2002). Equity, management, power sharing and sustainability – Issues of the "new tourism". *Tourism Management, 23*, 17–26.

Scheyvens, R. (2002). *Tourism for development: Empowering communities*. Upper Saddle River, NJ: Prentice Hall.

Schmidt-Soltau, K., & Brockington, D. (2007). Protected areas and resettlement: What scope for voluntary relocation? *World Development, 35*(12), 2182–2202.

Siemens, G. (2009). *Challenges faced by African universities in technology integration*. Retrieved May, 2010, from http://www.connectivism.ca/?paged=2

Sindiga, I. (1999). Alternative tourism and sustainable development in Kenya. *Journal of Sustainable Tourism, 7*(2), 108–127.

Sirakaya, E., Teye, V., & Sonmez, S. (2002). Understanding residents' support for tourism development in the central region of Ghana. *Journal of Travel Research, 41*, 57–67.

Sulaiman, M. (1996). Islands within islands: Exclusive tourism and sustainable utilization of coastal resources in Zanzibar. In L. Briguglio, R. Butler, D. Harrison, & W. Filho (Eds.), *Sustainable tourism in islands and small states: Case studies* (pp. 32–49). New York: Pinter.

Thompson, M., & Homewood, K. (2002). Entrepreneurs, elites and exclusion in Maasailand: Trends in wildlife conservation and pastoralist development. *Human Ecology, 30*(1), 107–138.

Timothy, D. (1999). Participatory planning: A view of tourism in Indonesia. *Annals of Tourism Research, 26*(2), 371–391.

Tribe, J. (2004). Knowing about tourism: Epistemological issues. In J. Phillimore & L. Goodson (Eds.), *Qualitative research in tourism: Ontologies, epistemologies and methodologies* (pp. 46–62). London: Routledge.

van Beck, W. (2003). African tourist encounters: Effects of tourism on two West African societies. *Africa, 73*(2), 251–289.

Victurine, R. (2000). Building tourism excellence at the community level: Capacity building for community-based entrepreneurs in Uganda. *Journal of Travel Research, 38*, 221–229.

Wang, Y., & Wall, G. (2007). Administrative arrangement and displacement compensation in top-down tourism planning – A case from Hainan Province, China. *Tourism Management, 28*, 70–82.

Wearing, W., & McDonald, M. (2002). The development of community-based tourism: Re-thinking the relationship between tour operators and development agents as intermediaries in rural and isolated area communities. *Journal of Sustainable Tourism, 1*(3), 191–206.

Witz, L., Rassool, C., & Minkley, G. (2001). Repackaging the past for South African tourism. *Daedalus, 130*(1), 277–296.

Yuksel, F., Bramwell, B., & Yuksel, A. (1999). Stakeholder interviews and tourism planning at Pamukkale, Turkey. *Tourism Management, 20*(3), 351–360.

A typology of governance and its implications for tourism policy analysis

C. Michael Hall[a,b,c]

[a]Department of Management, University of Canterbury, Christchurch, New Zealand; [b]Department of Geography, University of Oulu, Finland; [c]School of Business and Economics, Linneaus University, Kalmar, Sweden

Governance is a key concept in politics and public policy that is increasingly utilised in tourism. Using the notion of "policy as theory", a typology of governance suitable for tourism is systematically developed. Categorical variables are developed from the relationship between state intervention and self-regulation and the relationships between policy actors and steering modes. The resultant matrix identifies four governance types: hierarchies, markets, networks and communities. A 12-point framework of governance identifies core elements, including classifying characteristics, policy themes, policy standpoints, democratic models, primary focus, views of non-central actors, distinctions between policymaking and implementation, success criteria, implementation gaps, the reasons and solutions for those gaps and the primary policy instruments used. An example of the application is provided using an analysis of state party's implementation of the 1993 Convention on Biological Diversity. It is concluded that clear categorical variables contribute to improved formulation and evaluation of explanatory claims, help clarify key concepts and assist in the comparative analysis of governance and tourism policy between jurisdictions and over time.

Introduction

The role of government in tourism and the influence of state policy on tourism development has long been of interest to scholars (Bramwell & Lane, 2000; Hall, 1994; Hall & Jenkins, 1995; Jenkins, 1980; Jenkins & Henry, 1982). However, since the 1990s, there has been a gradual shift in approach in the tourism policy literature from the notion of government to that of governance (Beaumont & Dredge, 2010; Greenwood, 1993; Hall, 1999; Yüksel, Bramwell, & Yüksel, 2005). This shift has extremely significant implications for sustainable tourism, given that it influences such factors as the relationships between policy actors, the capacity of the state to act, the selection of policy instruments and indicators and, potentially, even the definition of policy problems (Bramwell, 2005; Dinica, 2009; Erkuş-Öztürk & Eraydin, 2010; Hall, 2008a; Hall, 2004; Pforr, 2002, 2006; Tyler & Dinan, 2001; Wesley & Pforr, 2010).

Conceptual frameworks, such as images, models and theories, are fundamental to the development of understanding public and private institutions and the relationships between them. In his very influential work, Morgan (1986, p. 12) emphasised "how many of our conventional ideas about organization and management build on a small number of taken-for-granted images, especially mechanical and biological ones". Judge, Stoker, and Wolman (1995, p. 3) also noted that conceptual frameworks "provide a language and frame of reference through which reality can be examined and lead theorists to ask questions that might not otherwise occur. The result, if successful, is new and fresh insights that other frameworks or perspectives might not have yielded".

By exploring different conceptual frameworks and images, it is possible to identify the ways in which theory influences how the world is analysed, understood and acted upon with respect to policymaking, and how, conversely, policymaking also affects the development of theory. In public policy terms, this notion is best illustrated by Pressman and Wildavsky's (1973, p. xv) insight that "policies imply theories" (see also Blume, 1977). Majone (1980, 1981) understood policies as theories in terms of their development in a quasi-autonomous space of objective intellectual constructs, of thoughts-in-themselves, equivalent to Popper's (1978) third "world" of reality. For Majone,

> A policy, like a theory, is a cluster of conclusions in search of a premise; not the least important task of analysis is discovering the premises that make a set of conclusions internally consistent, and convincing to the widest possible audience. (1981, p. 25)

Blume (1977, p. 253), while accepting that policies may be considered as implicitly embodying "implicit theories", highlighted the immediate problem of "theories about what?" Blume goes on to suggest that implicit theories usually cover both theories of the role of the state and the proper actions of government on the one hand, and theories of social interaction and change in social systems on the other. Such observations are extremely significant for gaining a better understanding of tourism policymaking, as it suggests that the ways in which policies are designed to act have implicit theoretical foundations and hence assumptions about, for instance, the appropriate role of the state, the relationship between the state and individual policy actors (businesses, associations and individuals), their responsibilities and how they are supposed to act politically.

The notion of governance as a theory has also been extremely significant in studies of governance (Ansell & Gash, 2008; Kooiman, 2003; Pierre, 2000a; Pierre & Peters, 2005), with Stoker (1998) emphasising that the contribution of the concept of governance was neither with respect to the level of causal analysis nor as a new normative theory. Instead, "the value of the governance perspective rests in its capacity to provide a framework for understanding changing processes of governing" (Stoker, 1998, p. 18). The various ways in which the term "governance" is used in tourism studies can therefore not be fully understood unless we also know its theoretical underpinnings and context.

This paper aims to identify how the instruments of state intervention in tourism, i.e. the tools used by government to achieve its policy goals (Hood, 2008), are framed by different constructs of governance. It will do this through the development of a typology of conceptual frameworks of governance. Typologies, an organised system of types, are an important means for analysing the formation and measurement of concepts that are widely used through the social sciences, including in tourism studies and political science (Bailey, 1994; Box-Steffensmeier, Brady, & Collier, 2008; George & Bennett, 2005). In policy terms, typologies are used for both descriptive and explanatory purposes and can focus on variables related to causes, institutions and/or outcomes (Collier, Laporte, & Seawright, 2008). Typologies play an important role as instruments in developing more general insights into the ways in which key concepts and ideas can be framed so as to facilitate comparative studies and map empirical and theoretical change, and, although usually associated with qualitative research, can also contribute to the quantitative analysis of categorical variables (Collier et al., 2008). Although a number of typologies have been applied to tourism policy settings (Anastasiadou, 2008; Beaumont & Dredge, 2010; Coccossis & Constantoglou, 2006, 2008; Hall, 2009; Pforr, 2005), they are usually applied at the organisational or instrumental level. The present paper seeks to connect a typology of the various ways in which tourism governance is conceptualised to different instruments of policy intervention.

The paper is divided into three main sections. The first discusses the definition of the concept of governance. The second section outlines the key issues involved in the development of a typology of governance with respect to tourism, and it identifies the four main conceptualisations of governance and their application. The paper concludes by noting the importance of typologies as an analytical tool, particularly in areas of policy and theoretical complexity such as governance.

Defining governance

Governance is the act of governing. Governance is an increasingly significant issue in the tourism public policy and planning literature (Beaumont & Dredge, 2010; Bramwell & Rawding, 1994; Cornelissen, 2005; Dredge, 2001, 2006a; Dredge & Jenkins, 2007; Dredge & Pforr, 2008; Göymen, 2000; Hall, 2005, 2007a, 2008a, 2008b; Wesley & Pforr, 2010; Yüksel et al., 2005). It has assumed importance as researchers have sought to understand how the state can best act to mediate contemporary tourism-related social, economic, political and environmental policy problems at a time when the role of the state has itself changed, given the dominance of neo-liberal policy discourse in many developed countries (Jessop, 1998, 2002; Larner, 2000). Attention to governance issues in tourism mirrors the broader growth of interest in, and development of, the concept in the policy sciences (Jordan, Wurzel, & Zito, 2005; Kersbergen & Waarden, 2004; Kooiman, 2003; Pierre, 2000a, 2000b; Pierre & Peters, 2005; Rhodes, 1997).

The growth of new supranational policy structures and multi-level scales of governance (Bache & Flinders, 2004; Hooghe & Marks, 2001, 2003) has also led to research with a more defined geo-political focus, especially with respect to the European Union (Gualini, 2004; Hooghe, 1996; Jordan, 2001; Kern & Bulkeley, 2009; Marks, Hooghe, & Blank, 1996; Sutcliffe, 1999). In addition, there is a growing literature on the influence of supra-national organisations in tourism governance, such as the United Nations World Tourism Organization (UNWTO), the United Nations Environment Programme (UNEP), the World Trade Organization (WTO) and the World Bank/International Monetary Fund (IMF; Hall, 2005, 2007b; Hawkins & Mann, 2007), as well as non-governmental organisations (Hall, 2008a; Medeiros de Araujo & Bramwell, 1999; Zapata, Hall, Lindo, & Vanderschaeghen, 2011).

There is no single accepted definition of governance. This is reflected in Kooiman's (2003, p. 4) concept of governance as "the totality of theoretical conceptions on govern-ing". Definitions tend to suggest a recognition of a change in political practices involv-ing, amongst other things, increasing globalisation, the rise of networks that cross the public–private divide, the marketisation of the state and increasing institutional fragmenta-tion (Kjaer, 2004; Pierre, 2000a; Pierre & Peters, 2005). Nevertheless, two broad meanings of governance can be recognised (Figure 1). Firstly, it is used to describe contemporary state adaptation to its economic and political environment with respect to how it operates. This is often referred to as "new governance". Yee (2004, p. 487) provided a very basic definition of this approach by describing new modes of governance as "new governing activities that do not occur solely through governments". In the European context, Heritier (2002) focuses

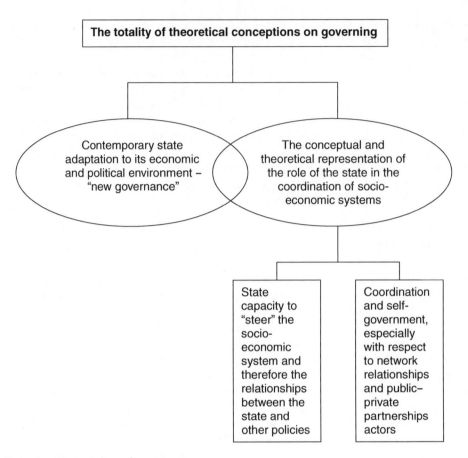

Figure 1.   The meanings of governance.

on new modes of governance that include private actors in policy formulation and/or while being based on public actors are only marginally based on regulative powers or not based on regulation at all. Some of the characteristics of the key elements of these so-called "new" modes of governance are indicated in Table 1 (Heritier, 2002; Scott & Trubek, 2002; Yee, 2004). Although as Treib, Bähr, and Falkner (2007, p. 16) note, it is not "appropriate to use the labels of 'old' and 'new' modes of governance for classificatory purposes. What is new in one area could be rather old in another field of study, which makes these labels inadequate as analytical categories".

   The second broad meaning of governance is that it is used to denote a conceptual and theoretical representation of the role of the state in the coordination of socio-economic systems. However, it should be noted that the two approaches are not mutually exclusive as the use of the term "governance" as a form of shorthand for new forms of governance in western societies is itself predicated on particular conceptions of what the role of the state should be in contemporary society and of the desirability and nature of state intervention. This second meaning can, in turn, be divided into two further categories (Peters, 2000). The first focuses on state capacity to "steer" the socio-economic system and therefore the relationships between the state and other policy actors (Pierre & Peters, 2000). The second focuses on coordination and self-government, especially with respect to network relationships and public–private partnerships (Rhodes, 1997).

Table 1. The characteristics of new modes of governance.

Elements	Characteristics
Participation and power-sharing	Policymaking is not considered as the sole domain of regulators, but private and public stakeholders from different levels are meant to participate in the policy process as part of public–private partnership.
Multi-level integration	Coordination between different levels of government needs to occur both horizontally and vertically and should involve private actors.
Diversity and decentralisation	Rather than a standard legislative or regulatory approach, a diverse range of coordinated approaches is instead encouraged.
Deliberation	Greater deliberation is encouraged between public and private stakeholders so as to improve democratic legitimation of policymaking processes.
Flexibility and revisability	Soft law measures are often applied that rely on flexible guidelines and open-ended standards that are implemented voluntarily and may be revised as policy circumstances change.
Experimentation and knowledge creation	Greater encouragement of local experimentation in governance measures as well as knowledge creation and sharing in connection with multi-lateral surveillance, benchmarking and the exchange of results and best practices.

Understanding how the institutional arrangements of governance are conceptualised is important as it determines the ways in which the state acts in the tourism policy arena and therefore selects instruments and indicators that are used to achieve policy goals. The focus of most discussions on policy instruments in tourism is on their utilisation or their effects rather than on the understandings of governance that led such instruments to be selected (Ayuso, 2007; Hall, 2008a; Pechlaner & Tschurtschenthaler, 2003). Literature on the relationships between different concepts or images of tourism policy processes and reasons for the selection of particular instruments is relatively limited. Beaumont and Dredge (2010) investigated the advantages and disadvantages of three different governance approaches at the local level: a council-led network governance structure, a participant-led community network governance structure and a local tourism organisation-led industry network governance structure. However, these comparisons, while useful at an operational level, did not then relate back to the conceptualisations of governance that underlie intervention and policy choice. With respect to the policy–action relationship, Hall (2009) identified three archetypes of implementation and their implications for tourism planning and policy: "top-down rational", "bottom-up" and "interactional network" models that are also related to different forms of intervention, but then did not go on to examine the broader contribution of such concepts for understanding tourism policy as a whole.

A typology of governance

Typologies have long been recognised as an important tool in helping to categorise policies "in such a way that the relationship between substance and process can be more clearly understood" (Steinberger, 1980, p. 185). The typological tradition in policy studies is considered as dating back to Lowi's (1964) extremely influential paper with respect to how different kinds of policies have different kinds of politics associated with them. According to Lowi (1972, p. 299), classification "reveals the hidden meanings and significance of the phenomena, suggesting what the important hypotheses ought to be concerned with". To

Lowi, such classification also leads to the identification of discrete areas of politics, each area characterised by its own political structure, policy process, elites and group relations, and power structures and policymaking processes that differ according to the type of issue they deal with (Hall, 2008a).

In order to develop an appropriate typology that classifies different frameworks of governance, it is helpful to include relatively well-delimited dimensions. Multi-dimensional typologies can be understood in terms of several elements (Collier et al., 2008, pp. 153, 156–157). Firstly, an overarching concept. This is the concept that is measured by the typology. Secondly, column and row variables that are cross-tabulated to form a matrix. Thirdly, the matrix. The cross-tabulation creates the familiar 2×2 matrix. Alternatively, more than two categories may be present on each variable, and/or more than two variables can be incorporated. This cross-tabulation creates new categorical variables that may be nominal, partially ordered or ordinal. It is also possible to create uni-dimensional typologies which are categorical variables organised around a single dimension. Many of the ideas about multi-dimensional typologies also apply to uni-dimensional typologies. Fourthly, the identification of types. The types located in each cell provide conceptual meaning that corresponds to their position in relation to the row and column variables. If typologies are to meet the norms for standard categorical scales, then scales should be mutually exclusive and collectively exhaustive.

A number of frameworks have been proposed for concept formation in political science. The work of Sartori (1970, 1984) has been especially influential in political science with respect to the identification of "data containers" employed in the research and the development of ladders of "abstraction". Sartori (1970) identified three main tasks. Firstly, paying careful attention to concepts given that they are the basic "data containers" of research. Secondly, understanding the semantic field in which conceptual reasoning is situated, i.e. the field of concepts and meanings that frame research. For the concept of governance, this field was briefly outlined in the previous section. Thirdly, recognising that concepts have a hierarchical structure, what Sartori (1970) referred to as a "ladder of abstraction". In contrast, Collier and Mahon (1993) used the term "ladder of generality", while Collier et al. (2008) used the term "kind hierarchy".

Core concepts of governance

The development of an appropriate typology of governance is therefore not based on a "haphazard shopping list" (Treib et al., 2007, p. 5) that is compiled on all possible dimensions noted in the policy and planning literature that characterise decision-making processes, outputs and outcomes. Instead, the criterion for the frameworks of governance should be systematically based on defining what dimensions are included and which are left out. The most common focus of most contributions to the governance debate in public policy terms is "the role of the state in society" (Pierre, 2000b, p. 4). Therefore, the core concept in governance in public policy terms is the relationship between state intervention (also referred to as public authority) and societal autonomy (self-regulation). This means that in order to avoiding political "concept stretching" (Collier & Mahon, 1993; Sartori, 1970), some dimensions of governance that have been suggested in the policy literature, such as Grosse's (2005) emphasis on transparency within the European Union's New Governance Project, operate at an instrumental scale and do not fundamentally add to an improved theoretical understanding of different frameworks or modes of governance (Treib et al., 2007).

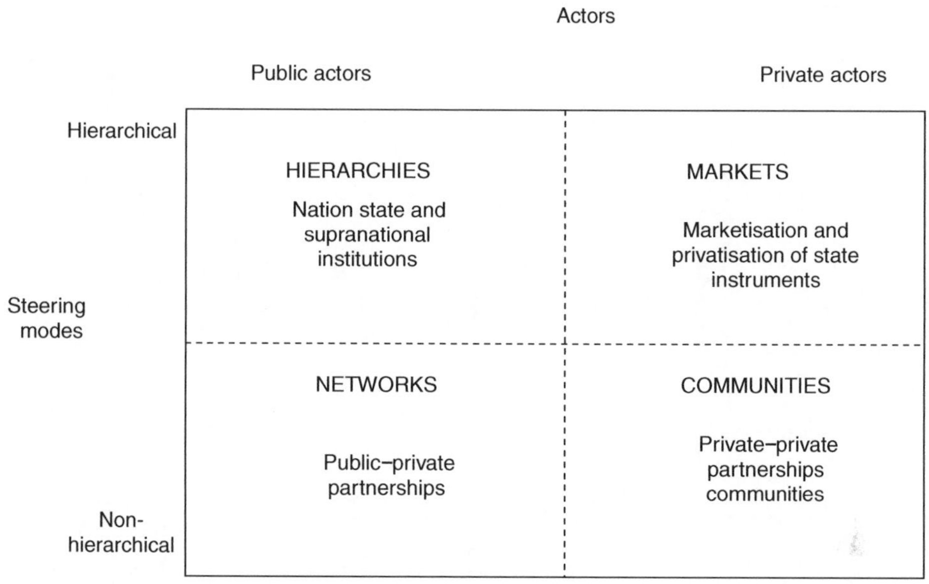

Actors

Public actors   Private actors

Hierarchical

HIERARCHIES Nation state and supranational institutions	**MARKETS** Marketisation and privatisation of state instruments
NETWORKS Public–private partnerships	**COMMUNITIES** Private–private partnerships communities

Steering modes

Non-hierarchical

Figure 2.   Frameworks of governance typology.

Knill and Lenschow's (2003) typology of modes of regulation in the European Union, which built upon their earlier work on the implementation of environmental policies in the European Union (Knill & Lenschow, 2000a, 2000b), has proven influential in the development of typologies of governance (Treib et al., 2007). Their typology utilises the dimensions of the level of obligation and the level of discretion with respect to the discretion European Union member states have to implement European Union rules. However, their framework focuses more on the regulatory instruments that are utilised by implementing actors "ranging from classical legal instruments to softer forms of steering the economy and society" (Knill & Lenschow, 2003, p. 1), rather than providing general types of governance.

In order to clarify the semantic field of governance for typology development, it is therefore necessary to identify the variables that serve to best clarify the core concept of governance. This can be done by reference to the relative use of hierarchical forms of regulation, i.e. legislation, and the relative power balance in the relationship between the state and other policy actors as categorical variables (Figure 2). Frances, Levačić, Mitchell, and Thompson (1991) recognised three different models of coordination, also referred to as meso-theoretical or intermediate theoretical categories, in western liberal democratic countries: hierarchies, markets and networks. These categories were found to be useful not only in national political life but also in analysing the external relationships between states. Therefore, according to Frances et al. (1991, p. 1), "the three forms of social organization have a general applicability that transcends any particular geographical space or temporal order. They exemplify genuine 'models' of coordination that can be characterized abstractly and then deployed in an analytical framework". To these categories, Pierre and Peters (2000) added a fourth common governance type which they termed "community".

Each of the conceptualisations of governance structures is related to the use of particular sets of policy instruments (Table 2). Given the artificiality of any policy–action divide (Barrett & Fudge, 1981), these instruments and modes of governance can also be connected to different conceptual approaches to implementation (Hall, 2009). Critical to the value of

Table 2. Frameworks of governance and their characteristics.

	Hierarchies	Communities	Networks	Markets
Classificatory type characteristics	Idealised model of democratic government and public administration	Notion that communities should resolve their common problems with minimum of state involvement	Facilitate coordination of public and private interests and resource allocation and therefore enhance efficiency of policy implementation	Belief in the market as the most efficient and just resource allocative mechanism
	Distinguishes between public and private policy space	Builds on a consensual image of community and the positive involvement of its members in collective concerns	Range from coherent policy communities/policy triangles through to single issue coalitions	Belief in the empowerment of citizens via their role as consumers
	Focus on public or common good	Governance without government	Regulate and coordinate policy areas according to the preferences of network actors than public policy considerations	Employment of monetary criteria to measure efficiency
	Command and control (i.e. "top-down" decision-making)	Fostering of civic spirit	Mutual dependence between network and state	Policy arena for economic actors where they cooperate to resolve common problems
	Hierarchical relations between different levels of the state			
Governance/ policy themes	Hierarchy, control, compliance	Complexity, local autonomy, devolved power, decentralised problem-solving	Networks, multi-level governance, steering, bargaining, exchange and negotiation	Markets, bargaining, exchange and negotiation
Policy standpoint	Top: policymakers; legislators; central government	Bottom: implementers, "street-level bureaucrats" and local officials	Where negotiation and bargaining take place	Where bargaining take place between consumers and producers
Underlying model of democracy	Elitist	Participatory	Hybrid/stakeholder; significant role given to interest groups	Consumer-determined; citizen empowerment
Primary focus	Effectiveness: to what extent are policy goals actually met?	What influences action in an issue area?	Bargained interplay between goals set centrally and actor (often local) innovations and constraints	Efficiency: markets will provide the most efficient outcome

Views of non-central (initiating) actors	Passive agents or potential impediments	Potentially policy innovators or problem shooters	Tries to account for the behaviour of all those who interact in the development and implementation of policy	Market participants are best suited to "solve" policy problems
Distinction between policy formulation and implementation	Actually and conceptually distinct; policy is made by the top and implemented by the bottom	Blurred distinction: policy is often made and then re-made by individual and institutional policy actors	Policy–action continuum: policymaking and implementation seen as a series of intentions around which bargaining takes place	Policy–action continuum
Criterion of success	When outputs/outcomes are consistent with a priori objectives	Achievement of actor (often local) goals.	Difficult to assess objectively, success depends on actor's perspectives	Market efficiency
Implementation gaps/deficits	Occur when outputs/outcomes fall short of a priori objectives	"Deficits" are a sign of policy change, not failure. They are inevitable	All policies are modified as a result of negotiation (there is no benchmark)	Occur when markets are not able to function
Reason for implementation gaps/deficits	Good ideas poorly executed	Bad ideas faithfully executed	"Deficits" are inevitable as abstract policy ideas are made more concrete	Market failure; inappropriate indicator selection
Solution to implementation gaps/deficits	Simplify the implementation structure; apply inducements and sanctions	"Deficits" are inevitable	"Deficits" are inevitable	Increase the capacity of the market
Primary policy instruments	Law Regulation Clear allocation and transfers of power between different levels of the state Development of a clear set of institutional arrangements Licensing, permits, consents and standards Removal of property rights	Self-regulation Public meetings/town hall meetings Public participation Non-intervention Voluntary instruments Information and education Volunteer associations	Self-regulation Accreditation schemes Codes of practice Industry associations Non-government organisations	Corporatisation and/or privatisation of state bodies Use of pricing, subsidies and tax incentives to encourage desired behaviours Use of regulatory and legal instruments to encourage market efficiencies Voluntary instruments Non-intervention

the different modes of governance are the relationships that exist between public and private policy actors and the steering modes that range from hierarchical top-down steering to non-hierarchical approaches. The main elements of the four models or frameworks of governance are outlined in Table 2, which identifies their key characteristics, the policy instruments associated with each concept of governance and various dimensions with respect to policymaking and implementation.

Hierarchical governance

In much of the tourism policy literature, the ongoing legislative and regulatory role of the state remains unassessed. Although much contemporary governance literature in tourism stresses public–private relationships (Bramwell, 2005; Dredge & Jenkins, 2007), hierarchical governance remains significant because of the continued role of the state in international relations, the development of institutions that enforce international and supranational law and the ongoing importance of legislation and regulation as part of the exercise of state control (Russell, Lafferty, & Loudon, 2008). "Governance conducted by and through vertically integrated state structures is an idealized model of democratic government and the public bureaucracy" (Pierre & Peters, 2000, p. 15), and provides the "traditional" model of state governance. However, this approach has been weakened by changes in the state environment, globalisation and the growth of the political powers of the local state.

There is very little direct discussion of hierarchical governance in tourism literature (Hall, 2011a; Viken, 2006), rather it tends to be subsumed under a more general discussion about the roles of government in tourism and the nature of state intervention (Hall, 2008a). Nevertheless, there is a substantial body of literature that discusses hierarchical governance in relation to environmental management, in which its implications for the sustainability of tourism activities are noted (e.g. Jentoft, 2007; Kluvánková-Oravská, Chobotová, Banaszak, Slavikova, & Trifunovova, 2009; Korda, Hills, & Gray, 2008; Meadowcroft, 2007).

Markets

The use of markets as a governance mechanism has been very much in political vogue since the mid-1980s (Pierre & Peters, 2000), including with respect to the corporatisation and privatisation of tourism functions that had previously been the domain of the state (Dredge & Jenkins, 2003, 2007; Hall, 1994, 1997, 2008a; Hall & Jenkins, 1995; Jenkins, 2000; Shone & Memon, 2008). The contemporary focus on the role of the market is very much associated with the influence of neoliberal political philosophy on considerations of the appropriate level of state intervention in socio-economic systems (Harvey, 2005). From this perspective,

> The market has come to be seen as everything Big Government is not; it is believed to be the most efficient and just allocative mechanism available since it does not allow for politics to allocate resources where they are not employed in the most efficient way. (Pierre & Peters, 2000, pp. 18–19)

The decision by the state to allow the market to act as a form of governance does not mean that government ceases to influence the market. Rather, instead of using imposed regulatory mechanisms, government may seek to use other forms of intervention, such as financial incentives, education and even the potential for future intervention, to encourage the tourism industry to move in particular directions, often via self-regulation. Examples of this approach include public subsidies and the provision of tax incentives for certain kinds of tourism activity (Bradshaw & Blakely, 1999; Hall & Williams, 2008; Jenkins, 1982; Wanhill, 1986). Nevertheless, the failure to achieve desirable outcomes as a result of self-regulation, market failure and the limits of the market as a form of governance has increasingly been recognised, especially with respect to the equity of policy outcomes (Schilcher, 2007) and the achievement of more sustainable forms of tourism (Gössling & Hall, 2008; Gössling, Hall, Peeters, & Scott, 2010; Hall, 2010c, 2011b).

Networks

The concept of networks, and public–private partnerships in particular, has received considerable attention in tourism policy and planning because of the ways in which they may facilitate coordination of public and private interests and resources (Beaumont & Dredge, 2010; Bramwell, 2005; Dredge, 2006a; Hall, 2008a; Pavlovich, 2001; Scott, Baggio, & Cooper, 2008). Policy networks vary widely with respect to their degree of cohesion, ranging from "sub-governments", "iron triangles"[1] and coherent policy communities through to issue specific coalitions (Gais, Peterson, & Walker, 1984; Jordan, 1981; Rhodes, 1997; Thatcher, 1998; van Waarden, 1992). Nevertheless, despite such variability in their organisation, network governance is often considered as a "middle way" or "third way" between hierarchical and market approaches to tourism governance (Scott, Cooper, & Baggio, 2008), while Hall (2009) presented networks in a similar fashion in relation to top-down and bottom-up approaches to implementation.

Networks have been proposed as a means to potentially integrate different policy perspectives, although integration capacity might depend on the inclusiveness of the planning process and the conditions influencing actors' perceived pay-offs from participation (Hovil & Stokke, 2007). However, the extent to which networks may act to serve self-interest rather than a larger collective interest poses major challenges for their utility as a policy instrument (Dredge, 2006b; Hall, 1999). Erkuş-Öztürk and Eraydin (2010) in a study of the contribution that networks may make to sustainable tourism in a Turkish destination suggested that, while there was an increase in local collaboration, environmental motivations fall far behind economic considerations in networking practices. "New governance" structures have strengthened the position of some policy networks (Pierre & Peters, 2005), although policy communities can also become solidified to the extent that policy alternatives are relatively closed with a policy arena forming sub-governments (Hall, 1999). Such a situation poses a dilemma for the contemporary state in that, while "it needs networks to bring societal actors into joint projects, it tends to see its policies obstructed by those networks" (Pierre & Peters, 2000, p. 20).

Communities

The fourth conceptualisation of governance is that of governance as communities. This approach is very much influenced by communitarianism and demands for more direct citizen involvement in governance. Communitarianism proposes that large-scale government should be replaced by smaller spatial units of governing that are closer to the "community" (Etzioni, 1993, 1995, 1998). Arguably, the most influential dimensions of communitarianism have been with respect to the focus on the significance of social capital in community and economic development (Putnam, 2001; Putnam, Leonardi, & Nanetti, 1993) and the development of alternative forms of consumption focused on the local region and voluntary simplicity (Doherty & Etzioni, 2003). However, in addition to the communitarian focus on the development of more appropriate scales of governance, the communities' framework also builds on traditions of deliberative and direct democracy. The former focused on improving mechanisms for greater direct public involvement in policymaking through enhancing debate and dialogue, while the latter via measures such as citizen-initiated referenda. All three dimensions of governance as communities highlight the importance of public participation in public policymaking (Pierre & Peters, 2000).

Community governance in tourism planning has been a significant theme in the tourism literature since the early 1980s (Murphy, 1983), before often becoming subsumed under general approaches towards sustainable tourism planning (Bramwell, 2005; Hall, 2008a). In some cases, interest in community-level governance developed because of the loss of local government authorities or powers as a result of political restructuring (O'Toole & Burdess, 2005), while the growing importance of the local state in tourism development and place competition within contemporary globalisation has also motivated interests in governance of the local state (Beaumont & Dredge, 2010; Thomas & Thomas, 1998). Although the framework has been criticised as being overly idealistic and exaggerating the benefits of perceived consensus (Hall, 2008a), community participation and even control over planning and decision-making remain an important issue in tourism planning and policymaking (Bramwell & Sharman, 1999; Dredge & Jenkins, 2007) and have become fundamental to much thinking about local governance with respect to voluntary tourism (Raymond & Hall, 2008), and the management of conservation and pro-poor tourism initiatives in less-developed countries (Nantongo, Byaruhanga, & Mugisha, 2007; Zapata et al., 2011).

Applications

Typologies are an important element of conducting analysis of public policy; the formal development of which has been hitherto little discussed in the tourism literature. "Working with typologies is crucial not only to the creation and refinement of concepts, but it also contributes to constructing categorical variables" (Box-Steffensmeier et al., 2008, p. 8). This paper has presented a typology of different frames of governance and their relationship to a range of policy elements. The significance of the typology is that it assists in the analysis of governance and policy both within and between different institutions, jurisdictions, policy domains and scales, and it reflects calls by authors, such as Young (2006), for greater comparative research of different policy choices and the selection of governance systems and institutional arrangements. This may be particularly important for a number of international environmental conventions that affect tourism and provide signatories with a substantial degree of flexibility in the development of policy and governance mechanisms in their implementation (Hall, 2011a). The case of the Convention on Biological Diversity (CBD) is discussed in the following section.

Applying a typology of governance to the CBD

The *Convention on Biological Diversity* (CBD) opened for signature on 5 June 1992 at the United Nations Conference on Environment and Development (UNCED; the Rio "Earth Summit"; Hall, 2010a). The convention entered into force on 29 December 1993 (United Nations, 1993). The objectives of the convention as stated in Article 1:

> are the conservation of biological diversity, the sustainable use of its components and the fair and equitable sharing of the benefits arising out of the utilization of genetic resources, including by appropriate access to genetic resources and by appropriate transfer of relevant technologies, taking into account all rights over those resources and to technologies, and by appropriate funding.

Table 3. Approaches to governance.

Governance approach	Examples	Percentage of responding countries adopting approach in full or part		
		In part	In full	Total
Hierarchy	Legislative change and development	12.4	14.9	27.3
	Improved risk assessment via environmental impact assessment	24	5.6	29.6
	Integrated the Guidelines on Biodiversity and Tourism	37.7	8	45.7
	Development in the development or review of national strategies and plans for tourism development, national biodiversity strategies and actions plans, and other related sectoral strategies			
Network	Mechanisms to coordinate national programmes	38.2 (under development)	11.4	49.6
	Sectoral cooperation in order to improve prevention, early detection, eradication and/or control of invasive alien species	52.8 (under consideration)	29.6	82.4
	Collaboration with trading partners and neighbouring countries to address threats of invasive alien species	46.3	21.1	67.4
Community	Indigenous and local communities provided with capacity-building and financial resources to support their participation in tourism policymaking, development planning, product development and management	46.3	3	49.3
Market	Development of financial measures to promote activities to reduce the threats of invasive species	36.9	1.6	38.5
	Education and training programmes in place for tourism operators on the impacts of tourism on biodiversity	25.9	43.9	69.8

Source: Derived from the third national report to the Secretariat of the CBD.

The reporting system of the CBD provides a means to analyse the extent to which state parties (the national and territorial governments that have ratified, acceded, approved or accepted the convention) have undertaken measures to implement it. As part of a regular reporting process, parties have to respond to a series of detailed questions from the CBD Secretariat with respect to the implementation of the CBD and the decisions and recommendations of the Conference of the Parties to the convention. At the end of 2009, the third national report provided by state parties was analysed with respect to their implementation of measures in Article 8(h) of the CBD which calls upon each Contracting Party to, "as far as possible and as appropriate" ... "Prevent the introduction of, control or eradicate those alien species which threaten ecosystems, habitats or species" in which tourism is a significant element (CBD, 2002; Hall, 2010b, 2011a), along with other tourism-specific measures related to the CBD (Hall, 2010a, 2010b).

The analysis of implementation measures of state parties to the CBD indicates that network approaches are given the greatest emphasis along with market- and community-based approaches (Table 3). Hierarchical regulatory mechanisms are not given as much weight with legislative change and development only being used by 27.3% of reporting state parties. This is particularly so given that national strategies and plans for tourism development, national biodiversity strategies and actions plans and other related sectoral strategies are usually voluntary rather than regulatory instruments (Hall, 2008a). The approach, and perhaps the relative success of the CBD, can be contrasted with other measures that affect international tourism such as the General Agreement on Tariffs and Trade (GATT) which entered into force with the establishment of the WTO in January 1995. Unlike the CBD, the GATT has a much stronger regulatory component, with the WTO providing a framework for dispute resolution as well as enforcing participants' adherence to WTO agreements that are ratified by the parliaments of member governments (Hall, 2011a). The hierarchical governance structure of the GATT therefore gives it a much stronger foundation for action and penalties for non-adherence under international law than the CBD.

Conclusion

This paper has investigated the conceptualisation of the construct of governance, a concept which is often referred to but which demonstrates a variety of different approaches in its understanding and application in tourism planning and policy studies. The study of governance concept formation has been undertaken through the systematic development of a typology. Within the context of political science and public policy studies, typologies are used for both descriptive and explanatory purposes with respect to the framing of key concepts and to contribute to the analysis of categorical variables (Box-Steffensmeier et al., 2008; Collier et al., 2008). In order to develop a typology of governance, an overarching concept was identified from the relevant literature with respect to the role of the state in society (Pierre, 2000b). Therefore, the overarching concept in governance in public policy terms is the relationship between state intervention/public authority and societal autonomy or self-regulation. The categorical variables that were selected to illustrate the concept of governance were the relative balance of the power relationships that exist between public and private policy actors and the steering modes that range from hierarchical top-down steering to non-hierarchical approaches. The resultant matrix identified the four frameworks or types of governance in the governance literature: hierarchies, markets, networks and communities. The core elements of these types were illustrated as well as the range of policy instruments that are normally associated with them. Employment of the typology does not mean that modes of governance are unchanging, rather it can assist in identifying how change occurs over time by providing a "snapshot" of the dynamic structures of governance and public policymaking.

Typologies contribute to conceptualising and describing empirical developments. They therefore serve as an appropriate analytical framework to structure analysis and comparison and can potentially be used for the development of quantitative as well as qualitative analysis. An example of the relative mix of governance measures in the implementation of the CBD that was dominated by non-hierarchical approaches was provided. However, like all maps, a typology of governance applies a simplifying lens to a complex reality. As Stoker (1998, p. 26) commented, "The issue is not that it has simplified matters but whether that simplification has illuminated our understanding and enabled us to find an appropriate path or direction".

The four types of governance that are identified are also not being described as "ideal types". As Collier et al. suggest, it is possible that scholars

> may be indirectly expressing the unease that readily arises when one seeks to fit cases into any scheme of classification. This unease may derive from the recognition that the cases grouped together in any one category usually cannot be understood as perfectly "equal". Rather, the claim is that they do indeed fit in a particular category, and not in another. (2008, p. 162)

In such a situation, the resolution is to perhaps recognise that abstraction and boundary definitions are an inevitable necessity of the process of classification. This is also not to deny the significance of boundary definition. As Rhodes (2005, p. 5) notes, some of "the most fascinating puzzles may be found at the boundaries of governing modes, both old and new, where they overlap, merge into one another and develop hybrid forms". Indeed, further comparative empirical research may likely assist the improved categorisation of governance types.

This analysis highlights the importance of accuracy and consistency in addressing key concepts in tourism as well as ensuring that they are used in a manner that allows for comparison in non-tourism fields. Given the considerable amount of research on governance in public policy, there is a clear need to ensure that concepts are being applied in a similar fashion in tourism studies. The value of the clear construction of categorical variables is that it allows for an assessment of change over time at various scales of assessment. This includes the overall semantic domain of governance as well as the utilisation of specific policy instruments. In the case of tourism planning and policy, it is apparent that there has been a strong focus on various elements of network governance since the late 1990s, but other dimensions of policy networks, such as policy communities and sub-governments, have not received the same level of attention. Although there are some notable exceptions (Beaumont & Dredge, 2010; Dredge, 2006b; Hall, 1999, 2008a; Pforr, 2005), the general focus on instruments such as collaboration and partnership in tourism networks, at the expense of critically understanding how governance is conceptualised or imagined and therefore why a governance approach is used when alternatives are ignored, means that the capacity to contribute to broader debates on governance has been substantially limited. In addition, key issues in the promotion of the virtues of certain governance frames, such as market governance and the application of democratic values to public–private partnerships (Pierre, 2009) and issues of equity, have also not been addressed.

Governance will clearly be a significant concept in tourism destination planning and policy in the foreseeable future. This paper advances our understanding of governance by emphasising the importance of having clear categorical variables in order to contribute to the formulation and evaluation of explanatory claims, clarify conceptual claims and assist comparative analysis and policy learning. It has also related concerns of tourism governance to the broader governance literature in public policy and political science. Importantly, it has stressed that the instruments of governance need to be understood as occurring within particular frames or images of governance rather than in isolation. To do so, it emphasises the critical importance of the understanding that not only do policies imply theories but governance implies theory as well. Therefore, for an improved understanding of tourism policy processes and outcomes, the empirical should not be divorced from the theoretical.

Acknowledgement

The assistance of Sandra Wilson in undertaking the analysis of national reports is gratefully acknowledged as are the valuable comments of the three anonymous referees.

Note

1. This is a term used by political scientists to describe a partnership of interest groups that come together for mutual support, usually consisting of elected politicians, state regulatory agencies and industry groups.

References

Anastasiadou, C. (2008). Tourism interest groups in the EU policy arena: Characteristics, relationships and challenges. *Current Issues in Tourism, 11*, 24–62.

Ansell, C., & Gash, A. (2008). Collaborative governance in theory and practice. *Journal of Public Administration Research and Theory, 18*, 543–571.

Ayuso, S. (2007). Comparing voluntary policy instruments for sustainable tourism: The experience of the Spanish hotel sector. *Journal of Sustainable Tourism, 15*, 144–159.

Bache, I., & Flinders, M. (Eds.). (2004). *Multi-level governance*. Oxford: Oxford University Press.

Bailey, K.D. (1994). *Typologies and taxonomies: An introduction to classification techniques*. Thousand Oaks, CA: Sage.

Barrett, S., & Fudge, C. (1981). *Policy and action*. London: Methuen.

Beaumont, N., & Dredge, D. (2010). Local tourism governance: A comparison of three network approaches. *Journal of Sustainable Tourism, 18*, 7–28.

Blume, S.S. (1977). Policy as theory. A framework for understanding the contribution of social science to welfare policy. *Acta Sociologica, 20*, 247–262.

Box-Steffensmeier, J.M., Brady, H.E., & Collier, D. (2008). Political science methodology. In J.M. Box-Steffensmeier, H.E. Brady, & D. Collier (Eds.), *The Oxford handbook of political methodology* (pp. 3–31). Oxford: Oxford University Press.

Bradshaw, T.K., & Blakely, E.J. (1999). What are "third-wave" state economic development efforts? From incentives to industrial policy. *Economic Development Quarterly, 13*, 229–244.

Bramwell, B. (2005). Interventions and policy instruments for sustainable tourism. In W. Theobold (Ed.), *Global tourism* (3rd ed., pp. 406–426). Oxford: Elsevier.

Bramwell, B., & Lane, B. (Eds.). (2000). *Tourism collaboration and partnerships: Politics, practice and sustainability*. Clevedon: Channel View Publications.

Bramwell, B., & Rawding, L. (1994). Tourism marketing organizations in industrial cities: Organizations, objectives and urban governance. *Tourism Management, 15*, 425–434.

Bramwell, B., & Sharman, A. (1999). Collaboration in local tourism policymaking. *Annals of Tourism Research, 26*, 392–415.

Coccossis, H., & Constantoglou, M.E. (2006). *The use of typologies in tourism planning: Problems and conflicts*. Paper presented at the 46th Congress of the European Regional Science Association (ERSA), Enlargement, Southern Europe and the Mediterranean, August 30 to September 2006, Department of Planning and Regional Development, University of Thessaly, Greece. Retrieved from http://www-sre.wu-wien.ac.at/ersa/ersaconfs/ersa06/papers/712.pdf

Coccossis, H., & Constantoglou, M.E. (2008). The use of typologies in tourism planning: Problems and conflicts. In H. Coccossis & Y. Psycharis (Eds.), *Regional analysis and policy: The Greek experience* (pp. 273–295). Heidelberg: Physica-Verlag.

Collier, D., Laporte, J., & Seawright, D. (2008). Typologies: Forming concepts and creating categorical variables. In J.M. Box-Steffensmeier, H.E. Brady, & D. Collier (Eds.), *The Oxford handbook of political methodology* (pp. 152–173). Oxford: Oxford University Press.

Collier, D., & Mahon, J.E., Jr. (1993). Conceptual "stretching" revisited: Adapting categories in comparative analysis. *American Political Science Review, 87,* 845–855.

Convention on Biological Diversity. (2002). *COP 6 Decision VI/23, Alien species that threaten ecosystems, habitats or species*. Retrieved from http://www.cbd.int/decision/cop/?id=7197

Cornelissen, S. (2005). *The global tourism system: Governance, development and lessons from South Africa*. Aldershot: Ashgate.

Dinica, V. (2009). Governance for sustainable tourism: A comparison of international and Dutch visions. *Journal of Sustainable Tourism, 17,* 583–603.

Doherty, D., & Etzioni, A. (2003). *Voluntary simplicity: Responding to consumer culture*. Lanham, MD: Rowman & Littlefield.

Dredge, D. (2001). Local government tourism planning and policy-making in New South Wales: Institutional development and historical legacies. *Current Issues in Tourism, 4,* 355–380.

Dredge, D. (2006a). Policy networks and the local organisation of tourism. *Tourism Management, 27,* 269–280.

Dredge, D. (2006b). Networks, conflict and collaborative communities. *Journal of Sustainable Tourism, 14*(6), 562–581.

Dredge, D., & Jenkins, J.M. (2003). Federal-state relations and tourism public policy, New South Wales, Australia. *Current Issues in Tourism, 6,* 415–443.

Dredge, D., & Jenkins, J.M. (2007). *Tourism planning and policy*. Milton: John Wiley.

Dredge, D., & Pforr, C. (2008). Policy networks and tourism governance. In N. Scott, R. Baggio, & C. Cooper (Eds.), *Network analysis and tourism: From theory to practice* (pp. 58–78). Clevedon: Channel View Publications.

Erkuş-Öztürk, H., & Eraydin, A. (2010). Environmental governance for sustainable tourism development: Collaborative networks and organisation building in the Antalya tourism region. *Tourism Management, 31,* 113–124.

Etzioni, A. (1993). *The spirit of community: Rights, responsibilities and the communitarian agenda*. New York: Crown.

Etzioni, A. (Ed.). (1995). *New communitarian thinking: Persons, virtues, institutions and communities*. Charlottesville: University Press of Virginia.

Etzioni, A. (Ed.). (1998). *The essential communitarian reader*. Lanham, MD: Rowman & Littlefield.

Frances, J., Levačić, R., Mitchell, J., & Thompson, G. (1991). Introduction. In G. Thompson, J. Frances, R. Levačić, & J. Mitchell (Eds.), *Markets, hierarchies and networks: The coordination of social life* (pp. 1–19). London: Sage.

Gais, T.L., Peterson, M.A., & Walker, J.L. (1984). Interest groups, iron triangles and representative institutions in American national government. *British Journal of Political Science, 14,* 161–185.

George, A., & Bennett, A. (2005). *Case studies and theory development in the social sciences*. Cambridge: MIT Press.

Gössling, S., & Hall, C.M. (2008). Swedish tourism and climate change mitigation: An emerging conflict? *Scandinavian Journal of Hospitality and Tourism, 8*(2), 141–158.

Gössling, S., Hall, C.M., Peeters, P., & Scott, D. (2010). The future of tourism: A climate change mitigation perspective. *Tourism Recreation Research, 35*(2), 119–130.

Göymen, K. (2000). Tourism and governance in Turkey. *Annals of Tourism Research, 27,* 1025–1048.

Greenwood, J. (1993). Business interest groups in tourism governance. *Tourism Management, 14,* 335–348.

Grosse, T.G. (2005). *Inception report: Democratization, capture of the state and new forms of governance in CEE countries (NEWGOV New Modes of Governance Project, Deliverable 17/D2)*. Warsaw: Institute of Public Affairs.

Gualini, E. (Ed.). (2004). *Multilevel governance and institutional change: The Europeanization of regional policy in Italy*. Aldershot: Ashgate.

Hall, C.M. (1994). *Tourism and politics: Policy, power and place*. Chichester: John Wiley.

Hall, C.M. (1997). Geography, marketing and the selling of places. *Journal of Travel and Tourism Marketing, 6*(3–4), 61–84.

Hall, C.M. (1999). Rethinking collaboration and partnership: A public policy perspective. *Journal of Sustainable Tourism, 7*, 274–289.

Hall, C.M. (2005). *Tourism: Rethinking the social science of mobility*. Harlow: Prentice-Hall.

Hall, C.M. (2007a). Tourism, governance and the (mis-)location of power. In A. Church & T. Coles (Eds.), *Tourism, power and space* (pp. 247–269). London: Routledge.

Hall, C.M. (2007b). Pro-poor tourism: Do "tourism exchanges benefit primarily the countries of the South"? *Current Issues in Tourism, 10*, 111–118.

Hall, C.M. (2008a). *Tourism planning: Policies, processes and relationships* (2nd ed.). London: Prentice-Hall.

Hall, C.M. (2008b). Regulating the international trade in tourism services. In T. Coles & C.M. Hall (Eds.), *International business and tourism: Global issues, contemporary interactions* (pp. 33–54). London: Routledge.

Hall, C.M. (2009). Archetypal approaches to implementation and their implications for tourism policy. *Tourism Recreation Research, 34*, 235–245.

Hall, C.M. (2010a). Tourism and the implementation of the Convention on Biological Diversity. *Journal of Heritage Tourism, 5*(4), 267–284.

Hall, C.M. (2010b). Tourism and biodiversity: More significant than climate change? *Journal of Heritage Tourism, 5*(4), 253–266.

Hall, C.M. (2010c). Changing paradigms and global change: From sustainable to steady-state tourism. *Tourism Recreation Research, 35*(2), 131–145.

Hall, C.M. (2011a). Biosecurity, tourism and mobility: Institutional arrangements for managing biological invasions. *Journal of Policy Research in Tourism, Leisure and Events, 3*(3). doi: 10.1080/19407963.2011.576868.

Hall, C.M. (2011b). Policy learning and policy failure in sustainable tourism governance: From first- and second-order to third-order change? *Journal of Sustainable Tourism, 19*(4–5), 649–671.

Hall, C.M., & Jenkins, J.M. (1995). *Tourism and public policy*. London: Routledge.

Hall, C.M., & Williams, A.M. (2008). *Tourism and innovation*. London: Routledge.

Hall, D.R. (Ed.). (2004). *Tourism and transition: Governance, transformation and development*. Wallingford: CABI.

Harvey, D. (2005). *A brief history of neoliberalism*. Oxford: Oxford University Press.

Hawkins, D.E., & Mann, S. (2007). The World Bank's role in tourism development. *Annals of Tourism Research, 34*, 348–363.

Heritier, A. (2002). New modes of governance in Europe: Policy-making without legislating? In A. Heritier (Ed.), *Common goods. Reinventing European and international governance* (pp. 186–206). Oxford: Rowman & Littlefield.

Hood, C. (2008). The tools of government in the information age. In M. Moran, M. Rein, & R.E. Goodin (Eds.), *The Oxford handbook of public policy* (pp. 469–481). Oxford: Oxford University Press.

Hooghe, L. (Ed.). (1996). *Cohesion policy and European integration: Building multi-level governance*. Oxford: Oxford University Press.

Hooghe, L., & Marks, G. (2001). *Multi-level governance and European integration*. Oxford: Rowman & Littlefield.

Hooghe, L., & Marks, G. (2003). Unraveling the central state, but how? Types of multi-level governance. *American Political Science Review, 97*, 233–243.

Hovil, S., & Stokke, K.B. (2007). Network governance and policy integration – The case of regional coastal zone planning in Norway. *European Planning Studies, 15*, 927–944.

Jenkins, C.J. (1980). Tourism policies in developing countries: A critique. *International Journal of Tourism Management, 1*, 22–29.

Jenkins, C.J. (1982). The use of investment incentives for tourism projects in developing countries. *Tourism Management, 3*(2), 91–97.

Jenkins, C.J., & Henry, B.M. (1982). Government involvement in tourism in developing countries. *Annals of Tourism Research, 9*, 499–521.

Jenkins, J.M. (2000). The dynamics of regional tourism organisations in New South Wales, Australia: History, structures and operations. *Current Issues in Tourism, 3*, 175–203.

Jentoft, S. (2007). Limits of governability: Institutional implications for fisheries and coastal governance. *Marine Policy, 31*, 360–370.

Jessop, B. (1998). The rise of governance and the risks of failure: The case of economic development. *International Social Science Journal, 50*(155), 29–45.

Jessop, B. (2002). Liberalism, neoliberalism, and urban governance: A state–theoretical perspective. *Antipode, 34*, 452–472.

Jordan, A.G. (1981). Iron triangles, woolly corporatism and elastic nets: Images of the policy process. *Journal of Public Policy, 1*, 95–123.

Jordan, A. (2001). The European Union: An evolving system of multi-level governance ... or government? *Policy & Politics, 29*, 193–208.

Jordan, A., Wurzel, R.K.W., & Zito, A. (2005). The rise of "new" policy instruments in comparative perspective: Has governance eclipsed government? *Political Studies, 53*, 477–496.

Judge, D., Stoker, G., & Wolman, H. (1995). Urban politics and theory: An introduction. In D. Judge, G. Stoker, & H. Wolman (Eds.), *Theories of urban politics* (pp. 1–13). London: Sage.

Kern, K., & Bulkeley, H. (2009). Cities, Europeanization and multi-level governance: Governing climate change through transnational municipal networks. *JCMS: Journal of Common Market Studies, 47*(2), 309–332.

Kersbergen, K.V., & Waarden, F.V. (2004). "Governance" as a bridge between disciplines: Cross-disciplinary inspiration regarding shifts in governance and problems of governability, accountability and legitimacy. *European Journal of Political Research, 43*, 143–171.

Kjaer, A. (2004). *Governance*. Cambridge: Polity Press.

Kluvánková-Oravská, T., Chobotová, V., Banaszak, I., Slavikova, L., & Trifunovova, S. (2009). From government to governance for biodiversity: The perspective of central and Eastern European transition countries. *Environmental Policy and Governance, 19*, 186–196.

Knill, C., & Lenschow, A. (Eds.). (2000a). *Implementing EU environmental policy. New directions and old problems*. Manchester: Manchester University Press.

Knill, C., & Lenschow, A. (2000b). Introduction: New approaches to reach effective implementation – Political rhetoric or sound concepts? In C. Knill & A. Lenschow (Eds.), *Implementing EU environmental policy. New directions and old problems* (pp. 3–8). Manchester: Manchester University Press.

Knill, C., & Lenschow, A. (2003). Modes of regulation in the governance of the European Union: Towards a comprehensive evaluation. *European Integration Online Papers (EIoP), 7*(1). Retrieved from http://eiop.or.at/eiop/texte/2003-001a.htm

Kooiman, J. (2003). *Governing as governance*. Los Angeles, CA: Sage.

Korda, R.C., Hills, J.M., & Gray, T.S. (2008). Fishery decline in Utila: Disentangling the web of governance. *Marine Policy, 32*, 968–979.

Larner, W. (2000). Neo-liberalism: Policy, ideology and governmentality. *Studies in Political Economy, 63*, 5–25.

Lowi, T. (1964). American business. Public policy, case studies, and political theory. *World Politics, 16*, 677–715.

Lowi, T.A. (1972). Four systems of policy, politics and choice. *Public Administration Review, 32*, 298–310.

Majone, G. (1980). The uses of policy analysis. In B.H. Raven (Ed.), *Policy studies review annual* (Vol. 4, pp. 161–180). Beverly Hills, CA: Sage.

Majone, G. (1981). Policies as theories. In I.L. Horowitz (Ed.), *Policy studies review annual* (Vol. 5, pp. 15–26). Beverly Hills, CA: Sage.

Marks, G., Hooghe, L., & Blank, K. (1996). European integration from the 1980s: State-centric v. multi-level governance. *JCMC: Journal of Common Market Studies, 34*, 341–378.

Meadowcroft, J. (2007). Who is in charge here? Governance for sustainable development in a complex world. *Journal of Environmental Policy & Planning, 9*, 299–314.

Medeiros de Araujo, L., & Bramwell, B. (1999). Stakeholder assessment and collaborative tourism planning: The case of Brazil's Costa Dourada project. *Journal of Sustainable Tourism, 7*, 356–378.

Morgan, G. (1986). *Images of organization*. Newbury Park, CA: Sage.

Murphy, P.E. (1983). Tourism as a community industry – An ecological model of tourism development. *Tourism Management, 4*, 180–193.

Nantongo, P., Byaruhanga, A., & Mugisha, A. (2007). Community-based conservation of critical sites: Uganda's experience. *Ostrich, 78*, 159–162.

O'Toole, K., & Burdess, N. (2005). Governance at community level: Small towns in rural Victoria. *Australian Journal of Political Science, 40*, 239–254.

Pavlovich, K. (2001). The twin landscapes of Waitomo: Tourism network and sustainability through the Landcare Group. *Journal of Sustainable Tourism, 9*, 491–504.

Pechlaner, H., & Tschurtschenthaler, P. (2003). Tourism policy, tourism organisations and change management in alpine regions and destinations: A European perspective. *Current Issues in Tourism, 6*, 508–539.

Peters, B.G. (2000). Governance and comparative politics. In J. Pierre (Ed.), *Debating governance: Authenticity, steering and democracy* (pp. 36–53). Oxford: Oxford University Press.

Pforr, C. (2002). The makers and the shakers of tourism policy in the Northern Territory of Australia: A policy network analysis of actors and their relational constellations. *Journal of Hospitality and Tourism Management, 9*, 134–151.

Pforr, C. (2005). Three lenses of analysis for the study of tourism public policy: A case from Northern Australia. *Current Issues in Tourism, 9*, 323–343.

Pforr, C. (2006). Tourism policy in the making: An Australian network study. *Annals of Tourism Research, 33*, 87–108.

Pierre, J. (Ed.). (2000a). *Debating governance: Authenticity, steering and democracy*. Oxford: Oxford University Press.

Pierre, J. (2000b). Introduction: Understanding governance. In J. Pierre (Ed.), *Debating governance: Authenticity, steering and democracy* (pp. 1–12). Oxford: Oxford University Press.

Pierre, J. (2009). Reinventing governance, reinventing democracy? *Policy & Politics, 37*, 591–609.

Pierre, J., & Peters, B.G. (2000). *Governance, politics and the state*. New York: St. Martin's Press.

Pierre, J., & Peters, B.G. (2005). *Governing complex societies: Trajectories and scenarios*. Basingstoke: Palgrave.

Popper, K. (1978). *Three worlds, the Tanner lecture on human values*. Lecture delivered at the University of Michigan (April 7). Retrieved April 1, 2010, from http://www.tannerlectures.utah.edu/lectures/documents/popper80.pdf

Pressman, J.L., & Wildavsky, A.B. (1973). *Implementation*. San Francisco, CA: University of California Press.

Putnam, R.D. (2001). *Bowling alone: The collapse and revival of American community*. New York, NY: Simon & Schuster.

Putnam, R.D., Leonardi, R., & Nanetti, R.Y. (1993). *Making democracy work: Civic traditions in modern Italy*. Princeton, NJ: Princeton University Press.

Raymond, E., & Hall, C.M. (2008). The development of cross-cultural (mis)understanding through volunteer tourism. *Journal of Sustainable Tourism, 16*, 530–543.

Rhodes, M. (2005). The scientific objectives of the NEWGOV Project. A Revised Framework. Paper presented at the NEWGOV Consortium Conference, 30–31 May 2005, European University Institute, Florence. Retrieved April 1, 2010, from http://www.eu-newgov.org/public/Consortium_Conference_2005.asp

Rhodes, R.A.W. (1997). *Understanding governance: Policy networks, governance, reflexivity and accountability*. Buckingham: Open University Press.

Russell, S.V., Lafferty, G., & Loudon, R. (2008). Examining tourism operators' responses to environmental regulation: The role of regulatory perceptions and relationships. *Current Issues in Tourism, 11*, 126–143.

Sartori, G. (1970). Concept misformation in comparative politics. *American Political Science Review, 64*(4), 1033–1053.

Sartori, G. (Ed.). (1984). *Social science concepts: A systematic analysis*. Beverly Hills, CA: Sage.

Schilcher, D. (2007). Growth versus equity: The continuum of pro-poor tourism and neoliberal governance. *Current Issues in Tourism, 10*, 166–193.

Scott, J., & Trubek, D.M. (2002). Mind the gap: Law and new approaches to governance in the European Union. *European Law Journal, 8*, 1–18.

Scott, N., Baggio, R., & Cooper, C. (Eds.). (2008). *Network analysis and tourism*. Clevedon: Channel View Publications.

Scott, N., Cooper, C., & Baggio, R. (2008). Destination networks: Four Australian cases. *Annals of Tourism Research, 35*, 169–188.

Shone, M.C., & Memon, P.A. (2008). Tourism, public policy and regional development: A turn from neo-liberalism to the new regionalism. *Local Economy, 23*, 290–304.

Steinberger, P.J. (1980). Typologies of public policy: Meaning construction and the policy process. *Social Science Quarterly, 61*, 185–197.

Stoker, G. (1998). Governance as theory. *International Social Science Journal, 50*(155), 17–28.

Sutcliffe, J.B. (1999). The 1999 reform of the structural fund regulations: Multi-level governance or renationalization? *Journal of European Public Policy, 7*, 290–309.

Thatcher, M. (1998). The development of policy network analyses: From modest origins to overarching frameworks. *Journal of Theoretical Politics, 10*(4), 389–416.

Thomas, H., & Thomas, R. (1998). The implications for tourism of shifts in British local governance. *Progress in Tourism and Hospitality Research, 4*(4), 295–306.

Treib, O., Bähr, H., & Falkner, G. (2007). Modes of governance: Towards a conceptual clarification. *Journal of European Public Policy, 14*(1), 1–20.

Tyler, D., & Dinan, C. (2001). The role of interested groups in England's emerging tourism policy network. *Current Issues in Tourism, 4*, 210–252.

United Nations. (1993). Convention on Biological Diversity (with annexes). Concluded at Rio de Janiero on 5 June 1992, No. 30619. *United Nations Treaty Series, 1760*(I-30619), 143–382.

Van Waarden, F. (1992). Dimensions and types of policy networks. *European Journal of Political Research, 21*(1–2), 29–52.

Viken, A. (2006). Svalbard, Norway. In G. Baldacchino (Ed.), *Extreme tourism. Lessons from the world's cold water islands* (pp. 129–144). Oxford: Elsevier.

Wanhill, S.R.C. (1986). Which investment incentives for tourism? *Tourism Management, 7*(1), 2–7.

Wesley, A., & Pforr, C. (2010). The governance of coastal tourism: Unravelling the layers of complexity at Smiths Beach, Western Australia. *Journal of Sustainable Tourism, 18*, 773–792.

Yee, A.S. (2004). Cross-national concepts in supranational governance: State-society relations and EU-policy making. *Governance – An International Journal of Policy and Administration, 17*, 487–524.

Young, O. (2006). Choosing governance systems: A plea for comparative research. In M. Moran, M. Rein, & R.E. Goodin (Eds.), *The Oxford handbook of public policy* (pp. 844–857). Oxford: Oxford University Press.

Yüksel, F., Bramwell, B., & Yüksel, A. (2005). Centralized and decentralized tourism governance in Turkey. *Annals of Tourism Research, 32*, 859–886.

Zapata, M.J., Hall, C.M., Lindo, P., & Vanderschaeghen, M. (2011). Can community-based tourism contribute to development and poverty alleviation? Lessons from Nicaragua. *Current Issues in Tourism.* doi:10.1080/13683500.2011.559200.

Governance, the state and sustainable tourism: a political economy approach

Bill Bramwell

Sheffield Business School, Sheffield Hallam University, Howard Street, Sheffield S1 1WB, UK

Collective actions are often needed to promote the objectives of sustainable tourism in destinations. Governance is the basis of these collective actions. This paper contends that research on the governance of tourism and sustainability would benefit from greater use of social theory. It shows how one social theory, a strategic-relational political economy approach, can offer insights into state interventions affecting tourism and sustainability in destinations. The paper uses a literature review and case studies incorporating ideas from this approach to understand the state's influences on tourism and sustainability. Case studies are taken from Germany, China, Malta, Turkey and the UK. A range of distinctive perspectives and themes associated with this approach are assessed. They include the approach's holistic, relational and dialectical perspective, its focus on the state's roles in regulating the economic and political systems, its concern with the interactions between agency and structure, and the adaptation of state activities at different spatial scales and at different times, together with the concepts of path dependence and path creation. These perspectives and themes are directions for future research on governance, the state and sustainable tourism.

Introduction

In order to develop and apply policies for tourism in destinations, there is usually a requirement for knowledge, thought, the application of power, resources and rules, and also coordination and cooperation among numerous actors. Together, these are key features of governance. This paper examines governance by state organisations that affects whether the management of tourism in destinations is either more or less sustainable. Much of the discussion focuses on explaining how a political economy approach provides distinctive research perspectives and themes to understand the state's activities that influence tourism and sustainability in destinations.

The term governance is widely used in a variety of academic and practitioner circles. It implies "systems of governing" and the ways in which societies are governed, ruled or "steered". It also suggests collective action and coordination. Rhodes (1996) describes governance as a condition of ordered rule or a method by which society is governed. He also suggests that governance processes provide the means for "authoritatively allocating resources and exercising control and co-ordination" (Rhodes, 1996, p. 653). In the specific context of tourist destinations, Baggio, Scott, and Cooper (2010, p. 52) indicate that in some circumstances "the governance system may be considered as the tool by which the destination adapts to change".

While the term government indicates a concern with the formal institutions and structures of the state, the concept of governance is broader and it draws attention to how governmental and non-governmental organisations often work together. The forms of governance can include hierarchical tiers of formal government, networks of actors beyond government, and markets and quasi-markets (Newman & Clarke, 2009). For the different forms of governance, attention is directed to how policy decisions are made and how power is distributed. There are important power relations around governance, with, for example, some groups in society having relatively more influence than others on government policy-making (Dredge & Jenkins, 2007; Hill, 1997).

The paper's first section explores the significance of governance, and particularly governance by the state, for tourism and sustainable development in destinations. Firstly, it considers why this topic deserves study. Secondly, it argues that in practice, the state is often a primary influence on governance, and consequently there is a requirement for further research on the state's influence on tourism and sustainability. The state involves an institutional ensemble that has political authority and power, including sovereignty, within a national, regional or more local territory. The state cannot be understood in isolation as it is dependent on its relationships with society, including societal groups seeking to influence its policies. Although the state has much power, it also has a responsibility for maintaining the cohesion of society within its territory (Dunleavy & O'Leary, 1987; Jessop, 2008; Weiss, 1998). A third argument in the paper's initial discussion is that there are likely to be benefits for research on the governance of tourism and sustainability if more use was made of social theory developed in the social sciences.

The bulk of the paper examines how one social theory, political economy, might be applied in order to understand the state's influences on tourism and sustainability in destinations. It also considers the distinctive research perspectives and themes that this approach can suggest. In political economy, the social system is considered to constitute a whole, so the various aspects of society are parts of the whole (Harvey, 2010; Peet, 1998). The driving force of change in the social system is considered to be the oppositions and conflicts within and between the elements of this whole (Jamal & Watt, 2011). Thus, the political sphere associated with governance is strongly related to the economic and social spheres. This approach also puts particular emphasis on the economic relations within which humans find themselves. A specific political economy perspective is also explained in the paper, i.e. Jessop's (2008) strategic-relational approach.

Short case studies are used to illustrate how political economy may be used to examine state interventions that affect tourism and sustainability in destinations, and the case studies also indicate the distinctive research perspectives and themes that can result. They are drawn from previously published studies by the author, often with a co-author, on state interventions that affect tourism and sustainability in destinations, and the original studies are informed to varying degrees by political economy. They reflect the author's attempts over recent years to understand how this social theory might assist in understanding government intervention in tourist destinations. Thus, the case studies indicate the author's personal journey, critical reflection and developing thinking around the application of political economy to tourism. A summary table, Table 1, lists the distinctive perspectives and themes associated with a strategic-relational political economy approach to governance in sustainable tourism.

The state and sustainable tourism in destinations

Governance and sustainable tourism

Destinations wanting to promote sustainable tourism are more likely to be successful when there is effective governance. Normally, this involves having good mechanisms for the coordination of collective action (Butler, 2010). But in practice there are substantial difficulties that can hinder effective governance for sustainable tourism. One reason why more studies of governance in this context are needed is to understand these difficulties and also, importantly, to find potential ways to overcome them.

One difficulty for the governance of sustainable tourism is that its concerns cut across sectors and span diverse policy domains, such as planning, transport, climate change, employment and regional development. Sustainable tourism policies need to be integrated with wider economic, social and environmental policy considerations within an overall sustainable development framework (Hall, 2008). Further, the policies affecting sustainable tourism are very often made in policy domains other than tourism, often with little attention paid to the implications for tourism. These characteristics of sustainable tourism governance mean that it is very difficult to secure a coordinated approach. There are also obstacles to securing coordination within the tourism sector itself. Williams and Shaw suggest that "the institutional setting for tourism policy is particularly weak due to fragmentation in the industry and weak interest group representation" (1998, p. 58). And, normally, most decisions in the tourism sector depend on private capital, and in practice, there are usually limits to the extent to which policies in the public sphere will influence commercial businesses and business decisions.

Another difficulty for the governance of sustainable tourism is that it requires cooperation and coordination among diverse actors from across varied sectors and policy domains, and these actors often have divergent interests, beliefs and priorities (Bramwell & Lane, 2000). The actors relevant to sustainable tourism are normally spread across the public, private, voluntary and community sectors. They are from elected government institutions as well as from commercial businesses, NGOs and the media. They include individuals and the wider public living in destination areas as well as tourists visiting these areas. They may be in global organisations and in national, regional and local ones. Securing cooperation and coordination among these varied actors is a challenge for the governance of any type of tourism, but it is an especial challenge for sustainable tourism as the relevant issues, and thus the relevant actors, cross so many sectors and policy domains. The actors might represent interests in, for example, business enterprise, energy, planning, employment, equality issues and environmental protection.

The influence of the state

In practice, government or the state is often a primary influence on governance, including policymaking for sustainable development. This is an important reason why more research is needed on the roles and activities of the state that affect tourism and sustainability in destinations. This paper focuses largely on state interventions.

The state may not promote democracy, efficient policymaking, equitable outcomes or the objectives of sustainability. Nevertheless, there are many potential reasons why the state is often a significant influence on governance. Its involvement is often justified, for example, on the grounds that the state is well placed to work for the collective interests of the population and that there may be opportunities to hold the state politically accountable for its actions, especially in democratic systems. By contrast, other governance arrangements may be less suitable as they could encourage partisan policies and be characterised by less transparency and accountability (Yüksel, Bramwell, & Yüksel, 2005). People can also look to government to seek to improve coordination across the breadth of issues and policy domains involved in sustainable tourism. Wearing and Neil assert that "The holistic ambitions of sustainable development and the multidisciplinary nature of tourism entail that only governments and public authorities can coordinate efforts in sustainable tourism policy at both the national and local levels" (2009, p. 44).

Further, the state may be in a position to offer incentives for actors to alter their behaviour so as to promote sustainability, or to impose requirements on actors to do this. These may be direct incentives of various kinds, or relate to overall fiscal policies and their indirect impacts on the tourism sector. Without government interventions, the objectives of sustainable tourism may be reliant on voluntary actions or self-regulation, and not all actors will respond positively. Actors may fail to respond to voluntary initiatives because of disinterest, because they object to the initiatives or because taking the required steps involves various costs. Tourism businesses may not accept these costs as it directly affects their profits and they fear that competitor businesses will not absorb them and thus might gain a market advantage. Such difficulties may explain why Williams and Montanari conclude that in the tourism sector, self-regulation "by itself is not a sufficient approach" (1999, p. 38).

Many researchers suggest, however, that over the last 30 years, the state in many countries has often become a less significant influence. The political direction has moved so that the state's activities increasingly occur through arm's length relationships, with a growing role for agencies, public–private sector partnerships, the voluntary sector, and markets and quasi-markets. The representative politics of government has also had a shrinking hold on public trust and engagement, and it has been supplemented by a greater use of public forums and consultation. Despite these trends, however, one cannot announce the state's demise (Newman & Clarke, 2009). Indeed, there is a risk of under-estimating the state's continuing significance in tourism governance. This risk is probably increased by government endorsements of tourism partnerships and community forums, and also by the proliferation of research on newer forms of tourism governance (Bramwell & Lane, 2000; Moore & Weiler, 2009). Some researchers contend that the government often remains powerful in contemporary governance, with the state retaining regulatory control over many organisations that at first can appear independent of it, and also over many functions that initially it may seem to have lost (Bramwell, 2010; Flynn, 2002; Jessop, 2008). The state's continuing influence can occur, for example, through subtle government steering of the priorities for action of the new agencies and partnerships. Such steering by the state might be achieved through its use of detailed contracts, competition for funding, performance indicators, audits and reviews (Kokx & van Kempen, 2010). The state can also maintain much influence by being a participant in the new partnerships.

The use of social theory

Research on tourism governance is likely to benefit if more use is made of social theory developed in the social sciences. Social theory consists of groupings of ideas concerned with finding broad explanations of the world (Panelli, 2004). Mowforth and Munt argue that some previous studies of governance in tourism are characterised by a "failure to set policy and action in a broader and more critical framework which acknowledges that there are competing interests" (2009, p. 297).

There is only limited use of social theory in some recent studies of tourism policy focused on network analysis techniques. In a study of tourism policy networks in Australia's Northern Territory, Pforr (2006, p. 90) maps the relevant actors, who are depicted as "nodes", and the presence of specific relationships between them, which are presented as connecting "lines" (Scott, 1991). These techniques are valuable for summarising specific policy network features, but they focus on the presence or absence of relationships rather than on their detailed character and inter-connections, and on specific points in time rather than on how they may evolve temporally (Börzel, 1998). A recent study of tourism policy networks using these techniques concludes that future research should "go beyond structure and relations to explore the dynamics associated with actor strategies, rules of conduct, levels of institutionalisation and power relations" (Presenza & Cipollina, 2010, p. 28).

One benefit of using social theory is that it functions as both a storage and a bridging device, storing the results of work on one topic or in one field of study in the form of broad ideas that can be transferred across the theoretical bridges to other study topics and other research fields. Research on the governance of sustainable tourism is likely to benefit if it puts more emphasis on its connections with broad frameworks or social theory (Hall, 2005). This would assist in developing new insights into its own topics and also in transcending its own subject boundaries so that it makes a fuller contribution to developing general social theory (Bramwell, 2007). However, there is much discussion and dispute in the social sciences about the relative merits of different social theories. This debate is necessary and important, and it reflects how profound consequences flow from the choice of social theory. This choice affects the perspectives and themes explored, the sources used, the methods employed, the interpretations and concepts developed, the recommendations suggested and also the political implications of research (Peet, 1998).

The paper next explains the potential applications of just one social theory to the study of state interventions affecting tourism and sustainability in destinations, and it also discusses the related distinctive research perspectives and themes that this social theory may suggest.

A political economy of state interventions

Political economy is a broad social theory that has been widely applied in the social sciences. It is used less frequently in tourism research, but there are several applications (Mosedale, 2011). They include Britton's (1982, 1991) work on unequal economic relations between peripheral tourist destinations and metropolitan economies, and Bianchi's (2002, 2009) use of the concepts of power and uneven development from political economy for evaluations of tourism development. Several papers exploring the relevance of political economy approaches to tourism were also recently brought together by Mosedale (2011). The applications of political economy, more specifically, to tourism governance are not extensive in number, but there are a few. Dredge and Jenkins assert that in relation to the potential use of political economy to understand the state's activities in tourism, "the field of tourism studies has grossly neglected this complex view of the state" (2007, p. 38). Among the relevant studies using ideas from political economy are Hall's work on the local state's roles in developing sport mega-events in cities (Hall, 1994, 2006), and Bianchi's (2004) assessment of the politics of tourism planning introduced by regional government in the Spanish Canary islands.

The discussion that follows elaborates on how political economy may be applied to gain an understanding of the state's roles and activities that affect tourism and sustainability in destinations. Space constraints mean that the account covers only certain features of political economy and it does not explain many of the criticisms of this research perspective. It also does not evaluate the different possible approaches to political economy. Mosedale (2011, p. 3), for example, identifies four such approaches within tourism research: Marxian, regulation theory, international comparative and post-structural. The particular variant of political economy used in this paper is based on Jessop's (2008) strategic-relational approach, although it also reflects Marxian ideas and regulation theory. The discussion considers how this approach can be applied to tourism and sustainability and how the approach may suggest distinctive research perspectives and themes, but it does not provide a full critical assessment. Certain features of the approach are described and several are illustrated through case studies drawn from previously published studies by the author, often with a co-author, on state interventions that affect tourism and sustainability in destinations. The original studies are informed to varying degrees by political economy.

A relational and materialist approach

In political economy, the social system is considered to constitute a whole, so the various aspects of society are parts of the whole (Harvey, 2010; Peet, 1998). Thus, the political sphere associated with governance is strongly related to the economic and social spheres. For Jessop (2008, pp. 1, 5), the strategic-relational approach to political economy "starts from the proposition that the state is a social relation", and from the idea that the state's "apparatuses and practices are materially interdependent with other institutional orders and social practices. In this sense it is socially embedded". This is a holistic and relational view of the social system and of the state within it, so that the "parts and wholes are mutually constitutive of each other" (Harvey, 1996, p. 53). This view would require research on the state's activities and tourism to adopt a broad horizon that considers the state within its wide relations with society, and for it to explore the multiple and reciprocal relations between tourism, the state, economy and society.

The materialist basis of political economy emphasises the economic relations within which humans find themselves. It presents workers in a capitalist society as active economic agents that transform nature through the labour process and achieve development by building productive forces. However, the social relations in a capitalist society include class relations, so that material benefits derived from hard work in the economy are unequally distributed to the disadvantage of the workers and the advantage of dominant groups. The conflicts around class relations involve relations of unequal power, and these conflicts provide a basis for change in society (Bianchi, 2011). Another dimension of the materialist basis of capitalism is that it is inherently expansionist due to constant economic pressures to increase surplus extraction and to accumulate capital (Bramwell & Meyer, 2007; Harvey, 2010). These economic pressures under capitalism can lead to the unsustainable loss of environmental, social and cultural features. This materialist perspective indicates that research on the state, tourism and sustainability needs to take account of their potential connections with the economy, which may not at first be readily apparent.

For political economy, a key driving force of change in the social system is considered to be the oppositions and contradictions within and between the elements of the whole. The social system and the elements within it are internally contradictory by virtue of the multiple processes that constitute them, and this leads to dialectical processes of change (Harvey, 1996). The interactions within and between the elements, with their oppositions and tensions, always occur in specific situations: "The dialectical resolution of conflict is a productive synthesis of the conflicting elements in a definite situation" (Peet, 1998, p. 79).

This significant empirical dimension "transforms it from an instrument of teleological ne-cessity to a way of analyzing a determinable but open historical process" (Peet, 1998, p. 79). The economic sphere is not determinant, even in the last instance, as social development is "constituted in and through contingent social practices", so that "a large part of macro-social development is anarchic or unplanned" (Jessop, 1990, p. 103). Thus, research on the state and tourism should examine the dialectical relations within this sphere and also between it and society's other elements, including the economy, and it should be sceptical about very simple cause and effect arguments, even when given feedback loops. Research should also focus on the relative weight of different institutions and social forces in determining specific outcomes in complex and changing specific situations or conjunctures.

The roles and activities of the state

Marx famously argued that market forces are inherently unstable. This is because they lead to capital over-accumulation and thus to periodic crises, and also because they encourage unstable social and political relations. When influenced by the regulation approach, political economy often focuses on how society may seek to regulate these instabilities (Cornelissen, 2011; Goodwin, 2001; Peet, 2007; Williams, 2004). Governance institutions, and notably state organisations, are important in regulating the economic and political systems in order to mitigate these instabilities, avert crises and promote the system's reproduction. The importance attributed to society's materialist basis means that a key role for the state is intervention to encourage capital accumulation and economic expansion (Bevir, 2009; Jessop, 1997a, 1997b, 2002). At the same time, the state must seek to ensure that it maintains its ability adequately to reflect the popular will and thus maintains its legitimacy (Goodwin & Painter, 1996; Peck & Tickell, 1992). If the state lacks legitimacy, then there will be social and political instability and sustained economic activity will not be possible. Purcell and Nevins suggest that "In order to maintain political legitimacy and effective authority over its people, the state must reproduce a politically stable relationship between state and citizen" (2005, pp. 212–213).

Political economy suggests that the state can tend to give priority to the economy as this produces the wealth, which provides income for the state and for the population that provides the state's political support (Jessop, 2008). Thus, the state may often intervene in favour of economic over environmental and socio-cultural priorities (Harvey, 2010). When priority is given to economic growth through tourism, then environmental and socio-cultural resources may be neglected or traded off. State interventions to support economic expansion in tourist areas can include enforcing the legal rights of property owners and marketing to attract tourists.

Political economy also indicates why the state may intervene to protect environmental and socio-cultural resources in destinations. One explanation is that the state may decide to protect these resources from tourism activities if it is considered that their loss or deteriora-tion may reduce the potential for future capital accumulation (While, Jonas, & Gibbs, 2010). Market forces often make actors focus on short-term economic returns to the detriment of environmental and socio-cultural resources, even if the resources are required to sustain their future economic returns, and thus this problem can prompt government intervention. The state, however, may also be more focused on securing immediate economic returns. Another explanation for state-sponsored environmental and socio-cultural protection is that there is usually an expectation that government will intervene to avert major instances of damage to society's collective assets (Gibbs, 1996; Gibbs & Jonas, 2000; Harvey, 1996). The state will usually intervene to secure some sort of balance between economic development, environment and local society because this is likely to gain quite wide public support, although this intervention will impinge on the interests of some groups and thus it may result in conflict. Such intervention is associated with the state's need to secure political legitimacy and to maintain authority.

Critics sometimes suggest that within political economy, the state ultimately makes decisions according to economic or structural necessity, and thus the approach is deterministic. But others assert that within this approach, state interventions are not determined by the economy or structures because they are also affected by policymakers' intentional decisions and by specific and at times unexpected circumstances at particular conjunctures, including the political situation (Bramwell, 2006). Thus, they suggest that policymakers actively consider the particular circumstances at specific times and also have some room to influence policy decisions. Policymaking is considered to reflect the political situation, including tensions between social classes and a range of lobby groups that reflect people's active and varying responses. There can be such tensions and conflicts between social groups around how the state regulates its priorities between tourism and environmental protection. Thus, "the intense commercial pressures to gain immediate economic returns mean that the tourism sector often opposes government interventions that aim to protect the environment" (Bramwell, 2004, p. 34). By contrast, environmental groups and community forums may oppose particular tourism schemes. Further, more powerful groups might seek to influence policies around tourism's environmental impacts in order to make sectional gains. Thus, with tourism-related governance, it is useful "to conceive of this political context as a multi-actor field, where different actors have their own specific interests, can espouse certain views, and have varying degrees of influence on the policy process and on the resulting policy direction" (Bramwell, 2004, p. 32).

Case studies using this relational and materialist approach

The two case studies examined here are drawn from previously published studies involving the author. Both use political economy to gain an understanding of the state's roles and activities that affect tourism and sustainability in destinations, and they indicate the distinctive research perspectives and themes that can result from applying this approach.

The first study, by Bramwell and Meyer (2007), applies a political economy approach to explore the relative balance between tourism development and environmental protection in the policies of two tiers of local government on the island of Rügen in former East Germany between 1990 and 2000. It explicitly adopts "a relational and dialectical approach focused on social relations" (p. 769). Policies for tourism and the environment in the case study area were affected by structural change in the economy and by shifts in politics and in the institutional arrangements for governance. The fundamental structural change was that from 1990, the former socialist East Germany joined the capitalist West in a reunified Germany. As a consequence, the island of Rügen rapidly had to adjust from being in a centrally planned socialist economy and a single-party political system to being within a free market capitalist economy and a political system based on representative democracy.

The shift to a capitalist economy initially meant that numerous sub-standard tourist facilities on the island closed down, partly because they lacked the West's quality standards, and Rügen's unemployment soared. At the same time, however, there was a revalorisation of local real estate as developers recognised investment opportunities due to the potential for escalating property prices and due to government support for private sector investment so as to promote economic development. The new investment opportunities meant that the former East Germany became known as "the golden east", with Rügen's tourism sector being seen as particularly attractive for investment and capital accumulation. Many of the island's new tourism business people were from former West Germany, but some had previously been influential in the former East Germany. Some became active in local politics and often supported proposals for new tourism developments.

The tourism development pressure on Rügen encouraged the sub-regional government, the Landkreis Rügen, to adopt policies for environmental protection and sustainable development. Its policies were supported by environmental groups and actors concerned about the increasing influence of external investors and the competition for established small tourism businesses from the new tourism schemes. However, the more local tier of government, the many municipalities, focused on policies to attract new investments in order to bring jobs, increase local tax revenues, and generally to secure economic development, as the area struggled to adjust to the market economy after its unification within Germany. The municipalities controlled the land-use planning system and the issue of planning permits for new developments. This meant that in practice the municipalities had much more influence than the sub-regional government on the development process, and much new tourism-related construction was allowed. Additionally, few local residents saw the environmental groups who opposed the new development projects as representing their interests. Instead, they considered that the environmentalists hindered the creation of the jobs which they saw as essential and that they were outsiders representing external interests. The responses of the residents, and thus the electorate, were also a significant political influence on the balance between tourism development and environmental protection.

The use of political economy helped the study to consider the potential influence of broad economic and political processes on local policies for tourism and the environment on the island of Rügen. Through detailed empirical investigation informed by these ideas, the effects on the state's policies of changes in the economic and political context, the related tourism development pressures, demands for investment in the local economy and the conflicting views between different groups of actors were all explored.

The second published study that draws on political economy to assess the state's influences on tourism and sustainability is by Yan and Bramwell (2008). It examines the approach taken by China's Communist Party-led central government to culture, heritage and tourism at Qufu in Shandong province, the historic home of Confucius and Confucianism and now a World Heritage Site. The approach by government is assessed in the study from Mao Zedong's communist revolution in 1949 to recent times. The empirical changes over this period in the central state's attitudes to cultural and tourist activities at Qufu encouraged the study to consider whether and how the changes reflected structural trends in China's politics, economy and society.

After Mao's communist revolution in 1949 and before 1978, China's central government actively suppressed the associations between Qufu and its Confucian past. During that period, Confucianism was strongly associated with the traditional values of China's feudal era, which were based on imperial dynasties and the exploitation by feudal elites of the majority in society; Confucianism was seen by the state as incompatible with the scientific and revolutionary socialism, which it intended should underpin the country's economy and society (Dardess, 1983; Ogden, 1995). During Mao's era, the authorities at Qufu feared the consequences from the Communist Party if it continued with Confucian traditions, and thus, it abandoned a traditional Confucian "cult ceremony" there. The state under Mao also discouraged domestic and international tourism, apart from very restricted numbers of tourists invited for propaganda purposes (Sofield & Li, 2011).

The situation began to change, however, following the 1978 "open-door" economic reforms introduced by Deng Xiaoping, which brought substantial marketisation and privatisation to the economy and created a state-manipulated market economy alongside communism that has delivered spectacular economic growth. With the 1978 reforms, the central state began to allow tourism to grow generally and at Qufu, and it also gradually accepted the revival of Qufu's Confucian "cult ceremony". The government became increasingly enthusiastic about tourism as a stimulus to economic growth (Sofield & Li, 2011). Deng Xiaoping gave much prominence to economic goals, and this economic argument has encouraged the rehabilitation of numerous traditional cultural sites, including those associated with Confucianism.

A second potential influence on the growth of tourism and the revival of the "cult ceremony" at Qufu was the new economic, social and political tensions in China that have arisen following the introduction of market forces in this socialist society. Because of these tensions, China's leaders seem to have felt it necessary to find new means to legitimise the incorporation of market forces and also to justify the Communist Party's continuing political dominance. One potential interpretation is that the national leadership recognised that a selective revival of traditional Chinese values, including Confucianism, might help to reduce growing tensions and questioning of socialist values. The position of the Communist Party might also be strengthened through a modest revival of traditional values because they can encourage the acceptance of established authority and leadership. These values have the potential to help to build among Chinese people a sense of social solidarity and self-confidence in their national history and identity. Potentially, the central state's changing attitudes to tourism and a Confucian ceremony at Qufu may have been influenced by the requirement for the state to maintain political legitimacy and effective authority over its citizens. This interpretation reflects the suggestion from political economy that the state needs to strive to maintain its political legitimacy and effective authority (Purcell & Nevins, 2005).

Agency–structure relations and strategic selectivity

A fundamental idea behind Jessop's strategic-relational approach to political economy is that social change is not the result of the deterministic unfolding of some inevitable economic or structural logic (Bianchi, 2011). He contends that the structural constraints in society should not be seen as absolute and unconditional, thus leaving no scope for people's individual subjective views and for their own personal decisions and associated actions. Jessop also rejects, however, the opposite idea that actors act completely on the basis of their own free will and subjectivity (Jessop, 2008). Instead, he brings together the structural constraints in society and the agency of actors through his idea of "strategic selectivity", a key concept for his strategic-relational approach to political economy. The argument behind this concept is that actors are reflexive, capable of taking a strategic view of the structural constraints and strategically able to select their specific actions within those constraints. Actors do this in the context of specific circumstances at particular conjunctures. Through these processes, actors can and do transform social structures, and thus, the structural constraints always operate through specific actors pursuing particular strategies in specific circumstances.

Jessop applies his strategic-relational view of structure and agency most fully to the roles of the state. He argues that the actors and organisations of the state engage in strategic selectivity in the context of the constraints found in their social environment. The state is considered "as a system of strategic selectivity and the nature of political struggle as a field of competing strategies for hegemony" (Jessop, 1990, p. 221). A key task for research about the state's influence would be to determine how the state and the actors in government privilege some strategies over others at particular times. The strategic choices of actors and organisations in the state are likely to be affected by the structural pressures in society, including the broad economic and socio-cultural changes and the lobbying by actors in civil society. But there is still room for choices and "strategic selectivity".

This approach suggests that research on the governance of tourism and sustainability should examine micro-scale agency, macro-scale structures and, most importantly, the dialectical relations between them based on the idea of strategic selectivity at particular conjunctures. This may help to avoid descriptive and static accounts of governance in this field, and also improve our understanding of causality and the processes of change.

A case study of relations between agency and structure

The next case study examines relations between the agency of actors and structural constraints on the Mediterranean islands of Malta. Bramwell (2006, pp. 959, 973) explores "the contingent and complex interplay between structures and actors", based on the assertion that, while large-scale structures are highly significant, actors still "have some room for manoeuvre, even under the most extreme structural constraints". These relations are assessed for government-appointed actors involved in selecting a limit or ceiling for future growth in the tourism sector on the Maltese islands. The study's focus on relations between structural pressures and active choices provides a distinctive perspective on why and how the policy took the precise form that it did.

In 1998, the government of Malta appointed a small working group to conduct a study to identify a limit to future tourism growth, and in 2001 the government endorsed the resulting strategy. The working group's decisions took account of key structural constraints, notably tourism's considerable importance for Malta's economy. It was also widely recognised in Malta that environmental groups were becoming active in opposing some tourism schemes and that some residents were becoming concerned about congestion during the main tourist season and also about the loss of scarce land due to tourism development. The working group's policy statement claimed that their choice of tourism growth limit was based on sustainable development principles, but the analysis of their considerations over the course of their decision process suggests that economic issues finally became the most prominent influence. The limit was fundamentally guided by business profitability and by the need to allow the tourism industry continuing opportunities for capital accumulation and to stimulate growth in Malta's economy.

Although the structural pressures for economic growth were a major influence on the working group's choice of growth limit, there were other influences on this choice. To use Jessop's terminology, there were varied influences on the policymakers' strategic selectivity. The working group's composition was one influence, especially because an hotelier and two tourist board officials in the working group were highly influential in making the final decision about the proposed growth limit. The limit was significantly influenced by the estimated number of tourists required for a target hotel bed occupancy rate, which clearly was advantageous for the island's existing hoteliers. After the strategy's publication, however, the association of Malta's hoteliers called for a moratorium on the construction of new hotels, except those already with permits, so as to help existing hotels secure higher bed occupancies, but the government rejected their proposals. This rejection might suggest that the government was concerned above all else with the national economy's broad health and with new investment opportunities, with these being more important than the profits of hotels already operating.

Another influence on the working group's choice of growth limit was the shifting priority it gave to the idea of sustainable development. In the early stages of the working group's activities, it had considered a range of socio-cultural, economic and environmental issues relevant to sustainable development. The breadth of this early research and deliberations had probably helped to secure wider acceptance of the approach taken to establishing the growth limit and also of the working group's final proposals. Arguably, this broad approach was eventually relegated more to a background influence on the final proposed limit due to the prominence given to economic concerns in the later stages. There also appears to have been dissenting voices among the working group members. One of them, a leading tourism industry representative, subsequently argued that the strategy "does not take into account that sustainable tourism needs to be based on longer term approaches and not focused on short term aims driven by economic aims" (Pollacco, 2003, p. 293).

Spatial features of state interventions

A political economy approach provides distinctive themes around spatial scales and temporal change that might help us to interpret state interventions around tourism and sustainability. Political economy is based on what Harvey (1996, p. 111) calls "historical-geographical materialism", so that the broad logics of political economy occur in different ways in different times and places. Thus, the state's activities differ within specific time horizons and at particular geographical or spatial scales. Both temporal change and spatial relations are central to political economy. In terms of the temporal dimensions of the state's operations, Jessop (1990, pp. 260–262) contends that

> the structure and modus operandi of the state system can be understood in terms of their production in and through past political strategies and struggles ... the current strategic selectivity of the state is in part the emergent effect of the interaction between its past patterns of strategic selectivity and the strategies adopted for its transformation.

The state also operates at one or more geographical or spatial scales, which may be transnational, national, regional or local, and the state's functions and activities often differ between these different spatial scales. Further, the state may adjust or reorganise its activities at these different spatial scales and also over time in order to reduce contradictions, lines of conflict and crisis tendencies in society. Jessop (2006) depicts these adjustments as "spatial fixes" and "temporal fixes". One temporal fix might be a government policy to encourage financial institutions to extend credit in order to defuse an economic crisis in the short term, although this may simply create a bigger crisis in the long term. The adjustments or fixes may be intended to secure relatively stable capital accumulation, coherent state action and social cohesion in society, although it can also intensify the problems or create new ones (Jessop, 2008).

The discussion turns first to some geographical or spatial features of state interventions, and subsequently, it considers aspects of their temporal features. Several researchers have noted that there are hierarchical spatial scales among the government institutions involved in tourism policymaking. Hall (2008, pp. 110–112) observes such spatial scales among the public sector institutions involved in ecotourism policymaking in Finland, Norway and Sweden. At the supranational scale, there are European Union (EU) agreements affecting the environment and tourism in EU nations, including the EU biodiversity programme Natura 2000. In Finland, among the organisations at the national scale, there is Metsähallitus, the Finnish Forest and Park Service, which encourages ecotourism where it does not endanger conservation objectives and there is wide participation in tourism strategy making. Finally, Hall notes that at the sub-national scale in the three countries, there can be involvement in ecotourism policy and planning by provinces, counties, communes and municipalities. Therefore, there is a need to appreciate the ecotourism policies and practices at all spatial levels in these three countries, as well as the related interactions within and between the levels. As Hall comments, "interorganisational relations occur not just horizontally, *within* the same level of government, but also vertically, *between* the different levels of government" (2008, p. 183).

One distinctive theme suggested by a political economy approach is the state's adjustments in its activities at different spatial scales in order to seek to reduce contradictions and conflict, to promote capital accumulation or to establish more stable social relations. As previously mentioned, Jessop (2006) depicts these adjustments as "spatial fixes". This might involve, for example, giving new powers to a spatial tier of government in a few places where there are emerging development opportunities or needs for capital and where government can assist with these developments. It could also entail the transferral of state competences, policy priorities or activities between spatial scales, such as from national government to supra-national or sub-national government, or to non-governmental entities or agencies at other scales (Oliveira & Breda-Vázquez, 2010). This is sometimes called "state re-scaling", and it may be associated with struggles for political control between different government tiers (Bulkeley, 2005). Hall comments on the rise of international government institutions that impinge on tourism and environmental issues and on their potential to "constrain the autonomy of nation states and limit their capability for exercising governance in a number of policy arenas that may have once been almost purely domestic considerations" (2005, p. 132). Jessop (2006) warns, however, that a spatial fix is likely only to be temporary as it tends to produce other crisis tendencies.

A case study of spatial features

The next case study involving the author illustrates how the state may adjust its activities through the transfer or re-scaling of state competences, in this case from the national to the local scale, and also to a non-government entity. It explores these issues through the development of the new coastal resort of Belek in Turkey, and it shows how such re-scaling can have implications for tourism and sustainable development. However, in the original study by Yüksel et al. (2005), there was very little overt use of political economy.

There is a long history of centralism in Turkey's public administration, but the pressure for rapid tourism growth to aid national development and the relative weakness of local government encouraged central government to experiment at times with new institutional arrangements when developing tourist destinations. This applies to the new resort of Belek, where in 1990 commercial businesses investing in hotels and other facilities joined in a new private sector company, the Belek Tourism Investors' Association (Betuyab), which worked with the Ministry of Tourism in funding, constructing and managing the resort's infrastructure. Betuyab contributed one third of the infrastructure costs and the Ministry of Tourism contributed two thirds. Previously these activities would have been undertaken by the Ministry of Tourism, and thus, certain state functions were re-scaled and part-privatised from central government to a local company. But the re-scaling of functions to this local company entailed only a moderate territorial transfer of power to Belek as many of the commercial funders were based in distant Ankara and Istanbul.

The approaches of Betuyab and the Ministry of Tourism influenced the resort's development and its implications for sustainability. Within the defined resort zones, development was carefully planned, building densities were strictly controlled, illegal construction was avoided and many jobs were created. However, there was local suspicion and resentment about Betuyab due to concerns about its corporatist relations with government, the transfer of state property to commercial businesses, the external sources of capital behind the resort's development and the exclusion of local people from policymaking. There was also resentment that the enclave form of tourism development that Betuyab had favoured had limited the number of jobs and other economic benefits available for local residents. Further, the central state's reluctance to devolve more powers and funding to local government outside the defined resort zones had created some significant environmental problems. In particular, the lack of funds available to local government in the surrounding areas had tempted it to raise revenue by issuing permits for new holiday homes, with many of these homes being built haphazardly and some lacking basic public utilities.

Temporal features of state interventions

There are also temporal features of state interventions that may be highlighted through a political economy or historical materialist approach, and these features can be relevant to state interventions affecting tourism and sustainability in destinations. Political economy can direct attention to historical trends in state interventions due to the dialectical inter-actions between structural pressures, such as the pressures for capital accumulation and the conflicts between classes, the working out of these pressures in practice at particular conjunctures and more specific influences and processes at those times. The more specific contingent influences may include the responses of individual government actors to issues at specific points in time.

Historical change relevant to the state can be examined using the idea of "path depen-dence" within a political economy approach. Path dependence occurs when state interven-tions move in the same direction as has occurred previously because past circumstances and legacies constrain subsequent developments. According to Kay, "A process is path-dependent if initial moves in one direction elicit further moves in that same direction; in other words ... the trajectory of change up to a certain point *constrains* the trajectory after that point" (2005, p. 553). Path-dependent sequences are also described as "marked by relatively deterministic causal patterns" (Mahoney, 2000, p. 511). Political economy may suggest several societal pressures or driving forces that potentially encourage path dependence. There are conditions, however, in which path dependence can be halted by a clearly new contingency, that is, by a shift to "path creation" or "path shaping" (Park & Lee, 2005). Path creation occurs when state interventions depart from past trends because of new contingencies, and do so in unexpected ways that cannot be explained by previ-ous circumstances (Jessop, 2008; Martin & Sunley, 2007; Park & Lee, 2005). Unexpected changes might occur, for example, when actors involved in government deliberately seek to disengage from an established path and structures.

Political economy and the ideas of path dependence and path creation can provide distinctive research themes for studies of state governance relevant to tourism and sustain-ability. They indicate, for instance, the potential for detailed studies of temporal trends in the interactions between state governance and the environment beyond, including wider pressures for economic growth and capital accumulation and the power of different social groups. They also encourage assessments of the specific circumstances leading to path cre-ation in spite of path-dependent legacies. This might occur, for example, when influential government actors use their agency to establish new precedents and innovations that depart from previous practices.

A case study of path dependence

The final case study, developed by Bramwell and Cox (2009), uses path dependence and path creation notions to examine temporal trends in the governance of tourism and sustainability, although the original study made only very limited use of political economy. Trends in governance are explored for a UK government agency, the Peak District National Park Authority, which had devolved aspects of policymaking for the Stanage area in the Peak District National Park to a local partnership organisation, the Stanage Steering Group. The case evaluates the extent to which policymaking and policies for tourism and conservation developed by this partnership were path dependent or path creating.

The Stanage Steering Group was established by the Park Authority to reduce conflicts around tourism and conservation at Stanage, an area intensively used for mountaineering and walking. Trends in the Steering Group's activities were considered in relation to internal processes and relevant external influences. Two aspects of the Steering Group's work were examined in relation to path dependency and path creation: the adoption of fairly intensive participatory working, involving diverse actors, and the relative priorities given to recreation activities and to environmental protection.

In practice, the Steering Group's activities demonstrated the elements of both path dependence and path creation. This was seen, firstly, in the fairly intensive approach to actor participation and negotiation in the Steering Group meetings. This was partly path dependent as it reflected a well-established trend in the United Kingdom away from direct state interventions and towards more diverse governance patterns involving more actors. At the same time, the intensity of the involvement of a broad range of partners in the Steering Group and their scope to develop policies that normally would be formulated by the Park Authority was path creating because it departed from past trends. The study concludes that "A somewhat surprising element of this partnership was that . . . there were very diverse groups participating in it, and that these groups, rather than the Park Authority, were allowed to formulate policies for the Stanage area" (Bramwell & Cox, 2009, p. 200). The mix of path-dependent and path-creating elements was also seen, secondly, in the partnership's policies. These were often path dependent, based on the historical legacy of the Park Authority's considerable influence, yet some would argue that the recreation groups involved in the partnership "have secured some significant concessions from the Park Authority as the constraints on access to the area . . . are very modest" (p. 202). The focus on path dependence also helped to identify key influences on these different paths. The unexpected level of participation by the varied actors in the Steering Group, for example, was strongly influenced by two individuals who were committed to promoting wide participation.

Conclusion

This paper argues that governance is important for tourist destinations seeking to promote sustainable development. Furthering sustainability objectives in destinations usually requires some collective action. But such governance faces major obstacles, because its concerns span many policy domains, numerous relevant policies are made in other policy domains, it can be difficult to influence private sector decisions and the relevant actors are diverse and have varied interests and priorities. These difficulties for the governance of sustainable tourism need to be much better understood in order to establish potential ways to overcome them.

The paper also contended that research on the governance of tourism and sustainability will benefit from greater use of social theory. Potentially, social theory can help create a better understanding of this topic, especially as it allows for the transfer of concepts and interpretations between research fields. An understanding of the relevant social theories is important, as the choice of social theory has substantial consequences for the interpretation of the case study and policy-relevant recommendations.

Fundamental ideas were explained behind one social theory, a strategic-relational view of political economy, and it was shown how this might be used to gain insights into state interventions affecting tourism and sustainability in destinations. This was achieved through a literature review and through case studies, which sought to use ideas related to this social theory to understand the government activities impacting on tourism and sustainability.

Space was too limited to undertake a full critical assessment of the value of a strategic-relational political economy approach. Instead, the paper focused on explaining the distinctive perspectives and themes associated with the use of this approach when researching state interventions that affect tourism and sustainable development. These distinctive perspectives and themes are brought together in Table 1. They include the approach's holistic, relational and dialectical perspective, its materialist but indeterminate basis, its focus on the state's roles in regulating the economic and political systems, its concern to understand

Table 1. Perspectives and themes associated with a strategic-relational political economy approach for research on the state's activities that affect tourism and sustainability.

1. A holistic, relational and dialectical perspective	A broad horizon would be used that considers the state's activities affecting tourism and sustainability within the state's overall relations with society, and thus it would explore the multiple and reciprocal relations between tourism, the state, economy and society.
2. Materialist but indeterminate	There would be consideration of the potential connections between the state, tourism, sustainability and the economy, with connections with the economy not always being immediately apparent. Change occurs through contingent social practices at specific conjunctures. Explanations which suggest that the economy is determinant would be rejected.
3. The state and regulation	The state's activities affecting tourism and sustainability would be considered in relation to the regulation of the economic and political systems in order to mitigate contradictions and to promote the system's reproduction.
4. Agency–structure relations and strategic selectivity	Research on the state's activities affecting tourism and sustainability would examine micro-scale agency, macro-scale structures and the dialectical relations between them. It would do this using the idea of strategic selectivity and it would consider this in specific conjunctures.
5. Spatial and temporal variations	The broad logics of political economy differ in time and place; research would examine how the state's activities affecting tourism and sustainability vary at different times and in different places.
6. Spatial and temporal adaptations	Consideration would be given to how the state may adjust or reorganise its activities affecting tourism and sustainability at different spatial scales and also over time in order to seek to reduce contradictions and conflicts in society. The adjustments can intensify the problems that they are intended to reduce.
7. Path dependence and path creation	Research on state interventions affecting tourism and sustainability would examine whether the interventions move in the same direction as has occurred previously due to past legacies constraining subsequent developments, or else depart from past trends due to new contingencies and in unexpected ways. Political economy may suggest several driving forces of change that affect these two trends.

the interactions between the agency of actors and social structures in specific conjunctures, the importance of spatial and temporal variations, the adaptation of state activities at different spatial scales and at different times, and the interpretation of path dependence and path creation. The paper indicated the relevance of these perspectives and themes for research on state activities affecting tourism and sustainability in destinations, and thus, Table 1 indicates some future research directions on this topic.

Case studies can be especially valuable for research on the governance of tourism and sustainability based on a political economy approach, and this is one reason that they were used in the paper. They allow for the careful weighing of the structural pressures and the contingent social practices based on specific actors at particular conjunctures. Case studies can encourage the constant tacking back and forth between provisional theoretical explanations and the specific case, thus allowing explanations to be revised along the way (Barnes, Peck, Sheppard, & Tickell, 2007). At the same time, with case studies, care must be taken not to become too empirical, thereby losing sight of the need to apply and challenge extant theory. Case studies may also assist us to evaluate the interactions between the diverse dimensions of tourism, sustainable development and governance at specific conjunctures. Finally, in case studies, it is possible to explore the context-specific character of sustainable tourism.

Acknowledgements

The suggestions provided by three anonymous referees and Bernard Lane are very gratefully acknowledged. They substantially helped in the process of improving the paper, although the interpretations of their suggestions are the author's.

References

Baggio, R., Scott, N., & Cooper, C. (2010). Improving tourism destination governance: A complexity science approach. *Tourism Review, 65*(4), 51–60.

Barnes, T., Peck, J., Sheppard, E., & Tickell, A. (2007). Methods matter: Transformations in economic geography. In A. Tickell, E. Sheppard, J. Peck, & T. Barnes (Eds.), *Politics and practice in economic geography* (pp. 1–24). London: Sage.

Bevir, M. (2009). *Key concepts in governance.* London: Sage.

Bianchi, R. (2002). Towards a new political economy of global tourism. In R. Sharpley & D. Telfer (Eds.), *Tourism and development. Concepts and issues* (pp. 265–299). Clevedon: Channel View Publications.

Bianchi, R. (2004). Tourism restructuring and the politics of sustainability: A critical view from the European periphery (The Canary Islands). *Journal of Sustainable Tourism, 12*(6), 495–529.

Bianchi, R. (2009). The "critical turn" in tourism studies: A radical critique. *Tourism Geographies, 11*(4), 484–504.

Bianchi, R. (2011). Tourism, capitalism and Marxist political economy. In J. Mosedale (Ed.), *Political economy of tourism. A critical perspective* (pp. 17–37). London: Routledge.

Börzel, T. (1998). Organizing Babylon: On the different conceptions of policy networks. *Public Administration, 76*, 253–273.

Bramwell, B. (2004). The policy context for tourism and sustainability in Southern Europe's coastal regions. In B. Bramwell (Ed.), *Coastal mass tourism. Diversification and sustainable development in Southern Europe* (pp. 32–47). Clevedon: Channel View Publications.

Bramwell, B. (2006). Actors, power, and discourses of growth limits. *Annals of Tourism Research, 33*(4), 957–978.

Bramwell, B. (2007). Opening up new spaces in the sustainable tourism debate. *Tourism Recreation Research, 32*(1), 1–9.

Bramwell, B. (2010). Participative planning and governance for sustainable tourism. *Tourism Recreation Research, 35*(3), 239–249.

Bramwell, B., & Cox, V. (2009). Stage and path dependence approaches to the evolution of a national park tourism partnership. *Journal of Sustainable Tourism, 17*(2), 191–206.

Bramwell, B., & Lane, B. (2000). *Tourism collaboration and partnerships: Politics, practice and sustainability*. Clevedon: Channel View Publications.

Bramwell, B., & Meyer, D. (2007). Power and tourism policy relations in transition. *Annals of Tourism Research, 34*(3), 766–788.

Britton, S. (1982). The political economy of tourism in the Third World. *Annals of Tourism Research, 9*(3), 331–358.

Britton, S. (1991). Tourism, dependency and place: Towards a critical geography of tourism development. *Environment and Planning D: Society and Place, 9*, 451–478.

Bulkeley, H. (2005). Reconfiguring environmental governance: Towards a politics of scales and networks. *Political Geography, 24*(8), 875–902.

Butler, R. (2010). Sustainability or stagnation? Limits, control, and the life cycle in tourist destinations. In E. Wickens & M. Soteriades (Eds.), *Sustainable tourism: Issues, debates and challenges. Conference proceedings* (pp. 23–31). Crete: Technological Educational Institute of Greece.

Cornelissen, S. (2011). Regulation theory and its evolution and limitations in tourism studies. In J. Mosedale (Ed.), *Political economy of tourism. A critical perspective* (pp. 39–54). London: Routledge.

Dardess, J. (1983). *Confucianism and autocracy: Professional elites in the founding of the Ming dynasty*. Berkeley: University of California Press.

Dredge, D., & Jenkins, J. (2007). *Tourism planning and policy*. Milton: Wiley.

Dunleavy, P., & O'Leary, B. (1987). *Theories of the state. The politics of liberal democracy*. Basingstoke: Palgrave Macmillan.

Flynn, R. (2002). Clinical governance and governmentality. *Health, Risk and Society, 4*(2), 155–173.

Gibbs, D. (1996). Integrating sustainable development and economic restructuring: A role for regulation theory? *Geoforum, 27*(1), 1–10.

Gibbs, D., & Jonas, A. (2000). Governance and regulation in local environmental policy: The utility of a regime approach. *Geoforum, 31*(3), 299–313.

Goodwin, M. (2001). Regulation as process: Regulation theory and comparative urban and regional research. *Journal of Housing and the Built Environment, 16*(1), 71–87.

Goodwin, M., & Painter, J. (1996). Local governance, the crises of Fordism and the changing geographies of regulation. *Transactions of the Institute of British Geographers, NS 21*(4), 635–648.

Hall, M. (1994). *Tourism and politics. Policy, power and place*. Chichester: Wiley.

Hall, M. (2005). *Tourism: Rethinking the social science of mobility*. Harlow: Pearson.

Hall, M. (2006). Urban entrepreneurship, corporate interests and sports mega-events: The thin policies of competitiveness within the hard outcomes of neoliberalism. *The Sociological Review, 54*(Suppl. S2), 59–70.

Hall, M. (2008). *Tourism planning. Policies, processes and relationships*. Harlow: Pearson.

Harvey, D. (1996). *Justice, nature and the geography of difference*. Oxford: Blackwell.

Harvey, D. (2010). *The enigma of capital and the crises of capitalism*. London: Profile Books.

Hill, M. (1997). *The policy process in the modern state* (3rd ed.). Harlow: Pearson.

Jamal, T., & Watt, M. (2011). Climate change pedagogy and performative action: Towards community-based destination governance. *Journal of Sustainable Tourism, 19*(4–5), 571–588.

Jessop, B. (1990). *State theory: Putting the capitalist state in its place*. Cambridge: Polity Press.

Jessop, B. (1997a). Twenty years of the (Parisian) regulation approach: The paradox of success and failure at home and abroad. *New Political Economy, 2*(3), 503–526.

Jessop, B. (1997b). A neo-Gramscian approach to the regulation of urban regimes. In M. Lauria (Ed.), *Reconstructing urban regime theory: Regulating urban politics in a global economy* (pp. 51–73). London: Sage.

Jessop, B. (2002). *The future of the capitalist state*. Cambridge: Polity Press.

Jessop, B. (2006). Spatial fixes, temporal fixes and spatio-temporal fixes. In N. Castree & D. Gregory (Eds.), *David Harvey. A critical reader* (pp. 142–166). Oxford: Blackwell.

Jessop, B. (2008). *State power. A strategic-relational approach*. Cambridge: Polity Press.

Kay, A. (2005). A critique of the use of path dependency in policy studies. *Public Administration, 83*(3), 553–571.

Kokx, A., & van Kempen, R. (2010). Dutch urban governance: Multi-level or multi-scalar? *European Urban and Regional Studies, 17*(4), 355–369.

Mahoney, J. (2000). Path dependence in historical sociology. *Theory and Society, 29*(4), 507–548.

Martin, R., & Sunley, P. (2007). Complexity thinking and evolutionary economic geography. *Journal of Economic Geography, 7*(5), 573–601.

Moore, S., & Weiler, B. (2009). Tourism-protected area partnerships: Stoking the fires of innovation. *Journal of Sustainable Tourism, 17*(2), 129–132.

Mosedale, J. (2011). Re-introducing tourism to political economy. In J. Mosedale (Ed.), *Political economy of tourism. A critical perspective* (pp. 1–13). London: Routledge.

Mowforth, M., & Munt, I. (2009). *Tourism and sustainability. Development, globalisation and new tourism in the third world*. London: Routledge.

Newman, J., & Clarke, J. (2009). *Publics, politics and power: Remaking the public in public services*. London: Sage.

Ogden, S. (1995). *China's unresolved issues: Politics, development and culture*. Englewood Cliffs, NJ: Prentice Hall.

Oliveira, C., & Breda-Vázquez, I. (2010). Contradictory rescaling: Confronting state restructuring and the building of new spatial policies. *European Urban and Regional Studies, 17*(4), 401–415.

Panelli, R. (2004). *Social geographies: From difference to action*. London: Sage.

Park, S., & Lee, S. (2005). The national and regional innovation systems in Finland: From the path dependency to the path creation approach. *AI and Society, 19*(2), 180–195.

Peck, J., & Tickell, A. (1992). Local modes of social regulation? Regulation theory, Thatcherism and uneven development. *Geoforum, 23*(3), 347–363.

Peet, R. (1998). *Modern geographical thought*. Oxford: Blackwell.

Peet, R. (2007). *Geography of power. The making of global economic policy*. London: Zed Books.

Pforr, C. (2006). Tourism policy in the making. An Australian network study. *Annals of Tourism Research, 33*(1), 87–108.

Pollacco, J. (2003). *The national interest: Towards a sustainable tourism industry in Malta*. Valletta: Fondazzjoni Tumas Fenech Ghall-Edukazzjoni Fil-Gurnalizmu.

Presenza, A., & Cipollina, M. (2010). Analysing tourism stakeholders networks. *Tourism Review, 65*(4), 17–30.

Purcell, M., & Nevins, J. (2005). Pushing the boundary: State restructuring, state theory, and the case of US – Mexico border enforcement in the 1990s. *Political Geography, 24*(2), 211–235.

Rhodes, R. (1996). The new governance: Governing without government. *Political Studies, 44*(4), 652–667.

Scott, J. (1991). *Social network analysis: A handbook*. London: Sage.

Sofield, T., & Li, S.M.F. (2011). Tourism governance and sustainable national development in China: A macro-level synthesis. *Journal of Sustainable Tourism, 19*(4–5), 501–534.

Wearing, S., & Neil, J. (2009). *Ecotourism: Impacts, potentials and possibilities*. Oxford: Butterworth-Heinemann.

Weiss, L. (1998). *The myth of the powerless state: Governing the economy in a global era*. Cambridge: Polity Press.

While, A., Jonas, A., & Gibbs, D. (2010). From sustainable development to carbon control: Eco-state restructuring and the politics of urban and regional development. *Transactions of the Institute of British Geographers, NS 35*(1), 76–93.

Williams, A. (2004). Toward a political economy of tourism. In A. Lew, M. Hall, & A. Williams (Eds.), *A companion to tourism* (pp. 61–73). Oxford: Blackwell.

Williams, A., & Montanari, A. (1999). Sustainability and self-regulation: Critical perspectives. *Tourism Geographies, 1*(1), 26–40.

Williams, A., & Shaw, G. (1998). Tourism and the environment: Sustainability and economic restructuring. In M. Hall & A. Lew (Eds.), *Sustainable tourism: A geographical perspective* (pp. 49–59). Harlow: Longman.

Yan, H., & Bramwell, B. (2008). Cultural tourism, ceremony and the state in China. *Annals of Tourism Research, 35*(4), 969–989.

Yüksel, F., Bramwell, B., & Yüksel, A. (2005). Centralized and decentralized tourism governance in Turkey. *Annals of Tourism Research, 32*(4), 859–886.

Event tourism governance and the public sphere

Dianne Dredge and Michelle Whitford

School of Tourism & Hospitality Management, Southern Cross University, Coolangatta, Australia

Political and sociological shifts have profoundly affected state, business and civil society relationships. This paper explores governance as a new form of public–private policy-making wherein stakeholders deliberate on and take action to achieve common goals. It examines how different public spheres facilitate (or not) sustainability debates, and specifically facilitate (or not) discussion about sustainable tourism. Using a case study of the 2009 Australian World Rally Championship, the paper explores the development of the public sphere. Tuckman's group development process – forming, storming, norming and performing – is employed as a lens to understand these processes. Key findings include: the way the public sphere is constituted has a major influence on the dialogue that takes place; citizens are currently reactive, rather than strategic and creative in their engagement; the "third way" project, seeking to empower communities, requires government commitment; there is a blurring of public–private interests; control of knowledge and expertise within the public sphere is largely controlled by corporate and state interests; fast action to secure events prevents debate and engagement; and a discursive public sphere is essential for transparent and accountable governance, and sustainable development, and to move beyond government by powerful corporate interests and extra-local rule systems.

Introduction

Governance has been widely discussed as a new form of public–private policymaking wherein stakeholders are able to deliberate on, and take action towards, the achievement of common goals (e.g. Agere, 2000; Rhodes, 1997; Sørensen & Torfing, 2005). In the 1990s, on balance, these discussions about governance were overwhelmingly positive; "good" governance was optimistically regarded as a mechanism to improve democratic participation in policymaking. From c.2000 onwards, increasing attention to governance practices in a variety of settings has led to more critical analyses and the initial enthusiasm has softened considerably (Bevir, Rhodes, & Weller, 2003; Klijn & Skelcher, 2007). One key point emerging from these discussions, and reinforced by an increasing body of case study research, is that pre-existing institutional structures, policymaking processes and underlying power structures quite often determine outcomes (e.g. Beaumont & Dredge, 2010; Bramwell & Cox, 2009). Not surprisingly, governance has received increasing criticism because it has neither necessarily improved democratic practices nor delivered open and transparent decision-making. Instead, "business as usual" practices that prioritise corporate interests and the economic dimensions of sustainability appear to have flourished under governance in practice (Klijn & Skelcher, 2007).

In the field of tourism, the organisational complexity of tourism and the currents of power that underpin governance practices have been highlighted by various authors (see Beaumont & Dredge, 2010; Bramwell & Cox, 2009; Bramwell & Pomfret, 2007; Dredge & Thomas, 2009; Dredge, 2010). Questioning whether governance can assist in implementing sustainable tourism, Dinica observes that there is

> a need to improve understanding about how specific "governance features" may pave the way toward sustainable development ... As neo-liberal political ideologies continue to expand worldwide and assume more varied forms and practices, it is important to understand [whether] interpretations of neo-liberalism have resulted in features of tourism governance that are more likely to facilitate the sustainable development of tourism [or not]. (2009, p. 602)

However, few researchers to date address this challenge and little is known about the ways in which governance facilitates or impedes sustainable tourism. This paper therefore aims to explore the characteristics of the public sphere – the space of dialogue and partici-pation – where governance takes place. It first considers the nature of the public sphere and its role within the broader sociological and political shifts taking place in western democra-cies. It goes on to use the governance applied to the Australian World Rally Championship (AWRC), 2009, as a case study in tourism event governance, assessing its institutional context, actors and agencies, the public sphere and its characteristics and its linkages to issues within sustainable tourism.

Globalisation, governance and the new public sphere

Shifts taking place over the twentieth century have had a profound effect on relationships between the state, business and civil society (see Held, 1989; Hirst, 2000; Pierre, 2000). By way of background, and summarising the detailed literature, economic and social restruc-turing associated with globalisation has given rise to increasingly mobile capital; global corporate interests have tended to dominate local interests; governments are losing control over local conditions as corporate interests beyond the reach of any single government shift their operations, investments and interests to take advantage of more favourable con-ditions; and local resistance in the form of an increasingly active citizenry is experimenting with new ways of engaging in political debate to protect local interests (Peck & Tickell, 2002).

At the same time, the breadth and depth of policy space and the complexity of policy issues have presented extraordinary challenges to governments at all levels. Free market principles and a freeing up of business from the constraints of regulation and bureaucracy have been, to varying degrees, a cornerstone of the new public management in most western democracies, whether of the left or the right, over the last three decades. Not surprisingly, there has been a breakdown and reinvention of government–business–civil society relations (Beck, 1994; Beck, Bonass, & Lau, 2003). In an effort to do "more with less", and to address negative criticisms that corporate interests have "taken over", governments are increasingly converging on a middle ground between left and right. Noted sociologist and advisor to the UK Blair governments, Anthony Giddens, called this the "Third Way" political project (Giddens, 1998, 2000). In this project, Giddens called for a renewal of social democracy and a reanimation of the public sphere wherein citizens are encouraged to actively and responsibly participate in a public debate.

The principles of the Third Way project have been adopted by numerous other western democracies, including the Obama (US), Rudd and Gillard governments (Australia). Moreover, in coming to power in 2010, UK Prime Minister, David Cameron, reiterated this project, calling for a "Big Society", one in which citizens are encouraged to take more responsibility for shaping their destinies by undertaking civic action to address "the big problems of our time" (Cameron, 2010). Sustainable development is one of these "big issues".

Much literature has explored the shifting nature of business–government relations, but the rise of the "Third Way" project and the "Big Society" suggests that the focus is now shifting to questions about the role of civil society and individuals and, in particular, the nature of the public sphere as the arena for discursive and participatory democracy. The "public sphere" has received considerable attention in cultural studies, sociology and political science and is generally understood to comprise the multiple spaces in which individuals and government agencies discuss and debate public matters. Arendt (1958) discussed the nature of the public realm in terms of two dimensions: "appearance" is that which is "seen and heard by others as well as by ourselves [and] constitutes reality" (p. 50) and the "public" which signifies that which is "common to all of as and distinguished from our privately owned place in it" (p. 52). In this conceptualisation, Arendt highlights two important factors, the artificial or contrived nature of a public sphere that is shaped by interests and the distinction between public and private interests.

Later, Habermas (1989) explored the public sphere as a theatre of democracy wherein political participation takes place, interrogating the conceptual triad of "public space", "discourse" and "reason". Habermas drew attention to the role of private interests and, as a corollary, the influence of subjectivity and cultural influences on private individuals acting in the public sphere (Habermas, 2004). Although now heavily critiqued (e.g. Freundlich, Hudson, & Rundell, 2004), amongst Habermas's main contributions was his reflection on the way in which the public sphere could be "appropriated by a public of private people making use of reason" (1989, p. 51). Private interests could make their way into public debates and be communicated so as to represent public interests. Herein lies what Habermas originally referred to as a blurring of public–private interests, later clarified to mean that the two complement each other; that is, public and private life become conflated as the focus of public debate is on exchange of ideas, opinion and reason rather than individual interests (Habermas, 2004).

In the context of the above-discussed shifts towards the "Big Society" and an increasingly active citizenry, explorations of the public sphere, and the way this public sphere shapes the capacity of individuals to act and raise issues according to one's own will, is deserving of greater attention (see Giddens, 1984). In particular, attention to how the public sphere is constituted, by whom and for what purposes and interests, could provide insights into issues of increasing importance to political scientists and sociologists engaged in critical debate about the health of western democracies, issues of social justice and the inequities of current development paradigms (Hajer & Wagenaar, 2003).

As a starting point, recognising the plurality of the public sphere, Strydom (2008) argues that public spheres may be understood according to the discourses of risk and responsibility for those risks identifying four basic types of public sphere:

- Public at rest – characterised by a low level of risk and limited systematic engagement between actors;

- Institutional public sphere – characterised by systematic structured dialogue between experts and organised interests around risks as perceived by the institutions of government;
- Liberal or mass public sphere – characterised by a dialogue between active members of society such as community, environmental and consumer groups, wherein they are responding to risks to "taken-for-granted-values" such as community values and lifestyle; and
- Discursive public sphere – characterised by engagement and mediation of actors and the presence of a balancing third point of view "over and above the ego and alter perspectives of institutional and civil society actors" (pp. 9–10).

A critical exploration of the public sphere in which tourism is debated and decisions are made has not yet received in-depth attention. Reflecting upon Dinica's (2009) call to better understand particular features of governance and Bramwell and Lane's (2010) suggestion that further attention needs to be placed on the role of government in governance, this paper explores the characteristics of the public sphere in one episode of governance associated with a major tourism event. Event tourism provides an interesting case study of governance, not only because of the increasing use of events to stimulate tourism, but also because of the compressed planning, implementation and evaluation cycle associated with the staging of a major event. The exploration of governance in this context provides opportunities to reflect on the characteristics of the public sphere in a well-defined temporal and spatial setting and provides important insights into governance and the public sphere in tourism destinations over more extended periods.

Research approach and methods

Approach

This paper explores the characteristics of the public sphere and its role in the governance of the 2009 AWRC. This major international event was held in the Northern Rivers region, an area that includes protected lands associated with the Gondwana World Heritage Area. The region is characterised by a spectacular rim of extinct volcanoes and high biodiversity and is one of Australia's iconic national landscapes. It is marketed in Australia and internationally as "the Green Cauldron", a nature-based tourism destination.

Two main objectives underpin the exploration of this case study. Firstly, the paper seeks to better understand the characteristics of the public space in which the staging of this major event was debated. The second objective is to explore the way in which different public spheres facilitate (or not) the raising and mediating of issues associated with sustainability. An important caveat to these objectives is that these public spheres are not the only interests at play within this episode of governance, nor are they mutually exclusive or homogenous in their membership. Our belief, informed by post-modern and post-structural discourses, is that there are multiple publics and multiple public domains and that the public–private dimensions of this space are relevant to the way in which sustainability issues are negotiated and valued within the discourse (see Dredge, 2006a, 2006b).

Before addressing these objectives, however, it is first important to set the context for the paper by defining key concepts. As a starting point, sustainability is a slippery term characterised by a large body of literature that has struggled to define it, let alone advance policy solutions (Lawrence, 2004, p. 3). Dovers (2005) explains the dilemma in that different stakeholders in a policy domain are in different stages of coming to terms with a range of environmental issues, which might include pollution, loss of biodiversity, sociocultural impacts or climate change. Only after each stakeholder develops an understanding of each individual issue, and then the interconnections between issues in the system, can the complex challenge of sustainability be appreciated. Moreover, because stakeholders have different levels of access to resources, expertise, knowledge and capacity to learn, the difficulty of dealing with the sustainability issues is exacerbated. As a result, stakeholders tend to deal with those immediate issues they can deal with or have the capacity to collaborate on, but the collective, longer-term societal issue of sustainability remains troublesome.

A key feature of current debates about sustainability is the need to invoke a collective policy response to both short-term environmental issues and the longer-term broader societal goal of sustainability. The need to work together and prioritise values gives rise to a range of tensions between environmental, social and economic issues. The public sphere is where these issues are identified and deliberated, decisions are made and joint action takes shape. In the context of event tourism, the sustainability challenge is further exacerbated by the compressed spatial and temporal characteristics of events, which inevitably impacts upon the public sphere, opportunities for participation and conditions for dialogue.

Figure 1 sets out the framework used in this research. The framework has been adapted from Dredge and Jenkins' (2007) framework and from the previous work of Hall and Jenkins (1995). In this framework, efforts to understand governance require that the researcher moves generally towards the centre of the diagram, but occasionally outwards to reflect upon previous understandings, to consider new cases and to incorporate new and emerging information (see also Dredge, Jenkins, & Whitford, 2011a). An understanding of governance necessarily incorporates an appreciation of the institutional context, the issue drivers and influences that get pushed onto the political agenda and into the public sphere (and those that do not) and the full range of actors and agencies directly and indirectly involved in tourism. From these understandings, an appreciation of the public sphere can be developed along with how this shapes the space of dialogue, communication and information-sharing. Moreover, events and circumstances change over time, so the influence of historical decisions and actions must also be considered. Researchers must also appreciate that micro, meso or macro scales are interrelated and that events occurring at one level are likely to affect what happens at other levels.

Case study

The researchers adopted a constructivist–interpretive case study approach, wherein a particular episode of governance was analysed to build insights into governance in practice. A case study approach is ideal for exploring complex social relations because governance is performed in practice (Hajer & Wagenaar, 2003). Case studies can help us understand what governance involves, how it is conducted, who wins and who loses, who holds the power and why it works or does not work (Flyvbjerg, 2001). They involve interpretation; they expand practical understandings, sharpen critical judgement and can contribute to reflective practice in the future (Dredge, Jenkins, & Whitford, 2011b; Hajer & Wagenaar, 2003). In this case, the temporal nature of the event placed pressure on stakeholders to quickly and effectively engage in the public sphere. This story can be described and analysed by using Tuckman's (1965) group development process – forming, (brain) storming, norming and performing – as a broad lens to understand these processes.

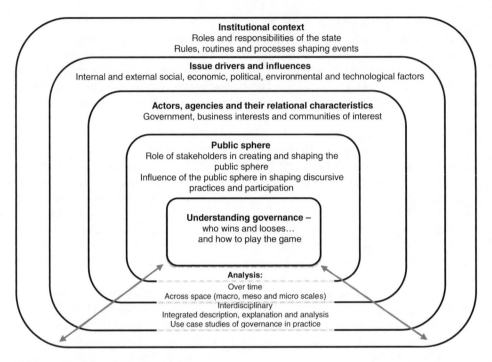

Figure 1.   Framework for the research.

Data collection and analysis

A mixed methods research approach was used (see Creswell, 2003), drawing upon multiple data sources to build a picture of event governance over time and across different spatial scales. Initially, media sources, parliamentary transcripts, council documents and archival resources were used to construct a case study background. These secondary data were augmented with 20 semi-structured interviews each between 30 and 60 minutes in duration and field notes recording observations and follow-up communications. Interview respondents were purposively selected to include local council staff, elected representatives, members of the Chamber of Commerce, tourism organisations and environmental and community groups from the two local government areas in which the event was staged. Importantly, State Government representatives and the event organisers declined to be interviewed, the main reason being that the situation was "too political". The absence of these voices was balanced with the use of parliamentary debates, government reports, council minutes and media releases to ascertain their public positions.

Interviews were audio recorded and transcribed. The researchers manually coded the interview transcripts, making constant comparisons with other interviews, literature and secondary data to draw out content and meaning. The familiarity with the transcripts in this reiterative, interpretive process helped to build deep understandings that go well beyond scientific notions of cause and effect (see Bevir et al., 2003) to explore complex and subjective processes of reasoning by individuals and how they engaged in the public sphere.

The Australian World Rally Championship

The World Rally Championship (WRC) is an international rallying series organised by the Fédération Internationale de l'Automobile (FIA). The first WRC was staged in 1973 and since then it has become one of the highest-profiled four-wheeled motor sport championships in the world. The current series consists of 24 events, staged in 12 countries over a two-year cycle. In 2002, 30.8 million people in 186 countries reportedly watched the three-day event on television (Cook, 2003). In 2007 the event reportedly attracted a combined worldwide TV audience of 816 million (International Sportsworld Communicators, 2007), although no data or methodology to arrive at these figures have been uncovered.

The Australian arm of the WRC (AWRC) is organised by Rally Australia, a not-for-profit company owned by the Confederation of Australian Motor Sport (CAMS). The first AWRC was held in the city of Perth, Western Australia (WA), in 1988. In conjunction with the CAMS, Tourism WA, a statutory corporation created by the State Government, managed the Rally through its events division, EventsCorp (Tourism Western Australia, 2005). Nineteen rallies were held in Perth from 1988 to 2006 producing an estimated economic return of $21.2 million in 1998 and $23 million in 1999 (Moore, 2000; Prior, 1999).

In 2004, a change in the methodology for the economic impact report revealed that the Rally only contributed $9.3 million to the WA economy. Concomitantly, public investment in hosting the event had grown significantly from $2.5 million in 1999 to $5.9 million in 2004. Return on investment in 2004 was calculated at 1:1.60, with the Tourism Minister admitting that "to make this event competitive with our other events, there would need to be either a 300% increase in revenue or a cost reduction of 62 percent" (World Rally Championship, 2005). Consequently, in March 2005, the WA State Government announced that they no longer wished to support the event, as it no longer delivered to WA an acceptable level of return on taxpayers' money (Glasson & Pedler, 2005).

In 2007, Events New South Wales (NSW) entered negotiations with the CAMS to stage the AWRC in the Northern Rivers region of NSW. After almost a year of private meetings between Events NSW (which is a private company wholly owned and funded by the NSW State Government) and Rally Australia (i.e. a private, not-for-profit company), it was officially announced on 10 September, 2008, that the AWRC would be staged in the Northern Rivers region every second year until 2017. The route would run over 340 kilometres of public roads through rural landscapes and protected areas and include 35 stages (see location map at http://media.gcbulletin.com.au/WRCMap.pdf). Table 1 shows an abbreviated timeline of events from the announcement to the staging of the 2009 AWRC.

Following the event, a media and communications consultant working on behalf of the Homebush Motor Racing Authority (a NSW State Government statutory corporation with responsibility for the management and conduct of works associated with an annual Supercar motor race in Sydney) prepared an evaluation for the NSW Department of State Development. Considerable controversy erupted over the consultant's expertise in conducting the evaluation, the independence of the Homebush Bay Motor Racing Authority and the lack of consultation and explicit concern over individual issues. Not surprisingly, shortly afterwards the NSW State Government and Rally Australia decided to move the event to Coffs Harbour, some 300 kilometres to the south.

Institutional context

The institutional context in which the event was debated and decisions were made was characterised by complex overlapping roles and responsibilities, which, like most western

Table 1.   Timeline of the AWRC 2009.

Date	Issue
10 September 2008	Announcement made by NSW State Government that the Rally would be held in the Northern Rivers.
7 February 2009	Details emerge that the route would cover 350 kilometres of roads in Tweed and Kyogle Shires, with around 10 kilometres passing through national parks.
23 February 2009	The North Coast Environment Council formally opposed the Rally's plans to hold the event in the Kyogle Shire, stating that they would rather see passive, environmentally friendly ventures in the area.
2 March 2009	100+ people turned out at "Rally against the Rally" protest.
May 2009	A series of impact reports, commissioned by the Rally organisers, were released.
15 May 2009	Kyogle Council Mayor expressed concern that time was running out to consider the Development Application for the event, which Rally Australia still had not yet lodged.
28 May 2009	The koala management plan gave rise to more criticism, with opposition claiming most protection measures would not be effective. Concerns led to another protest in Murwillumbah, this time attracting more than 300 people.
29 May 2009	NSW Government announced that they would introduce a special legislation to guarantee the running of the Rally event.
24 June 2009	Tickets for the event went on sale.
25 June 2009	The Motor Sports Bill 2009 passed, with the opposition managing to secure an amendment to review after one year (the draft legislation had not required an evaluation of the event).
11 July 2009	Representatives from the No Rally Group, 7th Generation (Kyogle), the Caldera Environment Centre (Murwillumbah) and Friends of the Koala gathered at the Lismore Regional Gallery on Wednesday, where Environment Minister Garrett opened a local artist's exhibition to remind him of his obligation to protect threatened wildlife and areas of national significance.
25 August 2009	Injunction lodged in Federal court on the grounds that the Rally would have a detrimental effect on species protected under Commonwealth legislation.
3–6 September 2009	The Rally was staged in the Northern Rivers of NSW.

developed economies, has been influenced by neo-liberalism and new public management. Since the 1980s, the NSW Government had been actively seeking economic development opportunities including tourism investment and the securing of major events (Dredge, 2005; Jenkins, 1993). In this case study, the State Government, through its privately owned corporation, Events NSW, was a key agency in attracting and securing the AWRC event. Being a privately owned corporation, it was free to operate outside normal codes of conduct and reporting expected of state government agencies, securing a commercial-in-confidence agreement free of public scrutiny with the event organiser. Once the event had been secured, it became apparent that the event would trigger a Development Application (DA) and the two local governments in which the event was to be held would be the consent agencies. Requirements for the DA process and associated public consultation were clearly outlined in legislation, and local councillors expected that they would have an opportunity to engage the public in debate (Respondents #12 and #8).

However, the complexity of this process quickly became apparent, and it was not long before special legislation was introduced to exempt the rally organiser from these requirements. Whilst the details of relationships and commercial-in-confidence agreements between Rally Australia, CAMS, and the NSW State Government remain off the public record, the removal of existing DA requirements illustrates the very powerful and privileged position of private corporate interests in state government decision-making in this instance. This institutional context had a significant influence on shaping the public sphere, in creating spaces of dialogue, and what individuals and agencies could contribute.

Issue drivers and influences on event tourism

Events and festivals are increasingly framed as tools that contribute to economic and community development objectives and improve the sustainability of rural and regional areas (Coaffee & Shaw, 2005; Gibson & Davidson, 2004). In this case study, the government's motivation for supporting the event was clearly framed in this light:

> Tourism generally brings New South Wales an estimated $27 billion a year and supports around 150,000 to 160,000 jobs ... When one looks at the loss of manufacturing industry in Australia, country areas in particular must rely on tourism in order for families to survive ... Events such as the rally support the backbone of one of the main and growing economic drivers of regional New South Wales. (Hon. Amanda Fazio, NSW Legislative Council, 3 September 2009)

Debates in the NSW parliament were liberal in their use of this rhetoric with the main benefits of holding the event cited as its short- and long-term contributions to tourism, employment generation, opportunities for place promotion and investment attraction (Dredge, Ford, Lamont, Phi, & Whitford, 2010). Moreover, despite attempts from local elected representatives to raise the interests of the Northern Rivers community, and the rally's "fit" with local values, environmental conditions and sense of place, the debates of the NSW legislative council focused on the public interest of NSW residents as a collective. As such, an important influence upon the debate was the scale at which public interest was conceptualised and the weight given to statewide public interests as opposed to local public interests (Dredge et al., 2010).

Another important driver of the event was the importance of the motor sports industry. Globally, motor sports events have grown considerably in recent decades in the number and size of events and in participation rates (Henderson, Foo, Lim, & Yip, 2010; Tranter & Keeffe, 2004). They have also become increasingly controversial (Gamage & Higgs, 1996; Lowes, 2004; Warren, 2002). Much of this criticism is derived from governments' prioritisation of economic development objectives combined and superficial public consultation practices (Fredline & Faulkner, 2001). Literature has focused on evaluating the impacts of motor sports events with increasing levels of sophistication in models and frameworks (e.g. see Burgan & Mules, 1992; Fredline & Faulkner, 2001; Jago & Dwyer, 2006). However, a comprehensive assessment of the impacts of motor sports events has not been forthcoming (e.g. Foley, McGillivray, & McPherson, 2009; Hede, 2008).

Actors and agencies

A range of actors and agencies were directly involved in the event, and an equally diverse range of actors and agencies were indirectly affected, or with an interest but with limited capacity to participate in the public sphere. The main actors and interests are summarised in Table 2.

Of note in this case, Events NSW lobbied for and secured the event, the staging of which was then facilitated by the NSW Department of Premier and Cabinet. That is, one

Table 2.   Key interests in the event.

Key interests	Roles/responsibilities
Events NSW	Private company created by NSW State Government with the aim of securing major events for the State.
NSW Department of Premier and Cabinet	Facilitated the staging of the event, liaising with State Government departments in planning and staging events.
Rally Australia	Event Organiser (not-for-profit company created by the CAMS).
CAMS	The CAMS operates under the auspices of the FIA and regulates the sport in a professional, streamlined and customer-focused manner as the delegated National Sporting Authority.
FIA	The FIA is the governing body for world motor sport and the federation of the world's motoring organisations.
Kyogle Shire Council – councillors, public sector workers	Rural local government area hosting part of the AWRC; contains world heritage rainforests, national parks and small rural towns (population 9800).
Tweed Shire Council	Coastal local government area hosting part of the AWRC; mountainous landscapes of high biodiversity included in world Heritage Area (population 89,000).
7th Generation	Community group in Kyogle Shire formed to lobby for a sustainable future for Kyogle residents.
No Rally Group	Community group formed to oppose the AWRC in Northern Rivers.
Community members	Rate payers and residents with various interests, directly and indirectly affected by the AWRC.
Githabul people	Indigenous people of the region.
Local and regional tourism organisations, economic development organisations, chambers of commerce	Various groups supporting tourism and economic development in the region
Homebush Bay Motor Racing Authority	A NSW State Government statutory corporation commissioned to undertake an evaluation of the event.

Note: FIA, Fédération Internationale de l'Automobile; CAMS, Confederation of Australian Motor Sport.

government agency became the proponent for the event and another agency within the same government became the arbiter of public debate and organising the necessary permissions to stage the event. Moreover, another state government agency was responsible for the evaluation of the event.

The public sphere in the AWRC event

Forming the public sphere

There can be little argument that the decision to stage the event in the Northern Rivers received a mixed response from stakeholders directly and indirectly impacted by the AWRC. The NSW State Government and Rally Australia announced their intention to hold the 2009 AWRC in the Northern Rivers region after closed-door negotiations and minimal contact with local governments and other key stakeholders in the region. The announcement, presented fait accompli, reflected the State's overarching priority of attracting major events for their economic development potential. But the decision to stage the rally came as a surprise, and even shock, to many in the region. According to one Council elected representative, the 2009 AWRC "was something that was given to Council as a little gift. (They said) here! You've got it. Now you have to deal with it" (Respondent #8).

Sides quickly formed. On the one hand, media reports claimed those in favour of the AWRC "could not wait for the Rally to roar into town", and the mooted economic benefits were widely cited in political circles and by the rally organiser:

> NSW is set to receive a $100 million boost to its economy [over the five events planned to 2017] by hosting the FIA World Rally Championships on the Northern Rivers. . . . This is a great coup for NSW . . . . This major event will drive tourism, create jobs and deliver significant economic benefits to the Northern Rivers region. (NSW Minister for State Development, cited in Rally Australia, 2009)

Local councils publicly supported the AWRC. Illustrating the blurring of public and private interests, however, the General Manager of Tweed Shire Council was appointed a board member of Rally Australia and the Council committed financial and in-kind support to the value of $120,000 every two years (Respondent #5). The Council's own code of conduct should have excluded the General Manager from taking on this role (Mr Ian Cohen MLA, NSW Legislative Council, 23 June 2009). However, not everyone saw this as a conflict of interest: one councillor observed, "It was probably better to have someone inside the tent than outside the tent, especially after council was removed from being the consent authority" (Respondent #12).

Despite Tweed Council's public position, some councillors expressed concern and made it known that the Council was deeply divided on the matter:

> In the same week we were elected, we had the launch of the Green Cauldron . . . as one of Australia's natural icons. It did seem that we were embracing this Green Cauldron concept . . . which was promoting the Tweed as a place of high biodiversity. At the same time it did seem a little bit difficult to, out in the community, to get too enthusiastic about the World Rally when we were just getting enthusiastic about the Green Cauldron . . . I mean there was a bit of a disconnect there. (Respondent #12)

Another spoke of the frustration that council support was assumed: "there was no survey or direct consultation with the councillors . . . whether council should support this or not. It was basically accepted . . . that the council . . . supported the proposal" (Respondent #10).

Community members against the AWRC voiced a range of concerns about the event. Despite little information about the rally being released (e.g. routes, environmental impacts, community implications), issues were quickly thrown into the public sphere for discussion and comment. Community members were concerned about disruptions to normal lifestyle, increased accidents due to copycat driving, excessive noise, waste and dust and impacts on wildlife in World Heritage listed rainforests (Respondents #8 and #20).

However, in keeping up the appearance of a commitment to consultation, the NSW State Government consistently claimed that consultation had been "extensive". Rally Australia offered *ex-poste* consultation after the announcement that the event would be held in the region: "the support of the community is of utmost importance to our event and we have targeted community consultation as a major priority as we start the countdown for the event" (Upson, 2009).

In sum, prior to the announcement that the event would take place in Northern Rivers, the public sphere was at rest. The shock announcement of the event profoundly affected by the way the public sphere developed. The lack of community engagement in or information about the potential of staging the event in the region meant that the AWRC was catapulted into public awareness. The controversy ignited concern over taken-for-granted values attached to local lifestyle, community and environmental values; values that had been acknowledged by a range of state and local government agencies in existing policies and plans. This formation of the public sphere would have lasting impacts on the "storming" phase.

"Storming" the public sphere

The (brain) storming phase is that phase of a group's development wherein ideas are identified, discussed and compete for consideration. In the context of the public sphere, storming refers to the process by which issues and concerns are raised and negotiated and collaborative networks emerge. Analysis of this phase highlights the emergence of different "publics" and public spheres and explains divergent orientations and actions of stakeholders.

Despite the shock announcement that the AWRC would be held in the Northern Rivers region, existing institutional arrangements still set the scene for the staging of the event. That is, despite its temporary nature, the event was technically "development" and therefore required a range of approvals under existing legislation. In all, 12 pieces of legislation were triggered. Developed over years of consultation, expert advice and legal drafting, this legislation included clearly defined processes for the application and consideration of changes in land use, environmental management and the use of public resources such as roads and public spaces. In addition, this legislation clearly outlined processes and opportunities for public consultation.

However, the confidence that existing legislation would protect public interests and provide opportunities for community consultation was short-lived. The compressed timeline from the announcement to the staging of the event (nine months) meant that timing was critical. The two councils directly involved commenced work immediately on defining the scope of an environmental impact assessment and a process of liaising with event organisers in order to streamline the approvals process (Respondents #6 and #9). Despite these efforts, a DA was not forthcoming.

On 29 May 2009, just three months before the Rally was to take place, the NSW State Government announced its intention to introduce special legislation to facilitate the event. The *Motor Sports* (*World Rally Championship*) *Act 2009* was passed on 24 June 2009, just nine weeks before the proposed event. This legislation effectively removed the requirement for approvals under existing NSW legislation including the *National Parks and Wildlife Act* (1974), the *Environmental Planning and Assessment Act* (1979), the *Crown Lands Act* (1989), the *Forestry Act* (1916), the *Water Management Act* (2000), the *Fisheries Management Act* (1994), the *Protection of the Environment Operations Act* (1997), the *Road Transport* (*General*) *Act* (2005), the *Road Transport* (*Safety and Traffic Management*) *Act* (1999), the *Motor Vehicle Sports* (*Public Safety Act, 1985*), the *Roads Act* (1993) and the *Local Government Act* (1993).

The NSW State Government's top-down approach during this storming phase had important implications on the space in which issues could be raised and negotiated. The stonewalling of the DA process by the event organiser and the NSW State Government meant that local government, whose established role was to look after public interests in the development process and undertake public consultation, had been taken away. According to one councillor:

> That (decision) was extraordinarily difficult for us and put many of us in a very compromising position. It became apparent, early in the piece that the DA wasn't going to come in with ample time for assessments, community consultations, and determination, and then to allow for serious planning. The [referral] agency forms were established before the Development Application had been lodged. At this stage, there was no discussion of any new legislation or anything like this and we were all ... still expecting a DA. We had seen some preliminary documentation prepared; we were patiently waiting, or anxiously, at this stage, waiting for the DA. (Respondent #14)

The Minister for State Development justified the intervention in terms of expediency:

> You need to be able to have legislation that can make the processes quicker and more expeditious and take the risk out of being able to hold these events. If we did not have the legislation in place, it's quite clear that some opponents up there would use the courts extensively to prevent the race being held. (McDonald, 2009)

Many local government councillors were not so accommodating about the introduction of special legislation. Sentiments were mixed about the autocratic approach of the NSW State Government with one councillor arguing "part of what Council was concerned about was that the DA process was taken away from Council and it probably did take away the opportunity from a lot of people to comment because there was no forum for them to comment in" (Respondent #13). According to another respondent:

> Residents were trying to find out more information ... (but the) information was unsatis-factory from both Rally Australia and our own council. The uncertainty about the planning approval went on for far too long, and created a lot of angst and uncertainty in the community. (Respondent #6)

This storming phase might be understood in terms of the process through which a fracturing of the public sphere took place wherein multiple publics and multiple public spheres galvanised. The NSW State Government sought to create an institutional public sphere to expedite the staging of the event. However, it was a contrived space, controlled and manipulated by special legislation and the actions of the event organiser. Interestingly, throughout the research process, the authors became aware that some public officers in other state government agencies and departments did not participate in or share this institutional space. Power relations and professional survival meant that these individuals with personal and professional concerns about the rally remained as silent voices.

Another public sphere emerged from the extensive efforts of local anti-rally protesters. Two key groups, the No Rally Group and 7th Generation, joined forces to share information and to collaborate on anti-rally actions and protest activities. Whilst the goals of these community organisations were different (the former to protest against the rally and included predominantly Tweed Shire residents and the latter to procure a more sustainable future for Kyogle residents), together they forged a collaborative partnership, shared information and discussed their approaches to, for example, media communications and legal avenues. They created an alternative mass public sphere and raised issues not included in the institutional public sphere, including the environmental impacts of the event, government accountability and transparency. However, not everyone in this mass public sphere was an anti-rally protester. Pro-rally supporters clashed with anti-rally groups at local protests and in the print media.

As the controversy escalated, according to one community member, the international motor racing body, FIA, became increasingly concerned about negative media coverage (Respondent #20). Community groups had managed to secure sympathetic media channels and international coverage of their fight, which could potentially affect consumer support for the event. Expediting special legislation was borne out of the State Governments' perception of risk and the need to illustrate that NSW was a competitive destination and a good business partner. The NSW State Government's concern with image suggests that it was subject to extra-local rule systems (see Peck & Tickell, 2002) and had little option but to pursue the AWRC agenda and ride out the political backlash. In other words, the pressures of global corporate interests, international competition for investment and place promotion and the perceived risks of being labelled uncompetitive overrode local issues. This situation had important implications for the "norming" stage.

Norming in the public sphere

The norming phase refers to the process through which a collaborative, dialogic space is created and stakeholders move towards joint action. In this phase, despite differences of opinion, stakeholders find common ground and take responsibility for the success of the group. The autocratic, top-down approach described above gave rise to a splintering of the public sphere into several arenas or spaces of common interests and values, that is, communities of interest. The collaborative actions undertaken in these communities of interest were underpinned by different agendas; they called upon different sources of power (e.g. the power of authority, the power of social action) and were implemented using different mechanisms (e.g. law, media, popular opinion, etc.). But even so, there was little clarity of purpose during the "norming" stage with typical comments from stakeholders such as "the lines of communication were very chaotic and I think all that stemmed from the lack of a defined assessment and approval process" (Respondent #14).

One elected representative observed that the roles of Council officers were unclear and that the new legislation had

> left everyone a little bit unsure of what the roles were. And so like when the event was on, there were food vendors setting up in the main street of Murwillumbah, our staff didn't know if they were authorised and if they were supposed to check them .... It was just the uncertainty if they were supposed to be doing it, or they had the right to do it, and whether they were doing it under the [special legislation] ... they couldn't do it under the Local Government Act because it has been modify for the event. (Respondent #10)

One elected representative of a local council further explained:

> our role is to look at economic and social sustainability issues, mostly economic issues .... We supported the Rally, but ... we didn't go out specifically and engage with the community to try to assess that, mostly because we didn't see that as our role. (Respondent #7)

In addition, it could be argued that "norming", if conceptualised as a unifying phase that results in a collective approach to dealing with the proposed event, was never achieved. However, if we conceive of the public sphere as a series of intersecting communities of interest wherein individuals galvanise over common platforms of understanding, behaviours, values and visions, then a number of public spheres emerged and/or were strengthened over the course of the AWRC.

During this phase, the blurring of public–private interests also became evident as individuals and groups, having moved through the forming and storming stages, took action. One individual, also an elected councillor, lodged a temporary injunction with the Federal Land and Environment Court on the grounds that the NSW Government's approval of the event was unconstitutional and it would threaten endangered species protected under the Commonwealth's *Environmental Protection and Biological Conservation Act* (1999). The injunction heard the week before the event, took just three hours to hear and was rejected. The event organiser pursued and was awarded costs against the individual. Since this action, however, anti-rally campaign supporters and others have used media to help raise funds to cover this debt, frequently (and correctly) referring to the individual as a Shire councillor. The Mayor concerned about the blurring of these lines sought to clarify the situation:

Over the past several months there have been numerous media articles, letters, TV reports and other statements that have referred to one of our colleagues as a councillor in a matter that was personal. This action was an injunction sought by [the councillor] in the Federal Court to stop the Repco World Rally. At no time did Council support, permit or fund this action. The action was undertaken by [the individual] in [their] personal capacity, rather than undertaken by [the] Councillor as a member of this elected body ... Further, the fundraising activity to provide financial support to [the individual] that is being promoted and advertised in the local press frequently refers to [that person] as a Tweed Shire Councillor, for a liability [this individual] incurred privately. (*Far North Coaster*, 2010)

This blurring of public and private interests in the way dialogue has played out illustrates the difficulty of separating public and private interests (Habermas, 1989) and how the two become conflated in appearance (Arendt, 1958). Another councillor reiterated the personal dilemma of public office:

So I guess a lot of the community thought "Oh she's pro-rally". But no, it's my responsibility to pull together the council and to make a decision to stand with this event. It wasn't whether I agree with this event. It wasn't whether I thought it was going to be a success. The reality was that the State had taken over. (Respondent #8)

Performing in the public sphere

The "performing" phase refers to the capacity of members in the group to function as a unit and to undertake activities without conflict or the need for external management. In this case study, "performing" can be understood both in terms of the performance of the public sphere as a space for participative democracy and the performance of the multiple public spheres and their effectiveness in raising and debating issues.

With respect to the institutional public sphere, rally organisers and the State Government claim the event was a resounding success. According to the official evaluation, the AWRC generated up to $16.9 million in new economic activity in the Northern Rivers region. Moreover, the report estimated that 20,000 visitors travelled to the Northern Rivers region in September 2009 to attend the event (Integrated Marketing Communications, 2010). However, the fact that the event was later relocated to a different region of the state as a result of continued controversy and local political activism also suggests that institutional public sphere performance was less than satisfactory.

In essence, the performance of the institutional public sphere revolved around issues of accountability, credibility and transparency. For instance, some policy actors believed the evaluation process and outcomes were unreliable because the review was conducted by a marketing and communications consultant, who inevitably sought to please the client, the NSW State Government, and to portray them in a good light. In short, there was a concern that the findings were inaccurately inflated to justify (amongst other things) the State Government intervention and public investment in the event.

The performance of the mass public sphere during the event was mixed. On one hand the anti-rally factions of the community fostered an engaged, active space of collaboration and information-sharing which galvanised political action. On the other hand, the pro-rally community was less well organised and frustrated at times with the strength and organisation apparent in the anti-rally sphere. Of particular concern was the absence of certain voices. These include the voices of Indigenous leaders of the Githabul people, who denied that they had agreed to give permission to run the AWRC through their lands. Their attempts to participate in the public sphere culminated in one Aboriginal elder from the Githabul people lodging an unsuccessful appeal to the Federal Environment Minister to stop the AWRC on the grounds that it would have a detrimental effect on local indigenous heritage.

Discussion

This case study has illustrated that the public sphere provides a useful heuristic device to explore and explain how spaces of dialogue and exchange take place in the planning and implementation of an event. The aim of this paper was to explore the characteristics of the public sphere and its role in the governance of a major tourism event. An important tenet of this research, informed by post-modern and post-structural perspectives on planning, policymaking and governance, is that there are multiple publics and multiple public spheres. These publics and spheres operate interdependently; they are not discrete in their membership or in the tools, techniques, strategies and sources of power used to pursue their interests and values. Moreover, conceptualising and exploring the way in which multiple publics and public spheres emerge, fracture and interact generates important insights into how event governance could be improved in practice.

Characteristics of the public sphere

The first objective of this paper was to better understand the characteristics of the public sphere in the staging of the event. Five key observations are drawn. Firstly, the way the public sphere is constituted has ongoing implications for community–government–business relations and the governance space. The instant creation of the institutional public sphere and the practices of the event organiser and State Government during the forming stage effectively restricted how and by whom issues could be raised and how they could be dealt with. Up until that point there had been a public sphere "at rest", but the need to create a dialogic space where issues could be raised, grievances heard and alternative actions formulated (i.e. to oppose the rally event) stimulated an alternative mass public sphere.

Secondly, the pluralisation of the public sphere observed in the storming phase is perhaps an expression of the structural transformations taking place in the roles and relationships between government, business and civil society. Earlier in this paper, the shifts taking place as a result of globalisation and the increasing domination of neo-liberal corporate interests were discussed and the emergence of the Third Way political project noted. In this case study, the organisation and co-ordination of local interests led to community action, the mobilisation of resources and the development of expertise in an effort to progress various overlapping interests. This reflects the emancipation of civil society from the confines of a narrowly defined institutional public sphere and a style of democratic participation approximating to the Third Way. Citizens were indeed taking responsibility and actively participating in the big issues in their local community, but it was reactive rather than strategic and creative.

Thirdly, and leading on from the above point, tensions in this case study between the institutional public sphere and the mass public sphere (populated by different communities of interest) reveal trouble in the Third Way project. This case study amply illustrates that whilst there was a proliferation of interests and increased participation within the public sphere, the State Government, through its special legislation and closed-door negotiations, also used mechanisms of political control and manipulation that excluded issues from being raised and prevented free and open participation from occurring.

Fourthly, the role of government in the creation and development of these alternative public spheres and healthy democratic practices is, therefore, important (see Habermas, 1989). Neo-institutionalists argue that governments are not independent arbitrators of public interest but are complicit in the development of the public sphere and in shaping the nature of exchange that takes place (e.g. Hirst, 2000; Reich, 2000; Sørensen & Torfing,

2005). In other words, governments can help to prepare the public sphere by laying the groundwork through policies, processes and resources. Over time, expectations are built up about the type of communication and dialogue that individuals can expect. In this case study, expectations built up and embedded over years in the development of legislation were swiftly removed by special legislation. The State Government had moved away from its citizens and its established position in relation to consultation, leaving citizens with a narrow range of avenues to engage in dialogue. Not surprisingly, alternative public spheres emerged: an active mass public sphere characterised by activism, political protest, and a critical awareness of how the media could be used. Questions about governments' readiness to embrace the implications of the Third Way therefore need to be raised. This case study reveals that the NSW State Government is still subject to extra-local rule systems that reduce the efficacy of the Third Way project.

Fifthly, the blurring of public–private interests occurred at organisational and individual levels, illustrating the increasing complexity of the governance context. At the organisational level, the corporatisation of the event agency and the distancing of the government from securing, staging and evaluating the event meant that, in this case study, the agency that secured the event (Events NSW) was not open to public scrutiny nor were its actions, use of resources and decision-making. These organisational arrangements also minimised community interests and reduced opportunities for transparency and accountability in public sector decision-making, criticisms that have also been observed in other cases (Andersson & Getz, 2008; Stokes & Jago, 2007).

The blurring of public–private interests was also noted at the individual level. Respondents articulated their professional opinions and organisational positions but also told stories of, for example, the moral conundrums they faced between personal feelings and organisational positions or the frustration at having information misrepresented but having no voice in the debate. Sometimes digressing from the semi-structured interview format, the researchers became increasingly aware of respondents' connections with other (multiple) communities of interests and the personal side (and costs) of their public representation. There were other instances where public and private interests became conflated, as in the case of one councillor who lodged an injunction as a personal action.

It also became increasingly clear that public and private interests played out in global–local relations. The NSW State Government experienced a kind of political, private sector lock-in because it risked being perceived as uncompetitive at an international level by the international motor racing body. In this way, the State Government was subject to the extra-local rules systems that made it difficult to address local public concerns (Peck & Tickell, 2002).

The public sphere and sustainability issues

The second objective of this paper was to explore the way in which different public spheres facilitate (or do not) debate associated with sustainability issues. The institutional public sphere would normally provide the dialogic space to identify, debate and mediate issues including the impacts on and management of environmental, social, cultural, economic and physical assets. Legislation, policies and plans lay the groundwork for this dialogic space providing a range of formal and informal opportunities to engage in public debate. In this case study, three key issues emerged that stymied the identification of sustainability issues and debate. Firstly, the introduction of special legislation resulted in a very narrow institutional public sphere that frustrated public debate by limiting opportunities for engagement. Moreover, the speed at which the process took place inhibited actors and agencies developing an appreciation and awareness of issues and opportunities to exchange information and ideas. There was also confusion over roles and responsibilities for facilitating public consultation, with local government, traditionally a key player in community engagement, being removed from this role.

Secondly, opportunities to raise and debate issues relating to the event's environmental, economic, social and cultural sustainability were also thwarted by the different levels of expertise and knowledge and the willingness of individuals and agencies to engage in debate. Dover's (2005) explanation of the challenge of implementing sustainable policies and management initiatives suggests that common knowledge and joint understanding between all stakeholders needs to be reached before the longer-term societal goal of sustainability can be actioned. In this case study, some individuals with knowledge about environmental and social impacts were excluded from the debate by virtue of the narrow definition of the institutional public sphere or because of their inability to publicly share their personal views and knowledge.

Thirdly, whilst sustainability issues ranging from the environmental impacts of the rally event, impacts on indigenous culture and sociocultural impacts were discussed to varying degrees in the mass public sphere, the tools and resources available to those operating in this sphere to share their understandings were unequally distributed, which in turn impeded the development of a common space of dialogue. Moreover, there were minimal opportunities for the institutional and mass public spheres to engage and for a meaningful discursive public sphere to emerge (Strydom, 2008). Further and more explicit consideration of the role of government in proactively creating this discursive public sphere is needed.

Conclusion

This paper has responded to a call for better insights into the features of governance and in particular the role of the public sphere in facilitating the sustainable planning and management of tourism events. Event tourism is characterised by critical time paths that in turn place pressure on the various stages of the event management cycle. Working within budget constraints, compressed and inflexible timelines, cycles of resourcing and complex public–private interest structures are some of the challenges associated with planning and managing a tourism event. Such challenges are often not conducive to the fostering of good dialogic space or meaningful exchange about issues such as sustainability. Short timeframes between winning a bid and hosting the event often influence policymakers to opt for quick solutions to realise pending deadlines, instead of adopting the more time consuming process of properly identifying and addressing issues and creating a discursive public sphere. Furthermore, a multitude of stakeholders, each with different interests, roles and responsibilities, are required to work together across organisational boundaries and across different geographical scales to share information and reach common collective understandings. The pressure to develop a discursive public sphere can be exacerbated where the dialogic space has not been prepared, there are no historical relationships, and where there is a lack of awareness as to what other stakeholders roles and relationships might be.

In sum, whilst Habermas (1989) might argue that government plays an important role in preparing and facilitating this dialogic space, the "Third Way" and "Big Society" political projects suggest that community also needs to take greater responsibility. However, unless government embraces the real meaning behind these political projects, and prepares and facilitates a discursive public sphere, governance will remain little more than rhetoric that empowers corporate interests and extra-local rule systems. What is clear then is that the challenge for researchers and practitioners is to build critical insights into governance by exploring its constituent features, to improve understandings about the roles that government play, the way that broader sociological and political shifts are impacting on public interests, public spheres, the quality and characteristics of exchange. This paper has demonstrated the public sphere is worthy of further attention.

References

Agere, S. (2000). *Promoting good governance: Principles, practices and perspectives*. London: Commonwealth Secretariat.

Andersson, T., & Getz, D. (2008). Sustainable festivals: On becoming an institution. *Event Management, 12*(1), 1–17.

Arendt, H. (1958). *The human condition*. Chicago, IL: University of Chicago Press. (Reprinted 1998).

Beaumont, N., & Dredge, D. (2010). Local tourism governance: A comparison of three network approaches. *Journal of Sustainable Tourism, 18*(1), 7–28.

Beck, U. (1994). The reinvention of politics: Towards a theory of reflexive modernization. In U. Beck, A. Giddens, & S. Lash (Eds.), *Reflexive modernization: Politics, tradition and aesthetics in the modern social order* (pp. 1–55). Cambridge: Polity Press.

Beck, U., Bonass, W., & Lau, C. (2003). The theory of reflexive modernization. *Theory, Culture and Society, 20*(2), 1–33.

Bevir, M., Rhodes, R.A.W., & Weller, P. (2003). Comparative governance: Prospects and lessons. *Public Administration, 18*(1), 191–210.

Bramwell, B., & Cox, V. (2009). Stage and path dependency approaches to the evolution of a national park tourism partnership. *Journal of Sustainable Tourism, 17*(2), 191–206.

Bramwell, B., & Lane, B. (2010). Editorial: Sustainable tourism and the evolving roles of government planning. *Journal of Sustainable Tourism, 18*(1), 1–5.

Bramwell, B., & Pomfret, G. (2007). Planning for lake and lake shore tourism: Complexity, coordination and adaptation. *Anatolia: An International Journal of Tourism and Hospitality Research, 18*(1), 43–66.

Burgan, B., & Mules, T. (1992). Economic impact of sporting events. *Annals of Tourism Research, 29*, 172–185.

Cameron, D. (2010). *David Cameron launches Tories' "big society" plan*. Retrieved December 20, 2010, from http://www.bbc.co.uk/news/uk-10680062

Coaffee, J., & Shaw, T. (2005). The liveability agenda: New regionalism, liveabilty and the untapped potential of sport and recreation. *Town Planning Review, 76*(2), 1–5.

Cook, T. (2003, September 4). *Rally drives events*. WA Business News. Retrieved August 16, 2010, from http://www.wabusinessnews.com.au/login.php?url=http%3A%2F%2Fwww.wabusiness news.com.au%2Farchivestory%2F13%2F12907%2FRally-drives-events%26year=2011%26P_ build=1%26pg=0%26P_author=%26P_headline=%26P_summary=kwik%26month=3%26 span=0

Creswell, J. (2003). *Research design: Qualitative, quantitative and mixed methods approaches*. Thousand Oaks & London: Sage.

Dinica, V. (2009). Governance for sustainable tourism: A comparison of international and Dutch visions. *Journal of Sustainable Tourism, 17*(5), 583–603.

Dovers, S. (2005). *Environment and sustainability policy*. Sydney: Federation Press.

Dredge, D. (2005). Local versus state-driven production of the region: Regional tourism policy in the Hunter, New South Wales, Australia. In A. Rainnie & M. Grobbelaar (Eds.), *New regionalism in Australia* (pp. 301–319). Aldershot, Hampshire: Ashgate.

Dredge, D. (2006a). Networks, conflict and collaborative communities. *Journal of Sustainable Tourism, 14*(6), 562–581.

Dredge, D. (2006b). Policy networks and the local organisation of tourism. *Tourism Management, 27*(2), 269–280.

Dredge, D. (2010). Place change and tourism development conflict: Evaluating public interest. *Tourism Management, 31*(1), 104–112.

Dredge, D., Ford, E.J., Lamont, M., Phi, G., & Whitford, M. (2010). *Event governance: Background to the world rally championship*. Northern Rivers, NSW/Tweed Heads, Coolangatta: Southern Cross University.

Dredge, D., & Jenkins, J. (2007). *Tourism policy and planning*. Milton: Wiley & Sons.

Dredge, D., Jenkins, J., & Whitford, M. (2011a). New spaces of tourism planning and policy. In D. Dredge, J. Jenkins, & M. Whitford (Eds.), *Stories of practice: Tourism planning and policy* (pp. 13–35). Surrey/Burlington: Ashgate.

Dredge, D., Jenkins, J., & Whitford, M. (2011b). *Stories of practice*. In D. Dredge, J. Jenkins, & M. Whitford (Eds.), *Stories of practice: Tourism planning and policy* (pp. 37–55). Surrey/Burlington: Ashgate.

Dredge, D., & Thomas, P. (2009). Mongrel management, public interest and protected area management in the Victorian Alps, Australia. *Journal of Sustainable Tourism, 17*(2), 249–267.

Far North Coaster. (2010). *Tweed Mayor distances council from Milne fundraising*. Retrieved January 20, 2010, from http://www.farnorthcoaster.com.au/news/7793/tweed-mayor-distances-council-from-milne-fundraising/

Fazio, A. (2009, September 3). *NSW parliamentary debates. Full day hansard transcript*. Sydney: Parliament of New South Wales.

Flyvbjerg, B. (2001). *Making social science matter: Why social inquiry fails and how it can succeed again*. Cambridge: Cambridge University Press.

Foley, M., McGillivray, D., & McPherson, G. (2009). Policy, politics and sustainable events. In R. Raj & J. Musgrave (Eds.), *Event management and sustainability* (pp. 13–21). Wallingford: CABI.

Fredline, L., & Faulkner, B. (2001). Variations in residents' perceptions of major motorsports events: Why residents perceive the impacts differently. *Event Management, 7*, 115–125.

Freundlich, D., Hudson, W., & Rundell, J. (Eds.). (2004). *Critical theory after Habermas*. Leiden/Boston: Brill.

Gamage, A., & Higgs, B. (1996). Economic of venue selection for the special sporting events: With special reference to the 1996 Melbourne Grand Prix. *Asia Pacific Journal of Tourism Research, 1*(2), 15–28.

Gibson, C., & Davidson, D. (2004). Tamworth, Australia's "Country Music Capital": Place marketing, rurality and resident reactions. *Journal of Rural Studies, 20*, 387–404.

Giddens, A. (1984). *The constitution of society: Outline of the theory of structuration*. Cambridge: Polity Press.

Giddens, A. (1998). *The third way: The renewal of social democracy*. Oxford: Polity.

Giddens, A. (2000). *The third way and its critics*. Malden, MA: Blackwell.

Glasson, M., & Pedler, R. (2005, October 24). Rally stays in WA as time runs out to find new venue. *The Western Australian*, p. 7.

Habermas, J. (1989). *The structural transformation of the public sphere: An inquiry into the category of bourgeois society* (Thomas Burger, Trans.). London: Policy Press.

Habermas, J. (2004). Public space and political public sphere – The biographical roots of two motifs in my thoughts. Kyoto, Commemorative Lecture, 11 November. Retrieved December 20, 2010, from http://homepage.mac.com/gedavis/JH/Kyoto_lecture_Nov_2004.pdf

Hajer, M., & Wagenaar, H. (2003). *Deliberative policy analysis: Understanding governance in the network society*. Cambridge: Cambridge University Press.

Hall, C.M., & Jenkins, J. (1995). *Tourism and public policy*. London: Routledge.

Hede, A. (2008). Managing special events in the new era of the triple bottom line. *Tourism Management, 11*(1/2), 13–22.

Held, D. (1989). *Political theory and the modern state: Essays on state, power and democracy*. Cambridge: Polity Press.

Henderson, J., Foo, K., Lim, H., & Yip, S. (2010). Sports events and tourism: The Singapore Formula One Grand Prix. *International Journal of Event and Festival Management, 1*(1), 60.

Hirst, P. (2000). Democracy and governance. In J. Pierre (Ed.), *Debating governance* (pp. 13–35). Oxford: Oxford University Press.

Integrated Marketing Communications. (2010). *A review of the impact on the Northern Rivers region of the World Rally Championship 2009: Repco rally*. Sydney, NSW: Homebush Bay Motor Racing Authority.

International Sportsworld Communicators. (2007). *2007 WRC fact book*. Retrieved February 24, 2010, from http://www.wrc.com/resources/2007WRCFactBook.pdf

Jago, L., & Dwyer, L. (2006). *Economic evaluation of special events: A practitioner's guide*. Gold Coast, Queensland: Sustainable Tourism CRC and Common Ground.

Jenkins, J. (1993). Tourism policy in rural New South Wales: Policy and research priorities. *GeoJournal, 29*(2), 281–290.

Klijn, E., & Skelcher, C. (2007). Democracy and governance networks: Compatible or not. *Public Administration, 85*(3), 587–608.

Lawrence, G. (2004). *Promoting sustainable development: The question of governance*. XI World Congress of Rural Sociology, Trondheim, Norway. Retrieved March 14, 2011, from http://www.irsa-world.org/prior/XI/program/Lawrence.pdf

Lowes, M. (2004). Neoliberal power politics and the controversial siting of the Australian Grand Prix motorsport event in an urban park. *Leisure and Society, 27*(1), 69–88.

McDonald, I. (2009, September 3). *7.30 Report*. Retrieved from http://www.abc.net.au/7.30/content/2009/s2673656.htm#

Moore, N. (2000). *Telstra rally Australia wins tourism award*. Retrieved May 17, 2010, from http://www.mediastatements.wa.gov.au/ArchivedStatements/Pages/CourtCoalitionGovernmentSearch.aspx?ItemId=113739&minister=Moore&admin=Court&page=2

Peck, J., & Tickell, A. (2002). Neoliberalising space. *Antipode, 34*, 208–216.

Pierre, J. (2000). *Debating governance*. New York: Oxford University Press.

Prior, N. (1999, November 6). Perth rallies to make annual event a success. *The Western Australian*, p. 68.

Rally Australia. (2009). *FIA world rally championship delivers for Northern NSW*. Retrieved May 16, 2010, from http://rallyaustralia.com/announcement-venue-for-rally-australia-2009

Reich, S. (2000). The four faces of institutionalism: Public policy and a pluralistic perspective. *Governance: An International Journal of Policy and Administration, 13*(4), 501–522.

Rhodes, R.A.W. (1997). *Understanding governance: Policy networks, governance, reflexivity and accountability*. Buckingham: Open University Press.

Sørensen, E., & Torfing, J. (2005). Network governance and post-liberal democracy. *Administrative Theory & Praxis, 27*(2), 197–237.

Stokes, R., & Jago, L. (2007). Australia's public sector environment for shaping event tourism strategy. *International Journal of Event Management Research, 3*(1), 42–53.

Strydom, P. (2008). Risk communication: World creation through collective learning under complex contingent conditions. *Journal of Risk Research, 11*(1/2), 5–22.

Tourism Western Australia. (2005). *Western Australian tourism commission annual report 2004–2005*. Retrieved March 18, 2010, from http://www.tourism.wa.gov.au/PublicationsLibrary/WesternAustralianTourismCommission2004_05AnnualReport.pdf

Tranter, P., & Keeffe, T. (2004). Motor racing in Australia's Parliamentary Zone: Successful event tourism or the Emperor's new clothes? *Urban Policy and Research, 22*(2), 169–187.

Tuckman, B. (1965). Developmental sequence in small groups. *Psychological Bulletin, 63*(6), 384–399.

Upson, G. (2009). *Rally Australia seeks community support*. Retrieved April 14, 2011, from http://www.rallysportmag.com.au/home/index.php?option=com_content&task=view&id=3357&Itemid=2775

Warren, I. (2002). Governance, protest and sport: An Australian perspective. *Entertainment Law, 1*(1), 67–94.

World Rally Championship. (2005). *Perth gives up rally Australia*. Retrieved May 12, 2010, from http://www.worldrallychampionship.net/features/index.php?id_display=9

Tourism governance and sustainable national development in China: a macro-level synthesis

Trevor Sofield[a,b] and Sarah Li[a]

[a]School of Management, University of Tasmania, Riverside, Tasmania, Australia; [b]School of Management, University of Tasmania, Launceston, Tasmania, Australia

This paper explores the macro-governance of the growth of China's tourism industry into the world's largest domestic tourist industry and the fourth largest international destination. It explains distinctive aspects of the political and economic changes that have driven China's tourism over the last 30 years. These include a gradualist approach to transition/transformation, the re-birth of entrepreneurship and the market economy, structural change and the retention but evolution of governance by the Chinese Communist Party. It also explains the power of China's 4000-year-old cultural and philosophical heritage that plays a key role in contemporary tourism governance and planning, with a special emphasis on Confucian/Daoist thought, *shan shui*, *feng shui* and *te-zhi*, and the Chinese search for harmony and a middle way. The paper charts the emergence of the concept of sustainable development for the economy as a whole, and since 1995, for tourism development, despite significant tensions between China's drive for "modernization" and "progress" rather than sustainable development. Sustainable tourism development is shown to have had positive influences on transport, wildlife and natural heritage conservation and regional development. The concept of tourism as a "keystone industry", analogous to ecology's concept of a "keystone species", is explored.

Introduction

In the last 30 years, tourism development in China has emerged from nowhere to overtake most other countries. With over 50 million international arrivals each year, it is now the fourth most visited destination in the world while its domestic tourism industry is perhaps unrivaled, reaching 1.9 billion visitations in 2009 (China National Tourism Administration [CNTA], 2010). The impact of tourism growth in China has been enormous in terms of its economy, its society, its culture and national identity, and its environment. This extraordinary growth has taken place in the context of another world first – that of a country in transition where, instead of the disruption that has accompanied the transition of most other former communist countries to a market economy (Organisation for Economic Co-Operation and Development [OECD], 2003), in China it has been accomplished in an environment of comparative stability. And a further world's first phenomenon is that tourism has been elevated and integrated into this transition by very specific government policy and planning in a way that has not occurred in any other socialist/communist country.

No other socialist country has elevated tourism to the status of a pillar industry recognized by its government as of primary importance. This paper, a study of macro-level tourism governance, explores China's evolving regime of governance and planning for tourism through a multidisciplinary perspective. It pays special attention to the evolving role of the state and its tourism governance systems. It also pays special attention to China's cultural and political heritage, and the value systems associated with that heritage, which is a powerful influence in decision-making in physical, generally, and tourism planning.

It must be noted that in examining the exceptional growth of tourism in China since 1978, there has been significant tensions between "progress" and "modernization" (driven largely by industrialization) on the one hand and sustainability on the other hand. China – in common with every country around the world – has had both successes and failures in the quest for sustainable tourism development. The communist ethos of modernization was embedded for more than 50 years as a priority over environmental considerations, with the tension between the two exacerbated by pressure arising from China's huge population and the perceived need by the communist regime to raise living standards as a key factor in the legitimacy of its governance (Grano, 2008). The old mentality of "pollute first, control later" (*xian wuran, hou zhili:* 先污染后治理) has been the mantra for pushing ahead with modernization. "Development", reads a Suzhou billboard, "is an Immutable Truth". (Suzhou is one of China's major tourist destinations, famous for its canals and traditional walled gardens and described as "The Venice of the East".) However, in the past decade, the government has begun to recognize the need for achieving a balance between its model of development and environmental concerns, and to grapple with issues of sustainability in all areas (energy, transport, manufacturing, mining, urban development, etc.). In this context, tourism has been one of the first proponents of a policy more attuned to western/international standards that incorporate sustainability in tourism planning, development and operations; we focus on this in detail later in this paper.

An explanation for the contemporary growth of tourism in China may be found in the particular path that the China Communist Party (CCP) has adopted since 1978 to move from a socialist state, where all economic activity was firmly and centrally controlled by the government, to a more open market economy. It has progressed along this path with characteristics that may be considered unique to China: a gradualist *transformation* to a market economy rather than a *transition* (Hall, 2008); the re-emergence of traditional Chinese expertise in commerce and entrepreneurship that had been almost totally suppressed under Mao Zedong (Naughton, 2007); structural change including massive investment in transport infrastructure; and the retention of the communist-party-led government with "incremental democracy" rather than embracing a form of western-style democracy (Naisbitt & Naisbitt, 2010; Yu, 2000, 2005). China's transformation challenges the conventional wisdom that free markets must always lead to western-style democratic societies (Pan, 2008). Several thousand books and perhaps hundreds of thousands of economic and political papers have been written about these four factors emphasizing the economic achievements of China's move away from socialism to a market economy, with little or no mention of tourism. Equally, the tourism literature on the role of tourism in this transformation has been limited: several books and a few hundred papers have covered different aspects of tourism in China, but few have taken a macro overview to synthesize the politico-economic deliberations that have dominated the analyses of the elevated role that tourism, through very focused government policy and planning, has played in the transformation of China. This paper fills that gap in the literature.

To understand the role of tourism, it is necessary to summarize the main themes of the post-1978 economic reforms in some detail. We can then better follow the evolution of tourism in China that has taken place in a relatively "greenfield" environment created by three decades of "non-tourism" under Mao. It allows observation of how tourism has capitalized on the re-emergence of traditional Chinese expertise in commerce and entrepreneurship, and its contributions to employment on a very considerable scale. It allows exploration of the scale of tourism's growth in China because of investment in transport infrastructure and at times the symbiotic relationship between transport and tourism where tourism has, in many cases, been the catalyst for such investment. This paper demonstrates the role of tourism in national development, with interventions by the Government to use tourism as a major tool to raise living standards in the comparatively poorer western provinces as compared with the wealthy eastern seaboard provinces, through a level of investment in tourism that is unprecedented anywhere else in the world. In drawing these disparate themes together, we advance the concept of tourism as a "keystone" industry, taking the analogy from ecology where a keystone species is fundamental to the health of its habitat as a whole.

Framework for analysis

A multidisciplinary approach is taken to examine tourism policy, planning and development in China drawing upon concepts from political science, economics and government studies. Our analysis is based on 17 years of research, consultancies and teaching in tourism planning and development in China in regions as disparate as Beijing and Shanghai, Guangzhou and Hangzhou, Lhasa and the Tibet Autonomous Region, Sha'anxi and Hunan, Hubei and Anhui, Zhejiang and Yunnan, Sichuan and Guilin, and many more. It benefits from numerous discussions over the years with CCP Province Deputy Secretaries and Governors, other Communist Party (CP) cadres, government dignitaries, senior officials and bureaucrats, industry representatives, academic colleagues, tourism industry practitioners and tourists, both domestic and international.

The evolution of China's economic structure, 1949–2010

China is undergoing a dual adjustment: (1) from a centrally planned economy to a more market-oriented economy "with Chinese characteristics" and (2) from a traditional agricultural to a modern industrial society. Tourism industry development and activity span both. In the words of Naughton (2007, p. 3), "The Chinese economy displays both unmatched dynamism and unrivalled complexity". For the past 30 years, China has been the world's fastest-growing economy, averaging 10% per annum for the last decade (OECD, 2006). By 2005, its gross domestic product (GDP) had reached US$2.225 trillion, surpassing the GDPs of Britain and France to become the fourth-largest economy in the world. It is currently the world's third-largest trading nation. It has the world's largest population at more than 1.3 billion despite a declining birthrate, and the combination of its rapid economic growth and massive human resources has propelled it to the forefront of world economies. Yet it is still fighting poverty, with more than 100 million people living at or below the subsistence level, and its GDP per capita income is only US$3678 per year compared with $46,500 per capita for the United States (IMF, 2009; World Bank, 2009). Its regions display significant diversity and disparity, from the highly developed wealthy eastern seaboard provinces with their mega-cities of Shanghai, Guangzhou, Beijing and Hangzhou to the disadvantaged western provinces. In the countryside, impoverished peasants struggle on subsistence incomes while the cities encompass the very rich by any standards, and where all modern conveniences and the Internet are integral to millions of households. In rural areas, wood- and coal-fired boilers co-exist with modern nuclear power stations and a space program. Huge state-owned enterprises (SOEs) with large bureaucracies not only continue to dominate parts of the economy but also compete with millions of entrepreneurs running privately owned small businesses and with large transnational corporations whose CEOs have degrees in business and management. As China has embraced major features of a market economy and powered into the twenty-first century, disparities in incomes and diversity in living standards have increased.

We may describe this complexity as a political economy: that is, a mix of the disciplines of economics, law, sociology and political science is required to explain how China's political institutions, the socio-political environment and its economic structures influence each other. Naughton (2007) suggests that the diversity arises from the fact that China is experiencing two incomplete transitions. The first is the gradual transformation from a centrally controlled economy ("bureaucratic socialism") to a market economy. And, the second is that China is in the middle of industrialization and a protracted transformation from a rural to an urban society. Since these changes are far from complete, China finds itself coping with "parts of the traditional, the socialist, the modern, and the market, all mixed up in a jumble of mind-boggling complexity" (Naughton, 2007, p. 4). Despite the complexities and difficulties, the World Bank (2000), commenting on the success of China in lifting more people out of poverty than any other country in a very short period of time, re-categorized China from "lower income" to "lower middle income" status. The Chinese themselves use an ancient saying to describe their steady, calculated progress: "Crossing the river by feeling underfoot for the stones".

China's unique set of circumstances

In reviewing a range of commentaries on why China's dramatic growth set it apart from other former socialist states that struggled to make the transition from planned economies to a market economy (e.g. Chow, 1997; Jones, 1997; Lin, 2004; Lin, Cai, & Li, 2003; Naughton, 2007; Perkins, 2002; Wei, 1993; World Bank, 2000, 2002), there is consensus on three key factors: a gradualist approach to transition/transformation, a re-birth of China's traditional commercial and entrepreneurship talents that had been suppressed under Mao, and a structural change. A fourth – on which there is less agreement – the continued hold of the CCP on government and its efficacy in charting the course for transition/transformation – will also be examined. Although each of these factors is considered separately in the following sections, in practice, they are totally integrated and intertwined with each other and this holistic reality needs to be constantly borne in mind.

Gradualist transformation

The first factor has been the incremental and gradualist approach to the transformation, rather than the "big bang" approach or shock therapy that was the theoretical and philosophical underpinning of the transition of the former East European and Soviet bloc economies to a market economy (Jefferson & Rawski, 1995; Lin, 2004; McKinnon, 1994). Hence, China's institutions, at most levels, have had time to adjust rather than collapse. In considering that the processes and dynamics of change in the "Middle Kingdom" have been substantively different from those in the former Soviet bloc countries, we believe that it is more appropriate to talk about China's "transformation" (after Derek Hall, 2008, commenting on developments in Eastern Europe) rather than "transition". Hall views transition as the replacement of an existing economic, social and political system by a new system, whereas transformation is modifying, amending and/or reforming that existing system. China's path has retained CP's governance and any move toward democracy has been very cautious and characterized as "incremental democracy" (Yu, 2000, 2005). It has also retained very large SOEs in another challenge to orthodoxy about transition states. Transformation rather than transition appears to be a more accurate description of what is happening in China.

Although argument still abounds over which approach is the better, that debate can be put to one side in noting that, for China, each time it has moved to make its markets more open, it has reaped significant benefits. The first "opening up" period, from 1978 to 2000, resulted in more people moving out of poverty faster and in greater numbers than any other country had achieved, while gross national product (GNP) rose dramatically. The second opening up began in 2001/2002 when China acceded to the World Trade Organization (WTO) and in the process had to make substantial structural changes in order to attain WTO membership. China's accession to the WTO, following 15 years of difficult negotiations,

> was a watershed event both for the WTO and its members and for China. The Chinese government . . . knew that accession would bring with it the necessity of a large number of reforms in domestic economic policies, many of which would require adapting the outlook of Chinese business establishments. . . . (but it knew that) WTO membership also brought with it the prospect to take advantage of new market access opportunities globally. (Gong, 2005, p. 169)

This second period from 2002 to the present, while exhibiting a slowing down due to the 2008/2009 global financial crisis (GFC), led to a further direct acceleration in growth. These transformational factors were accomplished in a climate of general macroeconomic and political stability that encouraged investment, that is, they interacted directly with structural factors. According to Naughton (2007, p. 8), the investment rate has been high "largely because the domestic savings rate is high; and the domestic savings rate is high largely because Chinese households and firms have experienced general macroeconomic stability and growth in the wake of a successful economic reform".

The role of SOEs illustrates the gradualism that has accompanied China's moves toward a more market-oriented economy. Under Mao, state-owned and collectively owned enterprises represented 77.6% and 22.4%, respectively, of China's then exclusively public ownership economy. The policy of reform and opening up provided extensive scope for the development of individual and private industrial enterprises, but by 1990, the state sector still accounted for about 70% of output. By 2002, the share in gross industrial output by state-owned and state-holding industries had decreased with the state-run enterprises themselves accounting for 46% of China's industrial output. Small- and medium-sized enterprises and non-public enterprises have become China's main job creators. As transformation proceeded, the Government reduced the number of SOEs mainly through amalgamation rather than closure, and instead of privatization, it embraced the concept of corporatization. By 2008, as GNP expanded, the SOE share decreased to just over 40%. Many surviving large- and medium-sized enterprises were converted into joint-stock companies with public ownership spread across a variety of state institutions and enterprises. In this way, majority "state" ownership is maintained, even though the central government has little or no direct role in running the company (World Bank, 2009). Corporatization fits well with Beijing's vision of a more dynamic state sector that dominates the key sectors of the economy and this approach differentiates China's transformation to a market economy from the East European experience wherein SOEs were quickly dismantled and/or privatized entirely.

CP's governance and democracy

The two other factors about which general agreement exists are internal to China and its particular set of circumstances: (1) traditional entrepreneurship and (2) structural change. And, these two have had a particular bearing on the formulation of policies and planning for tourism in China. We will return to examine these factors one by one shortly: but first we explore a fourth factor, less widely accepted, that in our view is valid and fundamentally important for ensuring stability during the dramatic and rapid economic changes accompanying the move to a market economy. This is the absence of any significant shift to western forms of democratic governance, a dynamic that has been considered by many analysts (including institutions such as the World Bank and the International Monetary Fund) as fundamental to a successful transition from communism to capitalism. The CCP at no stage contemplated political change as integral to economic change – and in the Chinese context, the legitimacy of the CCP Government is derived from being successful in implementing change that has benefited hundreds of millions of its people (Naisbitt & Naisbitt, 2010). Chinese tend to see the world in relational terms, that is, where nothing exists in isolation and where there is continuity and change between all things. In the same way, "history" is not consigned to the past, but is continuous, a living river that flows unendingly from ancestors through to the present and into the future (Li, 2005). On the basis of the teachings enshrined in the Analects of Confucius (unknown authors, circa 300–250 BC), Chinese society values social order and harmony where personal accountability is not as important as the quality of relationships with people around the individual whose desires will be subordinated to those of the greater whole. This is in stark contrast to western values that uphold individual freedoms as the pillar of their societies and democratic elections as bestowing legitimacy on a government. It is argued (Zhao, 2008) that despite the increasing awareness of democratic values, principles and practices among the Chinese public and politicians, the majority of the population is still obligated by Confucian values. As a result, Chinese society is to a certain extent organized in strong networks in which patron–client relationships play an overriding role in social and political relations. It is in these spheres that people are inclined to rely on consensus-making and the power of the authorities, which inhibit the development of a pluralist society. As Naisbitt and Naisbitt (2010, p. 43) state, "In the eyes of the West, justification for governing a country stands or falls on who is elected: in the eyes of the Chinese, justification for governance rests more on accomplishments".

Naisbitt and Naisbitt (2010) take this argument further, suggesting that had China established a western-style democracy as part of its transition toward a market economy, then energy would have gone into competing for elections among hundreds, possibly thousands, of candidates who would have presented an enormous array of programs to people with practically no history of democratic decision-making, thus deflecting and indeed making impossible the modernization of China and the alleviation of poverty that the CP has achieved. Dissent, disruption, disharmony and economic decline was the fate of the Soviet Union in the early years of its transition, and had China followed suit, there could have been chaos instead of successfully achieving "a gigantic transition in an astonishingly peaceful manner" (Naisbitt and Naisbitt, 2010, p. 46). Certainly, many sectors have benefited significantly from the consistency of policy frameworks over several decades that do not change like the swings and roundabouts of western democracies, and tourism has been one of them. The retention of the existing political system under the CCP reinforces the conclusion that China is undergoing transformation rather than transition.

The Chinese Government has increasingly moved away from strict adherence to the ideology of communism, and Mao's definition of socialism, to encompass all the main features of a market economy, making adjustments within the one-party system to accommodate the need for greater flexibility. President Hu Jintao (2007) has said that without less top-down autocracy, more bottom-up participation and "power that must be exercised in the sunshine to ensure that it is exercised correctly", China's modernization will falter. He expressed his willingness to deepen the political reform process by prioritizing democratization within the party and gradually increasing citizen participation in public affairs, especially at the grassroots level, under the rule of law. For the first time, he made it clear that he considered grassroots democracy as the fundamental engine of socialist-style market reform. However, this democracy would take place under the aegis of the CCP. This is reflected in a 300-page report produced by China's influential Central Party School – reportedly commissioned by the central leadership, according to Bergsten, Freeman, Lardy and Mitchell (2008) – which charges that the backwardness of the political system is affecting economic development and warns of serious social instability unless democratic reforms are implemented that strengthen supervision over the CCP (Zhou, Wang, & Wang, 2007). While there are still sometimes totalitarian ideological interventions in society because of the Government's fixation with political stability (Hutton, 2006), there is a greater tolerance of dissenting voices; a form of rural self-governance through direct election of village leaders by the villagers themselves (Ninth National Peoples Congress, 1998); relatively more open media reporting of some issues and events; widely publicized cases of prosecution of high-level corruption; and several thousand civil society organizations and Chinese non-government organizations (often linked to international NGOs) such as the World Wide Fund for Nature China (Howell, 2007). The Chinese themselves describe this as "incremental democracy" (Yu, 2005; Zhao, 2008), a term which was adopted by the 17th Communist Party Congress (CPC; October 2007). In fact, its roots may be found in Deng Xiaoping's (1983) speech when he intentionally initiated a revision of Mao's authoritarian view of "people democracy" for a more participatory model ("Emancipate the Mind; Seek Truth from Facts, and Unite as One to Look to the Future"). While the focus remains on a one-party state that is very different from western-style democracy, Naisbitt and Naisbitt (2010) define Deng's call for "emancipation of the mind" as one of the eight "mega trends" that characterize contemporary China: without this promotion of creativity and a degree of experimental thinking to replace mindless indoctrination, they suggest that China could not have embarked on transition/transformation. Tourism development has found fertile ground in this environment, identifying, valorizing and utilizing resources that previously had little or no capacity to generate income (e.g. caves, ancient monuments, temples and fortresses, traditional Chinese festivals, the tangible and intangible culture of minorities, etc.).

Traditional, commercial and entrepreneurial talents

A third major factor contributing to China's progress toward a market economy has been the re-emergence of the traditional, commercial and entrepreneurship talents in China that had been such a feature of China's millennia-long trading history and development (Naughton, 2007). These talents had been suppressed under Mao's regime. The re-emergence of en-trepreneurship domestically then led inevitably to the re-establishment of traditional economic relationships with Chinese compatriots in Hong Kong and Taiwan, and with overseas Chinese in Singapore, Malaysia, other Southeast Asian countries and western countries, and their contributions have also played a substantial part in China's successful graduation to a market economy. These trading and investment linkages led to WTO membership and facilitated China's integration into the global economy.

With reference to domestic entrepreneurship, the advent of the "open-door" policies of Deng began the move toward a market economy – tentatively at first and without formal state backing – through market-oriented "town and village enterprises" (TVEs), and subsequently a degree of privatization. During the Great Leap Forward (1958–1961) when China attempted to industrialize its largely rural economy over a five-year period, brigade- and commune-run industries established TVEs to support the rural areas. At that time, they played a limited role in the economy; were restricted to the production of cement, chemical fertilizers, farm tools and machinery, hydroelectric power, iron and steel; and operated under rigidly managed government allocations of resources and price controls. The 1978 reforms changed the nature of TVEs dramatically. They provided a ready-made structure to transform their commune business model into a more market-oriented version and expand into the new areas of economic activity. While still nominally under the purview of local town and village governing committees and theoretically under "collective ownership", they increasingly gave free reign to the centuries-old entrepreneurial skills of pre-communist China and devolved production quotas to individual households. Any above-quota outputs were allowed to be sold privately, thus incentivizing increased productivity. TVEs were quite flexible in terms of organizational structure. Although some were run by local governments, others were more genuinely independent in nature, and throughout the 1980s, most of the supposedly collective TVEs operated as private enterprises in practice (Wong, 1988). In this sense, "the use of the term 'collective' masked the privatization of rural enterprise at a time when it was ideologically subversive" (Saich, 2001, p. 44).

Indeed, according to Lin Yifu (2004), the government recognized in 1978 that solving managerial problems within the collective system was the key to improving farmers' incentives, but in the resolution adopted by the third Plenum of the Eleventh Central Committee of the CPC in 1978 that marked the start of transition in China, any type of household-based farming arrangement was explicitly prohibited.

> Nevertheless, a collective in a poverty-stricken area began to try out secretly a system of leasing a collective's land and dividing the obligatory procurement quotas to individual households in the collective in late 1978. That area was hit by a drought in that year. All other collectives reported sharp reduction in output. The output in that collective not only did not decline but increased 30 percent. Observing the advantage of the household-based farming system in improving agricultural production, the central authorities later conceded to the existence of this new form of farming ... (and granted) full official recognition of the household responsibility system as a "socialist" farming institution applicable to any collective in China in late 1982. By that time, 45% of the collectives in China had already been dismantled and had instituted the household responsibility system. By the end of 1983, 98% of agricultural collectives in China had adopted this new system. (Lin, 2004, p. 14)

This was the first crack in the centrally planned economy that led to initial reforms of the SOEs sector and paved the way for the establishment of TVEs in many different areas. TVE employment grew from 28 million in 1978 to a peak of 135 million in 1996 (Naughton, 2007) when there were perhaps as many as 22 million TVEs. According to Kung and Lin (2007, p. 573), "the political institutional environment favored these 'public' enterprises during the early years of reform, since private businesses faced severe restrictions and discrimination in terms of resources and regulations". Also, "the fiscal decentralization of the early 1980s gave greater decision-making power to local governments and linked fiscal revenue to the career potential of local officials, creating strong incentives for them to promote these enterprises" (Oi, 1992, p. 114).

The pent-up demand in China for a host of products and services provided ample profit-making opportunities for TVEs operating at this early juncture. Tourism as a newly approved economic activity resulted in thousands of TVEs being set up to develop rural sites as visitor attractions such as heritage sites, mountains, rivers, lakes and so forth (e.g. Li

& Sofield, 1994, a case study on the development of Ling Xiu caves in southern Guangdong Province), with concomitant service facilities such as restaurants, small hotels, coach tour companies, guiding, etc. (e.g. Sofield & Li, 1997, on rural tourism development in China). Tourism development policy encompassed a series of incentives such as tax exemptions of three to eight years for approved businesses, and under its preferential policies to improve the welfare of minorities, additional incentives were extended to include low land-use fees and even longer tax-free holidays. The "Five Together" policy initiated in 1984 was a successful exercise in partial privatization because it allowed government authorities – tourism administrations, individual government agencies, local governments, collectives and private individuals – to invest in the tourism industry. Some were TVEs, while others were more private sector oriented. As authority was devolved to local governments, many villages were designated by them as tourist zones and a wave of construction of scenic spots, folk villages, ethnic restaurants, minorities cultural shows and bed and breakfast homestays was established (Ge, 1995; Qiu, Chong, & Jenkins, 2002). Most of these were "greenfield" sites, with no prior tourism development.

Although SOEs and TVEs were dealing with their own set of reforms and changes, a third movement, that of privatization which in the 1980s was quite limited, began to gather momentum. As the government gradually decreased restrictions and controls at the macro-policy level, a more truly private sector began to expand and by 1995 it outrivaled TVEs. With increased market integration and competition, TVEs lost their protected position; the changes in the economic environment gradually reduced the benefits of public ownership and increased their costs. They experienced a dramatic decline in the face of increased competition and rewards accruing to the more efficient, better managed private operations and those that survived were forced to restructure substantially. By 1996, TVEs accounted for approximately 7% of GDP, down from about 30% at their peak. Privatization received a major boost from General Secretary Jiang Zemin's "Three Represents" theory, which was formally adopted as a guiding ideology of the CP at its 16th Party Congress in 2002. The Three Represents theory – that the party must always represent the development trend of China's advanced productive forces, the orientation of China's advanced culture and the fundamental interests of the overwhelming majority of the people – cleared the way for the admission of private entrepreneurs into CP membership and the introduction of a constitutional amendment to include the protection of private property (see Dickson, 2003, on "red capitalists" in China). This initiative was designed to bed down the economic reforms once and for all, but debate still continues as to whether reform is wrong and should be discarded or whether it has problems that need to be resolved (Bergsten et al., 2008). In this context, Hu Jintao at the 17th Party Congress in 2007 initiated another "Emancipation of the Mind" campaign to reinvigorate support for Deng's reforms.

These three parallel streams – (1) the continuation of SOEs, albeit transferred out from macro-policy to micro-policy with the devolution of management from central to local authorities; (2) the rise (and fall) of TVEs; and (3) gradual corporatization and privatization (still continuing but at an accelerated pace) – all operate concurrently in China within the context of transition/transformation to a market economy under the governance of the CP.

The three streams highlight a major difference from the transition of the East European countries to a market economy. There, the prescription was for immediate dismantling of the SOEs, the establishment of a private sector and the introduction of democratic government, with mixed results. However, China's political leadership did not question the feasibility or desirability of the socialist economic system or of the CP's governance. Rather, it simply wanted to improve the economic performance of SOEs and collectives through incentives, with the retention of power by the CP, a paramount concern. There was no clear blueprint for transition to a market economy, rather it has been characterized as "piecemeal, partial, incremental, and often experimental" (Lin et al., 2003, p. 1). This gradualist approach, which can be explained by the theory of induced institutional innovation (Hayami & Ruttan, 1984; Lin, 1989), has achieved success, however, and a new stream of resources was created by the micro-management system reforms begun in the 1980s that allowed China's transformation to a market economy to proceed with annual double-digit growth (Naisbitt & Naisbitt, 2010; Naughton, 2007).

It may also be concluded that China's example does not support "market fundamentalism" (i.e. where market forces as a "superior mechanism" are allowed free reign with limited government regulation) as a necessary requisite of the transition to a market economy, since some government coordination and control to make up for market failures has proved as important as the relentless expansion of free market forces (Naughton, 2007, p. 7). The GFC in 2008–2009, which saw governments all around the world become directly involved in the market with stimulus packages to combat capitalism's market failures, suggests that western governments appear increasingly to hold a partially similar view. The CCP, due in large part to fears of dire consequences if nothing was done to tackle the economic crisis, rushed through its multi-billion dollar economic stimulus package in November 2008. The plan cobbled together the existing and new initiatives focused on massive infrastructure development projects (designed, among other things, to soak up surplus steel, cement and labor capacity), tax cuts, green energy programs and rural development (Baker & Richmond, 2009). The pre-2008 literature's insistence on following the World Bank/IMF prescription for transition guided largely by free market forces may now not be quite so strongly held.

Structural factors

The final factor of the widely accepted triumvirate of factors that accounts for China's successful transformation is its consistent investment since 1978 in infrastructure with public good properties. In the early 1980s, China's road and railway system was limited, air travel even more so. Major investment has gone into transport infrastructure. Today, the entire country has multiple-lane divided highways, modernized rail (including some very fast trains) and several hundred airports. In response to the 2008–2009 GFC, China enacted a stimulus package that accelerated the input of billions of dollars into transport infrastructure that in 2009 amounted to some US$50 billion in railroad infrastructure, road works and plant (United Nations Economic Commission for Asian and the Pacific [UN ESCAP], 2009). Some key statistics on the development of rail, road, air and waterways are provided to emphasize the scale of modernization in China: tourism is of course dependent upon the modes of transport to provide access to destinations, attractions and other tourist facilities and services.

Railways

Rail is the major mode of transport in China and has attracted massive investment, which began under Mao (who was averse to travel by air and favored trains), and this accelerated rapidly under Deng's reforms. As the second-largest rail network in the world carrying about 25% of the world's railway transportation by volume along its total track length of 86,000 km in 2009, China's railway system is critical to its economy (Ministry of Railways, 2010). In 2008, Chinese railways carried 1.46 billion passengers (a 10.4% increase over 2007). Hundreds of millions of these are leisure travelers, especially traveling during China's

Golden Week holidays, and the Spring Festival or Lunar New Year, traditionally a time of family reunion.

Roads

In 2007–2008, China had a total road network of more than four million kilometers, of which 823,000 km were national highways that have been critical to China's economic growth. With the completion in 2008 of five north-south and the seven east-west national arterial highways, totaling 35,000 kms, Beijing and Shanghai were linked by major highways to the capitals of all provinces and autonomous regions of China, creating connections between more than 200 cities. China now has the second-longest expressway network in the world after the United States (Ministry of Transport, 2009).

Road usage has increased significantly. Annual automobile production first exceeded one million in 1992. In 2009, some 13.759 million motor vehicles were manufactured in China, surpassing Japan as the largest automobile maker in the world (Xinhua News Agency, 2010, citing data from the National Bureau of Statistics). In 2007, the country's 347,000 public buses carried 554 million passengers. Touring coaches are also increasing and millions of Chinese, overseas Chinese and foreign visitors now take guided bus tours to hundreds of destinations around the country. China leads all rivals in bus production and is expected to become the dominant global exporter (Rutkowski, 2009).

Air

In 1980, there were 55 paved airports; in 2007, there were 403. In 1990, the domestic commercial air fleet totaled 490 aircraft; by 2009, there were more than 1500, more than 1000 of them were jet aircrafts. In 2009, Beijing Airport handled 65.375 million passenger movements, Guangdong Province's two main airports (Guangzhou Baiyun and Shenzhen) handled 61.51 million passenger movements and Shanghai's two airports handled 56.99 million passenger movements. The 30 busiest airports handled more than 425 million passenger movements between them in 2009; a majority of them, 60%, were leisure travelers (Civil Aviation Administration of China, *2009 Final Statistics*).

Waterways

China has 123,000 km of navigable rivers, lakes and canals, more than any other country in the world. In 2007, these inland waterways carried nearly 1.6 trillion tons of freight and 228.4 million passengers to more than 5100 inland ports. In 2007, the Government released its *National Plan for Inland Waterways and Ports Layout* for the development of inland waterways and ports by 2020 as an integral part of the comprehensive transport system in China (Li & Fung Research Center, 2009). Passenger boats remain popular in some mountainous regions, where road and rail links are few and also for tourist destinations such as in Hubei and Chongqing, where a fleet of more than 65 small cruise ships (capacity 200–500) take more than three million tourists each year on a three-day journey through the Yangtze River lake, now formed by the Three Gorges Dam.

Sustainable development and environmental concerns

The consequences of China's rapid economic growth, industrialization and urbanization have not all been positive. These factors "have generated high pressures on the environment, with consequent damage to health and natural resources. . . . Air pollution in some Chinese cities reaches levels that are among the worst in the world, energy intensity is about 20% higher than the OECD average, and about a third of the watercourses are severely polluted. Challenges with waste management, desertification, and nature and biodiversity protection remain" (OECD, 2006, p. 2). However, following China's commitment to Agenda 21 on Sustainable Development and the Rio Declaration on Environment and Development arising from the 1992 United Nations Conference on Environment and Development ("Rio Earth Summit"), protection of the environment was adopted as a fundamental state policy (*jiben guoce* 基本国策) in 1993. China embarked on a rapid enactment of a comprehensive set of environmental laws and regulations (Morton, 2006, p. 67). The regulatory framework has continued to expand and environmental needs and priorities have been included in every state's Five-Year Plan for economic development since then (Grano, 2008). The budget for environmental protection as a percentage of GNP has risen from less than 1% in the ninth Five-Year Plan (1995–2000) to a pledged 2.5% for the 12th Five-Year Plan (2011–2015). To promote more balanced patterns of development, the CCP commenced a new ideological campaign in 2005 to shift the focus of the official agenda from "economic growth" to "social harmony" through its policy of harmonious development (*xietiao fazhan* 协调发展), coupled with the scientific development concept (*kexue fazhan guan* 科学发展观). These are the current official socio-economic policies guiding the CCP Government as it moves to integrate sustainable development, social welfare, a person-centerd society, increased democracy, and, ultimately, create a "harmonious society" (Grano, 2008, p. 4). They are extolled by the CCP as a progressive advance on Marxism–Leninism, Mao Zedong Thought, Deng Xiaoping Theory and the Three Represents of Jiang Jemin (Cann, Cann, & Gao, 2005; Day, 2005).

In 2006, the OECD stated that "China's comprehensive and modern set of environmental laws, together with its successive Five-Year Plans for National Economic and Social Development (FYPs) and Five-Year Environmental Plans (FYEPs), provide a high-quality framework for pursuing sustainable development and environmental progress" (OECD, 2006, p. 2). The OECD identified three new policy directions to confront environmental problems: "integrating environmental protection and economic decision-making and placing them on an equal footing, further decoupling pollutant emissions from economic growth, and applying a mix of instruments" such as pollution charges, user charges, emissions trading, incentives, campaigns and award schemes to support implementation at the local level, and working with NGOs to develop procedures for public participation in environmental impact assessment (EIA; OECD, 2006, p. 3).

The actual situation in China is not as hopeful as these developments might seem however, and despite significant action, efforts in pollution abatement, nature conservation and environmental improvement have often lacked effectiveness in the face of adverse pressures generated by China's continuing rapid economic growth. There is a substantial implementation gap (Dunsire, 1978) concerning the intended outcomes of the legislative and regulatory framework, evidenced by the failure to achieve some of the key objectives of the 11th Five-Year Plan and the continuing magnitude of environmental problems in different parts of the country (Economy, 2005). Despite endorsement by the highest levels of governance, the application of the two policies (harmonious development and the scientific development concept) has met with opposition from local governments and also from some members of the Politburo Standing Committee, who consider that the emphasis should remain on modernization and economic growth (Grano, 2008). Our own view, supported by a number of commentators (e.g. Baker & Richmond, 2009; Grano, 2008; Liu, 2010; OECD, 2006), is that the biggest obstacles to environmental policy implementation occur at the local level. The performance objectives of local leaders, the pressures to raise revenues locally to finance un-funded mandates and the limited accountability to local populations have generally meant that economic priorities have over-ridden environmental concerns (OECD, 2006). Grano (2008, p. 16) suggests that the low level of fines imposed on polluters by local authorities is considered as "small costs of doing business" rather than as a serious deterrent by many businesses, and payments to officials to turn a blind eye are perceived in the same vein. There is a need for much stronger monitoring, inspection and enforcement capabilities to establish a better mix of incentives and sanctions (OECD, 2006, p. 4). While there have been some successful interventions such as the 20-point program of environmental action undertaken by the central government and the Beijing City authorities for the 2008 Olympic Games at a national level, the structural problem remains: the central government devolution of responsibility to provincial, prefectures and county authorities in the last decade has resulted in a situation in which priorities for increased production, improvements in living standards and maintenance of social stability have often pushed the implementation of contrary policies on the environment and sustainability into a subordinate position in relation to economic growth.

Tourism as an approved form of development

Having completed the overview of China's transformation from socialism to a more market-oriented economy where sustainable development is emerging as integral to continued modernization, we now turn to tourism policy, planning and development to assess its role in this changing environment.

China's tourism policies after the establishment of the People's Republic of China have evolved from serving a political objective (showcasing the progress of China's communist regime) to an important tertiary industry aligned with Deng's reforms and now to a multi-purpose "pillar industry" of the twenty-first century that includes economic, social, political and environmental contributions to national development (Huang, 2010). The tourism industry gained a new acceptance as part of the open-door reforms; its foreign exchange earnings were recognized as being able to make a significant contribution to financing the "four modernizations". The Bamboo Curtain was pulled aside and the Chinese door opened to world tourism in a comprehensive way. The first national conference on tourism was held in 1978 to formulate the guidelines and organizational structures for its development (Gao & Zhang, 1982). Politically, tourism was justified in socialist terms as an acceptable industry because it would advance economic reforms and the policy of opening to the outside world, further friendship and mutual understanding between the Chinese proletariat and other people of the world, and contribute to world peace (Sofield & Li, 1998). In three different speeches in 1979, Deng stated the need for the swift growth and development of tourism (*Tourism Tribune*, 1992).

The adaptive response of successive Chinese Governments to tourism following the demise of Mao Zedong in 1976 and the "open-door" policies thus saw tourism for the first time embraced as a legitimate form of national and regional development. Unlike many governments (especially in western democracies!), the CCP Government understands the complex linkages of tourism with other sectors and its capacity to contribute to many other industries through the tourism supply chain. Thus, since 1978, it has formulated a range of policies for both international and domestic tourism development that have made tourism one of the most significant economic, social and cultural phenomenon in China in the past 30 years. These three decades have witnessed perhaps the strongest and most sustained rise of tourism of any country in the world as the Chinese Government has prioritized the sector and allocated substantial resources to it.

Although China has moved significantly beyond the highly centralized planning processes of the CP under Mao, its tourism planning remains to be characterized, to a certain extent, by top-down policymaking and strong government domination with limited participation by other stakeholders, even though there has been a significant devolution of power from Beijing to the provincial, prefecture and county levels of government (Airey & Chong, 2010; Qiu et al., 2002; Sofield & Li, 2007). In their detailed analysis of the key players and institutional processes involved in national policymaking for China's tourism sector, Airey and Chong (2010) emphasize the fragmented nature of tourism and the fragmented power structure that has resulted in policymaking being conducted by a variety of policy-makers with a diversity of values and interests. They acknowledge that decision-making is often accompanied with support from the state leaders because of a significant decrease in centralized power. However, our direct involvement in more than 30 tourism policy and planning development projects in China has made us aware of the way in which oversight in many cases is maintained by the national authorities, and where problems arise, in our experience the central authorities may quickly step in and coordinate a revised planning approach.

Furthermore, projects considered of national importance will be directly controlled by the central authorities, and the western development project or "Open up the West", which has a very large tourism component, is one such example (Sofield & Li, 2007). Launched in 2000, this large-scale exercise is aimed at narrowing the gap between the more highly developed eastern coastal provinces and the western interior of the country. China's "west" is generally defined as the poorer parts of China far away from the prosperous eastern seaboard and the rationale behind the project covers five separate agendas: "a quest for equality in the context of alarming growth in disparities between east and west, foreign investment, infrastructure investment, ethnic issues, and sustainable development" (Holbig, 2005, p. 21). In the decade following the launching of the strategy of western development, more than 100 important projects have been carried out with a total investment of RMB1250 billion (US$160 billion). These include more than 350,000 km of highways, major railway lines linking different ethnic regions (including the Qinghai-Lhasa railway), power stations and west-east gas pipelines. Since most of the provinces involved have significant minority populations (in some cases, they are the majority, such as in Yunnan, Xinjiang and Tibet), the program deals directly with the issue of underdevelopment in ethnic areas. In terms of tourism, the most ambitious is the "Greater Shangri-la Tourism Investment and Development Project" that covers all of the ethnic Tibetan areas from northern Yunnan to southwestern Sichuan and west into the Autonomous Region of Tibet (Sofield, 2002; Sofield & Li, 2007). Since policy and planning covers three provinces, numerous prefectures and even more counties, central coordination by the CNTA has been essential. The CNTA also exercises control over a set of tourism standards such as the classification of scenic sites (it has a four A rating system), the star rating of all hotels around China (with inspections on an annual basis) and national standards for ecotourism ventures, which incorporate the principles of sustainability such as carrying capacity and limits of acceptable change. And, in the past decade, it has coordinated a policy to produce a tourism master plan for every one of China's 26 provinces and autonomous regions. Nevertheless, in other instances, some policy-planning responsibilities and implementation of that planning have been devolved to the local level.

Tourism development has reflected this progression of change with what has been recognized within China as the "two phases" phenomenon: Phase one is known as "cultivation"

(1978–1991), when tourism emerged from the socialist planned economy, and Phase two is the "growth phase" (from 1992 to the present), when a private tourism sector began to emerge that has progressively adapted to a market economy (Zhao et al., 2006). We would preface these two phases, however, with the first phase that we have termed the embryonic phase of rigid restrictions that curbed travel under Mao Zedong from 1949 until Deng's open-door policies of 1978, a 30-year period during which tourism was not an approved form of development but was highly restricted and used as a tool of international diplomacy, and designed to showcase to "friends of China" the successes of the Mao regime. From 1949 to 1978, less than 250,000 international visitors were allowed behind the Bamboo Curtain. Domestically, citizens required a special pass, rarely granted, to leave their own place of residence. Unlike the former East European and Soviet Union communist societies in which workers were granted annual vacation leave in mega resorts provided by the state, in China, only highly ranked CP cadres were privileged to stay in Government guesthouses. In brief, under Mao, leisure travel was prohibited for all but a favored few (Li & Sofield, 1994).

It was this very deliberate policy of "non-tourism" that set mid-twentieth century China apart from virtually all other countries. There was no prior tourism development in many places that had to be taken into account when establishing the sector, no tourism "givens" that pre-determined, restricted, directed or otherwise curtailed how and what planners could consider. There was an absence of tourism in China. But then came the 1978 "open-door" policies that consigned the tumultuous decade of Mao Zedong's cultural revolution to history and charted a new course toward a market economy in which tourism was promoted as an acceptable form of development. Policymaking and planning for tourism in the last 32 years has thus taken place in a "greenfield" environment. The term is used here in a relative rather than in a literal sense, that is a greenfield site is an area of land that has never been developed or built up, but in this sense, we use it as a shorthand descriptor of the fact that all over China, under Mao, there were no sites developed specifically for tourism. Thus, after 1978, tourism planners had a relatively free hand. There were no existing tourism-specific structures even in many of the most famous sites. However, as travel has become an accepted component of everyday life in contemporary China, the huge population has had a paucity of sites to visit (Bao, 2008), and thus, we have been involved in planning and development for tourism of numerous, true greenfield sites where there has been no previous development of any kind, from Hubei to Sha'anxi Provinces, and from Yunnan and Sichuan to Xingjiang and Tibet. This has also maintained governance from the supply side, rather than the demand or market side of tourism – a situation unknown in the west since the 1970s.

Government policy has been the key driver that has elevated China to be one of the foremost tourism powerhouses in the world since Deng delivered a series of six keynote speeches on the merits of tourism as a tool for development just 30 years ago (CNTA, 2005). China's domestic tourism surpasses that of virtually all other countries despite a relatively low per capita income (by comparison with western standards of living), and its inbound tourism numbers rank it as the fourth most visited destination in the world. In 2009, it recorded 50.9 million international arrivals (down from 54.7 million in 2007 and 53 million in 2008, evidence of the "bite" of the GFC), with international tourism receipts totaling US$39.7 billion (United Nations World Tourism Organization [UNWTO], 2010). Domestic tourism was unfazed by the GFC and recorded an 11% increase in 2009 over 2008 figures as the Government pushed an aggressive "tour locally" policy to counteract the international arrivals downturn – 1.9 billion visitations with revenue exceeding RMB1 trillion (US$147.5 billion) for the first time. The CNTA attributed the increase not only to its policies of support for domestic tourism but also to a huge increase of investment in tourism-related industries and infrastructure, that is the State Council's "accelerating the development of the tourism industry program" (CNTA, 2010, p. 6), the tourism component of the four trillion yuan (US$586 billion) GFC national stimulus package. In 2006, the World Travel and Tourism Council (WTTC) reported that there were 72 million people directly employed in tourism, about 9% of the total workforce, making it one of the most labor-intensive industries in the country (WTTC, 2006).

In November 2009, the State Council issued a major policy statement that elevated tourism to the status of a "strategic pillar industry" of the national economy. To be declared a "pillar industry" denotes the importance of a particular industry or sector to the economy as a whole and it then may attract special government support, including preferential loans for investment and development, government-funded research and development (R&D) and strong policy support at the national, regional and local levels. Reporting on the new policy, the official newspaper *China Daily* (2009) said that the State Council executive meeting, chaired by Premier Wen Jiabao, called for improved service and management in the tourism sector, which consumes fewer resources and generates more job opportunities; more efforts should be made to improve tourism infrastructure and enhance training of personnel in the industry; and the Government would lower the market threshold to encourage social capital and enterprises of various ownership to invest in the sector on a fair basis. In demanding more efforts to protect ecosystems, indigenous environments and historical and cultural heritage, the Government also called for collaborative development between the tourism sector and related industries, including culture, sports, agriculture, industry, forestry, environmental protection and the meteorological sector. This policy statement clearly demonstrates the understanding of tourism as a system that has the capacity to contribute to a wide range of sectors.

How sustainable has China's tourism development been?

As noted earlier, China has begun to grapple with issues of sustainability in all areas (energy, transport, manufacturing, mining, urban development, etc.), and in this context, tourism has been one of the first proponents of a policy more attuned to western/international standards that incorporate sustainability in tourism planning, development and operations. It is difficult to date precisely the nationwide advent of this approach, but a key seminar took place in the Shanghai Institute of Tourism in October 1995. Organized by the CNTA and the WTO as part of the Government's commitment to implement a national Agenda 21 and incorporate the principles of sustainable development across sectors, all 88 Chinese tertiary institutions, then delivering courses in tourism, were invited to consider how to incorporate ecologically sustainable development (ESD) in tourism policy, planning and development (Sofield, 1995). At that time, there was no precise term for ESD in Chinese tourism semantics (although there was in the context of foreign affairs: *chixuxing shengtai fazhan* 持续性生态发展) and the seminar spent more than three hours in finding the characters to define it specifically for tourism. The result was *chixuxing luyou fazhan* 持续性旅游发展 , "sustainable tourism development (STD)" – a term that the CNTA then adopted nationally (Sofield, 1995). At that time, there was centralized control by CNTA over all tourism policy and planning, and so STD began to be incorporated into all terms of reference (ToR) for tourism projects. It is now a standard practice. For example, a current World-Bank-funded tourism project for Guizhou titled "Cultural and Natural Heritage Protection and Development Project for Community-Based Sustainable Tourism" includes in its ToR "the protection of physical, natural and intangible cultural heritage" by *inter alia* "the development of protection measures/regulations for land use, cultural landscapes, traditional architectural integrity and consistency, and acceptable limits of change" in order to achieve "sustainable cultural and ecotourism development" and "a sustainable tourism industry to benefit rural areas for poverty reduction" (Guizhou Provincial Government Project Management Office, 2010, p. 3).

The 2008 Olympic Games preparations, labeled as the "Green Oympics" by China, demonstrated a capacity by the central government to take decisive action to decrease the levels of pollution in and around Beijing. According to an assessment of improvements post-Olympics by the United Nations Environment Programme (UNEP, 2009), the Games organizers were successful across a broad range of activities, from reducing air pollution to the improvement of the city's transport infrastructure, investment in renewable energies, the upgrading of the waste system and the creation of 720 green spaces in central Beijing that covered 8800 hectares with more than 30 million trees and rose bushes. The Games also greatly increased public awareness of air quality in Beijing, leading the public to press for continued efforts to sustain the improved quality of life experienced during the Games, and UNEP (2009) considers that this heightened public awareness of environmental issues in China is a powerful legacy of the Games. China is estimated to have invested over US$17 billion on environmental projects for the Games.

Xu, Ding, and Packer (2008, p. 480) note that Chinese tourism researchers and the tourism industry "are often criticized as lacking concern for sustainability" (but) "the multiple goals of tourism for development were perceived right from the start of tourism planning". They acknowledge the tension between the reality of most tourism in China that is overwhelmingly mass domestic tourism and the sustainable alternative model promoted in the west, but argue that mass tourism "in the social, cultural and political contexts of China is a rational choice" since "It is only through mass tourism that modernization can be obtained and demonstrated" (2008, p. 480). This is fundamental in terms of China's governance and its adoption of tourism as a pillar industry because "without these observable indicators of modernization, tourism development cannot be supported and must be substituted for other modernization tools which could be sub-optimal for the region as a whole" (Xu et al., 2008, p. 481). In other words, tourism, they suggest, is relatively benign and sustainable in contrast to alternative forms of development such as industrialization. According to them, the challenge is to find ways to apply the best practice models to mass tourism to achieve sustainability outcomes and advocate more empirical research in China regarding integrated tourism planning and development for mass tourism and its application in different localities. Liu (2001, p. 1) provides some answers: "There is an urgent need to integrate ecology with human demography, behaviour, and socioeconomics in order to understand and manage ecological patterns and processes" because there are very few places left that have not been directly or indirectly affected by human activities. As a result, ecologists' traditional subjects of study (e.g. "natural" or pristine ecosystems) are disappearing, and human-dominated or human-influenced ecosystems inevitably require a new multidisciplinary focus of study.

The legacy of cultural value systems and beliefs

One issue that contributes to a rather different implementation of western concepts of sustainability via a Chinese approach is the general anthropocentrism and anthropomorphism inherent in the Chinese value system that is derived from Confucian philosophy and Daoism (Li, 2005, 2008). These twin foundations of Chinese society have continued to influence contemporary Chinese society (Sofield & Li, 1998; Yan & Bramwell, 2008) despite Mao's pursuit of "totalistic iconoclasm" to destroy completely "'the four olds" – religion, imperialism, feudal superstitions and customs and cultural heritage – during the Cultural Revolution, 1966–1976 (Lin, 1979, p. 1).

It is difficult to over-state the influence that Confucius has exercised over Chinese philosophy and the structuring of its society and its values. It has been said that "All of Chinese thinking is a series of commentaries on Confucius" (Hall & Ames, 1998, pp. 2–3). Fung Yu-lan (1952), one of the great twentieth century authorities in the history of Chinese thought, compares Confucius' influence in Chinese history with that of Socrates in the west. It is a fallacy of some western commentaries that Confucius was just a purveyor of trite moral truisms, when the validated historical record amply demonstrates that he was a founder of a social order which has lasted longer than any other in recorded history (Li, 1994). The accepted wisdom of Confucius established the tradition of Chinese culture practically for its entire intellectual heritage, from the time of his life during the fifth century BC to the Republican period in the early twentieth century AD (Ebrey, 2003; Lau & Ames, 1998). Confucianism was adopted as the state ideology in the second century BCE, and except for a period of Mongolian rule by the Yan Dynasty from 1279 AD to 1368 AD, the Confucian mandarin class dominated Chinese society until the overthrow of the imperial system in 1911 (Li, 2005, 2008).

Daoism stands alongside Confucianism as one of the two great religious/philosophical systems of China. It is difficult to define Daoism precisely because there are reputedly more than 100 schools of Daoist thought: only a brief outline is possible here. The umbrella term "Daoism" covers a range of doctrines similar to Confucianism, as well as assorted naturalistic or mystical religions. Ecological in its early form, it insisted that the relational definition of humankind advanced by Confucius had to extend to the natural world because the social, cultural and natural environments co-existed in continuous mutually shaping ways. Humans had to be "responsive to the cadence and flow of all of nature's complex orders. [They could not ignore their] responsibility to participate fully in the harmony of non-human surroundings" (Hall & Ames, 1998). Daoism accorded human emotions to inanimate objects such as mountains, natural elements such as rivers and lakes and non-human forms such as trees and animals, and encompassed the need for man and nature to bring opposing forces (*yin* and *yang*) into a symbiotic relationship in which "harmony" rather than "difference" or "opposites" was dominant (Rawson & Legeza, 1973). The essence of life itself, the cosmic force called *ch'i*, was the major determinant in the growth of all things, that is whether trees and crops would thrive, to what height a mountain reached and how fast a river flowed. Everything was in a constant dynamic state of change, even rocks, although the process of change in this instance was so slow that humans could not observe it (Eberhard & Morrison, 1973, p. 57). This is an anthropocentric perspective with an active sociological determinant that prescribes that because nature is imperfect, "man" has a responsibility to improve on nature (Chan, 1969; Elvin, 1973). Confucius decreed that harmony was to be achieved through "the middle way" ("*zhong yong zhi dao*") – avoiding extremes. This world view is thus distinct from a western perspective that separates nature and civilization (humans), which views wilderness ideally as free from artificiality and human intervention. Translated into the concept of sustainability, China's "middle way" accepts "improvements", "growth", "modernization" and "progress" that would possibly be rejected in western countries because of perceived negative impacts on the resource being "developed" (Dredge, 2004; Li, 2008; Sofield & Li, 2007). The continued relevance of this ancient life value is evidenced in the introduction in 2005 of the policy of "harmonious development" coupled with the scientific development concept, which together are intended to lead to a harmonious society.

Part of the problem identified by Xu et al. (2008) lies in the different indicators used to measure impacts. Western positivistic science uses physics and chemistry to measure pollution in soils, air and water; biology and ecology ascertain the impacts on living organisms and habitats; and mathematical modeling determines the rate of exploitation of a finite resource. By contrast, the Chinese perception of "harmony", which is often equated with sustainability, may encompass design principles of *feng shui* and *te-zhi* and 1600 centuries of *shan shui* literary, artistic and cultural heritage that in most instances and applications defy rational scientific measurement. These concepts are rarely understood by the western critics of Chinese development who utilize the etic perspective (outsider located), drawing upon their own value system, to cast judgment on another society. An emic perspective (insider located, drawing upon the indigenous value system) leads to an explanation of how *feng shui* and *te-zhi* contribute to the Daoist concept of harmony and the Confucian mantra of the middle way, and how *shan shui* art and literature has been a major vehicle for the transmission of those ideas and ideals through the centuries (Li, 2008). In this context, we would place China's value system based on its continuous two millennia-long socio-linguistic cultural heritage within the parameters of Liu's (2001) fields of behavior and socio-economics in order to analyze the Chinese approach to sustainability, governance and tourism development.

Daoism extended the concept of a unitary human-nature world to the mutual reciprocity of feelings that views nature as a living organic whole and has the capacity to empathize with human beings. Nature is related to humans through human sentiment: natural features will be imbued with human characteristics such as mountains with benevolence and rivers with wisdom (both from the *Analects* 论语, or "Sayings" of Confucius; Cai, 1994); a tree will not be valued because of its unique botanical qualities but due to its relational value to humans – cultural because it takes on human attributes (anthropomorphism), or functional as in terms of traditional medicines and shelter. This philosophy was manifested in the literary genre of *shan shui* (literally "mountains" and "water"). Thus, the *shan shui* paintings of the Song Dynasty artist, Guo Xi (1020–1090), often contained three types of trees. The lesser, bending trees Guo Xi described anthropomorphically as holding one's creeds within oneself; the crouching, gnarled trees were seen as analogous to an individual clinging to his own virtues; and the vertical trees were compared to those individuals who remain abreast of their environmental conditions (politics) and flourish (Li, 2005). *Shan shui* literature deeply influenced the esthetic image of landscape as culture for subsequent generations, as artwork, essays and poems in this genre, and the format of writing them has been passed down through the education system for generations. It is the foundation for much Chinese common knowledge. The *shan shui* movement captures the fusion between nature and culture, and while its antecedents span 1600 years to the time of the Tang Dynasty, it is still perhaps the most admired form of poetry today. Mao Zedong and Jiang Jemin were both contemporary practitioners of this art form. Standing as the archetype for *shan shui* poetry is the famous stanza "Green mountains" written by the poet Xin Quiji (1140–1207 AD):

> I see green mountains. How enchanting!
> I expect the green mountains see me in the same way.

(Translation by Li, F.M.S.)

This poem captures the essence of a culturally specific Chinese tourist gaze, as does Li Bai's poem about Mount Jinting where humans and mountain enjoy reciprocal empathy, their feelings permeating each other – an anthropomorphic mode from which to view the world (Li, 2005).

In this context, it may be said that the ultimate goal of tourism development – and therefore governance – in China is to induce the traveler to enter into a relationship of *mutual feeling* with nature, with all of the "Ten Thousand Things" (万事万物 *wanshi wanwu*, meaning both happenings/events as well as physical things) that in Daoism make up the cosmos, because the Chinese believe that all things are capable of feeling (Li, 2005, 2008). A Chinese tourist gaze thus encompasses anthropocentrism and anthropomorphism (Li, 2005). The famous Tang dynasty poet, Li Bai, has captured the Chinese essence of the symbiotic relationship of man-in-nature with his profound poem, "Alone on Mount Jingting":

> Man and mountain silently gaze in wonder at each other
> Neither is ever satiated
> Oh! Mount Jingting.

(Translation by Li, F.M.S.)

Weaving its way through the philosophy and religion of Daoism is the concept of *feng shui*. This guided the human relationship with the environment in a systematic way and impacted on the Chinese landscape at every level. Its origins are attributed to the early ruler, Fu Xi (circa 2800 BC) who "discovered" art and science according to popular Chinese wisdom and instituted *feng shui* "to sanctify the lives of his people, attune them to the moods and rhythms of nature and provide them with security and a sense of continuity" (Michell [sic], 1975, cited in Eitel, 1984, p. 5). Some of the rules for *feng shui* were recorded in the ancient text, *I Ching* (*The Book of Changes,* circa 2500 BCE, author(s) unknown). Yan (1965, p. 24) described *feng shui* as "a mystical combination of Chinese philosophical, religious, astrological, cosmological, mathematical and geographical concepts". The term literally means "wind" and "water". Since the endeavors of humans are subjected to the twin influences of the heaven and earth, *feng shui* was designed to provide a mechanism by which the *yin* and the *yang* of *ch'i* could identify where the forces of heaven and earth would be in harmony. Humans could then interact with them at prescribed places and times to achieve prosperity. Below the ground, the forces of *ch'i* flow through dragon's veins; above, they manifest chiefly as wind (*feng*) and water *(shui)*. Thus, features in the landscape are crucial to *feng shui*. For example, mountains – *yin,* passive, with ascribed characteristics of the dragon, tiger, turtle or phoenix – could be balanced by water – *yang,* active, able to attract and hold wealth; and their juxtaposition would determine the flow of forces or energy between them and whether a site was to be avoided or developed for a particular purpose (traditionally a town, a shrine, a grave, etc. – now extended to include a tourist attraction). This reflects the notion that "human alterations of the landscape do not simply occupy empty space. Rather, sites are *viewed* as manifesting certain properties which influence, even control, the fortunes of those who intrude upon the site" (Knapp, 1992, pp. 108–109, author's emphasis).

Feng shui became an official state science and was directed by the Board of Rites in Beijing. The national guidance of *feng shui* through governance ended with the overthrow of imperial rule in 1911, but continued to be practiced all over the country. Although officially banned by Mao Zedong as contrary to the scientific atheism of Marxism, it was integral to the Chinese landscape; it simply could not be banished or destroyed, although individual manifestations such as a *feng shui* shrine might be. Never fully suppressed, it flourishes today throughout China and among overseas Chinese, whether they are resident in Hong Kong, Singapore or California. Many tourism developments today are based on the *feng shui* analysis of the site that can determine the location of specific buildings and their orientation, placement of embankments or artificial hills, introduction of a body of water, tree-planting and so forth. It moves well beyond the esthetics that western architects and landscape specialists would apply (Li, 2005).

Governance practices based on *feng shui* are consistent with the principles of conservation and good land management. Williams and Webb (1994), describing the many examples of *feng shui* in rural China, note that ideally a village or house should be built on a south-facing slope flanked by the arms of encircling hills – the Dragon Mountains behind giving protection from cold northerly winds, the Green Tiger Hill on the right providing protection from easterly gales and the White Horse Hill to the left providing shelter from the westering sun and dust storms from the west. A *feng shui* grove of trees should be maintained on the uphill slope (Black Turtle Ridge) directly behind the village. This will provide further protection from the winds, lessen the risk of landslides, prevent soil erosion and regulate water flows (Williams & Webb, 1994, p. 113). There should be a meandering river in front of the village. This will provide a steady water supply and ensure that wealth accumulates – agriculturally likely at least, since it may deposit rich silt along its banks making farming prosperous, in contrast to a swiftly flowing river which will carry wealth away in floods (Li, 2005). The sites of thousands of villages and towns throughout China have been based on these *feng shui* principles.

The Daoist Purple Cloud (*Zi Xiao*) Temple in Wudangshan (made famous by the internationally acclaimed film "Crouching Tiger Hidden Dragon", 2000) is visited by more than one million Chinese each year and considered one of the best *feng shui* sites of any temple in China. Its construction on this favored site was ordered by the Song Emperor and first built between 1119 and 1125 AD. In terms of a Chinese tourist gaze, it is of interest that while the official guidebooks and pamphlets issued in both Chinese and English mention that Purple Cloud Temple is excellent *feng shui,* none of them provide any details as per the diagram and explanatory notes below. Through their "common knowledge", Chinese visitors, however, can see and read the site without the need for such interpretation (Li, 2005).

The Purple Cloud Temple demonstrates a classical *feng shui* arrangement of mountains and water.

- The temple is located facing south, with the Dragon Mountains and the Black Tortoise ridge encircling it and protecting it from the chill north winds.
- A *feng shui* forest covers the slope of the Black Tortoise ridge.
- The White Horse Hill on the west blocks the malignant glare of the western sun.
- The Green Tiger Hill on the east guards the site (easterly gales) and counterbalances the White Horse hill for increased harmony.
- The Red Phoenix in front (south) is low enough to allow a vista but high enough to protect the site from *shaqi* (evil) influences.
- The temple is located on a slope above the streams, small lake and river so it will thrive because its foundations will not be undermined.
- The temple faces the water, is embraced by the streams and so will enjoy prosperity. (A site in the bend of a body of flowing water will accumulate riches as the river slows down and deposits its wealth, whereas the one which is located on the banks of a straight flowing river will have its wealth swept away.)

(Li, 2005)

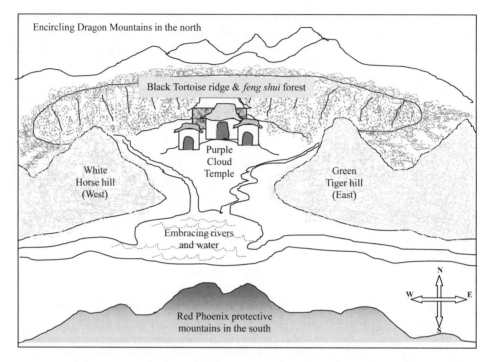

Figure 1.   The Purple Cloud Temple, Wudangshan – a classical *feng shui* arrangement of mountains and water. It is considered nationally as being located in one of the most harmonious *feng shui* sites of any temple in China.

The ideals of *feng shui*, stripped of their original packaging of mysticism, astrology, cosmology and Daoist concepts of *ch'i*, are largely consistent with the contemporary notion of ESD. Its fundamental tenet is the need for humans to harmonize with, not disrupt or destroy nature, although it also seeks to provide a measure of control by humans over natural forces. Tampering with nature might unleash adverse energies and disrupt equilibrium, and unplanned or indiscriminate modifications of the landscape could lead to unpredictable, perhaps disastrous, results. The goal of *feng shui* is to tap the earth's *ch'i* in ways which will achieve the desired harmony and its consequential sustainable prosperity (Li, 2005). The ancient practice of *feng shui* has resulted in major modification to the environment and has been a primary determinant in the pattern of human settlement in China. In tourism today, the landscapes of China hold a profound heritage, which is largely hidden from non-Chinese eyes and requires a carefully constructed interpretation to be revealed. One must be wary of being misled by romanticism about *feng shui* as ESD however, because it would be naive to expect that the ideals were always rigorously implemented, although they have represented the "best practice" and demonstrate a sensitivity toward sustainable development (Anderson & Anderson, 1973; Fan, 1992; Hammond, Adriaanse, Rodenburg, Bryant, & Woodward, 1995; Li, 2005).

Feng shui is making a resurgence in China and our work with tourism development planning projects in China has frequently included it. The Wolong National Nature Reserve, site of China's giant panda artificial breeding program and habitat for the largest remaining numbers of panda in the wild, became a World Heritage Site in 2005 and is such an example. The tourism master plan used *feng shui* to determine the best site for relocation of the artificial breeding station. A high alpine valley (Dongkoucao) was selected that met all of the fundamentals of *feng shui* principles – south-facing with protective Dragon Mountains to the north, encircling ranges that gave east and west protection (the White Horse and Tiger ridges), a heavily wooded slope directly behind the site (the Black Turtle Ridge with *feng shui* forest), two small streams flowing around the east and west sides of the valley to combine in a small lake at the entrance and a distant southern mountain range (the Phoenix). Good *feng shui*, we were advised, would enhance the prospects of success for the breeding program. The project is expected to attract 1.6 million visitors each year; sustainable ecotourism required harmony with the surrounding landscape (Aba Prefecture Jiuzhai Wolong Giant Panda Industry Co and Sichuan Province Forestry Department, 2006).

The Nanjing University started a course in *feng shui* in September 2005 and physical planners were one of the targeted recruitment areas (Li, 2005).

Planning principles

The value system derived from the Confucian/Daoist thought found expression in planning principles applied in China for centuries and is now being utilized in some planning for tourism development. The first principle to note is that for a mountain in China to be considered as beautiful, it needs to be "gazed at" holistically, that is the physical landscape must be permeated with human cultural and historic heritage. Without this, the essence of harmony is absent (Xie, 1988, p. 40). Since harmony is reliant on "man improving on nature", it is natural, indeed essential, for all types of human endeavor, from pavilions and temples, trails and stairways, rock cliff engravings and calligraphy, paintings and stone tablets, ponds and lakes and gardens, carvings and other arts and craftwork, to be located in natural landscapes, modifying the scenery. The evidence of such human endeavor is the "key esthetic" in Chinese landscapes (Xie, 1988, p. 41) and the application of the principles of *feng shui* ensures the achievement of harmony with the correct placement and orientation of human constructions in natural settings (Li, 2005).

Translated into contemporary tourism development in China, it results in *always* modifying natural environments with human-made construction of one form or another. The second principle, therefore, is that tourism development in landscapes in China is synonymous with building something or modifying the landscape through human intervention (Li, 2005). Nature is imperfect, to leave it untouched is to abrogate one's responsibility, and the words used to describe "wilderness", *huangye*, as "bad-lands" and its state as *yuanshi*, "primitive", express the fundamentals of a culturally specific Chinese tourist gaze. This principle forms the foundation of an anthropocentric approach to the development of natural landscapes for tourism, and it is combined with elements of the landscape (rocks, trees, and so on) being anthropomorphized, that is imbued with human characteristics (Li, 2005).

The third principle is that when developing tourism for China's natural areas, its planners will attempt to define the *tezhi* ("essence") of the landscape and then design accordingly. *Tezhi* connotes the intrinsic or indispensable properties that serve to characterize or identify the landscape (Xie, 1988, p. 37). But they are not properties of biodiversity or of geomorphology. They are properties embedded in human feelings, correlative and relational. Thus, a landscape will be identified as imposing 雄, or mysterious 奥, or elegant 秀, or dangerous 险, always in relation to the perspective of the emotions of the human onlooker (anthropomorphism). Design imperatives for human construction then flow from that given identity to match the design of nature, which, being imperfect, requires the addition of human-made elements for the benefit of humans (anthropocentrism). Thus, in scenic areas famous for their "imposing" image, buildings would normally be placed on ridges, peaks or cleared slopes, and in Chinese eyes, their highly visible presence will harmonize with and enhance the *tezhi*, the essence, of the landscape. The Yellow Crane Pagoda, for example, has occupied a strategic site above the Yangtze River in the ancient city of Wuhan for more than 2000 years (now in its sixth reconstruction), dominating the surrounding landscape. Its imposing presence has been the subject of poems and prose for centuries. The many temples adorning the slopes and summit of towering Tai Shan (sacred Daoist mountain) reflect its "orderly" and "splendid" *te-zhi* (Xie, 1988). The Dai Temple is located at the south piedmont looking back at Tai Shan peak, facing the flat plain with its central axis lined up with the peak, and its *feng shui* achieving harmonious balance with its setting.

In scenic areas famous for their elegant image, planners will strive to design buildings that are light, simple but elegant and in proportion to the surrounding landscape. The purpose is to lead visitors to calmly appreciate the view and add a delicate interest and charm to the scenery. In low undulating areas dominated by lakes, an elegant tower (pagoda) would be placed at the ridgeline of a small hill to break the smooth gentle outline of the view. The new pagoda on a low hill above West Lake, Hangzhou, is an example. It applies the need to improve on the imperfections of nature. A flat area needs a vantage point, and a round hill is not the ideal shape, which is that of a spire. By constructing a pagoda on the summit of a gently curving hill, man is not dominating nature (a western perspective) but is in harmony with nature through improving on it.

Shan shui, *feng shui* and *te-zhi* are all understood by Chinese as fundamental to the achievement of harmony and any consideration of sustainable development will, for Chinese, thus incorporate the values that support them. Their continued importance in tourism development in China underlines a vexed question: How are they to be measured with what indicators? And as a valid expression of deeply held Chinese values, that introduces another leading question: Are the so-called universal principles of sustainable development really universal? One could argue that operationalization of the western ideal of sustainability and the Chinese ideal of harmony are both equally fraught with difficulties. In terms of the Brundtland definition of sustainability (United Nations World Commission on Environment and Development [WCED], 1987), for example, how can one determine with any exactitude intergenerational equity, that is what level of exploitation of a resource will be appropriate to ensure that future generations enjoy the same level of access to a resource as the current society? In western-developed societies, we try to apply the cautionary approach when we are unable to determine the outcome of a particular development, but the application of this concept is very uneven and politics often over-ride environmental concerns. In China, traditional values confront western ESD values and the two do not always coincide. Planning for STD in China can seek ways to combine the two, in effect, a new demonstration of the Confucian "middle way".

Tourism – a keystone industry

To extend the understanding of tourism's governance and its contribution to China's transformation, this paper defines it as *a keystone industry*, a concept adapted from ecology. A keystone species is one that plays a critical role in maintaining the structure of an ecological community and whose impact on the community is greater than could be expected based on its relative abundance or total biomass. The activities of the keystone species determine the structure of the community. Whether a species is or is not a keystone species is most easily recognized by its removal. Such an organism plays a role in its ecosystem that is analogous to the role of a keystone in an arch. While the keystone is under the least pressure of any of the stones in an arch, the arch still collapses without it. Similarly, an ecosystem may experience a dramatic shift if a keystone species is removed. The phrase was coined in 1969 by an ecologist, Robert Paine, and it is now widely used in conservation biology studies.

Since Paine's original usage, the term has been generalized to cover a widening range of phenomena loosely grouped by the fact that they have important influences on some aspect of ecosystem structure or functioning (Power et al., 1996). Further refinements have introduced the concepts of "keystone mutualism", organisms that participate in mutually beneficial interactions, the loss of which would have a profound impact upon the ecosystem as a whole; and "keystone ecosystem engineers" whose physical activities impact across the ecosystem as a whole (Duffy & McGinley, 2008). It is precisely because the term keystone industry is capable of providing a nuanced indication of tourism's interrelationship with other sectors and society and the way in which it reinforces an understanding of tourism as a system, which we believe contributes to a better understanding of the term pillar industry. In the analogies discussed in the following sections, a destination is the equivalent of a habitat where the forms of tourism in different destinations will reflect the different species that exist in different habitats – and its degree of interaction/interdependence and its characteristics (general keystone, keystone mutualism or ecosystem engineering) could be measured more precisely. At each level of analysis, we believe that the concept has the capacity to tell us more about the role of tourism in China's transformation to a market economy.

Tourism as a keystone industry at the destination level

In some destinations in China, tourism is the mainstay of nearly all economic activity and warrants its description as a keystone industry. An unambiguous example of the absolute centrality of tourism to destination survival may be observed with Jiuzhaigou National Nature Reserve, Sichuan Province. When it was first opened up for tourism in 1984, the indigenous Tibetans living in six villages inside the boundary were impoverished pastoralists and herders. There was no other economic activity. In 2009, with 3.8 million tourists visiting the Park, the Tibetan communities enjoyed a per capita income of more than US$12,000 pa. from several tourist facilities including ownership or part ownership of the only (monopoly) bus company allowed to operate inside the park (now numbering more than 400 buses), the only restaurant located inside the Park (with a 5000 seat capacity), 180 Tibetan arts and crafts souvenir outlets (the only ones allowed inside the Park) and several performing cultural groups and accommodation units. Income generated from these activities makes them among the richest rural people in China and there has been a complete alleviation of poverty in the six villages (Li, 2006, figures updated in this paper to 2009). Tourism to the Park has resulted in the establishment of a new town where none existed before. Jiuzhaigou Township has more than 10,000 permanent residents, more than 150 hotels with a total of about 25,000 beds and numerous restaurants, shops of all kinds, vehicle service stations and so forth (Li, 2006). If tourism were removed from the scene, all of this economic activity would immediately cease. Not only is this an example of a keystone industry, but it is also a good example of a greenfield development as described earlier in this paper. It is also a striking illustration of the market economy at work in China and of the co-ordinating powers of centrally directed governance in China.

Tourism and keystone mutualism

Applying the concept of keystone mutualism to tourism at the level of a single sector, we find obvious links with infrastructure and modes of transport, perhaps the most symbiotic relationship occurring with airlines. Tourism drives the airline industry worldwide in terms of mass sales, and without airlines, thousands of destinations would be unable to achieve their current levels of visitation. In China, as the middle class has expanded, domestic tourism has taken to the skies in increasing numbers (as noted earlier), and without tourism, both destinations and airlines would suffer dramatically. Some destinations and some airline operations might well collapse. For China's domestic airline services, tourism meets all of the conditions required to define it as a keystone industry.

If we examine transport infrastructure in the context of tourism as a keystone industry, we find examples of both mutualism and ecosystem engineering. Many roads have been constructed specifically to provide tourism access, and from the more than 50 examples with which we are personally familiar, there is space for just two in this paper. We led the Yunnan Forest Conservation and Community Development Program (FCCDP) to formulate an ecotourism strategy for five newly created national parks in Yunnan Province in 1999 (four of which were true greenfield sites). Five new highways totaling about 1000 km in length were subsequently constructed to provide tourist access (Sofield, Li, & Khang, 2000). In the second example of tourism planning and the governance of the implementation process creating linkages, a two-lane highway, 450 km long, was constructed between 1996 and 1997 from Chengdu through the mountains of Sichuan Province to replace a single-lane unpaved road to open up the World Heritage listed Jiuzhaigou National Nature reserve, and visitor numbers doubled from 170,000 to 340,000 in the first year. By 2004, visitation had reached almost two million. In that year, a high altitude airport was constructed at Jiuzhaigou, reducing the 10-hour road journey from Chengdu to a 50-minute drive along a link road from the airport to the park entrance, and in 2009, visitation to the park reached 3.8 million, with approximately half arriving by air. The sole economic justification for the road/air infrastructure was tourism. The Chengdu–Jiuzhaigou road link is an example of not only keystone mutualism between tourism and road construction but keystone ecosystem engineering as well since the opening up of the highway has revolutionized the economic, productivity and trading environment of all of the many previously isolated hamlets, villages and towns en route.

Tourism, sustainability and natural heritage

We now turn to the role of tourism as a keystone industry in terms of its contribution to the principles of sustainability related to natural heritage. In 1980, China was one of the first signatories of the IUCN's World Conservation Strategy (IUCN, 1980). In 1988, China began the promulgation of a range of related laws for nature protection, thus protecting threatened fauna and flora and creating and managing nature reserves. By 2007, there were 2395 nature reserves of different types in China with a total area of 152 million ha, accounting for 15.1% of China's territory – well in excess of the world average of less than 9% and an increase from the 1972 figure of 54 reserves occupying less than 1% of China's total landmass (Liu, 2010). These programs are reinforced with a diversity of additional ecological initiatives covering numerous fields: they seek to make China "a country with sound ecology and environment by 2020" (State Forestry Administration, 2007). In brief, the Chinese Government has broad, ambitious legislation on nature reserves, biosphere reserves, wildlife management and conservation, which embraces the western values of sustainability. Whether it will reach its targets is a moot point. But tourism has been a major determinant in and a benefactor from the formulation of these regulations and legislation. This is graphically illustrated by examining the history of national nature reserves in China since 1998.

Many of China's reserves are under the governance of the National Forestry Administration devolved to provincial forestry departments. Following the disastrous floods of 1998, which many Chinese analysts blamed on deforestation and resultant soil erosion (e.g. Liu, Li, Ouyang, Tam, & Chen, 2008), the central government introduced "The Natural Forest Conservation Program" that banned all logging of natural forests (PRC State Council, 1998). With the cessation of logging, forestry departments all over China lost their main revenue stream to cover operating costs, and one of the major potential new sources of income was ecotourism. The authors of this paper were at the forefront of this "ecotourism revolution" in China when contracted in 1999 by the Yunnan Forestry Conservation and Community Development Project to develop an ecotourism strategy for five new nature reserves that had previously been logging forests in Yunnan Province (Sofield, Li, & Khang, 2000). This project helped to establish ecotourism guidelines based on the conservation of natural resources first and anthropocentric values (comfort of/benefits for humans in natural environments) second. We have participated in more than 15 subsequent tourism policy and planning projects in China under the auspices of the CNTA between 2000 and 2010, where ESD objectives have been central. They have included an ecotourism strategy for Hubei Province, site of the Three Gorges Dam (Bao, Xu, Sofield, & Li, 2001) and most recently (2009) for the WHS Three Parallel Rivers and Ninety Nine Dragon Pools Scenic Reserve in the Laojun Shan Tibetan Minority county of northwestern Yunnan with WWF China. One outcome from this work and contributions by other tourism planners was the adoption, six years ago, by the CNTA of environmental standards for public toilets and the management and disposal of solid and liquid wastes in nature reserves, heritage sites and other tourist attractions. Another was a CNTA project to develop national standards for accreditation as an ecotourism venture. In 2008, CNTA declared 2009 as the Year of Ecotourism in China with the slogan: "Be a green traveler and experience eco-civilization". The stated aim was to encourage resource-saving tourism operations and to build the Chinese tourism industry into a green industry with sustainable development (CNTA, 2008).

It is our hypothesis that tourism has been significantly influential in the conservation and protection of natural forests, flora and fauna in nature reserves all over China. Where tourism has been successful in terms of forestry-run reserves, it has replaced logging as the mainstay of income generation, entrance fees attaining many millions of dollars, allowing park administrators to implement sound management regimes (often based on a mix of Chinese and western best practice models – *vide* Jiuzhaiogou and its attainment of Green Globe accreditation combined with Chinese esthetics and *feng shui* in the location of several key facilities) and has thus exhibited a fundamental characteristic of a keystone industry in achieving sustainability. The strength of this income stream from nature-based/ecotourism again emphasizes the role of tourism as a keystone industry and underscores its contribution to the sustainability of the national parks system in China.

Wildlife conservation, tourism and sustainability

At the same time that the Chinese Government introduced its ban on the logging of natural forests, it also instigated a series of wildlife conservation programs and has moved increasingly to link these into viable tourism ventures to provide the necessary financial underpinnings for conservation and protection. Modern management of wildlife began in China in 1959 with the protection of the giant panda and other rare animals (Studley, 1999). Studley (1999, citing Edmonds, 1994; Zhu, 1989) noted that between 1989 and 1993, some 379 vertebrate species were protected under a two-class system. By 2000, the Government had established breeding centers for more than 60 animal species under the threat of extinction, a small group of which was prioritized as *The Seven Key Rescue Projects* (PRC National Environmental Protection Agency, 1999). They cover the endangered giant panda, crested ibis, Chinese alligator, Eld's deer, Pere David's deer, Saiga antelope and Wild horse.

Tourism has played a lead role in manifesting the principles of sustainability in China. These include contributions to the preparation of a tourism master plan for the development of the Wolong Giant Panda WHS nature reserve in Sichuan Province, already noted earlier (Sofield, Li, Xu, Mactaggart, & De Lacy, 2006). This iconic animal is of course automatically associated with China and is the internationally recognized symbol of the WWF. There are innumerable other tourism-linked wildlife projects. However, despite such activity, much well-designed legislation, numerous environmentally sound projects and commitment at the highest level to ESD, China's expanding industrialization and rapid development still leaves the implementation of its policies in many fields deficient in achieving the desired results. Tourism as a keystone industry however offers better prospects in general (but not in all cases) for a more sustainable future.

Conclusion

This paper has synthesized China's highly individualistic path from socialism to a market economy (a path we have described as transformation rather than transition) with an assessment of the contributions that tourism, and tourism governance, has played in this transformation. It addresses a key gap in the literature. In analyzing China's approach to sustainable development in the wider economy, we note that it has sound legislative, regulatory and governance regimes and environmental assessment of development planning and implementation became a fundamental state policy (*jiben guoce*) in 1993 after China acceded to the Agenda 21 agreement arising from the Earth Rio Summit. But often, and particularly at the local level, economic development priorities still take priority over issues of ESD. In analyzing tourism's specific responses to sustainability, we note the tensions that exist between international values associated with ESD and the profound, 4000-year-old Chinese traditional value system based around the Confucian and Daoist concepts of harmony (Li, 2005, 2008; Li & Sofield, 2008). And in this context, we have advanced the concept of tourism as a keystone industry to assist in unpacking its multiple and complex interrelationships with its surrounding economic, socio-cultural and political environments, and the direct contribution to conservation, protection and sustainability not only of the tourism sector but also of other sectors and the national parks system of China.

As part of becoming a "normal country", the governance, policy, planning and development of tourism since 1978 have played a significant role in China. Its contributions have been multi-faceted, providing early inputs into entrepreneurship and private enterprise as China took its first tentative steps toward a market economy. This development has often taken place in a relatively "greenfield" environment because, under the previous three decades of Mao Zedong, China followed a policy essentially of "non-tourism". We have shown that while central governance has remained powerful, and has retained and developed many traditional features of China's political and cultural values systems, it has also been an evolving governance process. It remains strongly linked to master planning and co-ordination – across regions and with other sectors of the economy. There are tourism master plans for each province and autonomous region, and broader plans such as the Greater Shangri-la Tourism Investment and Development Project, all attesting to the importance that the Chinese Government accords to tourism and coordinated governance.

Tourism has also made a valuable but often under-rated contribution to freedoms in China as the Government progressively relaxed its restrictions on travel for both international visitors and domestic tourist, an opening that has been not just physical but psychological and philosophical. The enthusiasm with which the Chinese have responded – in their hundreds of millions – to the opportunity to visit sites which they have been familiar through their Chinese "common knowledge" for centuries but for generations had been out of reach of ordinary citizens (Li, 2008), has produced perhaps the largest mass tourism the world has witnessed. The year-on-year growth of tourism in China over 30 years has been unparalleled. This extraordinary mobility, coupled with massive investment in supporting infrastructure and superstructure, has generated billions of dollars of revenue, resulted in the direct employment in tourism of about 9% of China's total workforce and many more indirectly through the multiplier effect and elevated tourism to the status of a pillar industry for China. A range of supporting policies and plans such as the specific government directives on Golden Week holidays constitutes the basis for releasing hundreds of millions of Chinese to participate in travel and tourism each year. Despite the massive growth, however, China's tourism remains a supply side dominated and governed industry. But the power of the market is growing and is likely to grow further. That growth is carefully governed, but can create issues for future governance.

A final word needs to be said about the politics of governance that has directed the structural and transformational changes in China. An influential western-oriented critique of transitional economies that move from socialism to a market economy is that SOEs must be dismantled, capitalist market forces must be given free reign and western-style democracy is inevitable. China's experience to date challenges some of these assumptions, especially that of market fundamentalism, and the CP retains government unchallenged, with SOEs still commanding some of the heights of the economy. Whether China's experience provides useful lessons for other transitional economies has generated strong debate. Some economists argue that China's success demonstrates the superiority of an evolutionary, experimental and bottom-up approach over the comprehensive top-down "shock therapy" approach that characterized the transition in Eastern Europe and the former Soviet Union (Jefferson & Rawski, 1995; McKinnon, 1994; Naisbitt & Naisbitt, 2010; Perkins, 2002). Other economists argue that it is neither gradualism nor experimentation, but rather China's unique initial conditions that have contributed to China's success (Chow, 1997; Jones, 1997; Lin, 2004; Lin et al., 2003; Naughton, 2007; Wei, 1993). According to these economists, China's experience has no general application because China's initial conditions are unique. One of the strengths of a transition/transformation economy is that there is not infrequently a political willingness to prioritize tourism in the national development agenda (Denman, 2005; Sofield & Mactaggart, 2005), and China has done that. Whatever the outcome of this debate, the specifics of China's changing socio-economic environment have provided fertile ground for an unprecedented development of tourism on a scale unmatched by any other country. In our view, it is doubtful that this phenomenon could have occurred at the pace and size that has eventuated without direct central government involvement.

References

Aba Prefecture Jiuzhai Wolong Giant Panda Industry Co. and Sichuan Province Forestry Department. (2006). *Wolong National Nature Reserve Dongkoucao Ecotourism Project: International bidding invitation*. Chengdu: Sichuan Province Government.

Airey, D., & Chong, K. (2010). National policy-makers for tourism in China. *Annals of Tourism Research, 37*(2), 295–314.

Anderson, E., & Anderson, M. (1973). *Mountains and water: Essays on the cultural ecology of South Coastal China*. Taipei: Chinese Association for Folklore.

Baker, R., & Richmond, J. (2009). *Internal divisions and the Chinese stimulus plan*. Austin, TX: Stratfor Global Commentary. Retrieved June 20, 2010, from http://www.futurebrief.com/Stratfor002.asp

Bao, J. (2008). *Personal communications with Professor Bao Jigang, Dean of the School of Geographical Sciences and Tourism Management*. Guangzhou: Sun Yat Sen University.

Bao, J., Xu, H.G., Sofield, T.H.B., & Li, F.M.S. (2001). *Master plan for tourism development for Hubei province. A report for Hubei provincial government*. Guangzhou: Center for Tourism Planning and Research, Zhongshan University.

Bergsten, C.F., Freeman, C., Lardy, N.R., & Mitchell, D.J. (2008). *China's rise: Challenges and opportunities*. Washington, DC: Petersen Institute for International Economics.

Cai, X. (1994). *Analects of Confucius with commentary*. Beijing: Sinolingua.

Cann, C.W., Cann, M.C., & Gao, S. (2005). China's road to sustainable development: An overview. In A.D. Kristen (Ed.), *China environment and the challenge of sustainable development* (pp. 3–34). New York: M.E. Sharpe.

Chan, W.-T. (1969). *A source book of Chinese philosophy*. New York: Colombia University Press.

China Daily. (2009, November 26). *China to make tourism a pillar industry*. Beijing: Xinhua News Agency. Retrieved March 22, 2010, from http://www.chinadaily.com.cn/bizchina/200911/26/content_9055876.htm

China National Tourism Administration. (2005). *Deng Xiaoping on tourism: Six speeches 1978–1979*. Beijing: Party Literature Research Office of the Central Committee of the Communist Party of China.

China National Tourism Administration. (2008, November 10). *2009 is Chinese eco-tourism year. Press release*. Beijing: Author.

China National Tourism Administration. (2010). *Yearbook of tourism statistics 2009*. Beijing: Author.

Chow, G.C. (1997). Challenges of China's economic system for economic theory. *American Economic Review, 87*(2), 321–327.

Day, K. (Ed.). (2005). *China's environment and the challenge of sustainable development*. New York: M.E. Sharpe.

Deng, X. (1983). Emancipate the mind; seek truth from facts, and uniting as one in looking to the future. In *Selected works of Deng Xiaoping* (pp. 144–146). Beijing: People's Publishing House.

Denman, R. (2005). *Policies and tools for sustainable tourism and their application to transitional (sic) economies*. Paper presented at the WTO European meeting on tourism: A tool for sustainable development in transition economies, Belgrade, Serbia.

Dickson, B.J. (2003). *Red Capitalists in China: The party, private enterpreneurs, and prospects for political change*. New York: Cambridge University Press.

Dredge, D. (2004). Development, economy and culture: Cultural heritage tourism planning, Liangzhu, China. *Asia Pacific Journal of Tourism Research, 9*(4), 405–422.

Duffy, J.E., & McGinley, M. (2008). Keystone species. In J.C. Cutler (Ed.), *Encyclopedia of Earth*. Washington, DC: Environmental Information Coalition, National Council for Science and the Environment. Retrieved April 30, 2010, from http://www.eoearth.org/article/Keystone_species

Dunsire, A. (1978). *Implementation in a bureaucracy*. Oxford: Martin Robertson.

Eberhard, W., & Morrison, H. (1973). *Hua Shan: The sacred mountain in West China: Its scenery, monasteries and monks*. Hong Kong: Vetch and Lee.

Ebrey, P.B. (Ed.). (2003). *A visual sourcebook of Chinese civilization*. New York: Washington University.

Economy, E. (2005). Environmental enforcement in China. In K. Day (Ed.), *China's environment and the challenge of sustainable development* (pp. 102–120). New York: M.E. Sharpe.

Edmonds, R.L. (1994). *Patterns of China's lost harmony*. London: Routledge.

Eitel, E. (1984). *Feng Shui*. Singapore: Graham Brash.

Elvin, M. (1973). *The pattern of the Chinese past*. Stamford, CT: Stamford University Press.

Fan, W. (1992). Village *Fengshui* principles. In R. Knapp (Ed.), *Chinese landscapes: The village as place* (pp. 35–46). Honolulu: University of Hawaii Press.

Fung, Y.-L. (1952). *History of Chinese philosophy*. Princeton, NJ: Princeton University Press.

Gao, D.-C., & Zhang, G. (1982). China's tourism: Policy and practice. *International Journal of Tourism Management, 4*(2), 75–84.

Ge, B. (1995). *A guide to investment, trade and tourism in China's border areas*. Beijing: China Audit Press.

Gong, B. (2005). Shanghai's WTO affairs consultation center: Working together to take advantage of WTO membership. In P. Gallagher, P. Low & A.L. Stoler (Eds.), *Managing the challenges of WTO participation – 45 case studies* (Chap. 11) (pp. 167–177). Cambridge: Cambridge University Press.

Grano, S.A. (2008). *China's environmental crisis: Why should we care?* Working Paper No. 28, Working papers in Contemporary Asian Studies. Lund: Centre for East and South-East Asian Studies, Lund University.

Guizhou Provincial Government Project Management Office. (2010). *Guizhou cultural and natural heritage protection and development project – Terms of reference: Consulting services for implementation support for community-based sustainable tourism*. Guiyang: Guizhou Provincial Government.

Hall, D. (2008). From "bricklaying" to "bricolage": Transition and tourism development in central and Eastern Europe. *Tourism Geographies, 10*(4), 410–428.

Hall, D.L., & Ames, R.T. (1998). *Thinking from the Han: Self, truth and transcendence in Chinese and Western culture*. Albany: SUNY Press.

Hammond, A., Adriaanse, A., Rodenburg, E., Bryant, D., & Woodward, R. (1995). *Environmental indicators: A systematic approach to measuring and reporting on environmental policy performance in the context of sustainable development*. Washington, DC: World Resources Institute.

Hayami, Y., & Ruttan, V.W. (1984). Towards a theory of induced institutional innovation. *Journal of Development Studies, 20*(4), 203–223.

Holbig, H. (2005). The emergence of the campaign to open up the west: Ideological formation, central decision making and the role of the provinces. In D.S.G. Goodman (Ed.), *2004 China's campaign to "open up the west": National, provincial and local perspectives* (pp. 4–21). Cambridge: Cambridge University Press.

Howell, J. (2007). Civil society in China: Chipping away at the edges. *Development, 50*(3), 18–21.

Hu, J. (2007, October 15). *Address to the plenary session of the 17th Communist Party Congress*, Beijing. Retrieved December 10, 2007, from http://www.china.org.cn/english/congress/225859.htm

Huang, S. (2010). Evolution of China's tourism policies. *International Journal of Tourism Policy, 3*(1), 78–84.

Hutton, W. (2006). *The writing on the wall: Why we must embrace China as a partner or face it as an enemy*. New York: Free Press.

IMF. (2009). *Report on the technical assistance evaluation mission to the people's Republic of China*. Washington: Author.

International Union for Conservation of Nature. (1980). *World conservation strategy*. Paris: IUCN-UNEP-WWF.

Jefferson, G., & Rawski, T. (1995). *How industrial reform worked in China: The role of innovation, competition, and property rights*. Proceedings of the World Bank annual conference on development economics 1994 (pp. 129–156). Washington, DC.

Jones, D.C. (1997). *The determinants of economic performance in transitional economies: The role of ownership, incentives and restructuring*. New York: UNU/WIDER Research for Action No. 39.

Knapp, R. (Ed.). (1992). *Chinese landscapes: The village as place*. Honolulu: University of Hawaii Press.

Kung, J.K.S., & Lin, Y.M. (2007). The decline of township-and-village enterprises in China's economic transition. *World Development, 35*(4), 569–584.

Lau, D.C., & Ames, R. (1998). *Yuan Dao: Tracing Dao to its source*. New York: Ballantine Publishing Group.

Li & Fung Research Center. (2009, April). An update on the transport infrastructure development in China: Water transportation. *China Distribution & Trading, 58*. Retrieved February 12, 2010, from http://www.idsgroup.com/profile/pdf/distributing/issue58.pdf

Li, F.M.S. (2005). *Chinese common knowledge, tourism, and natural landscapes: Gazing on "Bie you tian di" – "An altogether different world"* (PhD thesis). Murdoch University, Perth, Western Australia.

Li, F.M.S. (2006). Tourism development, empowerment and the Tibetan minority, Jiuzhaigou national nature reserve, China. In L. Anna & F. Alan (Eds.), *Managing world heritage sites* (pp. 226–238). London: Elsevier Science.

Li, F.M.S. (2008). Culture as a major determinant in tourism development of China. *Current Issues in Tourism, 11*(6), 493–514.

Li, F.M.S., & Sofield, T.H.B. (1994). Tourism development and socio-cultural change in rural China. In A.V. Seaton (Ed.), *Tourism: The state of the art* (pp. 854–868). Chichester: John Wiley & Sons.

Li, F.M.S., & Sofield, T. (2008). Huangshan – Cultural gazes. In C. Ryan & H. Gu (Eds.), *Tourism in China* (pp. 168–180). London: Elsevier.

Li, Z. (1994). *An overview of Chinese culture*. Beijing: Hua Wen Press.

Lin, J.Y. (1989). An economic theory of institutional change: Induced and imposed change. *Cato Journal, 9*(1), 1–33.

Lin, J.Y., Cai, F., & Li, Z. (2003). *China's miracle: Development strategy and economic reform* (Rev. ed.). Hong Kong: Chinese University Press, and Shanghai: Shanghai Sanlian Press.

Lin, Y. (2004, February 2). *Lessons of China's transition from a planned economy to a market economy*. Gothenburg: University of Gothenburg Seminar on China's Transition to a Market Economy.

Lin, Y.-S. (1979). *The crisis of Chinese consciousness*. Madison, WI: University of Wisconsin Press.

Liu, J. (2001). Integrating ecology with human demography, behavior, and socioeconomics: Needs and approaches. *Ecological Modelling, 140*(1-2), 1–8.

Liu, J. (2010). Policy forum: Environment: China's road to sustainability. *Science, 328*(5974), 50.

Liu, J., Li, S., Ouyang, Z., Tam, C., & Chen, X. (2008). Ecological and socio-economic effects of China's policies for ecosystem services. *Proceedings of the National Academy of Sciences, 105*, 9477–9482.

McKinnon, R.I. (1994). *Gradual versus rapid liberalization in socialist economies: Financial policies and macroeconomic stability in China and Russia compared*. In M. Bruno & B. Pleskovic (Eds.), Proceedings of the World Bank Annual Conference on Development Economics 1993 (pp. 63–94), Washington, DC: The World Bank.

Michell, J. (1975). *The earth spirit*. London: Thames & Hudson.

Ministry of Railways. (2010). *Annual report 2009*. Beijing: Author.

Ministry of Transport. (2009). *Annual report*. Beijing: Author.

Morton, K. (2006). Surviving an environmental crisis: Can China adapt? *Brown Journal of World Affairs, XIII*(1), 63–75.

Naisbitt, J., & Naisbitt, D. (2010). *China's megatrends: The 8 pillars of a new society*. New York: Harper Business.

Naughton, B. (2007). *The Chinese economy: Transitions and growth*. Cambridge: MIT Press.

Ninth National Peoples Congress. (1998, November 4). *Organic law of villagers committees of the Peoples Republic of China*. Beijing: Order No. 9 of the President of the Peoples Republic of China.

Oi, J. (1992). Fiscal reform and the economic foundations of local state corporatism. *World Politics, 45*(1), 99–126.

Organisation for Economic Co-Operation and Development. (2003). *Economic surveys: European economies in transition*. Paris: Author.

Organisation for Economic Co-Operation and Development. (2006, November 8–9). *Working party on environmental performance review of China: Conclusions and recommendations*. Beijing: Author.

Pan, P.P. (2008). *Out of Mao's shadow: The struggle for the soul of a new China*. New York: Simon & Schuster.

Perkins, D. (2002). The challenge China's economy poses for Chinese economists. *China Economic Review, 13*, 412–418.

Power, M.E., Tilman, D., Estes, J.A., Menge, B.A., Bond, W.J., Mills, L.S., et al. (1996). Challenges in the quest for keystones. *Bioscience, 46*, 609–620.

PRC National Environmental Protection Agency. (1999). *Seven key wildlife rescue projects*. Beijing: Author.

PRC State Council. (1998). *The natural forest conservation program*. Beijing: Author.

Qiu, H.Z., Chong, K., & Jenkins, C.L. (2002). Tourism policy implementation in mainland China: An enterprise perspective. *International Journal of Contemporary Hospitality Management, 14*(1), 38–42.

Rawson, P., & Legeza, L. (1973). *Tao: The Chinese philosophy of time and change*. New York: Bounty Books.

Rutkowski, R. (2009, November 4). China electrifies urban transit. *Asia Times On-Line: China Business section*. Retrieved July 2, 2010, from http://www.atimes.com/atimes/China_Business/KK04Cb01.html

Saich, A. (2001). *Governance and politics of China*. New York: Palgrave.

Sofield, T.H.B. (1995). *Ecologically sustainable development & ecotourism*. Keynote address delivered at "Educate the Educators" Seminar and Workshop (7–12 October), China National Tourism Administration Bureau and World Tourism Organization, Shanghai Institute of Tourism, Shanghai, PRC.

Sofield, T.H.B. (2002). The Greater Shangri-la area and Tibet: Analysis of prospects for international tourism. In J. Bao & H.G. Xu (Eds.), *Western China tourism development study for the Greater Shangri-la area*. Guangzhou: Center for Tourism Planning and Research, Zhongshan (Sun Yat Sen) University.

Sofield, T.H.B. (2009). *Re-visioning of Jin-Si-Xia National Forest Park, Shangnan County, Shaanxi Province, China*. Guangzhou: Centre for Tourism Planning and Research, Zhongshan University.

Sofield, T.H.B., & Li, F.M.S. (1997). Rural tourism in China. Development issues in perspective. In S.J. Page & D. Getz (Eds.), *The business of rural tourism: International perspectives* (pp. 120–142). London and New York: International Thomson Business Press.

Sofield, T.H.B., & Li, F.M.S. (1998). China: Tourism development and cultural policies. *Annals of Tourism Research, 25*(2), 362–392.

Sofield, T.H.B., & Li, F.M.S. (2007). China: Ecotourism and cultural tourism: Harmony or dissonance? In H. James (Ed.), *Critical issues in ecotourism: Confronting the challenges* (Chap. 18, pp. 368–385). London, Amsterdam: Elseveier Science & Butterworth Heinemann.

Sofield, T.H.B., Li, F.M.S., & Khang, Y. (2000). *An ecotourism strategy for Yunnan province, China. A report for the forest conservation and community development program*. Kunming: Sino-Dutch Accord and Brisbane: CRC Tourism.

Sofield, T.H.B., Li, F.M.S., Xu, H., Mactaggart, R., & De Lacy, T. (2006). *Wolong National Nature Reserve: Conceptual approach to integrated tourism development for Wolong*. Brisbane and Guangzhou: STCRC, GRM International and Zhongshan University.

Sofield, T.H.B., & Mactaggart, R. (2005, October 18). *Tourism as a tool for sustainable development in transition economies*. Paper presented at the DFID/GRM Conference on Development Learning in Transition Environments, London.

State Forestry Administration. (2007). *Forestry development in China*. Retrieved August 1, 2010, from http://www.china.org.cn/e-news/news071204-1.htm

State Statistical Bureau. (1995). *A statistical survey of China 1995*. Beijing: Zhongguo Tongji Chubanshe.

Studley, J. (1999). *Ecotourism in China: Endogenous paradigms for SW China's indigenous minority peoples*. Retrieved July 21, 2001, from http://ourworld.compuserve.com/homepages/john_studley

Tourism Tribune (1992, December). China must speed up tourism development: Deng Xiaoping. *Tourism Tribune, 7*(6), 1–2.

United Nations Economic Commission for Asian and the Pacific. (2009). *Statistical yearbook for Asia and the Pacific 2009*. Bangkok: Author.

United Nations Environment Programme. (2009). *Beijing 2008 Olympic games – Final environmental assessment*. Nairobi: Author.

United Nations World Commission on Environment and Development. (1987). *Our common future, report of the World Commission on Environment and Development*. New York: Author.

United Nations World Tourism Organization. (2010). *Yearbook of tourism statistics 2009*. Madrid: Author.

Wei, S. (1993). *Gradualism versus big bang: Speed and sustainability of reforms*. Harvard Working Paper Series, R93–2. Cambridge: Harvard University.

Williams, M., & Webb, R. (1994). Rural landscapes. In M. Williams (Ed.), *The Green Dragon: Hong Kong's living environment* (pp. 113–127). Hong Kong: Green Dragon Publishing.

Wong, C.P.W. (1988). Interpreting rural industrial growth in the post-Mao period. *Modern China, 14*(1), 3–30.

World Bank. (2000). *Peoples Republic of China annual report 1999*. Washington, DC: Author.

World Bank. (2002). *Transition: The First ten years, analysis and lessons for Eastern Europe and the former Soviet Union*. Washington, DC: Author.

World Bank. (2009). *Peoples Republic of China annual report 2008*. Washington, DC: Author.

World Travel and Tourism Council. (2006). *China Hong Kong SAR and China Macau SAR: Impact of travel & tourism on jobs and the economy*. London: Author.

Xie, N. (1988). Famous mountains in China. In W.H. Ding, Y.M. Xu, & Y.X. Lin (Eds.), *The study of natural scenery and heritage sites* (pp. 25–46). Shanghai: Tongji University Press.

Xinhua News Agency. (2010, February 24). *Citing data from the National Bureau of Statistics. China's auto production increases*. Retrieved May 3, 2010, from http://www.xinhuanet.com/english2010/

Xu, H., Ding, P., & Packer, J. (2008). Tourism research in China: Understanding the unique cultural contexts and complexities. *Current Issues in Tourism, 11*(6), 473–491.

Yan, H., & Bramwell, B. (2008). Cultural tourism, ceremony and the state in China. *Annals of Tourism Research, 35*(4), 969–989.

Yan, L. (1965). *Wuqiubeizhai Laozi jicheng, xubian*. Taipei: Yiwen yinshuguan.

Yu, K. (2000). *Toward an incremental democracy and governance: Chinese theories and assessment criteria*. Beijing: China Center for Comparative Politics & Economics.

Yu, K. (Ed.). (2005). *Government innovation: Theory and practice*. Hangzhou: Zhejiang People's Press.

Zhao, P., Liu, J., Yu, X.-C., Xu, C.-X., Wang, G.-X., Ma, H.-Y., et al. (2006, November). Study on China's tourism development: Leisure tourism in our times. *Tourism Tribune Monthly, 21*(11), 5–11.

Zhao, Y. (2008, June). China's new development agenda: Democracy Beijing-style. *The Broker, 6*, 4–7.

Zhou, T., Wang, C., & Wang, A. (2007). *A hard task: After the 17th party congress: China's political reform research report*. Xinjiang: Xinjiang Production and Construction Corps.

Zhu, J. (1989). Nature conservation in China. *Journal of Applied Ecology, 26*, 825–833.

Rethinking regional tourism governance: the principle of subsidiarity

Anne Louise Zahra

Department of Tourism and Hospitality Management, University of Waikato, Private Bag 3105, Hamilton 3240, New Zealand

This paper examines the governance of regional tourism organisations (RTOs) and relates governance to the principle of subsidiarity. The principle maintains that tasks and responsibilities should be accomplished by the lowest and most basic elements of any social organisation, and it is an injustice to assign to a larger and higher association what the lesser and subordinate associations can do. There is little research on understanding RTO governance, on how governance may contribute to RTO instability or on the application of the principle of subsidiarity in a tourism context. A New Zealand case study demonstrates a series of fundamental problems with typical RTO governance structures, linked to problems found in many tourism partnerships. Data collection methods for the case study of the Waikato RTO included observation, interviews, focus groups and document analysis. The paper concludes that the principle of subsidiarity can underpin an RTO governance system if the RTO adopts an ethos of service to the tourism sector and the wider community. This governance style requires open communication and consultation, must foster trust and legitimacy and contribute to securing the RTO's ongoing required resources. Such a governance structure would align well with the principles of sustainable tourism.

Introduction

Tourism governance is a complex issue involving multiple stakeholders in numerous relationships at a range of levels. Bramwell (2011) notes that complexity, and the ongoing power of the state, but stresses a further complexity: "the state ... operates at one or more geographical or spatial scales, which may be transnational, national, regional or local" (p. 470). Traditionally, proponents of sustainable tourism have sought to move governance powers down from the centre towards the community (Murphy, 1983). Beaumont and Dredge (2010) is a valuable recent example of the many studies of the operation of the local scale of governance and its dilemmas.

Regional governance generally is an important and growing issue in many countries (Pierre, 2000). This paper examines regional tourism governance, an important but rarely researched part of the spatial scaling of tourism governance. In tourism, governance at the regional level can bring together communities, local governments and industry stakeholders, thus creating cohesion and market relevance. Branding, infrastructure development, lobbying, training, partnership development and the on-site implementation of national policies can all be important functions for regional tourism governance (Jenkins, 2000; Pearce, 1992).

This paper explores key questions in the effective functioning of regional tourism organisations (RTOs). It does that through a study of New Zealand's RTOs and considers one RTO, Waikato, in depth. The paper reviews regional tourism governance through the lens of the principle of subsidiarity. The principle maintains that tasks and responsibilities should be primarily accomplished by the lowest and most basic elements of a social organisation and only in the case of failure is a higher organisation or community, such as local or central government or a large corporation, justified in stepping in to assist or take over (Melé, 2005). Subsidiarity places power at the organisation's lowest point (Handy, 1994). The application of the principle of subsidiarity recognises self-interest: however, this self-interest becomes fulfilled through concern for others (Fort, 1996). The principle also stresses the belief that social and commercial organisations should serve individuals and smaller communities and not destroy or absorb them. The paper concludes by discussing how the principle of subsidiarity could inform future governance arrangements for the Waikato and other RTOs.

RTOs have long been recognised as unstable and tenuous with disparity in their functions, structures and operations (Dredge, 2000, 2001; Dredge & Jenkins, 2003; Jenkins, 1995, 2000; Pearce, 1992; Ryan, 2002; Zahra, 2006), but there has been little research on understanding RTO governance structures. Members of RTO governance boards can include members not traditionally associated with the tourism industry (Dredge, 2000; Zahra, 2006). It can be difficult for RTOs and their governance bodies to identify key performance indicators (KPIs), and typically, they have no position of power or legal mandate to demand resources/funding from the public or private sector yet they are expected to meet both public and private interests. The key contributions of RTOs are often intangible, long term and cannot be measured in traditional corporate/market terms: coordinating a horizontally and vertically fragmented industry, with higher intermediaries such as state and national tourism organisations; providing leadership and vision for the tourism sector; and demonstrating expert knowledge in product development, domestic and international marketing and sustainability issues.

Tourism generally, and more specifically RTOs, are characterised by linkages, social, professional and exchange networks (Lynch & Morrison, 2007) and collaboration (Bramwell & Lane, 2000b). Tourism researchers have turned to collaboration, private–public partnerships and stakeholder and network theories to capture this fluidity and complexity. Hall (1999) cautioned the use of collaboration and partnerships as market solutions to tourism and resource production problems because of the implications on tourism governance. This paper will explore these governance implications in the context of RTOs.

Tourism collaboration stems from the notion of communicative action (Habermas, 1984), which assumes that unimpeded communication between tourism actors will deliver shared understanding, negotiation of trade-offs and thus consensus (Dredge, 2006a). Collaboration reflects the relationships between stakeholders seeking to resolve a common issue or problem within an agreed-upon set of norms and rules (Bramwell & Lane, 2000a). Within the tourism literature, collaboration has been proposed to facilitate sustainable tourism policy and planning (Bramwell & Lane, 2000a; Hall, 2000; Jamal & Getz, 1995; Timothy & Tosun, 2003; Vernon, Essex, Pinder, & Curry, 2005) and marketing (Fyall & Garrod, 2005; Palmer, 1998; Wang, 2008). The literature also recognises that the vested interests of stakeholders in collaborations can stifle innovations needed to solve problems (Bramwell & Lane, 2000a) and powerful stakeholders can dominate collaborative tourism planning processes (Bramwell, 2004; Dredge, 2006a; Lovelock, 2002).

Public–private sector partnerships have dominated tourism policy development over the last two decades (Bramwell, 2004; Eagles, 2009; Harvey, 2001; Ministry of Tourism, 2005; Svensson, Nordin, & Flagestad, 2005; Tourism Strategy Group, 2001; World Tourism Organisation [WTO], 1996; Zahra, 2006). This period has seen the state shift from being a "provider" to an "enabler" and from a "top-down" centralised to a "bottom-up" decentralised public administration, with the state seeking an inclusive form of governance (Hall, 2000). Vernon et al. (2005) found that the public sector, in these partnerships, has a leadership role in facilitating strategic direction and innovation when working with a fragmented tourism industry, and the public sector is justified in its dominant role of initiator, organiser and provider of resources for these partnerships. They also found that the role of partners does not remain static over time and can vary according to the ability of individual partners to influence outcomes. Public–private sector partnerships "have been heavily criticised for their narrow stakeholder and institutional base" (Hall, 2000, p. 149) and there is little evidence in the literature that these partnerships have made a positive contribution to RTO governance structures or their stability.

Both collaboration (Sautter & Leisen, 1999) and public–private sector partnerships incorporate stakeholder theory. The stakeholder theory is about the control and governance of an organisation's activities and recognises the mutuality of rights and obligations constructed around the notion of economic, social and political inclusion (Hutton, 1997). " 'Stakeholding' emerged as a political concept at a point when conflicts and differences of political interest and principle had to be recognised and negotiated" (Rustin, 1997, p. 76). The stakeholder theory has been examined in a range of tourism contexts (Caffyn & Jobbins, 2003; Cooper, Scott, & Baggio, 2009; Plummer & Fennell, 2009; Regional Tourism Organisations New Zealand [RTONZ], 2003; Robinson & Robinson, 1996; Sautter & Leisen, 1999; Sheehan & Ritchie, 2005; Yuksel, Bramwell, & Yuksel, 1999). Freeman's (1984) definition of a stakeholder is any group that has a legitimate interest in aspects of the organisations' activities, or alternatively, the organisation is a nexus of interests (Brummer, 1991). This definition is premised on self-interest in the organisation/firm by the stakeholder group (Donaldson & Preston, 1995). The stakeholder–RTO relationship is often determined by the stakeholder's interest in the RTO and its functions/activities rather than the RTO's interest in the stakeholder (Zahra, 2006). RTOs do however "recognize stakeholders as being important, because they supply or facilitate funding, provide tourism superstructure and product, participate in or generally support their programs, or influence governance" (Sheehan & Ritchie, 2005, p. 729).

Networks have evolved as a consequence of the "changing structures of government and a shift towards governance [which] has led to an interest in social relations between government, business and civil society" (Dredge, 2006b, p. 270). Researchers have provided evidence of network theory and its applications in a tourism context (Dredge, 2006a, 2006b; Pavlovich, 2001, 2003; Pforr, 2006; Timur & Getz, 2008; Wray, 2009). A key contribution of network theory to the governance of tourism is its recognition of the blurred distinction between private and public actions (Dredge, 2006b) and roles. Yet networks foster self-interest, do away with political responsibility and can create privileged oligarchies (Rhodes, 1999). The constraints of networks are individual interests, be they public or private sector, compounded by a competitive environment with an emphasis on organisational survival leading to the conditioning of network goals aligned with commercial outcomes and the reliance on one or a few people undertaking a leadership role: providing vision, motivation and facilitating communication (Hall, Lynch, Michael, & Mitchell, 2007).

Collaboration, private–public partnerships, stakeholder and network theories are all premised on the market model and self-interest, and to date have not provided a viable governance framework for RTOs. This paper commences with a background to the case study. This is followed by a literature review of RTO governance, a discussion of the principle of subsidiarity, the research methodology and the case study. The paper concludes with a call for fundamental changes to RTO governance.

Case study background

The academic literature has explored different dimensions of tourism at the local level in New Zealand, in terms of sustainability (Connell, Page, & Bentley, 2009; Dymond, 1997; Page & Thorn, 1997, 2002), local authority entrepreneurial activities (Ateljevic & Doorne, 2000) and tourism planning (Simpson, 2002). Blumberg (2005) examined the potential integration of destination marketing and destination management by a New Zealand RTO. Zahra (2006) examined the historical institutional arrangements, social and political dimensions that have shaped RTOs. There has been little academic research on New Zealand's RTO governance structures.

Until the 1980s, the New Zealand government had a centralist approach to both tourism and local government policies. The implementation of tourism policy was framed by the traditional public administration model and the delivery of a public good. RTOs were then created by the public sector supported by the private sector tourism industry association (Zahra, 2006) with centrally funded financial incentives characterising central government policy interest in regional tourism (Dredge & Jenkins, 2003) rather than bottom-up regional interests. The Waikato RTO was formed in this context, one of the 22 RTOs across the country (Zahra, 2006). The 1990s saw a shift to the corporatist model and from development, planning and policy to offshore marketing, thus re-shaping New Zealand's RTOs. The Government Tourism Department was downsized and restructured, tourism research was reduced and the responsibility for offshore marketing was transferred to the New Zealand Tourism Board (NZTB), a statutory authority, with a governance board with strong industry representation. Market forces replaced the notion of the public good. Inbound tourism, i.e. earning foreign exchange, became the policy focus. RTOs close to major inbound tourist destinations, such as the Waikato RTO, located between Auckland, the main gateway into New Zealand, and Rotorua, a major North Island tourist destination, benefited from the hub and spokes model (Pearce, 1992). RTOs with strong leadership and numerous inbound visitors prospered whilst others struggled. However, in the Waikato, domestic visitors far exceed international visitors: the region has the third-highest number of domestic visitors in the country amongst the 30 RTOs. Post-1990 central government tourism policy has ignored domestic tourism, thereby impacting many RTOs.

Since 2000, the formulation of central tourism policy advocated public–private sector partnerships, and the devolution of tourism responsibilities to local government, but with little or no tourism advocacy at the local level or administrative and financial support. There has been a backlash by local taxpayers against bearing the financial burden of central government policies: local elected representatives have policy agendas based on narrow local interests and local tax reductions. This has impacted on RTOs across New Zealand, which face funding problems and, therefore, a reduction in functions and credibility. Despite the state's increasing role as a facilitator, encouraging "partnership" between the public and private sectors, different levels of government and between business and civil society, few RTOs have benefited financially from this trend. Under new regional economic development policies, the Waikato Region received funding for agribusiness and biotechnology development, thus leveraging off the regions' successful agricultural sector. But the region has no significant agri-tourism sector.

RTOs were featured highly in the policy document *The New Zealand Tourism Strategy 2010* released in 2001. In response, RTOs formed a loose umbrella organisation called RTONZ (Zahra, 2006). In 2004, RTONZ commissioned research on the governance of RTOs (Catalyst Management Services Ltd., 2004). The RTONZ governance report identified the key functions of RTOs to be "Generic destination branding and promotion of the region to attract international and domestic visitors; advocating for and facilitating planning for destination management; and facilitating or providing support to the tourism industry for business development and/or product development" (Catalyst Management Services Ltd., 2004, p. 9). There was no mention of the alignment of public and private sector interests. A range of possible governance structures for RTOs included council departments and business units, council organisations and independent organisations (Catalyst Management Services Ltd., 2004). All of the governance structures proposed still left RTOs in a tenuous and vulnerable position (Zahra, 2006). The Catalyst report did not address the complex and problematic governance issues facing RTOs.

RTO governance

Regional tourism governance has been examined in the context of residents' perceptions towards local authority governance in regard to tourism development (Andriotis, 2002) and in the effectiveness of marketing tourism organisations in terms of loose and informal versus tight and formal governance structures (Palmer, 1998). Palmer (1998) recommended that newly formed RTOs adopt tight rather than the loose governance styles (generally associated with informal understandings, norms and implicit trust) and make strong leadership a priority. Vernon's et al. (2005) research recommended "bottom-up" forms of governance. Beritelli, Bieger, and Laesser (2007) examined six dimensions of governance, compared and contrasted them within community and corporate contexts and examined these dimensions in 12 tourist destinations in Switzerland. They found that the dimensions of transaction costs, power asymmetries, interdependence, trust/control, knowledge and informal, personal connections helped to shape the patterns of destination governance. The limitation of this study was its focus on corporate governance theories.

In an adaptive neo-liberal capitalist market context, governance "seems to indicate rules of bargaining over contingent future goods that escape contractual agreements" (Sison, 2008, p. 44). Falk (2005) argues that market forces organised around the energies of greed and self-interest dominate the policy-forming arenas at all levels of social organisation and they form a major obstruction to transparent and equitable governance. The overarching research question being raised in this paper is: Is there an alternative to these capitalist market assumptions to deliver transparent and equitable RTO governance?

For the purposes of this paper, a broad definition of governance from the Council of Rome in 1991 cited in Rosenau (2005) is felt to be relevant to a discussion of governance within an RTO context:

> We use the term governance to denote the command mechanism of a social system and its actions that endeavour to provide security, prosperity, coherence, order and continuity to the system ... Taken broadly the concept of governance should not be restricted to the national and international systems but should be used in relation to regional, provincial and local governments as well as other social systems such as education and the military, to private enterprises and even to the microcosm of the family. (p. 46)

Rosenau (2005), however, goes on to note that he does not like the word "command" as it implies hierarchy and authoritarian rule, thus preferring the word control or steering mechanisms, which highlight the purposeful nature of governance. He proposes that one should examine governance *in* the world rather than *of* the world. The former suggests the patterns of governance wherever they may be located – in communities, societies and non-governmental organisations. The latter implies a central authority that is doing the governing (Rosenau, 2005). This paper will question: Which form of governance: "governance in RTOs" or "governance of RTOs" would better serve regional tourism?

Not all definitions of governance are as embracing and conducive to the RTO environment. Wilkinson (2005) implies self-interest: he describes governance as an ongoing process through which conflicting or diverse interests may be accommodated and action taken either by formal institutions empowered to enforce compliance or informal arrangements that are perceived to be in the interest of individuals or groups. For Wilkinson (2005), governance is outcome-focused and should have the capacity to control and organise the resources it needs to realise its objectives. Most RTOs researched to date (Dredge, 2001; Jenkins, 2000; Zahra, 2006) do not have sufficient resources or control over the resources to realise their objectives, which Wilkinson sees as poor governance. This paper will ask: Do RTO governance bodies not only need to consider the delivery of outcomes but also have the ability to seek the resources to deliver these outcomes?

Weiss (2005) claims that an element of good governance is the devolution of resources and decision-making to the local level and the facilitation of meaningful participation by citizens in debating public policy. In a fluid complex postmodern world, governance control mechanisms can change rapidly. Those that evolve out of bottom-up rather than top-down processes are recognised as legitimate sooner and have increased support (Rosenau, 2005). At the local level, governance is there "to ensure that public administrators [for the purposes of this paper RTO governance bodies] deliver a higher level of transparency and equity in their actions that is comparable for all regional interests, which was not necessarily part of common practice in the past" (Hall et al., 2007, p. 146). This paper will discuss: What type of RTO governance structure will be seen as transparent and equitable in order to achieve legitimacy and widespread support?

Therefore, the Waikato RTO governance case study analysis can be framed around the following questions: Is there an alternative to these capitalist market assumptions to deliver transparent and equitable RTO governance? Which form of governance: "governance in RTOs" or "governance of RTOs" would better serve regional tourism? What type of RTO governance structure will be seen as transparent and equitable in order to achieve legitimacy and widespread support? Do RTO governance bodies not only need to consider the delivery of outcomes but also have the ability to seek the resources to deliver these outcomes?

The principle of subsidiarity

Subsidiarity is a principle of authority allocation. Subsidiarity can be defined as tasks being primarily accomplished by the lowest and most basic elements of social organisation (Paulus, 2008) and only in the case of failure is a higher organisation or community, such as the state or a large corporation, justified in offering assistance or taking over. Once any crisis is over, the higher community should end its intervention (Koyzis, 2003). Under the principle of subsidiarity, it is an injustice to assign to a larger/higher association what the lesser and subordinate associations can do. All social and commercial activities should serve individuals and smaller communities and not destroy or absorb them. Subsidiarity has been described as "'reverse delegation' – the delegation of the parts to the centre" (Handy, 1994, p. 134). Subsidiarity is different from empowerment. Empowerment implies that the higher power has the authority and chooses to give away that power. Subsidiarity, in contrast, implies that "the power properly belongs, in the first place, lower down or further out" (Handy, 1994, p. 146). Subsidiarity maintains power as close to the action as possible. Decisions are taken as close as possible to the level at which they can be effectively implemented (Wilkinson, 2005). *Bottom-up* approaches to tourism have been promoted to "devolve much of the decision-making processes that controls [tourism] development back to the affected communities" (Michael & Hall, 2007, p. 132). The challenge centres on how to put these ideals into practice within an RTO context.

The political concept of subsidiarity goes back to the anarcho-communitarian approach of the sixteenth century and reflects a holistic and exclusive vision of society (Collignon, 2003). "Holistic ideologies violate the normative claims of modern individualism and a modern market economy" (Collignon, 2003, p. 84), yet all societies contain both individualistic and holistic ideological elements. The principle of subsidiarity adopts an organic and holistic approach that recognises the needs and rights of individuals and small communities and that the larger communities and other forms of socio-economic organisations are there to serve them.

This principle can balance tensions often found between centralised and decentralised tourism decision-making processes, amongst stakeholders and various community groups. Franck (2008) proposes three *neutral principles* that can guide the application of subsidiarity when evaluating governance structures. The first is "nearer my law to thee": decisions affecting individuals or groups should be made by people closest to those affected. The second is "first do no harm", when there are redistributive ramifications. These need to be negotiated with the people they impinge on the most. If people or groups are differently situated, a common solution needs to be sought and take priority over existing differences. The third principle "responsive governance" implies that the locus of power needs to be responsive to the individuals and groups to whom governance is directed.

The principle of subsidiarity recognises that both the state (central or local) and intermediate groups such as an RTO have their own legitimate objectives and spheres of actions and they owe each other mutual respect. The state, often via local government, should promote and develop intermediary bodies, such as RTOs, and should not replace or absorb these organisations or misappropriate their functions (Sison, 2008). This process needs to foster mutual respect and trust. Caldwell and Karri (2005) claim that most organisational governance theories are fundamentally inadequate to build trust. Governance bodies need to have confidence in individual actors and groups, and these actors and groups need confidence in each other and the governance body (Handy, 1994). Hence, these processes need time and stability (Handy, 1994).

The principle of subsidiarity is used in many non-tourism contexts. Subsidiarity is a key term of reference in international law and the allocation of authority (Paulus, 2008): it provides legitimacy and "compliance pull" (Franck, 1990). It is central to many discussions within the European Union (EU). It "is commonly understood to mean that policy-making functions should always be exercised at the lowest possible level, and only 'if necessary' should they be delegated to a higher level" (Collignon, 2003, p. 85). The introduction of the notion of subsidiarity in the EU has its opponents. Davies (2006) argued that it should be interpreted as a technical functional rule rather than as a general principle. Davies claims that subsidiarity in the EU assumes that there is an agreement on the goal; therefore, when conflicts arise over priorities or goals, subsidiarity has no relevance, arguing that subsidiarity protects "the right of states to carry out missions in their own way. It does not protect their right to formulate their own mission or make substantive choices about values and policy" (2008, p. 97). In the WTO context, the principle of subsidiarity, coupled with the danger of loss of state regulatory autonomy, has prevented the direct application of

WTO law (von Bogdandy, 2002) and free-trade competition being imposed on nation states (Edward, 2002).

Subsidiarity is embedded in local government identity in New Zealand as "local government is charged with the responsibility of representing the interests of its own community. Local government supports the principle of subsidiarity of decision making" (Local Government New Zealand, 2001, p. 4).

Methodology

A case study "is not a methodological choice but a choice of what is to be studied. By whatever methods we choose to study a case" (Stake, 2000, p. 435). For this case study, data were collected from both primary and secondary sources. Primary sources were observation, interviews, focus groups and an online questionnaire. Secondary data sources included reports, media releases and media reports documenting interviews with key actors.

The data were obtained via observation at nine meetings, 12 industry and RTO forums and conferences and listening to speeches and presentations. These observations helped to understand the rich, complex and idiosyncratic nature of human operations (Cavana, Delahaye, & Sekaran, 2001), interrelations and politics associated with RTOs. Most observations were from an outsider's perspective, or that of a researcher/interpreter, rather than the emic observation, that of the insider (Jennings, 2001). The researcher was never perceived as being part of the RTO governance process at any time. She was allowed in, as an observer, but was never formally involved in the former RTO or in the evolving funding and governance process for the new RTO. Observations for this research investigation can be classified as "complete observer" (Junker, 1960), "total researcher" (Gans, 1982) and "peripheral membership" (Adler & Adler, 1983), but can still be categorised as participant observation (Jennings, 2001). The value and contribution of observation should not be underestimated: observation, living in, being immersed and part of the region, facilitated a holistic/inductive framework for the study. Through this observation and reflection, the researcher was able to unify the fragmented data gathered from other sources.

The role of participant observer was more pronounced when primary data were collected as part of an industry report conducted by the researcher after the demise of the first generation RTO; full details can be found in Zahra and Walter (2007). Interviews, focus groups and an online questionnaire captured the views of industry stakeholders within the tourism and hospitality sectors. In total, 125 tourism stakeholders participated in this research, either in one-on-one interviews, as part of a focus group, in an online questionnaire or through a combination of these methods. Interviews with tourism stakeholders from outside the Waikato Region included neighbouring RTO CEOs and Tourism New Zealand (TNZ; the National Tourism Organisation responsible for international marketing) and were undertaken to gather an understanding of the issues facing the Waikato in the context of the wider industry. Boundaries were set by the researcher; however, these boundaries were fluid and not clearly defined, especially between the phenomena and context (Yin, 1994). "A case study is both a process of inquiry about the case and the product of that inquiry" (Stake, 2000, p. 436). The limitation of this case study is that the RTO and, more specifically, its governance structure are still emerging and evolving. The process of establishing a formal RTO and a governance structure was taking place at the time of writing, and therefore, the application of the principle of subsidiarity can only be projected into the future.

Case study: the Waikato Region and its RTO

This study overviews the evolution, implosion and tentative resurrection of the Waikato RTO, in the western central part of the North Island of New Zealand. The Waikato Region, a pastoral area with a strong dairy farming heritage, comprises 22,000 km^2, predominantly valleys and rolling hills surrounding the Waikato River, New Zealand's longest river. It has beaches, but no major resort. Of its 400,000 people, over 200,000 live in the city of Hamilton. The former RTO, Tourism Waikato, which represented six local authorities, was formed in the early 1980s and disbanded in May 2006 when the major stakeholder and funder, Hamilton City Council, suddenly withdrew its funding. Resources and funding had bedevilled the RTO since the late 1990s. In this predominantly agricultural region dominated by a major regional urban centre, with very few export-ready tourism products, some sectors, especially the agricultural sector, do not think that tourism should be subsidised by local government (despite central government subsidising the agricultural sector, especially in research and development).

The one iconic tourism attraction in the region, the Waitomo caves, with its soft and hard adventure tourism offerings, is located in a sparsely populated rural community and its local authority, Waitomo District Council, is cash poor. The Waitomo District Council withdrew its funding for the RTO in the 1990s. Since then RTO legitimacy was questioned by the other local authorities. The former RTO's governance structure was a board composed of local authority representatives, who generally had little or no knowledge of tourism: some used this governance position to further personal political ambitions. The RTO had an additional Industry Advisory Board, made up of industry representatives that had some authority but no power.

The research for this paper found that the problems leading to the demise of the Waikato RTO closely followed the opening points on the list of potential partnership problems outlined in Table 1 in Bramwell and Lane (2000a, p. 9). The key points included the following:

A limited tradition of stakeholders participating in policy-making: The Waikato RTO was a first attempt at partnership working in a region with a fragmented tourism sector, a predominance of small operators with weak ties amongst and between the operators and local authorities.

The stifling of healthy conflict: For example, the post-2006 RTO collapse stakeholder report on regional tourism (Zahra & Walter, 2007) was politically sensitive as it highlighted the gap left by the RTO and the consequential implications of the uninformed, hasty and non-consultative decision to transfer funding from regional tourism to a Hamilton City focused events and branding strategy. The report was indirectly funded by Hamilton City Council, being the main funder of the Economic Development Agency that commissioned the report. The report was politically managed. It identified the economic significance of tourism to the region, the role of the RTO and how an events strategy needed to be supported by a robust regional tourism sector supplying accommodation, activities and attractions. Participants in the research were expecting a copy of the report. The researchers were requested to produce a public summary report that removed the politically sensitive issues from Hamilton City Council's perspective.

Collaborative efforts may be under-resourced: Much of the former RTO CEOs' time and energy was spent undertaking tourism advocacy and lobbying local authority councillors to continue funding the RTO. There was little or no funding to develop advocacy and community knowledge about tourism, a lack of technical tourism knowledge of both destination marketing and destination management and limited research in the region.

Actors may not be disposed to reduce their own power or work together: The decision by Hamilton City Council to cease funding the RTO in 2006 was taken by minority vested interests wanting to change the image of Hamilton from a rural provincial town to a modern progressive city. The rural-focused marketing and branding of the RTO "where the grass is greener" was not aligned to the City's new vision, and funding was needed by Hamilton for an events strategy and for a City branding campaign to lift the profile of the City, and more specifically for events sponsorship.

Stakeholders with less power may be excluded: When Hamilton City Council decided to withdraw its funding, the Industry Advisory Board was not consulted or informed. Some operators used their position on the Industry Advisory body to lever favourable marketing profiles and positions in the RTO's marketing publication, thus alienating other operators.

Power could pass to groups/individuals with more effective political skills: The last Tourism Waikato RTO CEO was a former employee of TNZ. TNZ's focus was predominantly on long haul international markets. Waikato had very few export-ready products and was operating in a highly competitive North Island market. This research investigation and its consultation with tourism stakeholders found that the former Tourism Waikato was perceived as not to be addressing local needs but was aligned to TNZ and was focusing on international marketing. One participant stated that they "don't want another Tourism Waikato like the last one. We need a different kind of regional coordination that is aimed at unique, smaller, authentic experiences".

Some partners might coerce others by threatening to leave: Hamilton City Council assumed greater informal power in the former RTO because of its higher proportion of funding (50% of the total, corresponding to its share of the population of the region). Hamilton carried out this process.

Impacts resulting from the RTO's demise

Nationally, the New Zealand tourism industry is organised and structured around RTOs and there was little or no international trade marketing and liaison with inbound tour operators for the Waikato after the demise of Tourism Waikato. The Ministry of Tourism research data are organised according to RTO geographical boundaries, and even though there was no Waikato RTO, the Ministry still produced the research data for the region. TNZ, responsible for marketing New Zealand internationally, was clear, since the demise of the former Tourism Waikato, that the region needed to come together collectively as they could not work with a number of smaller entities. TNZ outlined from the outset that the Waikato would miss out on international media opportunities and liaison with international travel and trade wholesalers as they were coordinated through the RTOs. RTOs were generally the link to TNZ's marketing website. The Great New Zealand Touring Route (GNZTR) was established in 2005 to cooperatively market member regions in the Central North Island of which the Waikato is part and the promotion of export-ready tourism products within these regions to international travel trade. The GNZTR is viewed by member RTOs to be a very effective and economical approach to international marketing. Some member RTOs conduct all their international marketing through the GNZTR. As there was no Waikato RTO since 2006, the Waikato had no representation at international travel shows, with travel trade or in the printed media from 2007 to 2010. Waitomo tourism operators could see the marketing implications of no Waikato presence in the GNZTR and rallied funding to include Waitomo so that they could continue accessing the marketing distribution channels.

The Zahra and Walter (2007) report concluded that stakeholders, including Waikato Region District Council Mayors and Councillors, wanted regional tourism coordination, facilitation and leadership to fill the vacuum that existed for both tourism expertise and knowledge and to facilitate product development, especially getting the current and potential tourism product export ready. Stakeholders wanted to see a Waikato tourism industry that has a clear vision, is sustainable and has a clear Waikato identity. Many of the suggestions from the focus groups of this research recognised the potential for tourism to be aligned to other major drivers of the Waikato economy: dairy processing, farming, forestry, equine, geothermal electricity generation and the education and scientific research community to provide an authentic Waikato visitor experience. Yet there are currently few or no linkages between tourism and other major sectors.

The implosion of the RTO allowed the local community, tourism operators to take a "bottom-up" self-determining approach. Attempts were made to reinvigorate the RTO, but there was a leadership vacuum, a lack of strategic management skills and most importantly no funding. In 2008, Waikato's tourism woes were compounded when Air Zealand announced that they were going to stop international flights to Australia in April 2009, the only international carrier out of Hamilton International Airport (and funded by five local authorities with 50% funding from Hamilton City Council). The airport had just undertaken a costly upgrade and refurbishment. To add to this woe, the Ministry of Tourism research data showed that 30,000 fewer people stayed in commercial accommodation in the former RTO boundary, the only region in the country to see a decline. The TNZ CEO addressed a Hamilton businesses network meeting in November 2008 highlighting the region's problems and the economic contribution of tourism to the region based on the data in the 2007 industry stakeholder report (Zahra & Walter, 2007). Hamilton Airport Chairman and TNZ's Development Manager coincidentally met and discussed the region's tourism problems. The outcome of this meeting was that the airport will take a leadership role in tourism and secure funding of $450,000 for two years from its five Hamilton Airport local authority shareholders, including Hamilton City Council, to appoint a regional tourism manager answerable to the airport board and also to boost regional tourism. The immediate tasks for the new manager, a former TNZ Development Manager with extensive experience in regional tourism and capability development, were to assist the Airport in attracting an international carrier and developing a business plan with the airport board.

The regional tourism manager has undertaken most RTO functions: liaison with TNZ, development of a website and development of marketing alliances. The airport commenced international flights again to Australia in September 2009 with another carrier. The region has secured $250,000 government funding only accessible to RTOs for marketing regional diversity in Australia. This government funding was matched by the private sector funding giving the RTO a $500,000 marketing budget. The regional tourism manager has been very active, re-establishing the RTO website, an image library, focusing on product development and has forayed into social network marketing. In 2010, the Waikato Region rejoined the rebranded GNZTR, Central Park. The next step is to secure ongoing funding and establish an official governance structure.

At the time of writing, the Waikato Region still does not have an official RTO. A plan has been presented to all seven Waikato local authorities to contribute to $820,000 a year RTO funding so that it can commence operations on 1 July 2011. Hamilton City Council would still provide a majority 40% share of $390,000, the Airport shareholder Councils will provide $100,000 per year and two smaller rural councils, Waitomo and South Waikato, funding $50,000 and $40,000 respectively. This funding and weighting was based on the number of operators in each council, guest nights, population and rates income. The plan is for the industry to contribute $450,000 to the RTOs' operational budget through their participation in specific projects rather than membership subscriptions as in the former

RTO. Hamilton City Council appears to support the proposed RTO funding arrangement with a new Mayor and new Council priorities, chiefly the reduction of debt. The Hamilton City Councils' events strategy is increasingly criticised by Councillors, the public and the media as contributing to the City's mounting debt.

Discussion and conclusion

The Waikato RTO case study is a specific example of the dispersed and fragmented nature of regional tourism development, marketing and governance providing further evidence of the need to find new approaches and solutions (Bramwell & Lane, 2000a). Funding arrangements appear to be progressing well for the new Waikato RTO. However, unless funding can be supported by a transparent and equitable governance structure, the RTO will fall back into its past pattern of instability. The challenge facing the Waikato RTO is the creation of a more inclusive and participatory governance mechanism, which is flexible enough to respond to new problems and new understandings of the old ones.

Is the principle of subsidiarity a viable alternative to underpin the new Waikato RTO? Which form of governance: "governance in RTOs" or "governance of RTOs" would better serve regional tourism? What type of RTO governance structure will be seen as transparent and equitable in order to achieve legitimacy and widespread support? Do RTO governance bodies not only need to consider the delivery of outcomes but also have the ability to seek the resources to deliver these outcomes?

The circumstances in the Waikato are conducive to the adoption of the principle of subsidiarity to underpin the new RTO governance structure. Given the mounting evidence that the region needs an RTO, local government now see the need to financially support the RTO. Local government in New Zealand advocates the principle of subsidiarity in managing and identifying their rights, responsibilities and authority allocation with central government. They should equally acknowledge the principle of subsidiarity's application to an RTO recognising the rights and powers of the RTO governance body, with the seven local authorities recognising the new RTO governance body as the legitimate authority in identifying the strategic objectives and operations of the RTO and not interfere and misappropriate the RTO resources and functions for their own ends. Trust and mutual respect needs to be fostered and continually nurtured. Hamilton City Council's actions in 2006 were an injustice according to the principle of subsidiarity as it destroyed and absorbed a subordinate association and assigned to itself the tasks that a lesser organisation, in this case an RTO, was capable of accomplishing.

The nature and style of the new RTO governance mechanism still needs to be addressed. Should this board take on a "command-style" approach involving hierarchy and authoritarian rule or adopt more of a control or steering style of governance? RTO governance bodies without a purpose and an end are inept and dysfunctional bodies. It is argued here that the RTO's purpose is to meet the needs of the public and private sectors and the community: those ends are very much in line with the key principles of sustainable tourism. Thus, an RTO governance board guided by the principle of subsidiarity would seek to take on local social meanings and place attachment (Dredge, 2010) besides the expected economic objectives of product development, infrastructure and marketing. An RTO governance board should try to identify and locate themselves in the local context seeking governance *in* the jurisdiction they serve (Rosenau, 2005). An RTO board driven by purely economic objectives and measurable KPIs would adopt a more authoritarian style of governance or the governance *of* regional tourism (Rosenau, 2005) not aligned to the principle of subsidiarity and service to the wider community that are indirectly funding the RTO through the taxes they pay to their local authority.

The proposed new RTO appears to be following the same historical funding pattern as the former RTO. Perhaps, past Waikato RTO traditions and cultures have been severed in the five-year period with no RTO and tensions have settled, especially for Hamilton City Council, a major player. Historical precedents demonstrated that it is difficult to bring diverse operators and local authorities together to find common ground. Marketing and promotion are often canvassed as the major uniting force for an RTO but this favours major tourist attractions and players, which further alienates smaller and complementary tourism operators. RTOs have been accused of becoming distant and alienated from their constituency (Dredge, 2000). The challenge for the new governing body is to deliver a governance structure that is seen as transparent and equitable in order to achieve legitimacy and widespread support. The principle of subsidiarity advances that the RTO governance body is there to serve individual tourism operators, communities/local authorities, within which the tourism product is consumed, and other interested groups. An ethos of service to others, especially subordinate individuals and entities, embodied in the RTO governance culture, rather than self-interest and the promotion of personal and political agendas, could contribute to legitimacy, trust and widespread support for the RTO. This ethos of service should be evidenced in deeds and processes, with a governance ethos of open communication channels, fostering more contact with constituents, clearly articulating the benefits and relevance of working with the RTO, especially with small tourism operators. The principle of subsidiarity can facilitate trust and possibly mitigate the free-rider effect so typical of RTOs. The former Tourism Waikato had a membership structure, and therefore, non-members enjoyed the benefits paid for by others but it also fostered inadvertent exclusion that did generate at best apathy or at worst active disinterest. The proposed RTO funding structure will not have membership subscriptions. Thus, all parties may be willing to contribute to the RTO consultation and communication process, which can also in turn further strengthen legitimacy.

Governance is not only about process. Individuals in governance bodies have positions of influence and are ultimately responsible for dealing with substantive issues and the identification and delivery of outcomes. RTO governance cannot be divorced from power, and in the end, power must be exercised and responsibility be acknowledged. Is it the responsibility of the RTO governance board to not only focus on the delivery of outcomes but also ensure that the resources are available for the realisation of the outcomes? The regional tourism manager and the Hamilton Airport Governance Board appear to have secured funding for the new RTO but as the case study has highlighted, local authority funding is tenuous and continuous funding is not assured. The proposed arrangement for the private sector to fund specific projects is another financial resource for the RTO, but this also may not be ongoing. However, in a regional tourism governance context, it is generally the funders either from the public or from the private sector such as local authorities and tourism operators (generally larger tourism operators), who have legitimacy on RTO governance bodies over non-funders. RTO managers generally give priority to communicating with, informing and meeting the needs of funders over non-funders, as they are the ones to whom they are accountable to as agents and if they are perceived as ineffective not only their job but also the organisation can be jeopardised, as was demonstrated by the demise of Tourism Waikato. This tension is a reality and needs to be acknowledged. However, the legitimacy of the RTO is derived not only from funders but also from non-funders, the media and the community that vote for local politicians who ultimately decide on continued funding for the RTO. The challenge remains of how to continually build and maintain trust. Trust goes beyond an economic transaction, involves a personal and social relationship and is "based on shared expectations and common goals" (Hall et al., 2007, p. 150). The principle of subsidiarity can foster trust and therefore can aid the governance body to source resources for the RTO.

This paper has limitations. It has focused on the application of the principle of subsidiarity to guide tourism governance in developed countries characterised by democratic accountability and a history of decentralisation. It has not considered the application of this principle to governance structures in developing countries, often characterised by highly centralised bureaucracies responsible for tourism development and policy formulation coupled with local authorities with few resources (Yuksel, Bramwell, & Yuksel, 2005). The research has assumed that governance bodies will agree to serve the constituents they represent and diversity and differences can be negotiated away for the greater good and consensus. However, some authors argue that RTO governance representatives will only negotiate on the issues for which consensus will be reached (Dredge, 2006a; McGuirk, 2000). Flyvbjerg (1998) argues that avoiding conflict and seeking consensus will weaken democratic civil society; therefore, further research is required to explore the applicability of the principle of subsidiarity in governance conflict.

This paper has argued the case for a change in governance approaches based on a *principle*. A principle is a statement that is taken to be true at all times and all places where it is applicable. The notion of truth is contestable in a relativistic postmodern academic environment. It is beyond the scope of this paper to explore these tensions and philosophical implications, yet it merits further research. This paper has also not adequately addressed the concept of "good" governance for which there is extensive literature (Curtin & Wessel, 2005; Poluha & Rosendahl, 2002) and has implied that the process of local communities participating in and debating public policy is a reflection of good governance. The principle of subsidiarity can be investigated further in the context of the (good) governance debate.

Governance under collaboration, private–public sector partnerships, network and stakeholder theory is about changing the structure of control in an RTO and redirecting its actions towards other goals such as social, community and environmental sustainability. However, in a tourism context, governance structures have not been addressed. This paper has proposed a fundamental change in a premise of the market system that shifts interest from *self*, a key driver of enterprise, to *other* and the role of service. A governance framework underpinned by the principle of subsidiarity is a step towards this direction, removing the public–private sector divide and fostering the governance role of service to society for those who hold governance positions in RTOs. The principle of subsidiarity perceives RTO governance as a service to the smaller entities such as tourism operators, local communities and visitors rather than assuming positions of power and control and taking over the identity of the RTO to further self-interest.

References

Adler, P.A., & Adler, P. (1983). Shifts and oscillations in deviant careers: The case upper-level drug dealers and smugglers. *Social Problems, 31*(2), 195–207.

Andriotis, K. (2002). Residents' satisfaction or dissatisfaction with public sector governance: The Cretan case. *Tourism and Hospitality Research, 4*(1), 53–68.

Ateljevic, I., & Doorne, S. (2000). Local government and tourism development: Issues and constraints of public sector entrepreneurship. *New Zealand Geographer, 56*(2), 25–31.

Beaumont, N., & Dredge, D. (2010). Local tourism governance: A comparison of three network approaches. *Journal of Sustainable Tourism, 18*(1), 7–28.

Beritelli, P., Bieger, T., & Laesser, C. (2007). Destination governance: Using corporate governance theories as a foundation for effective destination management. *Journal of Travel Research, 46*(1), 96–107.

Blumberg, K. (2005). Tourism destination marketing – A tool for destination management? A case study from Nelson/Tasman Region, New Zealand. *Asia Pacific Journal of Tourism Research, 10*(1), 45–57.

Bramwell, B. (2004). Partnerships, participation and social science research in tourism planning. In A.L. Lew, C.M. Hall, & A.M. Williams (Eds.), *A companion to tourism* (pp. 541–545). Oxford: Blackwell.

Bramwell, B. (2011). Governance, the state, and sustainable tourism: A political economy approach. *Journal of Sustainable Tourism, 19*(4–5), 459–477.

Bramwell, B., & Lane, B. (2000a). Collaboration and partnerships in tourism planning. In B. Bramwell & B. Lane (Eds.), *Tourism collaboration and partnerships: Politics, practice and sustainability* (pp. 1–19). Clevedon: Channel View Publications.

Bramwell, B., & Lane, B. (Eds.). (2000b). *Tourism collaboration and partnerships: Politics, practice and sustainability*. Clevedon: Channel View.

Brummer, J.J. (1991). *Corporate responsibility and legitimacy: An interdisciplinary analysis*. New York: Greenwood.

Caffyn, A., & Jobbins, G. (2003). Governance capacity and stakeholder interactions in the development and management of coastal tourism: Examples from Morocco and Tunisia. *Journal of Sustainable Tourism, 11*(2–3), 224.

Caldwell, C., & Karri, R. (2005). Organizational governance and ethical systems: A covenantal approach to building trust. *Journal of Business Ethics, 58*(1–3), 249.

Catalyst Management Services Ltd. (2004). *Recommended good practice for governance of regional tourism organisations*. Wellington: Local Government New Zealand.

Cavana, R., Delahaye, B., & Sekaran, U. (2001). *Applied business research: Qualitative and quantitative methods*. Milton: Wiley.

Collignon, S. (2003). *The European republic: Reflections on the political economy of a future constitution*. London: Kogan Page.

Connell, J., Page, S.J., & Bentley, T. (2009). Towards sustainable tourism planning in New Zealand: Monitoring local government planning under the Resources Management Act. *Tourism Management, 30*(6), 867–877.

Cooper, C., Scott, N., & Baggio, R. (2009). Network position and perceptions of destination stakeholder importance. *Anatolia: An International Journal of Tourism & Hospitality Research, 20*(1), 33–45.

Curtin, D.M., & Wessel, R.A. (2005). *Good governance and the European Union: Reflections on concepts, institutions and substance*. Antwerp: Intersentia.

Davies, G. (2006). Subsidiarity: The wrong idea, in the wrong place, at the wrong time. *Common Market Law Review, 43*(1), 63–84.

Davies, G. (2008). Subsidiarity as a method of policy centralisation. In T. Broude & Y. Shany (Eds.), *The shifting allocation of authority in international law: Considering sovereignty, supramacy and subsidiarity* (pp. 79–98). Oxford: Hart Publishing.

Donaldson, T., & Preston, L.E. (1995). The stakeholder theory of the corporation: Concepts, evidence and implications. *Academy of Management Review, 20*(1), 65–91.

Dredge, D. (2000). The dynamics of regional tourism organisations in New South Wales. *Current Issues in Tourism, 3*(3), 175–203.

Dredge, D. (2001). Local government tourism planning and policy-making in New South Wales: Institutional development and historical legacies. *Current Issues in Tourism, 4*(2), 355–380.

Dredge, D. (2006a). Networks, conflict and collaborative communities. *Journal of Sustainable Tourism, 14*(6), 562–581.

Dredge, D. (2006b). Policy networks and the local organisation of tourism. *Tourism Management, 27*(1), 269–280.

Dredge, D. (2010). Place change and tourism development conflict: Evaluating public interest. *Tourism Management, 31*(1), 104–112.

Dredge, D., & Jenkins, J. (2003). Destination place identity and regional tourism policy. *Tourism Geographies, 5*(4), 383–407.

Dymond, S. (1997). Indicators of sustainable tourism in New Zealand: A local government perspective. *Journal of Sustainable Tourism, 5*(4), 279–293.

Eagles, P.F.J. (2009). Governance of recreation and tourism partnerships in parks and protected areas. *Journal of Sustainable Tourism, 17*(2), 231–248.

Edward, D. (2002). Competition and national rule making. In A. Von Bogdandy, P.C. Mavroidis, & Y. Meny (Eds.), *European integration and international co-ordination* (pp. 129–138). The Hague: Kluwer Law International.

Falk, R. (2005). Humane governance for the world: Reviving the quest. In R. Wilkinson (Ed.), *The global governance reader* (pp. 105–119). London: Routledge.

Flyvbjerg, B. (1998). Empowering civil society: Habermas, Foucault, and the question of conflict. In M. Douglass & J. Friedmann (Eds.), *Cities for citizens: Planning and the rise of civil society in a global age* (pp. 185–211). Chichester: John Wiley.

Fort, T.L. (1996). Business as mediating institution. *Business Ethics Quarterly, 6*(2), 149–163.

Franck, T. (1990). *The power of legitimacy among nations.* Oxford: Clarendon Press.

Franck, T. (2008). The centripede and the centrifuge: Principles for the centralisation and decentralisation of governance. In T. Broude & Y. Shany (Eds.), *The shifting allocation of authority in international law: Considering sovereignty, supramacy and subsidiarity* (pp. 19–32). Oxford: Hart Publishing.

Freeman, R.E. (1984). *Strategic management: A stakeholder approach.* Boston, MA: Pitman.

Fyall, A., & Garrod, B. (2005). *Tourism marketing: A collaborative approach.* Clevedon: Channel View Publications.

Gans, H.J. (1982). The participant observer as human being: Observations on the personal aspects of fieldwork. In R.G. Burgess (Ed.), *Field research: A sourcebook and field manual* (pp. 80–93). Boston, MA: Allen & Unwin.

Habermas, J. (1984). *Theory of communicative action: Reason and rationalisation of society.* Boston, MA: Beacon.

Hall, C.M. (1999). Rethinking collaboration and partnership: A public policy perspective. *Journal of Sustainable Tourism, 7*(3–4), 274–289.

Hall, C.M. (2000). Rethinking collaboration and partnership: A public policy perspective. In B. Bramwell & B. Lane (Eds.), *Tourism collaboration and partnerships* (pp. 143–158). Clevedon: Channel View Publications.

Hall, C.M., Lynch, P., Michael, E.J., & Mitchell, R. (2007). The contribution of the micro-cluster approach. In E.J. Michael (Ed.), *Micro-clusters and networks: The growth of tourism* (pp. 141–152). Amsterdam: Elsevier.

Handy, C.B. (1994). *The age of paradox.* Boston, MA: Harvard Business School Press.

Harvey, D. (2001). *Spaces of capital: Towards a critical geography.* New York: Routledge.

Hutton, W. (1997). An overview of stakeholding. In G. Kelly, D. Kelly, & A. Gamble (Eds.), *Stakeholder capitalism* (pp. 3–9). London: Macmillan Press.

Jamal, T., & Getz, D. (1995). Collaboration theory and community tourism planning. *Annals of Tourism Research, 22*(1), 186–204.

Jenkins, J. (1995). A comparative study of tourist organisations in Australia and Canada. *Australian-Canadian Studies, 13*(1), 73–107.

Jenkins, J. (2000). The dynamics of regional tourism organisations in New South Wales, Australia: History, structures and operations. *Current Issues in Tourism, 3*(3), 175–203.

Jennings, J. (2001). *Tourism research.* Milton: John Wiley.

Junker, B.H. (1960). *Fieldwork: An introduction to the social sciences.* Chicago, IL: University of Chicago Press.

Koyzis, D. (2003). *Political visions and illusions.* Downers Grove, IL: InterVarsity Press.

Local Government New Zealand. (2001). *Tourism and local government: A proposal for enhanced local government participation in tourism.* Wellington: Author.

Lovelock, B. (2002). Why it's good to be bad: The role of conflict in contributing to sustainable tourism in protected areas. *Journal of Sustainable Tourism, 10*(1), 5–31.

Lynch, P., & Morrison, A. (2007). The role of networks. In E.J. Michael (Ed.), *Micro-clusters and networks: The growth of tourism* (pp. 43–60). Amsterdam: Elsevier.

McGuirk, C. (2000). Power and policy networks in urban governance: Local government and property led regeneration in Dublin. *Urban Studies, 37*(4), 651–672.

Melé, D. (2005). Exploring the principle of subsidiarity in organisational forms. *Journal of Business Ethics, 60*(3), 293–305.

Michael, E.J., & Hall, C.M. (2007). A path for policy. In E.J. Michael (Ed.), *Micro-clusters and networks: The growth of tourism* (pp. 127–140). Amsterdam: Elsevier.

Ministry of Tourism. (2005). *Regional tourism organisations of New Zealand: RTO/Maori tourism group partnerships.* Retrieved July 7, 2005, from www.tourism.govt.nz/rto/rtonz-mrtg-partnership.html

Murphy, P.E. (1983). Tourism as a community industry – An ecological model of tourism development. *Tourism Management, 4*, 180–193.

Page, S.J., & Thorn, K.J. (1997). Towards sustainable tourism planning in New Zealand: Public sector planning responses. *Journal of Sustainable Tourism, 5*(1), 59–77.

Page, S.J., & Thorn, K.J. (2002). Towards sustainable tourism development and planning in New Zealand: The public sector response revisited. *Journal of Sustainable Tourism, 10*(3), 222–238.

Palmer, A. (1998). Evaluating the governance style of marketing groups. *Annals of Tourism Research, 25*(1), 185–201.

Paulus, A.L. (2008). Subsidiarity, fragmentation and democracy: Towards the demise of general international law. In T. Broude & Y. Shany (Eds.), *The shifting allocation of authority in international law: Considering sovereignty, supramacy and subsidiarity* (pp. 193–216). Oxford: Hart Publishing.

Pavlovich, K. (2001). The twin landscapes of Waitomo: Tourism network and sustainability through the Landcare Group. *Journal of Sustainable Tourism, 9*(6), 491–504.

Pavlovich, K. (2003). The evolution and transformation of a tourism destination network: The Waitomo Caves, New Zealand. *Tourism Management, 24*(2), 203–216.

Pearce, D. (1992). *Tourist organisations.* Harlow: Longman Scientific and Technical.

Pforr, C. (2006). Tourism policy in the making: An Australian network study. *Annals of Tourism Research, 33*(1), 87–108.

Pierre, J. (2000). *Debating governance: Authority, steering, and democracy.* Oxford: Oxford University Press.

Plummer, R., & Fennell, D.A. (2009). Managing protected areas for sustainable tourism: Prospects for adaptive co-management. *Journal of Sustainable Tourism, 17*(2), 149–168.

Poluha, E., & Rosendahl, M. (2002). *Contesting "good" governance: Crosscultural perspectives on representation, accountability and public space.* London: Routledge Curzon.

Regional Tourism Organisations New Zealand. (2003). *Further tourism strategy response: Building of stakeholder understanding of tourism.* Wellington: Author.

Rhodes, R.A.W. (1999). *Understanding governance, policy networks, reflexivity and accountability.* Buckingham: Open University Press.

Robinson, J., & Robinson, I. (1996). From shareholders to stakeholders: Critical issues for tourism marketers. *Tourism Management, 17*(7), 533–540.

Rosenau, J.N. (2005). Governance in the twenty first century. In R. Wilkinson (Ed.), *The global governance reader* (pp. 45–88). London: Routledge.

Rustin, M. (1997). Stakeholding and the public sector. In G. Kelly, D. Kelly, & A. Gamble (Eds.), *Stakeholder capitalism* (pp. 72–81). London: Macmillan.

Ryan, C. (2002). The politics of promoting cities and regions – A case study of New Zealand's Regional Tourist Organisations. In N. Morgan & A. Pritchard (Eds.), *Destination banding: Creating the unique destination proposition* (pp. 66–86). London: Continuum Books.

Sautter, E.T., & Leisen, B. (1999). Managing stakeholders: A tourism planning model. *Annals of Tourism Research, 26*(2), 312–328.

Sheehan, L., & Ritchie, J. (2005). Destination stakeholders: Exploring identity and salience. *Annals of Tourism Research, 32*(3), 711–734.

Simpson, K. (2002). Tourism planning at subnational levels: A New Zealand case study. *Pacific Tourism Review: An Interdisciplinary Journal, 6*(1), 3–21.

Sison, A.G. (2008). *Corporate governance and ethics: An Aristotelian perspective.* Cheltenham: Edward Elgar.

Stake, R.E. (2000). Case studies. In N.K. Denzin & Y.S. Lincoln (Eds.), *Handbook of qualitative research* (pp. 435–454). Thousand Oaks, CA: Sage.

Svensson, B., Nordin, S., & Flagestad, A. (2005). A governance perspective on destination development – Exploring partnerships, clusters and innovation systems. *Tourism Review, 60*(2), 32–37.

Timothy, D.J., & Tosun, C. (2003). Appropriate planning for tourism in destination communities: Participation, incremental growth and collaboration. In S. Singh, D.J. Timothy, & R.K. Dowling (Eds.), *Tourism in destination communities* (pp. 181–204). Wallingford: CABI.

Timur, S., & Getz, D. (2008). A network perspective on managing stakeholders for sustainable urban tourism. *International Journal of Contemporary Hospitality Management, 20*(4), 445–461.

Tourism Strategy Group. (2001). *New Zealand tourism strategy 2010*. Wellington: Author.

Vernon, J., Essex, S., Pinder, D., & Curry, K. (2005). Collaborative policymaking: Local sustainable projects. *Annals of Tourism Research, 32*(2), 325–345.

von Bogdandy, A. (2002). Legal equality, legal certainty and subsidiarity in transnational economic law-decentralized application of Art 81.3 EC and WTO law: Why and why not. In A. von Bogdandy, P.C. Mavroidis, & Y. Meny (Eds.), *European integration and international co-ordination* (pp. 13–38). The Hague: Kluwer Law International.

Wang, W. (2008). Collaborative destination marketing: Roles and strategies of convention and visitors bureaus. *Journal of Vacation Marketing, 14*(3), 191–209.

Weiss, T.G. (2005). Governance, good governance and global governance: Conceptual and actual challenges. In R. Wilkinson (Ed.), *The global governance reader* (pp. 68–88). London: Routledge.

Wilkinson, R. (2005). Introduction: Concepts and issues in global governance. In R. Wilkinson (Ed.), *The global governance reader* (pp. 1–22). London: Routledge.

World Tourism Organisation. (1996). *Towards new forms of public-private sector partnership. The changing role, structure and activities of National Tourism Administrations*. Madrid: Author.

Wray, M. (2009). Policy communities, networks and issue cycles in tourism destination systems. *Journal of Sustainable Tourism, 17*(6), 673–690.

Yin, R. (1994). *Case study research, design and methods* (2nd ed., Vol. 5). Thousand Oaks, CA: Sage.

Yuksel, F., Bramwell, B., & Yuksel, A. (1999). Stakeholder interviews and tourism planning at Pamukkale, Turkey. *Tourism Management, 20*(3), 351–360.

Yuksel, F., Bramwell, B., & Yuksel, A. (2005). Centralized and decentralized tourism governance in Turkey. *Annals of Tourism Research, 32*(4), 859–886.

Zahra, A. (2006). *Regional tourism organisations in New Zealand 1980–2005: Process of transition and change* (PhD thesis). University of Waikato, Hamilton, New Zealand.

Zahra, A., & Walter, N. (2007). *The Waikato region: Major tourism issues and opportunities to facilitate tourism development*. Hamilton: University of Waikato.

Death by a thousand cuts: governance and environmental trade-offs in ecotourism development at Kangaroo Island, South Australia

Freya Higgins-Desbiolles

School of Management, University of South Australia, GPO Box 2471, Adelaide, South Australia 5001, Australia

In the wake of the Brundtland Report's articulation of the concept of sustainable development (1987), ecotourism has been promoted as an optimum way to achieve sustainable development in the tourism sphere. Ecotourism, as a subset of sustainable tourism, is touted as a win-win endeavour – a high-yield, low-volume strategy is often pursued in the hope of achieving good economic returns for local communities while simultaneously creating fewer negative environmental impacts than other economic development options. However, the concept of sustainable development contains the tensions of an oxymoron as the conservation implied in "sustainability" conflicts with the growth and resource use implied in "development". In an era where market imperatives dominate, this results in "trade-offs" between requirements for environmental conservation and demands for greater economic growth through tourism. This paper narrates the story of governance and the development approval process for an ecolodge on Kangaroo Island (KI) in order to explore the nature of such trade-offs. Evidence suggests that the requirements of environmental protection are "traded off" in the pursuit of tourism development and the income and employment it provides. Is sustainability possible when such incremental development, in fact, results in "death by a thousand cuts"?

Introduction

Ecotourism has been credited with numerous beneficial impacts, including conservation of environments, sustainable development opportunities for local communities, education of tourists and revenue for governments to implement environmental management and protection processes (Weaver, 2008). Local regions like the Kangaroo Island (KI) in South Australia turn to ecotourism in order to capitalise on their natural assets and achieve viable economies while being assured they do not irreparably degrade their natural environment. As the concept of sustainable development has become widely accepted in tourism policy and planning following its articulation in the Report of the Brundtland Commission (1987), ecotourism is often touted as a win-win solution in circumstances such as these.

However, it has long been recognised that even the more benign niche of ecotourism may bring environmental degradation as profits are secured by providing ecotourists, particularly the upmarket niche, with ever closer access to the world's remaining pristine areas for intense nature experiences. The environmental literature has noted the tensions inherent in the concept of sustainable development that arise from the efforts to sustain environmental integrity while simultaneously attempting to extract wealth for development, arguing that this results in "environment-development trade-offs" (Lee, 2007). In addition, the tourism literature suggests that the quest for profits may override concerns for environmental sustainability or community wellbeing when ecotourism development is undertaken (McLaren, 2003; Mowforth & Munt, 2003; Wheeller, 2005).

This paper explores such environment-development trade-offs through a case study analysis of the planning approval process for the Southern Ocean Lodge (SOL), an upmarket "ecolodge" on the pristine southwest coast of KI, in order to investigate the discourse on sustainable ecotourism development employed by the stakeholders and to identify trade-offs that resulted from the development approval process. The key research question concerned how these tensions were manifested and managed in the development approval process for the SOL and what outcomes resulted from these processes.

Additional research questions pursued included:

- Can sustainable approaches to development occur in the pro-growth and pro-development context of market-driven economies?
- In the neoliberal context, do industry interests achieve a disproportionate amount of attention in the policy process?

Evidence from this case study suggests that the requirements of environmental protection were "traded off" in the pursuit of tourism development and the income and employment it provides. This paper poses this challenging question: is sustainability possible when such incremental development, in fact, results in "death by a thousand cuts"?

Ecotourism

Ecotourism developed out of the twin dynamics of the rise of the environmental movement and the articulation of the concept of sustainable development. In terms of the former, Honey noted how ecotourism grew in the 1970s as an offshoot of environmental consciousness that had been awakened by green movements, which were active in alerting people to what was interpreted as an impending ecological crisis (1999, p. 19). The concept of sustainable development emerged from the Report of the Brundtland Commission (1987) entitled *Our Common Future* which highlighted the need to pursue development options that did not permanently degrade the environment in such a way as to curtail the development options and wellbeing of future generations. Since then, sustainability has been a main driver for doing tourism differently by focusing on limiting the negative environmental impacts of tourism and developing ways of securing its economic benefits in less damaging ways. It is in this effort that ecotourism has been promoted as one of the optimum ways of securing environmental sustainability while pursuing economic development. Although there are numerous and diverse definitions of ecotourism, the World Conservation Union's (IUCN) definition is a rigorous and widely accepted one. It reads:

> Ecotourism is environmentally responsible travel and visitation to relatively undisturbed natural areas, in order to enjoy and appreciate nature (and any accompanying cultural features – both past and present) that promotes conservation, has low negative visitor impact, and provides for beneficially active socio-economic involvement of local populations. (Ceballos-Lascuráin, 2001)

Richardson's definition from a popular guidebook adds a requirement of ecological sustainability: "Ecologically sustainable tourism in natural areas that interprets the local environments and cultures, furthers the tourists' understanding of them, fosters conservation and adds to the well being of the local community" (1993, p. 8). Often, ecotourism is associated with protected areas, as the conservation efforts to conserve the world's remaining natural and wilderness areas create an attraction for tourists who are increasingly seeking out natural areas for escape from urbanised lifestyles.

One way to experience ecotourism is through the accommodation offered by an "ecolodge". Perhaps the most rigorous assessment of ecotourism accommodation was developed by Wight in the 1990s, who noted a small but potentially lucrative market for the luxury ecolodge niche (1997). As Higgins has noted, "the recent construction of inclusive ecolodges on private nature reserves with quality guides and eco-packaging has created alternative ecotourism products" (2001, p. 543). The International Ecotourism Society (TIES) has defined ecolodge as a term used by the tourism industry "to identify a nature-dependent tourist lodge that meets the philosophy of ecotourism" (TIES, as cited in Ceballos-Lascuráin, 2003, p. x). Ceballos-Lascurain argues:

> At a purist level an ecolodge will offer a tourist an educational and participatory experience, be developed and managed in an environmentally sensitive manner and protect its operating environment. An ecolodge is different from mainstream lodges, like fishing and ski lodges and luxury retreats. (2003, p. x)

However, what exactly qualifies as a proper ecolodge is more difficult to distinguish in practice despite these rigorous guidelines, as a continuum of soft to hard ecotourism has been identified. As Page and Dowling note, "accommodation providers can be situated along a continuum meeting the needs of hard to soft types of ecotourists with different types of accommodation available" (2002, p. 141). In fact, Weaver and Lawton (2007) arrived at a category of "structured ecotourists" from a survey they conducted of ecolodge clients at the Gold Coast of Australia, which suggests that ecolodge participants appreciate a softer and more luxurious ecotourism. Weaver and Lawton describe soft ecotourism as "being associated with a high level of services and facilities to mediate encounters between venues and potentially large numbers of visitors more casually engaged with the natural environment" (2007, p. 1170). With such flexibility in practice, five star luxury lodges such as Couran Cove Resort in Australia with its 567 units is admitted to the list of ecolodges (Page & Dowling, 2002, p. 144).

Despite this heightened profile of ecotourism, sustainability and the enjoyment of protected areas, ecotourism stands accused of being "greenwash" as the tourism industry adopts the language of environmental responsibility but effectively continues business as usual. For example, Shaw and Williams claim that ecotourism promoters in the industry have been charged with employing "a promotional discourse using the language of 'greenspeak'" (2002, p. 299). Wall has characterised much of ecotourism as "new wine in old bottles", and he alleges that the tourism industry has endorsed it to promote a "clean and green image, which is occasionally deserved but, more often, is little more than a marketing gimmick" (1997, p. 487). Weaver states that:

> Deliberate misrepresentation [of ecotourism] is commonplace, given the current lack of accreditation schemes that are familiar to the public, the public's lack of familiarity with ecotourism criteria, and the absence of any legal restrictions that govern the use of terms such as "ecotourism". (2008, p. 91)

Additionally, some ecotourists are complicit in this process as they seek highly luxurious and exclusive access to pristine nature in order to enhance their social status, becoming what Mowforth and Munt characterise as "egotourists" (2003, pp. 121–124).

As Butler (1999b) has asserted, contemporary definitions of sustainability in tourism can be interpreted as meaning sustaining the tourism industry rather than limiting it to protect the environment or cultures and societies. Butler has noted the tendency of the tourism industry to ignore the implications of the limits that the sustainability concept implies, including limiting tourist numbers, infrastructure development and landscape changes (1999a, p. 15). Fennell and Ebert say that a call to apply the precautionary principle to tourism "has led to a backlash . . . because it accentuates the process of pulling back the reins on unfettered growth" (2004, p. 475).

Specifically, on ecolodges, Wheeller's analysis alerts us to be sceptical of the claims of ecological sensitivity and sustainability when these luxury retreats, instead of offering a true encounter with nature, offer the "safety of the environmental bubble" (2005, p. 268). Wheeller's analysis (2005) touches on the often ignored and politically sensitive topics in tourism/ecotourism development of political corruption, hasty development in pursuit of quick economic gains and elitist consumption by wealthy ecotourists/egotourists.

Seen through the lens of the neoliberal market economy, it is clear that government authorities are pressing protected area managers to engage in partnerships with private tour operators in order to secure conservation aims from private sector funds, as funds from the public purse are reduced. As Buckley notes, "tourism interests . . . see the protected area estate as a resource for tourism, and push for increased access, activities and facilities" (2004, p. 77). In countries such as Australia, this may result in greater impacts in protected areas, which protected area managers can only manage by ironically entering into commercial arrangements with private tourism operators to secure funding for further conservation efforts. "Effectively, they are forced to lease rights over part of the protected area estate so as to provide funds to protect and manage the remainder; a political firesale of public assets" (Buckley, 2004, p. 76).

Wight noted that ecolodges and ecoresorts may also potentially play a particularly negative role because of the trend to want to site the development in the heart of the natural area to create a unique experience with nature through the accommodation:

> The concern that ecotourism may lead the way to the devastation of natural areas may yet be realised if the trend to building larger, internationally funded and managed facilities in the heart of the resource continues – "as ecotourism grows, so does the demand for new resorts in faraway, pristine lands". (Shundich, as cited in Wight, 1997, p. 217)

This brief literature review indicates the contested nature of contemporary ecotourism and sustainability issues in tourism. The case study that follows from an ecolodge development on KI indicates how these tensions are manifested in a community hoping to harness ecotourism for its developmental needs.

Background

Kangaroo Island sits off the mainland of South Australia, and it is 155 kilometres long and up to 55 kilometres wide. It retains almost half of its original native vegetation, of which half again is conserved in national and conservation parks. There are just over 4400 residents on KI and a significant and increasing number of non-resident landowners.

KI has been branded as a tourist destination on the basis of the beauty of its natural environment and its wildlife. In 2003, 150,915 people visited KI, of which 26% were international visitors (Jack & Duka, n.d.). The development of tourism has occurred in the context of a declining agricultural sector on the island and concern about retaining young people in the community. However, a rise in visitor numbers since the late 1990s drew the concern of both the community and planners. As Miller and Twining-Ward state:

It became evident that without clear observation and understanding of the motivations and changes brought about by the tourism industry, visitor impacts both on the environment and community, coupled with economic worries and emigrations of youth could easily take their toll on the future sustainability of the island. (2005, p. 203)

Realising the need to manage tourism development, KI planners and policymakers decided that, rather than using the then existing tools of visitor management such as the Limits of Acceptable Change (LAC) model, they would develop their own "broader and more integrated approach", which was called the Tourism Optimisation Management Model (TOMM) (Miller & Twining-Ward, 2005, p. 204). Of significance to the rejection of the LAC was the resistance of the tourism industry to the concept of "limits" being applied to tourism development. As a result, the TOMM planners opted for establishing parameters of "optimal uses" of resources instead (Jack, n.d.). Proponents of the TOMM argue that it sets out optimal conditions that "cover the broad spectrum of the economic, market opportunity, ecological, experiential and socio-cultural factors and as such, reflect the entire tourism system ... [in] contrast to the LAC ... which tend[s] to focus on one specific aspect of a tourism system [the ecological]" (Jack, n.d.). As Jack and Duka state:

The vision of TOMM is to achieve best practice in the sustainable management of Kanga-roo Island as a tourism destination for the benefit of both residents and visitors. TOMM was developed as a collaborative management and monitoring program, based upon a series of indicators, covering the health of the environment, the health of the Kangaroo Island commu-nity, health of the economy; the number and type of tourists visiting; the type of experience visitors are having and visitor satisfaction levels. Data is now collected in relation to each of these indicators and this information is presented to the stakeholders in a simple way to show whether current practice is viable or not. (n.d)

Although TOMM has been presented as "a unique example of a 'community' driven, visitor management system" (Jack, n.d.), it should not be forgotten that the creation of TOMM was in part designed to appease the tourism industry, which might otherwise have seen management efforts under a LAC model as detrimental to their interests. These tensions between tourism development and environmental protection are perennial, even in ecotourism, and achieving the correct balance is rarely easy. In fact, it was noted as early as in the mid-1990s that "ecotourism and nature based tourism pose a number of potential threats to the island's biodiversity values" (Lynch, 1996). Before introducing the empirical case study which is the focus of this paper, a brief outline of the methodology is in order.

Methodology

This project evolved from an observation of tourism development dynamics on KI. A case study methodology was selected in order to observe the stakeholder dynamics concern-ing the SOL development proposal and to analyse the significance of these events. As Yin claimed, "a case study is an empirical enquiry that investigates a contemporary phe-nomenon within its real-life context, especially when the boundaries between phenomenon and context are not clearly evident" (1994, p. 13).

This project used the case study technique to corroborate narratives and triangulate the data by reviewing documentary evidence, interviews and using a reflexive research technique. Primary documents included government policies and plans; development ap-plication materials; public, government agency and non-government agency submissions to the planning approval process; government documents obtained through freedom of information requests; and letters to the editor written to the local newspaper when the development proposal was under consideration. In 2009, 26 focused interviews were conducted either face-to-face, via telephone or via email with stakeholders, including the developer, community members both in favour of the development and against it, representatives of government agencies who contributed to the planning approval process, former members of the KI Council, politicians, KI tourism operators, environmentalists and experts who participated in these events.

One weakness of this research project was that the interviews were conducted some two years after the SOL received conditional approval and almost one year after it opened. This made locating participants in these events somewhat difficult, their memories potentially less accurate and the ability to piece together events retrospectively more problematic. On the contrary, the passions and the anger felt by some remained surprisingly fresh. A small number of potential informants declined to be interviewed. For instance, one opponent of the development declined an interview, stating that it would bring up distressing memories that s/he wished to avoid. Also, it must be mentioned that the KI Council prohibited interviewing of any of its current staff and councillors, claiming that the people sought for interview had had "very little to do with the decisions on this matter. It was a major project status and hence was not ultimately Council's decision" (email communication from Carmel Noon, CEO of KI Council, February 17, 2009). Former members of the KI Council have disputed this interpretation, thereby indicating the political sensitivity of this research project. Because interviewees living in such a small community would be easily identifiable by their roles, it was decided that participants would not be interviewed under conditions of anonymity. Permission was obtained to cite informants verbatim and to have such citations attributed, and a right to preview such citations was offered to all informants.

Conducting research in such contested circumstances, when passions and suspicions run high, is neither easy nor unproblematic. However, the rich results yielded by this research proved worth the time and difficulties that had to be overcome to engage these diverse stakeholders in an interview process that collected their narratives of tourism development and of the tourism governance processes.

The development of Southern Ocean Lodge

The $10 million development proposal for the SOL included 25 accommodation suites and associated facilities, including a main lodge, spa retreat and staff village, created on one hectare of cleared land (Planning South Australia, 2005, p. 5) (Figure 1). The site was flanked by Flinders Chase National Park to the west and the Kelly Hill Caves Conservation Park and Cape Bouger Wilderness Protection Area to the east (Figure 2). The development area was situated in the Coastal Landscape Zone on the western end of the island between two conservation zones.

The SOL development proposal was described as being a "major new development proposal which would provide a premium nature based tourism experience for Kangaroo Island" (Major Developments Panel, 2005, p. 5). Award-winning, locally born architect Max Pritchard was engaged to design the development, which he promised would be a "model development in South Australia ... [with] nothing like it in existence anywhere in the State" (The Islander, 2005, pp. 1–2). Its design and luxurious features were intended to attract more exclusive clientele from overseas and around Australia to South Australia's only six star resort.[1] The ecological features of its pristine location were the key assets the SOL developers hoped to capitalise on:

Figure 1.   Site plan of the proposed SOL development (used with the permission of Max Pritchard, architect).

> Floating atop a secluded cliff on a rugged stretch of coast, the lodge commands peerless views of the wild Southern Ocean and pristine Kangaroo Island wilderness. Sensitive, intimate and sophisticated, Southern Ocean Lodge is a sanctuary of refined comfort and luxe, Kangaroo Island style. (SOL, n.d.b)

It was originally estimated that the development would represent a capital investment of $10 million and once in operation would sustain 20 jobs (Major Developments Panel, 2005).

It is important to view this proposed development against the provisions of the *KI Development Plan*. The sections of the Plan focused on tourism development and the coastal landscape zone set the context for a development of the type proposed. The Plan states that "tourist developments should not be located within areas of conservation value, indigenous cultural value, high landscape quality or significant scenic beauty", and these "should not require substantial modification to the landform, particularly in visually prominent locations", and when "outside townships should . . . not result in the clearance of valuable native vegetation" (KI Council, 2009, p. 59). The site selected for the SOL was situated in the Coastal Landscape Zone which specifies non-complying tourism development would exceed 25 "tourist accommodation units" and be within 100 metres of the high-tide mark. The SOL proposal stayed just within the limits of these provisions. However, with plans to clear one hectare of native vegetation and an added seven staff accommodation units included in the plan, debate on whether the proposal was compliant with the spirit of the *KI Development Plan* was inevitable.

It is also important to note the results of a 2004 resident survey entitled "Mapping the future of Kangaroo Island" by Brown and Hale, which found:

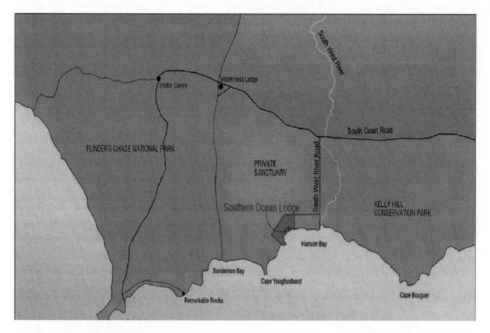

Figure 2.   Site map of the proposed Southern Ocean Lodge development (used with the permission of the developer, James Baillie).

> When asked about developing visitor accommodation "in a limited number of coastal strategic locations provided they are attractively situated, small to medium scale, and achieve excellence in environmental design and management", about 62 percent of respondents believe this is a good idea while 33 percent believe it is a bad idea. Given the highly favourable wording of this question toward coastal development, it is significant that one-third of residents still oppose any future tourism development in the coastal zones. *Any tourism development in the coastal zone, even if supported by the majority of KI residents, will likely meet significant opposition.* (2005, p. 3, emphasis added)

These observations foreshadowed the contentious climate that would engulf the SOL development proposal.

Baille Lodges planned to submit a development application to the KI Council's Development Assessment Panel by the end of 2004. However, considerable opposition arose because of the development's site in a pristine area of the island. In June 2005, the proposed development of the SOL was declared a "major development" by the Minister for Urban Development and Planning. As a result, the proposal was removed from the local development approval process and placed in the South Australian state government's development approval process under Section 46 of the Development Act 1993. This occurs when the Minister "believes such a declaration appropriate or necessary for proper assessment of the proposed development, and where the proposal is considered to be of major economic, social or environmental importance" (Planning South Australia, 2007). Once the Minister declares a proposal a "major development", the development proposal is referred to an independent statutory authority, the Development Assessment Commission. For a diagram showing the full assessment process for "major developments" in South Australia, see Figure 3.

The Development Assessment Commission determines the level of assessment that is required for the proposal, and it issues formal assessment guidelines. The three possible levels of assessment that can be required are:

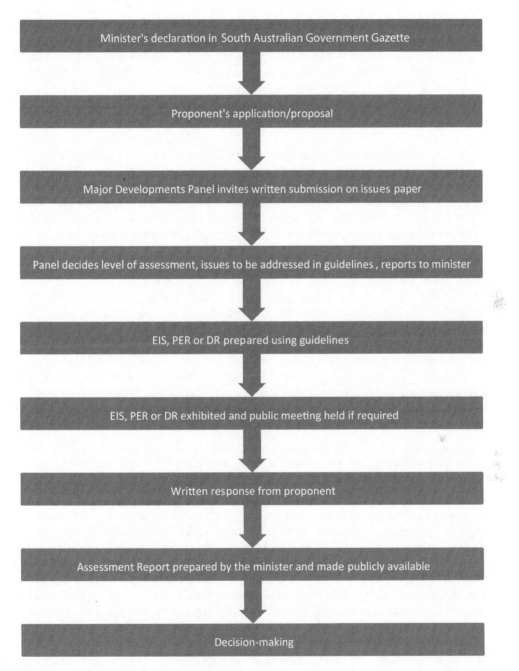

Figure 3.   Major developments or projects – assessment processes and decision-making (Planning South Australia, 2007).

- Environmental Impact Statement (EIS) – required for the most complex proposals, where there is a wide range of issues to be investigated in depth;
- Public Environmental Report (PER) – sometimes referred to as a "targeted EIS", required where the issues surrounding the proposal need investigation in depth but are narrower in scope and relatively well known;
- Development Report (DR) – the least complex level of assessment, which relies principally on existing information (Planning South Australia, 2007).

In January 2006, the Development Assessment Commission determined that a PER level of assessment was appropriate for the development proposal and released the guidelines to the proponent, which set out what issues the PER should address. The choice of a PER over an EIS assessment process was a major source of controversy in the assessment process.

In January 2006, the KI Council voiced "its first protest over the proposed SOL development" and passed a resolution informing the State Government that a PER level of environmental assessment was insufficient and a full EIS was necessary (*The Islander*, 2006a). Planning South Australia responded that a PER was sufficient because "the proposal and its associated activities are relatively 'limited in scale' and that a wide range of issues did not require significant investigation" (*The Islander*, 2006b). One of the KI councillors was described as stating that the "State Government had taken the project out of the council's hands by declaring it a Major Development" and that "he spoke for a large number of people who were not necessarily against the proposed six-star development, just the site they had chosen" (*The Islander*, 2006a).

In April 2006, the proponent of the development released the PER for six weeks of public comment. Two hundred and twenty-three submissions were received from the public, with 11 of these from government agencies and the council. As the developer's Response Report states:

> 10 were in full support of the proposal, nine raised issues or made comment on the proposal but were not opposed, 11 were in favour of the proposal if it were in a different location on Kangaroo Island and 193 were opposed to the proposal. (SOL, 2006)

Despite this level of community opposition to the proposed development at the site and the concern voiced by key government agencies, such as the Department of Environment and Heritage (DEH) and the Native Vegetation Council (NVC), during the PER consultation process, the project proposal was approved following the recommendation of the minister in mid-October 2006.

Significant to this outcome was the role of the South Australian Tourism Commission (SATC) that supported the development proposal and helped the developers navigate the planning approval process (SATC, 2007, p. 28).[2] This difference in governmental departmental positions is not surprising and provides one example of bureaucratic politics in tourism governance. Rather than focusing on these issues, this analysis will examine the dialogues and trade-offs that resulted as stakeholders weighed up the requirements of environmental protection versus the promises of this ecotourism development.[3]

Environmental trade-offs in ecotourism development

It is undisputed that the area proposed for development is one of spectacular natural beauty. Indeed, Baillie noted that when he first investigated the site in 2002 he mistakenly assumed it must be part of the national park: "I still remember saying to Hayley: wow this would be the most amazing spot for a lodge if it wasn't national park, because I just assumed that's where it was" (James Baillie, personal communication, May 29, 2009).[4] As Bill Haddrill of the Department of Environment and Heritage (DEH) described the site:

> it was and remains one of the most intact sections of natural environment on Kangaroo Island. The site sits directly between Flinders Chase National Park and Kelly Hills Conservation Park in a fantastic corridor between those areas and one of the most intact sections of the coastline. (personal communication, May 25, 2009)

It was these very qualities that were the issue, as the former Chair of the NVC noted, "the SOL application advocated clearance in an absolutely pristine area and this was the biggest problem, because the Native Vegetation Act had no capacity to authorise clearance of pristine native vegetation. That is exactly the vegetation we were set up to protect" (John Roger, personal communication, May 29, 2009). It was widely recognised by both critics and supporters alike that the Baillies had credentials in developing environmentally sensitive resorts; the concern was with their choice of this unspoilt location.

According to the acting executive officer of the NVC:

> The agency and myself . . . provided consistent advice to the proponents that an application to clear native vegetation lodged under Section 28 of the Native Vegetation Act would be very difficult for the NVC to approve in recognition that the native vegetation on site would in all likelihood be considered to be "intact" as defined by the Native Vegetation Act. The Act prevents the NVC from granting consent to the clearance of substantially intact native vegetation. The Native Vegetation Regulations 2003 provide a mechanism for the clearance of intact native vegetation only in specific circumstances. (Craig Whisson, personal communication, June 12, 2009)

The only way to avoid the prohibition of native vegetation clearance that the Native Vegetation Act stipulated was to have the proposed development declared a "major development" so that Regulation 5(1)(c) could be invoked, allowing "clearance associated with a Major Project" (Craig Whisson, personal communication, June 12, 2009). Once the development was declared a "major development", the role of the NVC became limited to:

> providing comment on the Public Environment Report document prepared consistent with the declaration of the development as a Major Project under Section 48 of the Development Act 1993 ensuring that any clearance of native vegetation for a development approved by the Governor would be: "undertaken in accordance with a management plan that has been approved by the NVC that results in a significant environmental benefit". (Craig Whisson, personal communication, June 12, 2009)

Craig Whisson described the process and outcomes regarding the establishment of the "significant environmental benefit" in accordance with the provisions of Section 21(6) of the Native Vegetation Act:

> The outcome was negotiated between the NVC and the proponent following the site inspection by the NVC and a meeting with the proponent. The Significant Environment Benefit involved the protection of the balance of the vegetation on the land owned by the developer being safeguarded under the terms of a Heritage Agreement, and the establishment of a fund to finance conservation projects on Kangaroo Island. (personal communication, June 12, 2009)

This fund was called the SOL Environment Fund, which the developer suggested might deliver between $20,000 to $50,000 (partly funded by visitor tariffs) per annum over the life of a 10-year agreement for KI environmental projects. A board made up of representatives of DEH, KI Natural Resources Management, NVC and the SOL manages the fund. According to the Tourism Minister Jane Lomax-Smith, "the Environment Fund is a great example of the mutually beneficial alliance that can be achieved between tourism and conservation" (Rann, 2007). Baillie was likewise quoted as stating that the agreement set a "new benchmark for public/private collaboration in SA and demonstrates how tourism could benefit conservation" (Rann, 2007). Similarly, David Crinion of SATC stated:

> SATC regards SOL to be an excellent model of new private development contributing benefits to the natural environment – a characteristic of eco-tourism. This is consistent with SATC and DEH's Responsible Nature-based Tourism Strategy. It is particularly important as a model in light of the increasing needs and diminishing public resources for environmental management. (personal communication, June 9, 2009)

The DEH found itself in similar circumstances to the NVC, playing its prescribed role in the policy process:

> The department certainly provided comments in relation to the likely impact of the clearance of native vegetation required for the construction of the development. Our comments were objective, based on what would be the direct loss of native vegetation and what impact that might have on particularly our threatened species, our flora and fauna and impact on the landscape. (Bill Haddrill, personal communication, May 25, 2009)

It is also significant that the development proposal triggered the provisions of the Environment Protection and Biodiversity Conservation Act 1999 as a "controlled action" because it had potential impact on nationally threatened species. However, rather than running its own assessment process, the Commonwealth Department of Environment and Heritage accredited the process of the PER run by the South Australian government. On 20 December 2006, the development received approval to proceed under the Environment Protection and Biodiversity Conservation Act.

Whatever environmental concerns DEH and NVC may have had about the SOL, the professional practice of public service within the processes of governance requires a neutral approach in all interactions:

> It's really important to note that whatever the decision . . . the best outcome ongoing into the future is for an organisation such as DEH to work with SOL. You know, once the approval was provided, we could have quite easily turned our backs on it and said "We don't agree" or "We don't approve of the approvals process – we're walking away and not having anything to do with it"; far from that. The best thing for us to do is to work with SOL and we continued to work with SOL through the construction phase . . . that was the change in mindset that we took and that has stood both us and SOL well in continuing to work with them. (Bill Haddrill, personal communication, May 25, 2009)

As evidence of this change in mindset, it was agreed to give a 12-month trial of pre-opening access to Seal Bay Conservation Park, a site that allows visitors to walk supervised among Australian sea lions resting on the beach which is their only breeding site on KI. The agreement provided the SOL clients with an "exclusive" experience led by the SOL naturalist, rather than DEH personnel as is the norm. It appears that this access was initially offered exclusively to the SOL but with protest in the newspaper *The Islander* by Fraser Vickery, the tours were opened up to other KI tour operators (Vickery, personal communication, July 15, 2009). DEH has provided a training and accreditation programme to the SOL to ensure it complies with the appropriate practice at this site. Although the offer was opened up to others, so far the SOL is the "only commercial tour operator or accommodation house which is availing themselves of that tour" (Bill Haddrill, personal communication, July 25, 2009). The SOL is charged an additional fee (above the standard entrance fee per person) of $50 per tour group for this access. Given that the Australian sea lion is on the threatened species list under the Environment Protection and Biodiversity Conservation Act, and this new arrangement increases their exposure to human pressures, the concession to the SOL clients is evidence of a shift in attitude in conservation agencies such as DEH away from rigid conservation goals to more tourism-industry-friendly agendas.

Discussion

Whether the SOL is in fact a proper ecotourism ecolodge is open for debate. It certainly is a nature-based facility as its location in a pristine natural environment on the wild Southern Ocean is its key marketing attraction. It also clearly fits Weaver and Lawton's (2007) description of a structured ecotourism experience catering to the softer and more luxury-seeking end of the ecotourism market. Examination of media and marketing materials on the SOL witnesses a change in terminology from ecolodge, to luxury lodge, to wilderness lodge. The advertising for the SOL appears sensitive to walking a fine line between taking advantage of the market for encounters with nature while not actually committing the ecolodge to the rigours of ecotourism criteria. However, government representatives in the SATC clearly wish to promote it as an ecotourism development and to market it as an example of a model of private sector contributions to conservation agendas. If one accepts a notion of an ecotourism spectrum, the SOL clearly sits at the softer end of the spectrum.

Accepting the SOL as a soft version of an ecolodge, this case study analysis suggests that ecotourism, rather than being the win-win situation many present, is in fact a phenomenon that often results in trade-offs between environmental conservation and economic development. In today's context of market-based economies with their demands for economic growth and economic development, it would seem that environmental agencies of governments are often having to compromise on their mandates and negotiate the best outcomes they can as the economic, trade and developmental government agencies hold the upper hand in policy dialogues.

It is in this context that the SOL fund must be understood. The irony that clearance of a pristine site in the middle of a significant wildlife corridor can be allowed because the developer promises to fund environmental projects on the island demonstrates the limitations of the NVC and the native vegetation regulations. As the preceding quote from Crinion of the SATC indicates, environmental agencies are forced to accept such trade-offs because "of the increasing needs and diminishing public resources for environmental management" (personal communication, June 9, 2009). This exclusive access granted to the SOL clients to the sea lions at Seal Bay is perhaps another example of such a trade-off.

Additionally, we see the developers of the SOL appropriating this "environment" fund for their greenwashing purposes. It is clear that the fund was created as a result of the legislative requirements of the Native Vegetation Act to provide a "significant environment benefit" in exchange for permission to clear vegetation on the selected site, and yet the SOL has presented this as the centre of its commitment to environmental sustainability (SOL, n.d.a). Such publicity helps the SOL present its green credentials and works to erase the environmental controversies that engulfed its approval process.

Additionally, Baillie Lodges promotes its "sustainable management policy" in its marketing materials for the SOL, including its brochures and website. This document records SOL's commitment to environmental sustainability by reviewing its design and construction facets and detailing its ongoing energy, waste and water management practices. To its clients, these materials may reassure them that their luxury is not at the expense of the environment, as solar energy systems, organic composting systems and wastewater treatment systems are detailed in the two-page fact sheet (Baillie Lodges, n.d.). But when this is read critically, one can easily identify additional greenwashing. This is done in two ways: poor sustainability practices are overlooked and good practices that were pressed on the developers in the planning approval process are spun for their marketing potential. As an example of the former, the fact sheet fails to discuss the development's reliance on diesel generators that are less than environmentally friendly. As an example of the latter, the SOL development is positioned as a protector of its habitat as the document talks about clearance of only 1% of the 102 hectare property, while the remaining 99% is "protected to guarantee its pristine state for future generations". However, as noted previously, this protection of the remaining vegetation was mandated by the NVC as a condition for their permission to clear native vegetation on the building site to build the lodge – therefore, it could be characterised as disingenuous to present it as evidence of a conservation ethos. In addition, SOL's sustainable management policy notes that the SOL "is situated on an important wildlife corridor between two National Parks" and "encumbrances are now secured on adjoining land limiting future development and protecting the wildlife corridor". No mention is made about how this long, extended ecolodge development with its continuous human occupancy, bright lighting and numerous walking trails interferes with wildlife movement through this special corridor. Also, the document mentions management plans to protect endangered wildlife, such as the much publicised osprey, through "buffer zones and strict access controls, guest awareness programs, signage and ongoing monitoring", but such material also acts to market these endangered fauna as attractions. Despite this apparent care to cordon off these vulnerable birds' nesting sites, a hosted travel journalist boasted she "walked along the clifftop to see an osprey's nest" (Kurosawa, 2008, p. 3).

Taking a more strategic view, one might ask just how important this one ecolodge on these few hectares of pristine bush is? Asked this very question, former Chair of the NVC John Rogers stated:

> When you look at KI as a whole, there is only a relatively small percentage of native vegetation that remains; I believe it is only around ten percent. That is one of the real problems with this part of SA ... The level that you need to retain native species habitat for flora and fauna is a minimum of ten percent. So we cannot keep encroaching on pristine areas with this "death by a thousand cuts" and that is what it is; that's what the NV Act has been set up for. The Act allows for development but it does not allow for further incursion into pristine areas. Because that has already happened; our forefathers already did it and now we are dealing with the remnants. (personal communication, May 29, 2009)

According to KI ecotourism operator and environmentalist Fraser Vickery, the notion that a developer could economically compensate for such vegetation clearance is unacceptable:

> You cannot replace intact stratum that has been cleared by paying money into a fund or revegetating an open paddock, because basically that vegetation [intact stratum] has been untouched pretty much for thousands of years, except for fire and natural processes. So you are actually intervening and destroying something that is priceless; you cannot put a price on pristine habitats on a place like KI. (personal communication, July 15, 2009)

But in a market economy, everything comes to be measured in financial terms and as a result, as Butler (1999b) argues, sustainability comes to mean sustaining tourism and resisting limits imposed on environmental grounds. Placing an economic value on environmental "assets" results in a view that money can be used to compensate when the environment is compromised. However, from an ecological perspective, if these habitats once removed (along with the threatened species they nurture) are irreplaceable, do we understand what we have traded off? Compounding this dilemma is the fact that KI is one zone of tourism development among many around the globe where these "deaths by a thousand cuts" are also occurring on a daily basis. Do we actually know the full extent of our impacts as we accept each ad hoc case oblivious to the larger vantage point? The concept of the precautionary principle is very unlikely to be applied in such circumstances when limits to development are resisted by tourism industry interests and their government collaborators (Fennell & Ebert, 2004, p. 475).

Compounding the gravity of the decision to approve the SOL was the fact that there were alternative sites available to the developers, and opposition would have been greatly reduced if such a site had been selected. As Rogers noted:

> There were sites right next door that were [environmentally] degraded to which we [the NVC] would have given total consent. The problem was they wanted to pick a particular plot because it was the most pristine and had the biggest views. But there was a place right next door that had just about the same views though it was degraded[5] and only a matter of kilometres away from where they finally built SOL. (John Rogers, personal communication, May 29, 2009)

It is clear from this analysis of the SOL development approval process that the balance between economic development and environmental protection is not as easy to achieve as the ecotourism advocates might claim.

Conclusion

We live in an era when the key issue is unsustainable human demands on a finite environment. Although ecotourism promises to deliver economic development while conserving precious environments, we can see in this case study that in an era of reduced government funding and forced public–private sector partnerships in our current neoliberal context, this is not so easily achieved. The interests of business predominate and this plays out in unusual ways for such upmarket "ecolodges". Ecolodges like the SOL appear to be trying to have it both ways. They want the environmental credentials of ecotourism and yet want to attract the profits attained by more mainstream tourism enterprises. Such dynamics is confirmed in the literature; Weaver notes that Couran Cove Resort abandoned its ecotourism origins to diversify its client base as the "ecotourism image was too narrow to sustain a 300-room facility and implied a rusticity that did not reflect the luxurious nature of its product" (2008, p. 167).

More significantly, such structured and luxury-focused ecolodge developments are increasingly driven to be sited directly within the natural resource rather than settling for being based adjacent to it in more degraded locations; this is part of creating a unique experience for discerning and high-spending tourists. Wight warned of such tendencies over a decade ago:

> Resorts (or ecoresorts) certainly have a place in the ecotourism accommodation spectrum, but outside the resource, where they should act as base camps for ecotourists, rather than be located in the heart of pristine areas. Environmentally sensitive construction and operational technologies, and unobtrusive architecture may otherwise be used as a justification for an inappropriate location. (1997, p. 217)

As this study of the SOL development has demonstrated, key provisions intended to secure conservation in environmental legislation can be overturned by other legislation focused on facilitating development. These trade-offs seem to only work one way in our current situation of the market economy – in favour of development at the expense of the environment. Assessing the position of bodies such as the DEH and NVC, it is clear that agencies focused on environmental protection can be compelled to accept limits to their capacities in a time of tighter budgetary constraints, and this limits their impact in the policy debates with their colleagues in the economic agencies of government.

It is clear in such circumstances that environmental conservation will be slowly undermined as ecological interests are traded off in the interest of promoting economic development. For effective implementation of sustainable tourism policies to occur, we all must recognise these dynamics and determine to change contemporary political practice and institute effective and rigorous legislation that actually recognises the precautionary principle and determines to implement meaningful limits to development. This is unlikely to occur when we fail to gain an insight into the bigger picture, which can happen because these developments occur ad hoc and their impacts accrue incrementally. Although case study analyses such as this are helpful in gaining in-depth insights that assist in realising the nature of the challenges we are facing, they in fact work inadvertently to reinforce a focus on the micro-level, which blinds us to the larger dynamics. A dedicated research agenda which investigates the macro-effects of these micro-level decisions is essential to underpin the development of a truly sustainable tourism/ecotourism industry in a future featuring ever greater challenges of resource constraints.

Although governing is usually described as the art of compromise, this case study raises the disconcerting question of whether trade-offs are really an adequate response to protecting a finite environment. If we are in fact succumbing to a future of a "death by a thousand cuts" in our current tourism management practice as suggested by this case study, then sustainable tourism seems to be a vain hope that will continue to elude us.

Notes

1. When the SOL opened its doors on 9 June 2008, it hosted visitors for a minimum two-night stay at a tariff of $900 per night twin share.
2. In the 2006–2007 and 2007–2008 budget cycles, the SATC allocated $1 million for infrastructure for the SOL (Mark Blyth, personal communication, SATC, September 29, 2008).
3. I have examined the policy context and planning approval process for the SOL more fully in a book chapter (Higgins-Desbiolles, 2011).
4. In fact, on its website, the SOL advertising material appears to imply a national park location: "In March 2008 the world-class Southern Ocean Lodge on Kangaroo Island opened as South Australia's new icon. The dramatic coastal national park location, architectural integrity, locally influenced cuisine and personalised interpretive adventures ensures this new entrant immediate success as an international destination of choice" (http://southernoceanlodge.com.au/about.asp).
5. SOL's "environment fund" could have then been used to rehabilitate this degraded site and thereby clearly earned the SOL a reputation for corporate environmental responsibility if this alternative site had been selected.

References

Baillie Lodges. (n.d.). *Baillie Lodges sustainable management policy*. Retrieved December 3, 2010, from http://southernoceanlodge.com.au/downloads.asp

Brown, G., & Hale, S. (2005). *The future of Kangaroo Island*. Retrieved November 7, 2008, from http://www.unisanet.unisa.edu.au/Resources/gregbrown/Greg%20Home%20Page/Research/Australia%20(Kangaroo%20Island)/Survey%20Results/Final%20Survey%20Results%20Summary%20(PDF).pdf.

Buckley, R. (2004). Partnerships in ecotourism: Australian political frameworks. *International Journal of Tourism Research*, 6(2), 75–83.

Butler, R.W. (1999a). Sustainable tourism: A state-of-the-art review. *Tourism Geographies*, *1*(1), 7–25.

Butler, R.W. (1999b). Tourism: An evolutionary perspective. In J.G. Nelson, R. Butler, & G. Wall (Eds.), *Tourism and sustainable development: A civic approach* (pp. 33–62). Waterloo, Ontario: University of Waterloo.

Ceballos-Lascuráin, A.H. (2001). *Comments to IYE 2002 International Ecotourism forum*. Retrieved May 15, 2001, from http://groups.yahoo.com/group/iye2002/message60

Ceballos-Lascuráin, A.H. (2003). Preface. In M. Luck and T. Kirstges (Eds.), *Global ecotourism policies and case studies: Perspectives and constraints* (pp. viii–xii). Clevedon: Channel View Publications.

Fennell, D.A., & Ebert, K. (2004). Tourism and the precautionary principle. *Journal of Sustainable Tourism*, *12*(6), 461–479.

Higgins, B.R. (2001). Tour operators. In D.B. Weaver (Ed.), *The encyclopedia of ecotourism* (pp. 535–548). Wallingford: CABI.

Higgins-Desbiolles, F. (2011). Development on Kangaroo Island: The controversy over Southern Ocean Lodge. In D. Dredge & J. Jenkins (Eds.), *Stories of practice: Tourism planning and policy* (pp. 105–131). London: Ashgate.

Honey, M. (1999). *Ecotourism and sustainable development: Who owns paradise?* Washington, DC: Island Press.

Jack, L. (n.d.). *Development and application of the Kangaroo Island TOMM*. Retrieved November 19, 2010, from http://www.regional.org.au/au/countrytowns/options/jack.htm

Jack, L., & Duka, T. (n.d.). *Kangaroo Island tourism optimization management model*. Retrieved August 5, 2008, from www.sustainabletourism.com.au/pdf_docs/tomm_aug31.pdf

KI Council. (2009). *KI Development Plan*. Retrieved May 5, 2009, from http://www.planning.sa.gov.au/edp/pdf/KI.PDF

Kurosawa, S. (2008, May 31). Sunrise with sea lions. *The Australian*. Retrieved December 2, 2010, from http://www.southernoceanlodge.com.au/press/TheWeekendAustralianJun089639.pdf

Lee, D.R. (2007). Environment-development tradeoffs: A developing country perspective. In J. Pretty, A. Ball, T. Benton, & J. Guivant (Eds.), *The Sage handbook of environment and society* (pp. 181–190). London: Sage.

Lynch, H. (1996). *Kangaroo Island tourism case study*. Canberra: CSIRO Division of Wildlife and Ecology. Retrieved March 3, 2009, from http://www.environment.gov.au/biodiversity/publications/series/paper9/appnd2_5.html

Major Developments Panel. (2005, September). *Issues paper: Southern Ocean Lodge, Hanson Bay, Kangaroo Island proposal*. Adelaide: Planning South Australia.

McLaren, D. (2003). *Rethinking tourism and ecotravel* (2nd ed.). Bloomfield, CT: Kumarian.

Miller, G., & Twining-Ward, L. (2005). Tourism optimization management model. In G. Miller & L. Twining-Ward (Eds.), *Monitoring for a sustainable tourism transition* (pp. 201–232). Wallingford: CABI.

Mowforth, M., & Munt, I. (2003). *Tourism and sustainability: Development and new tourism in the Third World* (2nd ed.). London: Routledge.

Page, S.J., & Dowling, R.K. (2002). *Ecotourism*. Harlow: Pearson.

Planning South Australia (2005). *Information sheet: "Southern Ocean Lodge" proposal at Hanson Bay, Kangaroo Island*. Retrieved March 1, 2008, from http://www.planning.sa.gov.au/index.cfm?objectId=B0D6F25D-96B8-CC2B-63BE28584A11F809

Planning South Australia (2007). *Assessment processes for proposals declared major developments and how to have your say*. Retrieved March 1, 2008, from http://www.planning.sa.gov.au/index.cfm?objectId=B0D6F25D-96B8-CC2B-63BE28584A11F809

Rann, M.(Premier of South Australia). (2007, March 16). *Kangaroo Island to benefit from environment fund [media release]*. Retrieved May 4, 2009, from http://www.ministers.sa.gov.au/news.php?id=1381&print=1

Report of the Brundtland Commission. (1987). *Our common future*. Oxford: Oxford University Press.

Richardson, J. (1993). *Ecotourism and nature-based holidays*. Sydney: Simon and Schuster.

Shaw, G., & Williams, A.M. (2002). *Critical issues in tourism: A geographical perspective* (2nd ed.). Oxford: Blackwell.

SOL. (n.d.a). Managing our wilderness footprints. Sustainable management policy brochure.

SOL. (n.d.b). *Southern Ocean Lodge website*. Retrieved May 3, 2009, from http://southernoceanlodge.com.au/

SOL. (2006). *SOL public environmental report response document* [prepared by Parsons Brinckerhoff on behalf of Baillie Lodges]. Retrieved from www.planning.sa.gov.au/.../publications/Southern%20Ocean%20Lodge%20Response%20Document%20txt.pdf.

South Australian Tourism Commission. (2007). *SATC 2006*. Retrieved March 1, 2008, from http://www.tourism.sa.gov.au/Publications/Ann_Rep_06_07.pdf

The Islander. (2005, August 11). Full steam ahead for $10m "Lodge". pp. 1–2.

The Islander. (2006a, January 27). *Council protest on lodge*. Retrieved May 27, 2009, from http://kangarooisland.yourguide.com.au/news/local/news/general/council-protest-on-lodge/362531.aspx

The Islander. (2006b, March 16). *Council slams "cop out" response*. Retrieved June 5, 2009, from http://kangarooisland.yourguide.com.au/news/local/news/general/council-slams-cop-out-response/183180.aspx

Wall, G. (1997). Is ecotourism sustainable? *Environmental Management, 21*(4), 483–491.

Weaver, D. (2008). *Ecotourism* (2nd ed.). Milton, Queensland: John Wiley.

Weaver, D.B., & Lawton, L.J. (2007). Twenty years on: The state of contemporary ecotourism research. *Tourism Management, 28*(5), 1168–1179.

Wheeller, B. (2005). Ecotourism/egotourism and development. In C.M. Hall & S. Boyd (Eds.), *Nature-based tourism in peripheral areas: Development or disaster?* (pp. 263–272). Clevedon: Channel View.

Wight, P.A. (1997). Ecotourism accommodation spectrum: Does supply match the demand? *Tourism Management, 18*(4), 209–220.

Yin, R.K. (1994). *Case study research: Design and methods* (2nd ed.). Thousand Oaks, CA: Sage.

Climate change pedagogy and performative action: toward community-based destination governance

Tazim Jamal[a] and E. Melanie Watt[b]

[a]Department of Recreation, Park and Tourism Sciences, Texas A&M University, College Station, Texas, USA; [b]Biosphere Institute of the Bow Valley, Canmore, Alberta, Canada

Despite urgent sustainability imperatives, tourism providers and destination managers are slow to undertake initiatives that enable: (1) an informed public (tourists) and (2) an engaged citizenry (residents) to manage resource use, conservation and climate change. This paper draws on concepts from two renowned political theorists, Carole Pateman and Hannah Arendt, and especially from Arendt's theory of human action, which offers insights for a *performative* and pluralistic theory of civic engagement, multi-stakeholder learning and collaboration. It helps to explore emerging forms of participatory action and climate change pedagogy in the mountain resort of Canmore (Canada), facilitated by the Biosphere Institute, a local nongovernmental organization, that indicate a strong potential. The Mountain Air program involves schoolchildren and businesses in tackling clean air and idling impacts from local transport (including taxis used by visitors). The results of a door-to-door community social marketing campaign, Sustainable Action Canmore, are also discussed. Detailed and ongoing requirements of participatory action are described, and the results of the two programs are analyzed. Links between governance for tourists and residents are explained, and potential lessons for destination managers discussed. In addition, the paper notes the relevance of the Natural Step program, a comprehensive model for planning sustainable development in complex systems.

Introduction

Globalization and the trans-national mobilities of capital, finance, labor, migrations and travel have vastly increased the complexity of tourism destination governance. Even greater challenges lie ahead with respect to climate change and sustainability. Tourism research in those fields is focusing on adaptation and mitigation strategies, and policies based on sustainable production and consumption (e.g. Becken & Hay, 2007), but attention is surprisingly lacking on the roles and responsibilities of destination managers (including local government, national park services and destination marketing organizations) toward engaging both residents and visitors in sustainable destination management. Newly formed partnerships and initiatives are emerging to fill this void but, as illustrated below, significant pedagogic action is needed in order to facilitate an informed and involved civil society. New theoretical paradigms are also required to address emerging forms of civic engagement and pedagogic action at the local destination level.

This paper focuses on local-level participatory governance for sustainable destination management, with respect to resource use, behavioral change, conservation, and climate change. It draws its framework and direction from the work of two important political theorists, Carole Pateman and Hannah Arendt, both relatively unknown in tourism studies. It links local resident governance with tourism governance. It takes, as a case study in good practice, the resort town of Canmore, Alberta, Canada, where a hybrid form of governance appears to be emerging, aided by a local nongovernmental organization (NGO), the Biosphere Institute of the Bow Valley, that is applying community-based pedagogic approaches to inform and involve full-time residents, as well as short and long-term visitors, in sustainability initiatives. It illustrates the detail and complexities involved in engaging local people and tourists in participatory governance.

The paper argues in its first section that Hannah Arendt's political theory of action offers a *performative* approach to understand and improve local governance, civic participation and public pedagogy to address critical issues like climate change. The second section offers a critique of local participation related to various global sustainability initiatives and reveals the need to re-examine participatory governance and collaborative action. The Canmore case study and related theoretical discussion offers insights for future research and theory building on sustainable destination governance and collaborative action learning related to climate change management. The conclusion links the theory and practice in the paper to wider issues and change in tourism destination governance.

Political perspectives on governance and participatory democracy

The term "governance" has undergone a metamorphosis over the years, from traditional notions of governance used in the context of political governance by government, to broader notions of the political as involving multiple stakeholders actively engaged in the task of influencing government policy and rule, or in the control and management of specific domains. Recent applications of this broader notion include "forest governance" such as Nepal's Community Forest Program, wherein Community Forest User groups have been organized nationally to enable local people to directly participate in the control and management of over a million hectares of forested land (Ojha, 2006). As Ojha, Persha, and Chhatre (2009) explained, the development of a strong civil society network was critical to the success of community forestry, and a technocratic, interventionist approach has given way to a collaborative learning process and participatory decision-making.

It is certainly not unreasonable in a participatory theory of democracy to claim that the necessary condition for establishing a democratic polity is a participatory society, as political theorist Carole Pateman (1970), now a distinguished professor at the UCLA, puts forward. Participatory theory argues that the experience of participation itself will develop and foster the qualities needed for a successful democratic system, that is, a "democratic" personality. As Pateman (1970) points out, it is unlikely that the average citizen would be as interested in national level decisions as in local ones closer to home, but the important point here is that direct participation opens avenues to become an educated, public citizen in addition to a private individual. The existence of a participatory society at the local level, therefore, means better civic ability to appreciate the connectedness of the public and private spheres, and to assess and weigh decisions of national level representatives who impact a citizen's everyday life and environment (Pateman, 1970). Pateman draws on Jean

Jacques Rousseau's educative theory of democracy (taking education in the broadest sense) to support this participatory perspective. Rousseau's political theory saw multiple benefits in doing so, including an integrative function in which citizens would more strongly feel that they belonged to their community, and would also feel (and actually be) free (Pateman, 1970). Participation affords the opportunity for control over one's life and environment, for though "man is born free, everywhere he is in chains" (Rousseau, 1762/1902).

In addition to the freedom dimension, Rousseau also felt that the participation of civic society was especially important to ensure that the government addressed the general will of the public (i.e. public interest),[1] and would not have it co-opted by scientific, technical or other rule by experts (Habermas, 1978, 1984, addresses this in his work on knowledge constitutive interests and communicative action in the public sphere). The above views offer fuller theoretical insights into the popular planning reference to Arnstein's (1969) ladder of participation, wherein Arnstein argues for full and direct involvement in decision-making in the planning domain (rather than risk tokenism or exclusion of key interests in "consultation" processes). What Arnstein's ladder does not address is the characteristic of such participation and power relations involved, nor the precursors to effective participation. Participation enables the possibility of genuine civic freedom, belonging and expression, as Pateman and Rousseau advance in the discussion above, and opportunity to understand the intersections between the public and the private spheres. Governance refers to "a set of rules, norms, procedures and practices that determines how power is exercised, for what purpose, and how it is shared and weighed during decision-making" (United Nations, 2005, p. 17). Involving the poor and the marginalized (including minority groups) fairly and equitably into the socioeconomic decision-making processes of the state, and allowing for difference are essential to good governance (United Nations, 2005), but what factors enable (or prevent) good governance? More specifically, what qualities and capacities are needed to develop a participatory civil society?

In her influential treatise, *The Human Condition,* political theorist Hannah Arendt (1958/1998) forwarded a participatory politics whose characteristics are detailed in her theory of human action. The public space of action is a *performative* space that must be continually created by action, when actors come together to discuss, deliberate or undertake some common project. It comes into being through the performance of deeds or utterance of words in the *vita activa* (the world of human action), a practice that presupposes and is actualized through interaction and *speech* with others, and establishes itself through the "web" of human relationships and interests that lie between people. Arendt emphasizes this in terms of *inter-esse* (or *inter-est* as translated in Arendt, 1998, pp. 182–183), which lies between people and can therefore bind them together (Arendt, 1998, p. 182).

Hannah Arendt was born in Germany in 1906, moving later to the USA, and became the first woman at the USA's prestigious and fourth-oldest University, Princeton, to be appointed to a full professorship. She died in 1975. She championed a participatory politics that stresses plurality and freedom as conditions that correspond to action. To act is to take the initiative and to introduce something new and unexpected, and cannot be done independently of the presence of a plurality of actors who, as human beings, are sufficiently alike to understand one another but yet uniquely different with their own perspective and biographies.[2] A proper political view of the world is therefore pluralistic, relativistic and sensitive to difference (see Young, 1995). "This kind of understanding – seeing the world (as we rather tritely say today) from the other fellow's point of view – is the political insight par excellence" (Arendt, 1990, p. 84, as cited in Dolan, 2000, p. 268). Arendt disagreed with Rousseau's point on politicians implementing the "general will" of the people, as she felt it important to address and nurture plural, diverse perspectives – arguments among these may be agonistic and polemic, but must rise above the mere clash of interests to engage in performative action, through dialogue, rational persuasion and consent (Disch, 1994; Villa, 2000).[2]

Action and speech or dialogue are thus closely related for Arendt, and are central to her characterization of power. Power springs up between people who act in concert through words and deeds; it is not the property of an individual but rather that of a plurality of people who come together *freely* to initiate something new, and the outcomes of their actions are not based on violence but on consent and rational persuasion.[3] Human beings do not possess freedom, rather, they have the capacity to initiate, to begin and to act – hence, for Arendt, to be free and to act are synonymous. It is this capacity to initiate that makes freedom a performative aspect of doing and acting, and distinguishes genuine action from behavior that is rote, habituated, regulated or automated (Yar, 2001/2005). Freedom is located in the social (household and society) and enacted in action (*praxis*) in the public space of appearance (Arendt, 1998, p. 195).

Arendt also emphasizes the importance of narrative in human action (via speech and words in deeds and performance). Action, as constituted through the web of human relationships, "produces" stories with or without intention, enabling retrospective insight and sources of inspiration for the future (Arendt, 1998, p. 184). Arendt is drawing on the Greek *polis* here, to argue for the importance of developing forms of remembrance and "communities of memory", wherein organized remembrance can take place, as every citizen can engage freely in that participatory space of action and speech, be a witness and a potential narrator, and leave a record or a testament for future generations of the outcomes of their communicative acts. The Arendtian *polis*, however, is not the city-state in its physical location; it is "the organization of the people as it arises out of acting and speaking together, and its true space lies between people living together for this purpose, no matter where they happen to be" (Arendt, 1998, p. 198).

Arendt's *performative* approach to participatory democracy along with Pateman's (1970) perspectives offer theoretical insights and support for direct civic involvement and collective deliberation to influence policy and planning (see Arnstein, 1969) with respect to "public interest" (in this case, the public good – its wellbeing as related to sustainability and climate change).[4] Arendt's theory of action alerts us to closely examine the nature and character of civic participation in destination governance and management of "public interest" as related to climate change and resource sustainability. The insights from the above sections comport well with the Canmore case described in detail further below, wherein a local NGO, drawing funding from local government and other stakeholders, is implementing community-based, participatory initiatives to engage residents, resident tourists and other tourism stakeholders in sustainability and climate change management. Action with respect to deeds and performance is occurring in the public (community spaces), such as in the *Mountain Air* program and the *Mountain Idle* movie made by schoolchildren acting in concert, and on the thresholds between public and private spheres (in a dialogue on the doorstep of local residents) in the *Sustainable Action Canmore* (SAC) social marketing exercise.[5] In these various community initiatives, the conditions of freedom and plurality, and characteristics of dialogue, rational persuasion, storytelling and remembrance for future generations (via the formation of movies, website portals and on-line documents) are evident. These also make evident the potential for the participants to engage further in participatory political action, through being directly involved and better informed in climate change and sustainability management.

A number of global initiatives have paved the way for such local participation in destination development, planning and policy setting. Several initiatives that are directly pertinent to sustainable destination management and climate change governance are summarized briefly below. Together with the above theoretical discussion, they help to ground the subsequent discussion on civic involvement and stakeholder collaboration in Canmore, Canada, which has historically experienced prolonged conflict over resort development and population growth, and is engaging actively and creatively in sustainability action.

Sustainable destination governance and local participation

A brief look at the sustainability discourses since the Brundtland Commission's foundational report on sustainable development, entitled "Our Common Future" (World Commission on Environment and Development [WCED], 1987), provides some historical context to both progress and omissions in destination sustainability and local governance. The Brundtland Commission's influential report was aimed at balancing economic/business and environmental issues in sustainable development; the World Tourism Organization (UNWTO, 2004) framed sustainable tourism development very similarly in terms of aspiring toward a "suitable balance" between economy, environment and social–cultural aspects, but did little to address implementation or governance. The 1992 United Nations Conference on Environment and Development held in Rio de Janeiro ("the Rio Summit") subsequently established *Agenda 21* to implement sustainable development, followed by *Local Agenda 21*, which focused on local-level implementation of the sustainable development agenda, along with a procedural goal of encouraging local participation in sustainability-related planning and decision-making. Feichtinger and Pregernig (2005) discovered varying modes of Local Agenda 21 implementation, including deliberative and expert-led approaches. Study of Local Agenda 21 and the role of local government indicate that successful movement toward local sustainability will require "visionary political leadership, supportive administrations, networks of experience sharing, alliances with nongovernmental organizations and local industry, and effective community mobilization" (Voisey, Beuermann, Sverdrup, & O'Riordan, 1996, p. 33). Subsequent studies indicate that an emphasis on participatory decision-making (community mobilization to act in the public sphere) may be especially important where the benefits (actual or perceived) of sustainability efforts are low (Owen & Videras, 2008).

The 2002 Cape Town Conference on Responsible Tourism (a side event preceding the UN World Summit on Sustainable Development in Johannesburg, which emphasized poverty alleviation) was attended by 280 delegates from 20 countries. The resulting Cape Town Declaration on Responsible Tourism noted the importance of the *local* level and of collaborative governance (http://www.icrtourism.org/Capetown.shtml):

> Recognizing that dialogue, partnerships and multi-stakeholder processes – involving government, business and local communities – to make better places for hosts and guests can only be realized at the local level, and that all stakeholders have different, albeit interdependent, responsibilities; tourism can only be managed for sustainability at the destination level.

But even this declaration says little about the specific roles and responsibilities of local stakeholders, residents or tourists with respect to destination governance. The challenge is exacerbated by the complexity of the tourism domain, the diversity of stakeholders, values and interests, as well as the scale, scope and interdependencies between sectors and processes involved in travel and tourism. Jamal and Jamrozy (2006) argue that vital destination functions are fragmented rather than well networked, so that marketing, land use planning, resource use and conservation have tended to operate in isolation from each other and from societal values and resident/visitor needs. Some strategic planning and policy efforts toward integrated destination management are indeed being initiated from the local to the global level, but concerted local action is clearly needed to facilitate the emergence of an informed civic society and participatory public sphere to assist with sustainable destination governance and the urgencies of climate change.

As Scott and Becken (2010) point out, the Davos Declaration on Climate Change and Tourism declared that climate change "must be considered the greatest challenge to the sustainability of tourism in the 21st century" (UNWTO, 2008, p. 4).

Local climate change action and pedagogy

How does social responsibility, pedagogy and public interest play out in this interrelated, fragmented tourism domain, in which climate change impacts are exacerbating destination complexity and sustainability? Becken and Hay (2007) discuss underlying institutional relationships, policy principles and business practices for managing climate change. Scott and Lemieux (2005, as cited in Becken & Hay, 2007, p. 245) address capacity building and awareness as an important component of a climate change adaptation portfolio for protected areas and agencies. In addition to improved partnerships/collaboration with greater (regional) park ecosystems and in the local–global domain, these authors note the importance of ensuring public acceptance for climate change adaptation. Belle and Bramwell's (2005) survey of tourism managers in Barbados similarly showed that managers showed most support for those strategies to increase public awareness, policy formulation and collaborative work across sectors. However, the general public tends to be poorly involved and poorly informed about the impacts of transportation choices and travel actions in relation to climate change and the destination's carbon footprint (Becken, 2007; Camargo & Jamal, 2009; Eijgelaar, Thaper, & Peeters, 2010; McKercher, Prideaux, Cheung, & Law, 2010).

Earlier in this paper, discussion on local governance and Arendt's political theory of action suggests that destination governance is a *performative* endeavor, enabling a flourishing public sphere of informed stakeholders participating in a joint dialogue and action for sustainability and climate change management. Arendt's political theory of action is especially fitting here as she is a strong proponent of narrative and storytelling that encourage critical understanding, thinking and "visiting" unfamiliar issues – stories that make oneself "less at home in the familiar world" (Disch, 1994, p. 189). The players in the dialogic space are not passive recipients but rather active co-creators of knowledge, understanding and action. From this perspective, it is not a matter of actor "A" (e.g. marketer) influencing "B" (e.g. consumer), but it is a *performative* act involving communicative action and relational power – language, dialogue and negotiation co-construct action and behavior. Agonistic negotiation and debate in such political spaces is seen as potentially positive by Arendt and other political theorists like Bonnie Honig (1993), who recognize both consensus and contestation as important aspects of democratic politics.

Seeing marketing as a performative act reveals the valuable role it can play in destination governance; consider, for instance, the role of *social marketing* to address and encourage action on sustainability issues for societal good. Andreasen (1995), Kotler (2004) and Kotler, Roberto, and Lee (2002), among others, view social marketing as a practical endeavor aimed at obtaining social goods through behavior change.[6] At the local level, a community-based social marketing approach offers significant potential to inform and enable civic engagement and social action for sustainable destination management. At the community level, such a social marketing approach involves identifying barriers and benefits to sustainable behavior, designing a strategy that utilizes behavior change tools, implementing it across the community and subsequently evaluating the program's impacts (McKenzie-Mohr & Smith, 1999). In Arendtian terms, behavior adaptation would be viewed as part of the performative act enabled by participatory engagement in the community social marketing program. The case study of Canmore discussed below illustrates two of a number of initiatives to address sustainability and climate change through community-based social marketing and participatory local action – facilitating joint learning and collaborative governance. The information summarized below is based on participatory action research (Fals-Borda & Rahman, 1991; Reason, 1998), a field in which one of this paper's authors has been directly engaged in fundraising, facilitating and taking management responsibility for much of the work described below.

Social marketing and climate change pedagogy in Canmore

Case setting and background

The mountain community of Canmore is located in the Bow Valley region of Alberta, Canada, about 100 kilometers from the city of Calgary (Figure 1). Canmore is adjacent to the Canadian Rocky Mountain Parks World Heritage Site, which is a UNESCO designated World Heritage Site. Nestled in the front ranges of the Rockies, it shares boundaries with Banff National Park and Kananaskis Country (a provincial park and multi-use area). Canmore is a popular destination for amenity migrants, tourists, recreational day users and second home owners. It experienced a rapid growth of the permanent population in the 1990s followed by a rapid growth of the non-permanent population in the 2000s, which now makes up 32% of its total population of 17,970 persons. "Non-permanent residents" are defined as persons with a permanent address elsewhere who usually occupy the household on a non-permanent basis (2009 Canmore Census). The broadness of this definition means that there is a wide degree of frequencies of visits, that is, some use their recreational property every weekend while others may visit only once per year. The impacts of even these occasionally used homes are not negligible in terms of climate change. The mountain resort of Aspen, USA, which has 57.7% of its homes as second homes, found that 61% of its residential emissions are attributable to second homes. This is partially due to second homes being somewhat larger and having more elaborate appliances that owners tend to leave on during their absence (Heede, 2007).

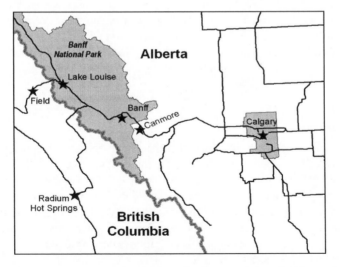

Figure 1.   Location map of Canmore, Alberta (Canada). Source: Adapted with permission from the Biosphere Institution.

Tourism and related activities provide much of Canmore's economic base. There are over 71 kilometres of multi-use trails within the town, while the surrounding regions host the world-class Canmore Nordic Centre, five major ski resorts, hiking, scrambling, climbing, mountain biking, kayaking, canoeing, rafting and many other outdoor activities (see www.tourismcanmore.com).

The Bow Valley, with its visibly receding glaciers, illustrates the tangible effects of climate change. In the near future, climate warming through its effects on glaciers, snowpack and evaporation in combination with cyclic drought and rapidly increasing human activity is predicted to result in a water quality and quantity crisis locally and beyond (Schindler & Donahue, 2006; Scott, 2006). The rapid pace of settlement growth in the Bow Valley and the associated environmental pressures emerged as a significant concern for Bow Valley residents in the late 1980s. In 1995, after years of local debate over resort development and rapid growth, the Town of Canmore's Growth Management Strategy (Town of Canmore, 1995) was formed to develop a collaborative process, which helped confront and resolve many controversial issues. The community-wide Growth Management Committee that was convened to develop the Growth Management Strategy report was an exercise in collaborative governance, and was highly agonistic, to use Arendt's term (Jamal & Getz, 1999). In part, because of this process, the Biosphere Institute of the Bow Valley (www.biosphereinstitute.org) was created, as a nonprofit organization, to serve as a public clearing house for a wide range of ecological, economic and social information pertinent to decisions.

Registered as a nonprofit society in 1997 and awarded charitable status in 2003, the award-winning Biosphere Institute works with all levels of government, industry, a variety of nonprofits and the general public in fulfilling its mission. It is guided by a volunteer Board of Directors from the public, private and nonprofit sectors, and is funded from several sources both for its core activities and its specific projects, including municipal, provincial and national governments, foundations, corporations and individuals. Dedicated to ensuring the ecological integrity of the Bow Valley for the wellbeing of the ecosystem and those who live there, through education, research and outreach, the institute compiles, catalogs and makes accessible ecosystem information through its Canmore resource center, library and website; it facilitates, encourages and coordinates ecological, economic and social research on the region's ecosystem; it supports and implements outreach and education programs that assist individuals, businesses and other organizations to learn about and to adopt ecologically sustainable behaviors; and it facilitates information sharing and analysis in support of collaborative solutions to ecological issues. The Biosphere Institute also works with organizations and communities elsewhere to share methodologies, practices and products developed in the Bow Valley.

Climate change initiatives and local action

In addition to programs on environmental management and visitor education programs (e.g. education to better handle human–wildlife interaction – see its WildSmart program, www.wildsmart.ca), the institute tries to raise community awareness and learning about sustainability issues. Influencing community-wide behaviors is seen as an important step *before* trying to influence policy change in the community. A number of local initiatives had been undertaken by the Biosphere Institute in this regard, some directly related to climate change while others covering broader sustainability issues. Among a host of networking activities, the Biosphere Institute was involved in the Alberta Sustainable Tourism Initiative Working Group in 2009. Government-sponsored programs such as Canada's *One Tonne Challenge* (part of Canada's 2002 Climate Change Plan) resulted in participation of 40 communities (see http://www.trea.ca/one_Ton_challenge.htm). This Environment Canada program challenged each Canadian to reduce their greenhouse gas emissions by one ton of CO_2 or about 20% of their current emissions. The Biosphere Institute was the *One-Tonne Challenge* community coordinator for the towns of Banff and Canmore. Residents in these two adjacent mountain communities participated actively in the Challenge, totaling 1% of all Canadians and almost 10% of all Albertans taking on the *One-Tonne Challenge*. The program was highly complementary to the greenhouse gas reduction goals of both the towns of Banff and Canmore.

In addition to federal-level initiatives were local initiatives that helped to inform and engage local government in sustainability action. The Natural Step to a Sustainable Canmore was a program introduced to the community through the Biosphere Institute. This Swedish-based program was aimed to help communities, organizations and individuals to understand, design and implement sustainability-oriented practices and behaviors (see Gill & Williams, 2011 and www.thenaturalstep.org/canada). After a two-day workshop and site visit by the Natural Step program organizers, a $300,000 program commenced in 2004.[7] Municipal staff and early adopters were trained in this program, including Tourism Canmore, the local destination management organization. The Natural Step to a Sustainable Canmore provided a framework for learning, discussion and action. All town employees are introduced to the Natural Step process where it is used as a tool for decision-making. The town has also identified completed, current and future Natural Step initiatives by department, and the Natural Step system conditions are used in capital budget justifications.

Through these programs and many others, the Biosphere Institute has helped inform and involve the community about issues such as climate change, sustainability and ecological integrity. These early national and local-level efforts set the stage for community-wide engagement of youth and adult resident populations in clean air, climate change and direct home-based actions toward more sustainable lifestyles. For this paper, we will focus on two examples of local community level initiatives that involve education, awareness and behavioral change linked to sustainability and climate change that were undertaken. They directly involved local citizenry (residents as well as resident-tourists) as well as key tourism-related stakeholders, notably taxi drivers. Both provided the measured results reported here.

Project funding for these two programs came from a variety of sources, including Natural Resources Canada through its ecoENERGY program, the Calgary Foundation, Alberta Real Estate Foundation and the towns of Banff and Canmore.

The Mountain Air program

The Bow Valley Mountain Air program focused on transportation issues that related to green house gases (GHGs). Six locations in Canmore and Banff that were known for high automobile engine idling times were selected for monitoring. A record was kept of how many cars were idling and the total idling minutes for each time period. Comparisons were made of idling at each location pre-and post-communication campaign. Pledge forms were another method of measurement to determine what specific behaviors individuals would undertake following a series of education events. These included commitments to actions such as regularly checking tire pressure, reducing idling by specific amount per day and reducing driving by specific amount after making carpool connections.

The community-wide communication campaign was purposely multifaceted and was targeted at a variety of audiences, including tourists, part-time and full-time residents, and therefore it was impossible to determine which parts of the campaign caused the specific measurable change. Part of the program included working with taxi services, heavily used by tourists in Banff and Canmore. The Banff Taxis management company displayed IDLE FREE BANFF license plates on all taxis. Through a Biosphere Institute program, taxi company staff received a presentation by a commercial vehicle specialist to discuss biodiesel and other methods of decreasing fleet GHGs. There are many Canmore taxi companies, but at least one put IDLE FREE CANMORE plates on its vehicles. To show both tourists and residents that the municipalities were behind the idle-free initiatives, both the Town of Banff and the Town of Canmore put IDLE FREE plates on all fleet vehicles. Canmore put huge Idle Free signs on its garbage trucks. The Town of Banff put up 6 feet tall IDLE FREE banners along the main street at the entrance to town. Local businesses and schools also placed idle-free signs at locations throughout the community. The Town of Canmore put many "Turn off engine" signs by railway crossings and other high idle places. Canmore even put a large sign under the big Welcome to Canmore sign at the town entrance that said: *Canmore is an Idle Free Community*.

To capitalize on customer loyalty, the Biosphere Institute also made business-specific anti-idle signs for local businesses that have quite a "weekender" following, including the movie rental shop and coffee shops and convenience store (i.e. "The Summit Cafe would like you to turn your engine off when you come in to enjoy our coffee"). To specifically educate tourists, the Biosphere Institute made rear-view mirror hangers for rental car agencies and gas stations that included specific actions which tourist could take to reduce their GHG emission while visiting the destination community (i.e. reduce idling time, use a block heater in cold weather, reduce speed, drive less aggressively).

The Biosphere Institute's 2008/2009 Bow Valley Mountain Air Program activities thus included anti-idle programs, anti-idle signs and license plates, a speakers' series, a walk to school program, carpool linkages and efficient driving education. In addition, youth involvement in developing environmental films and videos was sought. The anti-idle programs included working with students from a local Middle School on monitoring idling vehicles before and after a community-wide communication campaign, producing radio spots, an anti-idling song contest and production of the student-made *Mountain Idle*. Students collectively explored and jointly came to share their understandings of climate change, engaging in storytelling and developed a nine-minute film narrative (enabling Arendt's notion of future remembrance). The film can be viewed on: http://www.youtube.com/watch?v=xt8x6M20Hvo&feature=player_embedded

Collaborative learning is also evident in this process, indicated by comments following the main story lines shown in the video:

> If everyone in Canada cut their idling time by 3 minutes a day that would save $630 million per year!

> If you idle – you might as well shred your money.

Total measured reductions of GHGs for all components of the program, including pledged commitments, and actual measured reductions, such as comparison of idling at specific locations, were over 69 tonnes per year.

Measured results also include number of minutes of idling reduced at the six specific locations surveyed both before and after the anti-idling campaign. Total reductions were extrapolated to annual amount of 2573 liters of fuel saved and over 240,000 minutes of idling reduced. This represents 6 tonnes of GHGs reduced on an annual basis. Commitments were made by 20 Banff Taxi and other commercial personal transport drivers to reduce GHG emissions by 3.25 tonnes per year.

Other results from the program are less measurable, but not less important. Local businesses, such as the largest hotel in the region, requested anti-idling signage. The rear-view mirror hangers were well used, with the rental car agencies and garages requesting more for distribution. In addition, the local student-made Mountain Idle movie was selected and shown at a national film festival, at a provincial film festival and posted on the National Resources Canada website. The Calgary Police Service requested permission to use the video in their staff training on idling.

Sustainable Action Canmore (SAC)

In 2009, the Biosphere Institute and the Town of Canmore embarked on SAC: Community Based Social Marketing for Urban Change – a door-to-door community-wide social marketing program. Funding for the project came from several sources including foundations and the Town of Canmore. The town also provided administrative payroll services for the canvassers, helped hire the canvassers, supplied their transportation and helped provide canvasser training, as well as consulting and advertising for the program.

This unique project involved an entire community and multiple domains of action. After a small, successful pilot test, canvassers strove to visit every Canmore home and asked residents to commit to at least one of four sustainable actions (waste reduction, water conservation, energy savings or fuel efficiency). In return, each resident received a free Sustainable Action Item to help them take immediate concrete actions such as changing a light bulb, installing a low-flow showerhead, using reusable bags and checking vehicle tire pressures. It should be noted here that, as in the other examples above, the process was highly participatory. The canvassers each had a script that was conversational in nature and dialogue was oriented toward "rational persuasion" in the form of commitment and consent to self-mobilizing action. Residents were asked to take a role in Canmore's sustainability and to help bring sustainability to life by partnering to commit to one sustainable action. They were then asked which of the actions they would commit to, and then given the corresponding item (showerhead, tire pressure gauge, cloth shopping bag, energy-efficient light bulb). They signed a pledge form that they would use the item, or if they already had those items, then they signed a pledge form that they would continue to take sustainable actions. In order to remove barriers to action, some items were immediately replaced (i.e. canvassers waited while homeowners put in the new showerhead and provided tips and plumbers' tape for installation, and then took away the old showerhead), while others required help to use the item such as how to find their vehicle's tire pressure information. They were asked to display the prompt sticker (i.e. Check Tire Pressure) for their chosen action, to help them remember to do it, and were given project stickers to show neighbors that they were participating, thus helping to create a discussion and develop social norms.

A *Sustainability at Home* toolkit booklet was also provided to give suggestions to the participants to take other sustainable actions. Contact information was requested to allow follow-ups that included encouraging participants to commit to further actions and checking that they had undertaken their pledged action. This type of written commitment and promised follow-up has been shown to increase action in social marketing campaigns (McKenzie-Mohr & Smith, 1999).

In order to undertake a true community-wide social marketing program that included both permanent and non-permanent residences, canvassers attempted to knock on the doors of every home in Canmore. Property managers of buildings that did not normally allow public access were contacted to request access for the canvassers. Homes were excluded only when canvasser access was denied or when project managers could not be reached to provide access to units. To help ensure high participation levels, canvassers were active on evenings and weekends, including holiday weekends (many resident tourists visit only on weekends/holidays); when the first visit did not result in contact, a second visit was made; booths were set up at easy access venues throughout the community (i.e. grocery stores) to allow people who missed the home visits to participate. Addresses were cross-checked from these events to ensure that each household's participation was only counted once.

After all the canvassing was completed, a follow-up survey was conducted through phone calls/emails for each of the households to encourage further sustainable actions and help evaluate the program's impacts. To decrease the number of dishonest positive responses, on suggestion of Doug MacKenzie-Mohr, participants were told: "We are continuing to look at the program and would like you to be frank with us about whether you used the item yet or not" (Doug McKenzie-Mohr, personal communication, April 1, 2010). The survey also asked those who had not yet used the item if they would commit to using it in the following week. Participants were also asked if they would be willing to commit to another action, to specify which action and then asked if they wanted to join an email list.

Over 6100 homes were visited and a response rate (those personally contacted after one or two visits) of 51% was achieved. Participation rates were very high: 92% of the 3138 households with people at their home during canvassing participated. This included 83% who took and pledged to use a Sustainable Action item and another 9% who already had all items, and therefore signed the sustainability pledge forms. Feedback was very positive.

An additional 521 households participated via booths at local grocery stores, the Civic Centre, community events and drop-ins. Overall 3404 different households committed to the program. The follow-up phone call/email survey conducted had a response rate of 31%, with 92% of the respondents indicating that they used the sustainable action item. Of those who had not yet used the item, 25% committed to using it in the following week. Over 65% of all respondents committed to taking another specific measurable action as specified (Figure 2). Interest in learning more about sustainability was also high: 437 people agreed to be included on the Biosphere Institute's email list.

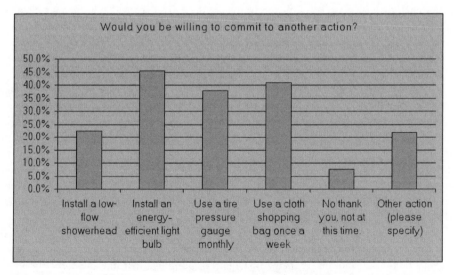

Figure 2.   Respondents committed to taking another specific measurable action in the social action Canmore program follow-up survey.

Overall, the follow-up results of the Mountain Air program and the follow-up survey of the SAC results indicate significant behavioral change toward greater sustainability and climate change adaptation practices. However, reaching second home owners was difficult. Further collaborative planning and governance strategies will need to be developed to engage resident tourists to take part in these programs and to provide a feedback.

New pedagogies, new approaches for destination governance

This paper offers preliminary theoretical and practical insights into community-based destination governance. From a theoretical perspective, following Hannah Arendt, collaborative governance is a dialogic and pluralistic space, where public interest is governed by multiple civic participants (stakeholders) who come together freely to inform political action through communicative consent and rational persuasion (which can be agonistic at times, as was the community collaboration that was convened to address growth management [Jamal & Getz, 1999], which helped lead to the creation of the Biosphere Institute). The urgencies of climate change and other sustainability challenges have led to calls for direct public involvement as described earlier in the paper. The Canmore case, described earlier, shows that civic action, education, awareness and behavior change in relation to sustainability and climate change are being undertaken freely through pluralistic dialogue, rational persuasion and multiple narratives. Drawing from Arendt (1998), it can be argued that these qualities of participatory action are integral steps toward developing a flourishing public sphere and community-based destination governance wherein social responsibility does not lie in the hands of a bureaucratic elite, or technical, scientific and managerial experts, but in the hands of a well-informed and directly engaged citizenry, facilitated by partnerships and collaboration with public, private and nonprofit organizations.

The Biosphere Institute in Canmore has undertaken significant efforts to enable a participatory and informed public at the local destination level to tackle climate change and resource conservation priorities – acting as a "bridging organization" (Brown, 1991) to engage multiple destination stakeholders in a "web" of relations (as Arendt discusses) toward sustainability-oriented action. The actions and outcomes shown above indicate the nurturing of qualities that can lead toward participatory democracy, as advocated by Arendt and Pateman, among others. The *Mountain Air* program and the *Mountain Idle* film initiatives comport well with Arendt's theory of human action, wherein the human capacity to initiate, to begin and to act is facilitated by interaction and speech with many other participants in public spaces and, we argue, in hybrid public–private intersections such as on the thresholds of households engaged in *Sustainable Action Canmore*, enabling bridging of public and private spheres (a concern of both Pateman and Arendt). Freedom and belonging is enabled through action and speech: active engagement, participation and joint dialogue in public and private–public spaces have helped to facilitate learning, understanding, as well as a participatory ethos in the community of Canmore. Residents, resident tourists, taxi drivers, schoolchildren as well as other stakeholders in the local governance domain "struggled" (strove) to understand unfamiliar stories related to energy efficiency and carbon management, and to engage in behavior change both at home (SAC campaign) and on the street (*Mountain Idle* program). Power in this dialogic domain is relational rather than top-down, and joint dialogue, learning, storytelling and an action-oriented pedagogy are key features of participatory and communicative action to address a local–global interest – climate change and resource sustainability. Changes in behavior and perceptions about sustainability and climate change are also evident in the Canmore case (e.g., see schoolchildren's dialogue in the *Mountain Idle* film). All of the above, we argue, provide for an informed and involved citizenry that can engage in future political action and projects that further their common interests (or "public interest") in addressing climate change, resource use and conservation-related issues.

Following Arendt (1990), and Disch (1994) on Arendt, local engagement in participatory democracy, storytelling and pluralistic human action is important for destination governance (also see Pateman, 1970). Their theoretical insights, together with the discussion on sustainable tourism and climate change governance initiatives, indicate the need for new pedagogies and processes to enable a participatory public sphere (including residents and tourists) in climate change adaptation and sustainable destination governance. The Biosphere Institute's community-based social marketing initiatives illustrate performative, pluralistic dialogue and action in collaborative governance of the local sustainability domain.

However, effective sustainability-oriented action in the public sphere also involves pedagogic learning and change. In his influential book, *Public Opinion*, Lippmann (1922) was highly concerned about the quality of information needed for democracy to be effective: it demands a well-informed public. The Biosphere Institute in Canmore facilitated a number of programs (such as The Natural Step) that engaged local government and other stakeholders in sustainability-related action. These provided learning-based opportunities and led to comprehensive projects including those described above which were community-based and engaged a wide cross-section of the public. Public support and direct participation can be solicited from such an informed and engaged visitor and citizen population, for future sustainability planning and policy setting. In addition, the Biosphere Institute actively facilitates an ongoing youth environmental movie-making initiative, which included fostering speech and performance in the collaborative creation of the *Mountain Idle* film and enabling future remembrance and re-telling (as per Arendt, 1998).

This paper raises an important question: what are the pedagogic responsibilities of the tourism "industry" and destination managers (private and public sector, including destination marketing/management organizations) in facilitating collaborative learning and citizen (resident, resident tourist and tourist, as well as other stakeholders in the local domain) involvement in climate change management and sustainable destination governance? Can the powerful experiential and interpretive aspects of tourism and travel be called up to do more than is being done at present to enable action and change in the sustainability domain? What might encourage destination managers (and academics and other tourism practitioners) toward enabling an informed public and a flourishing public sphere that can engage in a participatory action in tourism-related issues and destinations? The conclusions below draw on the Canmore case study and related discussion:

- Tourism stakeholders can play a strong pedagogic role in adaptive planning, for instance, challenging tourists (and residents): "How do you behave in this destination?" Through the recently implemented Mountain Air program, both visitors to Canmore and residents can learn through community signage and the other media that discussed how to reduce their climate change impacts by simple means. Additional media strategies for visitors can include in-accommodation interpretive venues (e.g. information posted on hotel's website or television channel, or print material left at each bedside), and web-based, positive pre-visit information delivery. Visitors to Canmore can also learn about human–wildlife impacts and how to minimize their impacts via the Biosphere Institute's WildSmart program (www.wildsmart.ca), not discussed here. There are powerful pedagogic tools available to managers that are relevant, or adaptable, to travel and tourism.

- In addition to destination managers, destination residents must also "walk the talk" in managing environmental and climate change impacts – the local community must also be actively pursuing actions and activities to reduce carbon impacts, pollution, fossil fuel use and pursue energy efficient alternatives. Supporters of the "Sustainable Action Canmore" program can act as role models for new visitors, although they may need some guidance about how best to do that.
- The above case also illustrates the important role that NGOs can play in "engaged governance" (United Nations, 2005) and in assisting local destination managers. The Biosphere Institute plays a vital role in sustainability funding and partnerships with local–regional stakeholders to enable collaborative and enthusiastic local action. Its multiple, complex and detailed work offers valuable lessons for destination managers and planners.

Communities are storied places of learning and dwelling, and yield stories of planning practice as well as pedagogic actions for community-based destination governance of the sustainability domain (see Dredge & Jenkins, 2011). Hannah Arendt's theory of human action, while it has been subject to criticism, can be seen to offer insights into the qualities and characteristics needed for nurturing such a participatory democracy, from which concerted action can occur to tackle diverse sustainability challenges. It is also a powerful reminder of participatory processes as dialogic spaces that are richly experiential as well as existential, involving performative acts of identity, freedom and belonging to place and community.

As this paper was going through final edits, the Biosphere Institute of the Bow Valley won the Green Communities Canada 2011 Innovation Award for designing and implementing a suite of programs that demonstrate cutting-edge approaches to sustainable development, incorporating the principles of social marketing, obtaining high and diverse community engagement, and effective results (www.greencommunitiescanada.org).

Acknowledgements
We thank the School of Tourism and Hospitality, Southern Cross University, for the opportunity to present a portion of this paper at their 2011 Research Symposium: Sustainability, Collaborative Governance and Tourism, February 17–18, Coolangatta, Queensland. Thanks to Bart Robinson for his vision of SAC. Major partners and funders for the programs discussed here include the Town of Canmore, The Calgary Foundation, Natural Resources Canada, Alberta Real Estate Foundation and the Town of Banff. The Melbern G. Glasscock Center for Humanities Research, Texas A&M University, assisted with some research funding. Our sincere thanks to the JOST editors for their patient editing and support on this agonistic task of introducing Arendt to Canmore!

Notes
1. Dredge and Thomas (2009, p. 251) describe public interest broadly as "the interests of all members of society with a direct or indirect interest in the issue" and include "stakeholders and interest groups, and both present and future generations".
2. Dredge and Pforr's (2008) notion of governance alludes to such pluralism as they discuss the relationships between the state, civil society and economic interests through which decisions are made that direct a society. They draw on Giddens's (1998) call for a third-way politics to develop new relationships between communities and governments, wherein greater responsibilities are assumed by individuals, small groups, communities and the voluntary sector.
3. Eward N. Zalta (Ed.). Section on Hannah Arendt, Stanford Encyclopedia of Philosophy, last updated fall 2008. http://plato.stanford.edu/cgi-bin/encyclopedia/archinfo.cgi?entry=arendt.

4. Public interest, for Arendt, relates to the interest of a public world, which we share and which we can enjoy and partake in only by going beyond our own private self-interests (Arendt, 1998, 1990).
5. Social marketing is based on the premise that initiatives that promote behavior change are often most effective when they are carried out at the community level and involve direct contact with people (McKenzie-Mohr & Smith, 1999).
6. See García-Rosell (2009) for a critical look at performativity; also see Jamal, Everett, and Dann (2003).
7. For more information on the Natural Step, see: http://www.biosphereinstitute.org/?q=p-natural-step.

Notes on contributors

Tazim Jamal is an Associate Professor in the Department of Recreation, Park and Tourism Sciences, Texas A&M University. Her main research areas are community-based tourism planning, collaborative processes for sustainable development, and theoretical as well as methodological issues related to tourism and sustainability.

E. Melanie Watt is the Executive Director of the Biosphere Institute of the Bow Valley in Canmore. She is also a Lecturer in the Department of Biological Sciences at the University of Calgary in Alberta. Her work focuses on community sustainability and ecological integrity.

References

Andreasen, A.R. (1995). *Marketing social change: Changing behavior to promote health, social development, and the environment*. San Francisco, CA: Jossey-Bass.
Arendt, H. (1990). Philosophy and politics. *Social Research, 57*(1), 73–103.
Arendt, H. (1998). *The human condition* (2nd ed.). Chicago, IL: University of Chicago Press. (Original work published 1958)
Arnstein, S.R. (1969). A ladder of citizen participation. *JAIP, 35*(4), 216–224.
Becken, S. (2007). Tourists' perceptions of international air travel's impact on the global climate and potential climate change policies. *Journal of Sustainable Tourism, 15*, 351–368.
Becken, S., & Hay, J.E. (2007). *Tourism and climate change: Risks and opportunities*. Clevedon: Channel View Publications.
Belle, N., & Bramwell, B. (2005). Climate change and small island tourism: Policy maker and industry perspectives in Barbados. *Journal of Travel Research, 44*, 32–41.
Brown, L.D. (1991). Bridging organizations and sustainable development. *Human Relations, 44*(8), 807–831.
Camargo, B., & Jamal, T. (2009, July). *An eco-cultural approach to destination management, climate change and tourism: New pedagogies, new structures*. Paper presented at the 7th International Symposium on Tourism and Sustainability: Travel & Tourism in the Age of Climate Change, University of Brighton, UK.
Disch, L.J. (1994). *Hannah Arendt and the limits of philosophy*. Ithaca, NY: Cornell University Press.
Dolan, F.M. (2000). Arendt on philosophy and politics. In D. Villa (Ed.), *The Cambridge companion to Hannah Arendt* (pp. 261–276). Cambridge: Cambridge University Press.
Dredge, D., & Jenkins, J. (2011). *Stories of practice: Tourism policy and planning*. Burlington, VT: Ashgate.
Dredge, D., & Pforr, C. (2008). Policy networks and tourism governance. In N. Scott, R. Baggio, & C. Cooper (Eds.), *Network analysis and tourism: From theory to practice* (pp. 58–78). Clevedon: Channel View Publications.
Dredge, D., & Thomas, P. (2009). Mongrel management, public interest and protected areas management in the Victorian Alps, Australia. *Journal of Sustainable Tourism, 17*(2), 249–267.
Eijgelaar, E., Thaper, C., & Peeters, P. (2010). Antarctic cruise tourism: The paradoxes of ambassadorship, "last chance tourism" and greenhouse gas emissions. *Journal of Sustainable Tourism, 18*(3), 337–354.
Fals-Borda, O., & Rahman, M.A. (Eds.). (1991). *Action and knowledge: Breaking the monopoly with participatory action-research*. New York: Apex Press.

Feichtinger, J., & Pregernig, M. (2005). Imagined cities and participation: Local Agenda 21 in two communities in Sweden and Austria. *Local Environment, 10*(3), 229–242.

García-Rosell, J.C. (2009). *A multi-stakeholder perspective on sustainable marketing* (dissertation). University of Oulu, Oulun Yliopisto, Oulu.

Giddens, A. (1998). *The third way: The renewal of democracy*. Oxford: Polity Press.

Gill, A.M., & Williams, P. (2011). Rethinking resort growth: Understanding evolving governance strategies in Whistler, British Columbia. *Journal of Sustainable Tourism, 19*(4–5), 629–648.

Habermas, J. (1978). *Knowledge and human interests* (2nd ed.). Boston, MA: Beacon Press.

Habermas, J. (1984). *The theory of communicative action*. Cambridge: Polity Press.

Heede, R. (2007). *Energy consumption and carbon emissions from second homes in Aspen. Aspen second homes energy study (ASHES)*. Preliminary Report commissioned by the Sopris Foundation. Retrieved February 3, 2011, from http://www.soprisfoundation.org/PDFs/ASHESrptSep07.pdf

Honig, B. (1993). *Political theory and the displacement of politics*. Ithaca, NY: Cornell University Press.

Jamal, T., Everett, J., & Dann, G.M. (2003). Ecological rationalization and performative resistance in natural area destinations. *Tourist Studies, 3*(2), 143–169.

Jamal, T., & Getz, D. (1999). Community-based roundtables for tourism-related conflicts: The dialectics of consensus and process structures. *Journal of Sustainable Tourism, 3*(4), 290–314.

Jamal, T., & Jamrozy, U. (2006). Collaborative networks and partnerships for integrated destination management. In D. Buhalis & C. Costa (Eds.), *Tourism management dynamics* (pp. 164–172). Amsterdam: Elsevier.

Kotler, P. (2004). Wrestling with ethics: Is marketing ethics an oxymoron? *Marketing Management, 13*(6), 30–35.

Kotler, P., Roberto, E.L., & Lee, N. (2002). *Social marketing: Strategies for changing public behavior*. Thousand Oaks, CA: Sage.

Lippmann, W. (1922). *Public opinion*. New York, NY: Harcourt.

McKenzie-Mohr, D., & Smith, W. (1999). *Fostering sustainable behavior: An introduction to community-based social marketing*. Gabriola Island, BC: New Society Publishers.

McKercher, B., Prideaux, B., Cheung, C., & Law, R. (2010). Achieving voluntary reductions in the carbon footprint of tourism and climate change. *Journal of Sustainable Tourism, 18*(3), 297–317.

Ojha, H. (2006). Techno-bureaucratic doxa and the challenges of deliberative governance – The case of community forestry policy and practice in Nepal. *Policy and Society, 25*(2), 131–175.

Ojha, H., Persha, L., & Chhatre, A. (2009, November). *Community forestry in Nepal: A policy innovation for local livelihoods* (IFPRI Discussion Paper 00913, 2020 Vision for Food, Agriculture and the Environment). Washington, DC: International Food Policy Research Institute (IFPRI). Retrieved June 6, 2010, from http://www.ifpri.org/publication/community-forestry-nepal

Owen, A.L., & Videras, J. (2008). Trust, cooperation, and implementation of sustainability programs: The case of Local Agenda 21. *Ecological Economics, 68*(1–2), 259–272.

Pateman, C. (1970). *Participation and democratic theory*. Cambridge: Cambridge University Press.

Reason, P. (1998). Three approaches to participative inquiry. In N.K. Denzin & Y.S. Lincoln (Eds.), *Strategies of qualitative inquiry* (pp. 261–291). Thousand Oaks, CA: Sage.

Rousseau, J.J. (1902). *The social contract* (3rd ed.). (Henry J. Tozer, Trans.). London: Swan Sonenschein. (Original work published 1762)

Schindler, D.W., & Donahue, W.F. (2006). An impending water crisis in Canada's western prairie provinces. *Proceedings of the National Academy of Sciences USA, 103*(19), 7210–7216.

Scott, D. (2006). Global environmental change and mountain tourism. In S. Gössling & C.M. Hall (Eds.), *Tourism and global environmental change: Ecological, social, economic and political relationships* (pp. 54–75). New York: Routledge.

Scott, D., & Becken, S. (2010). Adapting to climate change and climate policy: Progress, problems and potentials. *Journal of Sustainable Tourism, 18*(3), 283–295.

Scott, D., & Lemieux, C. (2005). Climate change and protected area policy and planning in Canada. *The Forestry Chronicle, 81*(5), 691–703.

Town of Canmore. (1995). *Town of Canmore Growth Management Committee 1995 strategy report*. Canmore, Alberta: Author.

United Nations. (2005). *"Engaged governance": A strategy for mainstreaming citizens into the public policy process* (ST/ESA/PAD/SER.E/73). New York: Department of Economic and Social Affairs, United Nations.

UNWTO. (2004). *Sustainable development of tourism.* Retrieved June 6, 2010, from http://www.unwto.org/sdt/mission/en/mission.php

UNWTO. (2008). *Climate change and tourism – Responding to global challenges.* Madrid: UNWTO.

Villa, D. (2000). *The Cambridge companion to Hannah Arendt.* Cambridge: Cambridge University Press.

Voisey, H., Beuermann, C., Sverdrup, L.A., & O'Riordan, T. (1996). The political significance of Local Agenda 21: The early stages of some European experience. *Local Environment, 1*(1), 33–50.

World Commission on Environment and Development (WCED). (1987). *Our common future.* New York, NY: Oxford University Press.

Yar, M. (2005). *Internet encyclopedia of philosophy.* (Original work published 2001). Retrieved June 6, 2010, from http://www.iep.utm.edu/arendt/

Young, I.M. (1995). The ideal of community and the politics of difference. In P.A. Weiss & M. Friedman (Eds.), *Feminism and community* (pp. 233–258). Philadelphia, PA: Temple University Press.

Global regulations and local practices: the politics and governance of animal welfare in elephant tourism

Rosaleen Duffy and Lorraine Moore

Department of Politics, Manchester University, Arthur Lewis Building, Oxford Road, Manchester M13 9PL, UK

This paper examines challenges associated with global regulation of the tourism industry via an analysis of the use of elephants for trekking and safaris in Thailand and Botswana. It highlights inherent problems in applying universal principles in diverse locations; it unpicks the North–South power dynamics involved in drawing up global standards for elephant welfare in tourism. The development and expansion of elephant riding raise important ethical issues around questions of animal welfare, especially definitions of acceptable and appropriate standards for working animals. This paper uses a political economy approach to understandings of global governance to analyse who has the power to govern, at what scale and with what effects. It examines the role of animal welfare NGOs as key epistemic communities shaping the debate on elephant welfare. It discusses the highly variable practices of working with elephants in Botswana and in Thailand. It concludes that attempts at global regulation need to seriously engage with local level practices if global standards are to be workable and acceptable for tour operators, animal welfare NGOs, elephant camp owners and tourists alike. It raises leading global governance issues and discussions of the role of NGOs in governance, in general.

Introduction

This paper examines the power dynamics involved in global regulation via an analysis of local practices of using animals for the tourism industry. The tourism industry is adept at designing and creating new commodities for which clients will pay to see or experience. It relies on the transformation of places into desirable "must see" locations and the development of new "must do" activities for which people will pay to experience. This includes the production of new sensory experiences centred on close encounters with animals (Bulbeck, 2004; Cohen, 2008, pp. 135–179). However, these new products raise important ethical issues, especially around questions of animal welfare and how we define appropriate and acceptable use of animals for human entertainment.

This paper focuses on questions around who has the power to define international standards for animal welfare in the tourism industry, and why. A range of interests is involved, including donors, NGOs, local people, the international tourism industry and destination governments, each with differences in outlook. It is also clear that there is a growing

179

shift towards cooperation with each other to produce mutually agreed outcomes, particularly in the South. Conservation and animal welfare NGOs constitute important epistemic communities, producing "expert knowledge" on what constitutes good practice for animal welfare (Demeritt, 2006; Haas, 1992; Litfin, 1994). However, this paper demonstrates real and potential clashes among calls for global regulation, standardisation of animal working conditions and locally based practices. Major dilemmas are posed by attempts to devise universal principles for a diverse range of contexts. This challenge faces wider forms of global tourism regulation: the case of elephant welfare provides vital lessons about the efficacy of "one size fits all" forms of global regulation and indicates the need for locally acceptable and context-specific regulations that take account of variations within and between countries.

This paper critically examines the international transmission and standardisation of values for animal welfare in Thailand and Botswana. In both countries, tourists are offered elephant riding as part of the holiday experience; both locations present different challenges to international standardisation of elephant welfare. Several international animal welfare organisations, including Born Free Foundation (BFF), International Fund for Animal Welfare (IFAW), The Humane Society International (HSI) and People for the Ethical Treatment of Animals (PETA), strongly argue that elephant trekking is inherently cruel and that captive trained elephants should be re-trained for release into the wild. The tourism industry is responding to these concerns in various ways. This paper investigates the challenges in producing global regulations for elephant welfare and argues that international regulations need to engage with and be sensitive to the realities of working with elephants in very different locations.

Global governance

There have been increasing calls for global-level regulation to certify tourism products as "ethical", related to wider shifts in the international system often referred to as "global governance". Since the end of the Cold War, analysts have grappled with understanding a new world order characterised by multiple sites of power and authority. Numerous denser, multi-sited and increasingly transnational forms of governance have arisen from shifts in the relationships between states and markets, and between public and private international bodies (Newell, 2008, pp. 507–511). Global governance is a useful framework for examining how multiple interest groups operate together to govern and regulate the tourism industry. Global governance is "the patchwork of formal and informal arrangements among states, international organisations and various public-private partnerships" (Weiss, 2009, p. 254). Global governance differs from Government, ordinarily the preserve of states, because it encompasses the range of formal and informal arrangements to which individuals and organisations adhere. The move towards governance rather than government recognises that power and authority can be exercised by multiple actors, including international institutions, private companies, NGOs and community-based organisations, and not just states (Commission on Global Governance, 1995; also see Dingwerth, 2008; Dingwerth & Pattberg, 2009; Hewson & Sinclair, 1999; Rosenau & Czempiel, 1992; Weiss, 2009; Young, 1997).

The nature of global governance is well debated elsewhere, and there are subtle differences in the ways it is understood (Murphy, 2000). This paper takes a political economy perspective that asks what is to be governed (and what is not), who governs and who is governed, how do they govern, on whose behalf and with what implications (Bulkeley, 2005; Liverman, 2004, p. 734; Newell, 2008). It is clear that emergent forms of global governance, especially in the environmental arena, have been "privatised" out into a range of non-state networks that draw together NGOs and private businesses. Tollefson, Gale, and Haley argue that "we are witnessing fundamental change in the nature of governance and regulation and in the respective roles of government, business and civil society" (2008, p. 4). New forms of governance are emerging in private arenas, free from public participation and scrutiny, allowing stakeholders to settle political questions in a technical manner. A good example is the growing emphasis on voluntary codes of conduct, which shift focus away from states as the regulator (or site of governance) towards private actors. This shift is also marked by the fetishisation of ideas of partnership and engagement with "stakeholders" as key actors (Newell, 2008, pp. 521–523). Certification is one facet of governance through the private sphere, marking the convergence of global civil society and market forces to regulate the distribution and use of resources. Certification relies on markets to distinguish between goods that have been produced in accordance with agreed, standardised regulations and draws on the idea of the responsible producer (corporate social responsibility) and the responsible citizen (through consumption choices) (Barrientos & Dolan, 2006).

However, in debates about global governance, there is very little critical engagement with how new systems of regulation, certification and standardisation intersect with North–South power dynamics. Dingwerth (2008, p. 607) argues that "analysts are interested in the exercise of private authority beyond the state, but the role of stakeholders in the southern hemisphere as *subjects* and *objects* of private transnational governance is rarely addressed" (also see Bäckstrand, 2006; Pattberg, 2006). This paper addresses this gap in our understanding of North–South dynamics of international regulation by examining global standards for animal welfare in the tourism industry. It examines the ways in which Northern-based international actors attempt to shape standards for the tourism industry in a diverse range of contexts in the South. The analysis reveals the complex power dynamics involved in global standardisation that are often made invisible in structures of global governance.

Civil society actors (in this case animal welfare NGOs) are in a uniquely powerful position to determine standards for certification of ethical practices in the tourism industry. Newell suggests that we need to pay attention to the material, discursive and organisational elements of power, including recognising the powerful role played by "experts" (including animal welfare NGOs) in shaping, defining and producing new international regulations (Demeritt, 2006; Haas, 1992; Litfin, 1994; Newell, 2008, pp. 523–525). We need to question who has the power to define those international standards for animal welfare and why. Conservation and animal welfare NGOs present themselves as key experts capable of defining and producing new governance structures regulating the use of animals in tourism. They are important knowledge brokers, deciding appropriate and inappropriate use of animals in the tourism industry. NGOs claim that they are not tainted by the government or corporate thinking, and that their research, approaches and policies are neutral, scientific and in the best interests of animals. People are more likely to be influenced by the information presented by IFAW or BFF, while suspecting that national governments or private businesses have their own interests and agendas to protect. NGOs are particularly influential in how the public views elephants and what is seen as humane treatment.

Animal welfare NGOs and the elephant trekking industry

This paper examines the encounter between calls for international standardisation and locally based practices in the South through examination of the use of elephants in tourist activities in Botswana and Thailand. The proliferation of elephant riding experiences is one example in which international NGOs have actively pursued global standards for animal welfare so that tour operators and tourists can know that they are not supporting cruel practices. However, there is a potential clash between the calls for global regulation and standardisation of animal working conditions and locally based practices. This is in part the result of very different understandings of the role of animals in the tourism industry. There is a clear division between Northern-based animal welfare NGOs that see elephants as "wild" animals versus local-level practices that value elephants as working animals, especially in Thailand. This provides important wider lessons about developing universal principles for regulating the tourism industry in diverse contexts. In this section, we set out the positions of four of the most active animal welfare organisations campaigning for the rights of elephants working in the tourism industry. We also examine the complex ways in which Southern actors are the subjects and objects of attempts to govern from Northern positions on animal welfare (see Dingwerth, 2008; Pattberg, 2006).

Conservation NGOs tend to focus on wild elephant populations, leaving working elephants to animal welfare and animal rights organisations. NGOs campaigning against the elephant back safari industry have a common approach, to prevent cruelty, and a stated aim to free animals from captivity in the future. NGOs are important actors in networks of global governance because they push forward the debate on the need for global regulation and standardisation of elephant welfare in the tourism industry. This raises questions about the material and discursive dimensions of NGO power in designing and implementing new systems of governance, drawing attention to questions of who has the power to govern, at what scale and with what effects (Bulkeley, 2005; Liverman, 2004; Newell, 2008).

The IFAW has 1.2 million supporters worldwide; its aim is "to create a better world for animals". It campaigned against culling harp seal pups for fur in Canada in the 1960s. Its philosophy rejects the notion that the interests of humans and animals are separate; IFAW sees them as inextricably linked (IFAW, n.d.a). Recently, IFAW has campaigned against elephant back safaris in southern Africa. Its stated position is that "elephant tourism is not responsible tourism, and should not be supported in any shape or form", and that it has no conservation value and is cruel and exploitative (IFAW, 2006a). IFAW claims that the elephant tourism industry in the region is rapidly increasing, with 25% more elephants in captivity for commercial use, rising from 89 to 112 between 2005 and 2007 (IFAW, 2007). IFAW is also concerned about the elephants captured from the wild for training for this new "luxury" tourism product in southern Africa and the lack of regulation of training facilities. IFAW claims that tourists were at risk from badly trained, potentially dangerous elephants. Between 2005 and 2007, at least three handlers were killed, and incidents occurred when tourists were injured while riding the elephants (IFAW, 2006a, 2006b, 2007).

IFAW is a powerful voice shaping global standards for the welfare of working elephants, calling for better legislation to manage the elephant safari industry. In 2007, it released its report entitled "An Overview of the Commercial Use of Elephants in Captivity in South Africa", claiming that lack of standards and regulation in the elephant back safari industry in southern Africa meant that elephant tourist rides "were accidents waiting to happen". The Southern Africa Director of IFAW, Jason Bell-Leask, has stated that IFAW would like to ban the industry altogether; it views the industry as cruel, wrong, exploitative and driven by greed. IFAW devotes its energies into developing regulations to prevent further growth in elephant back riding and to ensure that captive elephants are well cared for (IFAW, 2007, n.d.b). This includes guidance on the size of area that elephants should have access to and stipulates that:

No person may train a captive elephant unless they have relevant knowledge and a minimum of five years experience of working with elephants ... (and) there being a minimum of one handler permanently and exclusively allocated to the care of the elephant. (Government of South Africa, 2008; IFAW, 2008)

There are commonalities between IFAW and BFF, both of which promote a similar message about elephant back safaris, especially in Africa. BFF is a UK-based NGO campaigning against the suffering of wildlife and seeking protection for species in the wild. Founded by the actress Virginia McKenna after her role in the film, *Born Free*, its Chief Executive is her son, Will Travers (Born Free Foundation, n.d.a). One of its primary concerns is the use of animals in circuses, shows and tourist activities. It runs a zoo check programme on cruel treatment of animals in zoos and campaigns against keeping wild animals in zoos. It is a source of expertise on the welfare of captive and working animals and opposes the elephant back safari industry (Born Free Foundation, n.d.b). It also campaigns against the use of wild animals in all shows, arguing that the animals are stressed because they are kept in cramped conditions, moved too frequently when part of travelling shows, and that the training of animals to perform tricks is demeaning and cruel (Born Free Foundation, n.d.c).

BFF is an important actor in the elephant welfare debate, shaping and defining appropriate standards for using elephants as working animals in the tourism industry. It is a key expert knowledge broker on elephant welfare working with global tour operators to shape standards and policies. It is also indicative of North–South dynamics of governance of the tourism industry because the standards were drawn up by an alliance of Northern NGOs and Northern-based international tour operators separate from potential partners and interest groups in Southern contexts in which the elephant rides operate. BFF is one of the NGO partners of Thomson, a part of Touristik Union International (TUI), one of the world's largest travel companies, operating in 180 countries and serving 30 million tourists every year (TUI, n.d.). One of its airlines, Thomsonfly, shows a short film by BFF on its flights as a fundraiser. Cabin crew collect donations from passengers on board, raising £2.5 million in 2007 alone (Born Free Foundation, n.d.d). Kuoni, another BFF tourism partner, has developed a "Born Free experience" holiday in Kenya (Born Free Foundation, n.d.e). Both Thomson and Kuoni offer holidays in Asia and Africa that include elephant back safaris. BFF aims to push forward global standards for the elephant riding industry, with the ultimate goal of ensuring that all elephants are wild rather than captive or working.

The HSI is one of the most vocal organisations for elephant welfare. HSI is the international coordinator for the Humane Society of the US (HSUS) and partner organisations around the world. Established in 1954, it has over 10 million supporters, one in every 30 Americans (HSUS, n.d.a). It works with national and jurisdictional governments, humane organisations and individual animal protectionists in countries globally to "find practical, culturally sensitive and long-term solutions to common animal issues, and to share an ethic of respect and compassion for all life" (HSUS, n.d.a). Dr Andrew Rowan, the Chief Executive Officer of the HSI, argues that the use of animals is cruel and unethical. A Northern-based NGO, HSI plays an important role in setting standards and shaping governance structures in the tourism industry, and campaigns for better regulations for elephants used in elephant back safari tourism in southern Africa (HSUS, 2008). HSI opposes elephant back safaris, claiming that in 2009 it played a significant role in ending the capture and training of elephants for safaris in South Africa (HSUS, n.d.b). This is a further example of North–South power relations in global tourism governance.

PETA opposes keeping elephants in captivity because that denies everything that is natural and important to them (PETA, n.d.a). In 2002, PETA called for a total boycott of tourism in Thailand because they claimed that the elephants were tortured to make them perform tricks in circuses and shows, and to provide rides for tourists. PETA continues to campaign against the training of elephants in Thailand, stating that "still-nursing baby elephants are literally dragged from their mothers, kicking and screaming. They are immobilised, beaten mercilessly and gouged with nails for days at a time. These ritualized 'training' sessions leave the elephants badly injured, traumatised or even dead" (Kontogeorgopoulos, 2009a; PETA, n.d.b, n.d.c). PETA remains opposed to elephant riding and actively campaigns for an end to keeping elephants in captivity.

In conclusion, animal welfare NGOs have a clear message about the use of elephants in the tourism industry. IFAW, BFF, PETA and HSI all oppose the capture of wild elephants for captivity, training of captive elephants, their use in circuses and shows, and their use for elephant rides. They all share a commitment to the idea that elephants should ideally be in the wild, and, if in captivity, then their welfare should be paramount. Their underlying approach informs and shapes the campaigns they run and the character of the advice they give to governments, tour operators and tourists about the use of elephants in tourism. They have an important role to play as epistemic communities in drawing up global standards for elephant welfare in the tourism industry, which are then implemented in Southern contexts (Demeritt, 2006; Haas, 1992; Litfin, 1994). But their role also reveals North–South dynamics, because animal welfare NGOs operate as agents of global governance, pushing forward international regulation and standardisation in particular local contexts. We need to have a greater degree of understanding of how these governance systems impact on and affect Southern actors as objects and subjects of governance (the elephant riding industry in Thailand and Botswana in this case) (Dingwerth, 2008; Newell, 2008; Pattberg, 2006). However, as discussed below, the concerns raised by animal welfare NGOs more readily map onto the profile of the elephant back safari industry in southern Africa but present more challenges when they are applied to the case of elephant riding in Thailand, where there is a much longer history of using elephants as working animals and the profile of the tourism industry is much more diverse. In Thailand, it is not feasible to simply move elephants out of the tourism industry and release them into the wild. Captive working elephants are not always suitable for "re-wilding": they are unable to adapt to the wild, there is insufficient space to accommodate them in existing national parks and there are important considerations around how mahouts will earn a living without captive elephants (see Lair, 2004). These complexities are lost in blanket statements that elephants should ideally be in the wild. In Botswana, there is possibly less of a problem because very few elephants are captive working animals operating in the safari industry; those that are used for elephant riding are equally difficult to release into the wild because they are accustomed to captivity and may not be able to integrate into wild herds. This is the subject of an on-going research project at Abu Camp in Botswana, run by Dr Kate Evans at the Bristol University (Evans, n.d.; Dr Kate Evans, personal communication, June 23, 2008).

This paper uses fieldwork by the authors who spent four months in Thailand and three months in Botswana during 2008–2009. The study compares and contrasts nature-based tourism, elephant riding, in two very different contexts. We conducted 75 interviews in Kasane, Maun and Gaborone (Botswana) and in Bangkok and Chiang Mai (Thailand). Kasane, Maun and Chiang Mai are the main areas for elephant riding in each country, and undertaking research in the capital cities of Gaborone and Bangkok enabled us to access relevant wildlife, conservation and tourism authorities. Interviewees were drawn from a wide range of stakeholders, including wildlife and human rights NGOs, tour operators, lodge and camp owners, tourist guides and the tourists themselves. Some of the interviews have been anonymised to protect the identities of participants; some interviewees criticised the industry in which they were employed, and revealing their identity exposes them to risks of reprisals. Interviews were not taped; instead, extensive notes were taken and typed up shortly after each interview. This was the most productive method because it put interviewees at ease; however, we take full responsibility for any errors in the information, as the notes were our interpretations of the interviewees' statements. These methods were the most suitable because they are adaptable in the field (which is particularly important when discussing sensitive topics such as elephant culling in Botswana). We also undertook participant observation at tourist sites such as elephant shows and elephant riding tours. We used these qualitative methods as the most appropriate and effective means to understand the complexities of the elephant riding industry in both countries. Research ethics were a key issue for this project. We conducted the research according to the code of ethics produced by the Manchester University, but we also consulted the ethical guidelines of various professional bodies, including the International Sociological Association and the Royal Geographic Society's Geography Outdoors (which provides expedition and training advice).

The profile of elephant back safaris in Botswana and Thailand

Elephant back safaris have become important aspects of the tourism industries in Botswana and Thailand. But there are considerable differences between those countries and their use of elephants. It is critical that organisations involved in promoting a global governance approach to elephant welfare take a nuanced view of local-level practices.

The tourism industry in Botswana is heavily focused on a "wilderness" brand, with wildlife safaris as the core product, including photographic tourism and sport hunting safaris (interview with District Wildlife Co-ordinator, Maun, October 31, 2008; interview with Wilderness Safaris, Maun, October 29, 2008; also see Keitumetse, 2009; Mbaiwa, 2008). Elephant back safaris are now promoted as a means of getting "up close and personal" with wildlife. These experiences have become a high-end/luxury tourism product in the last decade, and are now found in South Africa, Botswana, Zimbabwe and Zambia. Elephant rides cost upwards of US$150 per person per hour; in Botswana, close interactions with elephants are sold as part of an accommodation package in fly-in luxury camps costing between US$500 and US$2000 per night (LWE, n.d.a; Sanctuary Lodges, n.d.; Wilderness Safaris, n.d.). Botswana's camps claim that it is possible to get closer to wildlife on elephant back because it is more "natural" than using a vehicle. Abu Camp was the first operator to offer elephant back safaris in southern Africa in the early 1990s; it is now run by a large South African operator, Wilderness Safaris, promoting itself as a "responsible eco-tourism and conservation company".

> Guests at Abu Camp are invited to become part of the elephant herd during their stay: watching the evening feeding, sharing the simple joy of a frolicking youngster, and accompanying them on foot as they move through the bush. These elephant encounters provide unforgettable magical moments. (Wilderness Safaris, n.d.; also see interview with researcher and former manager of Seba Camp, October 23, 2008)

A former manager and researcher at Seba Camp commented that tourists show a lot of interest in the elephants and want to know more about the research programmes at Abu Camp, which include work on releasing captive elephants back into the wild (interview with researcher and former manager of Seba Camp, October 23, 2008; also Dr Kate Evans, personal communication, June 23, 2008).

Equally, Living With Elephants (LWE) is an NGO that engages in educational outreach and provides high-end/luxury experiences for guests at Baines and Stanley's Camp in the Okavango Delta. The camps are run by Sanctuary Lodges, a division of the global safari operator Abercrombie and Kent (Sanctuary Retreats, n.d.). LWE offers walking with elephants as a means of educating tourists about elephant conservation issues (Abu Camp, n.d.; LWE, n.d.a; Sanctuary Lodges, n.d.; interview with Sandi Groves, Living with Elephants, Maun, May 28, 2008; Randall Moore, personal communication, May 26, 2008). LWE's mission statement states that it is "dedicated to creating harmonious relationships between people and elephants. Doug and Sandi have striven to find ways in which their foster elephants can act as ambassadors for their wild counterparts". The key motivation for LWE is to "reduce competition between elephants and human populations in Botswana" (LWE, n.d.b). Captive elephants are seen as a method for ensuring conservation of their wild counterparts through the "re-education" of African communities into understanding elephants. Although LWE's elephants are working animals, they do not offer rides for tourist entertainment or as a safari experience. Instead, they offer walking with elephants as an "educational experience"; they use elephants not suited to release in the wild because of their experiences in captivity.

Thailand is very different. It has c. 3000 elephants, 2000 of them privately owned working animals (Cohen, 2008, p. 136; Kontogeorgopoulos, 2009a). Each elephant is owned by someone: either the mahout (its driver and often lifelong keeper) or an owner who hires the elephant with its mahout. The government authorities responsible for elephants are the Department of Livestock, Department of Transport and the Forest Industry Organisation, rather than the Department of National Parks or Ministry of Environment. Elephants are regarded as working animals rather than as wildlife (see Lair, 2004, pp. 15–30).

Captive working elephants are important in long-term elephant conservation in Thailand. Without them, the long-term survival of Thailand's elephants would be at risk. Any attempt to close down the elephant trekking industry would have to grapple with the possibility that it would spell the end for Thailand's elephants. Without careful consideration of how captive elephants would be re-wilded (including where they would live and who would pay for re-wilding and management), Thailand could be left with a fragmented and non-viable wild population, while the much larger captive population dies off over time. Unlike other countries where most elephants are in national parks or "wild", two-thirds of Thailand's elephants are captive. Masakazu Kashio, the Forest Resources Officer for the FAO Asian office, argued that this was a key challenge for the future of elephants in Asia. He pointed out that many Asian elephants are captive working animals, but that they have a close relationship with their wild counterparts; it is helpful to treat the two populations as separate as many conservation NGOs do (Lair, 2004, p. 5; interview with Masakazu Kashio, Forest Resources Officer, FAO Regional Office For Asia and the Pacific [RAP], Bangkok, March 4, 2008).

Thailand has a much more diverse tourism product than Botswana. It includes standard sun, sea and sand packages, sex tourism, cultural tourism, adventure tourism (e.g. scuba diving, sea kayaking) and nature-based tourism (visiting national parks, wildlife viewing) (see Cohen, 2008). Elephant trekking is a central image in the *Amazing Thailand* tourism marketing campaign (TAT, n.d.a, n.d.b; also see Kontogeorgopoulos [1999] for further discussion). Thailand is one of the few places where tourists have close personal interactions with elephants. Experiences with elephants range from watching elephants perform in shows to training to be a mahout for 1–30 days. The elephant shows vary in style from circus-style shows in package holiday destinations to displays of skills used in the logging industry (stacking and pulling logs), to the Elephant Orchestra where elephants play tunes by hitting a glockenspiel (interview with Somchat Changkarn, Mahout Training School, Thai Elephant Conservation Center [TECC], Lampang, March 20, 2008; Anchalee Kalmapijit, personal communication, March 13, 2008; interview with Prasop Tipprasert, Elephant Specialist, Forest Industry Organisation/Chief of the Training School for Thai Elephants and Mahouts, TECC, Lampang, March 20, 2008; also see Cohen, 2008, pp. 135–179). This paper concentrates on elephant camps offering elephant rides and trekking, rather than circuses and shows. These experiences are offered by tourism operators ranging from upscale luxury hotels with their own elephant camps to luxury private non-residential elephant camps and non-residential camps aimed at mass/package tourists. Some state institutions offer basic home-stay accommodation (such as the Thai Elephant Conservation Centre) to tour operators that offer short elephant rides as part of a longer day trip (Anantara, n.d.; Chiang Do, n.d.; Mae Sa Elephant Camp, n.d.; TECC, n.d.). Unlike Botswana, the elephant trekking industry serves a wide range of markets.

In southern Africa, the removal of wild elephants for training for the safari industry has been a major source of concern for animal welfare organisations. However, although IFAW and other NGOs celebrated the ban on wild capture in 2008 in South Africa, sources of elephants for training are varied. One reason for developing elephant trekking was that culling operations had produced orphaned calves and there were also elephants available that were no longer suitable to work in circuses, or were kept in poor conditions in zoos. These animals could not easily be returned to the wild, but training them for elephant trekking could improve their fate (interview with researcher, Maun, October 23, 2008). LWE explained that their operations began in this way (LWE, n.d.a; interview with Sandi Groves, Living with Elephants, Maun, May 28, 2008).

In Thailand, the elephants used in the trekking industry also come from very different sources and their status as trained working animals produces a critical challenge for attempts to standardise the industry at a global level. Prior to 1989, elephants were primarily used in teak logging, but following the 1989 ban on logging, elephants in the logging camps faced an uncertain future. Many elephants and their mahouts were put out of work. As many mahouts have a lifelong commitment to their elephants, alternative work was essential to pay for their upkeep; they can eat 120–200 kg of food per day (Kontogeorgopoulos, 2009a).

Following the logging ban, some elephants were released, but the amount of land under national parks provides insufficient habitat for all the elephants in Thailand. In the initial years after the ban, a few elephants were funnelled into the illegal logging industry—often working for long hours and during the night to avoid detection. A second problem was the phenomenon of "street wandering elephants"—unemployed elephants and mahouts coming to big cities and tourist areas to beg on the streets (interview with Prasop Tipprasert, Elephant Specialist, Forest Industry Organisation/Chief of the Training School for Thai Elephants and Mahouts, TECC, Lampang, March 20, 2008; Pornsawan Pongsopawijit, personal communication, March 17, 2008). In Bangkok, this became a real public safety issue because of the dangers posed to traffic and pedestrians.

Although elephants have an important cultural status in Thailand, there were concerns that they would not be looked after once they were unable to earn a wage. One interviewee explained that a mahout abandoned his elephant at the elephant hospital in TECC because he believed it would no longer be able to work for a living (anonymous interview, Maetaman Elephant Camp, owner, April 7–8, 2008). One mahout commented on the street-wandering elephants that it was desperation which drove mahouts to take their elephants to beg in urban areas and tourist resorts; they were aware that the elephants found the environment stressful but felt that they had no choice and did this to survive (interview with mahout 1 from Surin, interviewed in Chiang Saen, April 24–25, 2008; mahout 2 also from Surin, interviewed in Chiang Saen, April, 24–25, 2008). Any attempt to create global standards of elephant/tourism governance must recognise and solve these problems. Equally, the idea that all elephants should be in the wild fails to constructively engage with the everyday realities of elephant conservation in Thailand. Further, not all working elephants are suitable to be released into the wild because of a lack of available habitat and because they are unable to adapt after a life as working animals.

Since the 1989 logging ban, the promotion of elephant trekking as a tourist experience has been regarded as a potential answer for conservation from diverse organisations from tour operators to the Thai Governments Forest Industry Organisation to the global Food and Agricultural Organisation. One of the first examples of elephant-based tourism in Thailand came from the Government-run Thai Elephant Conservation Centre. It started out as the "Young Elephant Training Centre", to train mahouts and provide short courses for officials who might encounter elephants as part of their duties (such as police officers who confiscated elephants in urban areas or zookeepers) (interview with Prasop Tipprasert, Elephant Specialist, Forest Industry Organisation/Chief of the Training School for Thai Elephants and Mahouts, TECC, Lampang, March 20, 2008; Cohen, 2008, pp. 135–179). The TECC began to offer elephant rides for tourists and displays of elephants' skills such as skidding and piling up logs. Since then, a number of elephant camps have opened in the Chiang Mai area, aimed at the international tourist market (interview with Richard Lair, Thai Elephant Conservation Centre, Lampang, March 13, 2008). They offer much the same tourist product as the TECC: elephant rides and elephant shows; they retail elephant paintings or the opportunity to experience mahout training for one or more days. This is one example in which a locally based institution attempted to tackle welfare issues posed by working elephants in the tourism industry. Such local initiatives might mirror international efforts to draw up industry standards. However, where they diverge is in the commitment to a future without captive working elephants, which is central to the approach taken by the key Northern-based NGOs, namely HSI, PETA, BFF and IFAW. This also reveals the problems associated with implementation of Northern-inspired global standards in Southern contexts. Northern NGOs approach elephants with the notion of "intrinsic value" of individual animals. Southern organisations approach captive elephants as working animals with important economic, spiritual and culture uses or value. In a sense, they are regarded in a more utilitarian way. There is an important disjuncture between Northern and Southern approaches, arising from their fundamental approach to understanding animals and their place in nature. This clash of values makes cooperation difficult in the longer term (Bentrupperbäumer, 2005; Butcher, 2007). It reveals North–South power relations in global governance and how Southern partners are both the objects and subjects of governance (Dingwerth, 2008; Newell, 2008; Pattberg, 2006).

Kontogeorgopoulos (2009b, p. 430) points out important objections to the ways in which some elephant training relies on the use of physical force. One of the main criticisms levelled against the elephant back safari industry by animal welfare NGOs is that training elephants for work inevitably involves cruelty. There are well-documented and high-profile examples of cruelty during training in southern Africa, but the Asian case is a little more challenging. NGOs such as IFAW and BFF point to the use of the mahout's hook, or *ankus*; they argue that the hook is used extensively in training and management, which inflicts pain and causes suffering for elephants. However, a number of camp managers and mahouts in Thailand contest this, arguing that the *ankus* is used sparingly and only when the elephant poses a danger to itself, to the mahout or to the tourists. They claim that training increasingly relies on rewards and incentives rather than on physical punishment (e.g. see interviews with Anchalee Kalampimjit, April 7–8, 2008). But some mahout trainers and camp owners do still rely on using the *ankus* and on the practice of "breaking" (*phajaan*) baby elephants, confined in a crate for a number of days and sometimes poked, burned, hit or cut to make it "safe" for working life (Kontogeorgopoulos, 2009a). In 2002, PETA released an undercover footage of the breaking ceremony in Thailand that caused international outrage. Thai organisations challenged the footage. They accepted that the ceremony still took place in remote areas but was very rare. The Government of Thailand said that such practices were outlawed in Thailand and that the cruelty may have been "staged" for the *National Geographic* journalist who filmed it (Ministry of Foreign Affairs, 2003; *The Times*, 2002). Critics also object to male elephants in Asia being chained for many weeks during musth because they become unpredictable and violent; mahouts point out that this is the only way to manage musth in captive elephants, otherwise they pose a real danger to themselves, other elephants and to the people (Kontogeorgopoulos, 2009b, p. 430).

Animal welfare NGOs have also criticised the working and living conditions of captive elephants in Africa and Asia. But there are important variations in those conditions. Thailand (and other Asian elephant range states) has a long history associated with using captive trained elephants (Cohen, 2008, pp. 135–179; Duffy & Moore, 2010), whereas Africa does not. There are concerns about how elephants are housed and treated in safari facilities in southern Africa, because the region lacks long-term knowledge of working with elephants compared with Asia. These concerns have led to the creation of the Elephant Management and Owners Association (EMOA) to draw up standards for the elephant back safari industry (African Conservation Foundation, n.d.; EMOA, n.d.). As one interviewee put it, there is a need for standards in terms of keeping and managing elephants, including levels of exercise, provision of food and acceptable working hours. As this is a new industry, elephant owners and managers lack experience and may not know how to properly manage captive elephants (anonymous interviewee, UK, June, 2008). One interviewee who worked with trained elephants suggested that one of the problems in southern Africa was that there was little understanding of the lifelong commitment attached for working with elephants (anonymous interviewee, Maun, May, 2008). A researcher expressed concerns that many of the elephant riding experiences were popping up in southern Africa, but they were run by people with little or no experience of animal training or working with elephants (anonymous interviewee, UK, June 2008). Another interviewee raised concerns that there was a real problem with taking older elephants from the wild to be trained for riding, especially 8- to 10-year-old elephants, because "training is harder on the people and on the elephants, two to three years olds are easier to train, as are elephants born in captivity" (anonymous interviewee, UK, June, 2008). This indicates that there are local concerns about animal welfare that intersect with and mirror the approach of international NGOs. If international NGOs were able to effectively link with local interest groups, global standards that were more workable and acceptable in local contexts could be drawn up.

Deaths and injuries caused by trained elephants used in the safari industry have been singled out by critics; this is partly because the industry is a new initiative with no long-term cultural history. Working with large animals such as elephants sometimes results in injuries and deaths in Asia as well as in southern Africa. One interviewee who worked with trained elephants stated that they were concerned that it would only be a matter of time before a tourist was killed by an African elephant (anonymous interviewee, Maun, May, 2008).

A criticism levelled at the elephant riding industry in Botswana is that it is an industry driven by profit and not by concerns about elephant welfare and conservation. This is a potential problem in Thailand and Botswana, and indicates the need to regulate working hours and conditions for trained elephants. One interviewee stated that there was a perception that you could make "big bucks" from elephant riding, partly because of the high prices charged by lodges in Botswana. Inexperienced private operators have been drawn in—and the results were distressed elephants and mahouts who were injured or killed (anonymous interviewee, Maun, May 2008). A recent study of elephants used for elephant back safaris in Letsatsing Game Reserve in South Africa revealed that elephants secreted a slightly higher level of glucocorticoids, which indicated a higher level of stress on days when they interacted with tourists as compared with days when they were not working (Millspaugh et al., 2007).

It is also important to recognise the differences between elephant camps in Thailand. Because the camps are not defined as tour operators, the Tourism Authority of Thailand has no power to regulate the camps and they are characterised by a high level of variability in size and quality (Kontogeorgopoulos, 2009a). They are not a singular phenomenon that offers a homogeneous experience that is produced and managed in the same way, and each kind of camp produces differing problems and benefits for working elephants. For example, Khun Lek, the owner of the Elephant Nature Park in Chiang Mai, campaigns against the use of elephants for tourist rides and has a stated commitment to allowing elephants to live as close to the "wild" as possible (http://www.elephantnaturepark.org/). This also draws our attention to the important variations within and between countries that offer tourist experiences with elephants, and raises even greater challenges for drawing universally applicable standards for the tourism industry. In the eco-tourism literature, we are accustomed to the argument that "small is beautiful", and one of the key defining characteristics of eco-tourist businesses is that they are locally owned or community-oriented. The case of elephant camps in Thailand leads us to question these assumptions, as smaller and larger camps have differing benefits and problems. Community-oriented or village-owned elephant camps may not provide the best conditions for elephants or their mahouts, but their elephants and mahouts are not employed at long distances from their homes (as is the case for Karen mahouts and elephants employed in international resorts in Pattaya and Phuket). Although smaller camps cannot provide large-scale facilities for elephants, they can provide space in different ways. Smaller camps often temporarily allow the vegetation to recover as elephants are moved, whereas permanent camps are not big enough to allow areas to be rested in the same way (Pornsawan Pongsopawijit, personal communication, March 17, 2008; interview with Richard Lair, Thai Elephant Conservation Centre, Lampang, March 13, 2008). But larger camps can afford better facilities and are easier to regulate.

The conditions for working elephants and their access to accommodation, appropriate food and veterinary care are highly variable within Thailand, and there is an even greater level of variation between Botswana and Thailand. Any attempt to draw up global regulations must capture and respond to these localised variations. The variability in local practices is not necessarily detrimental to elephant welfare; instead, differences at the local level clearly offer different costs and benefits for captive working elephants. The push for global regulation of the elephant back safari industry needs to take account of this rather than advancing a "one size fits all" solution driven by the singular approach of Northern-based animal welfare NGOs. This is vitally important if international regulations are to be made credible for local practitioners, tour operators, tourists and animal welfare NGOs. It is also important to ensure that any global standards are workable at the local level.

Conclusion

The case for global standardisation of elephant welfare raises important challenges for the tourism industry and requires us to refine our understanding of mechanisms of global governance. There are increasing calls for global level regulation to verify tourism products as "ethical". These developments are related to wider shifts in the global system, often referred to as global governance, which denote a shift in the location of power and authority away from states and towards a wider range of actors, including international organisations, civil society and the private sector. These shifts need careful analysis to uncover how global attempts at regulation intersect with North–South power dynamics. In particular, it is important to examine how global regulations are drawn up by alliances of Northern-based animal welfare NGOs and global tour operators, and how they engage with highly variable local contexts. This study of elephant riding reveals real difficulties with drawing up global standards for ethical certification and tourism products and activities. Our research highlights the need to engage with locally specific conditions, especially the viability of returning elephants to the wild and the recognition of variations within and between countries that offer elephant riding to tourists. It indicates major real-world challenges associated with devising, and implementing, universal global governance standards. This provides important lessons for other forms of global regulation of the tourism industry, especially at the local level. The framework of global governance provides a useful approach for understanding the myriad of actors in the international system. The shift towards global governance makes it essential to examine the powers of non-state actors in the international system. We have highlighted the problems associated with the privatisation of global governance by expert knowledge brokers, in this case, Northern-based animal welfare NGOs. Our analysis reveals that animal welfare NGOs have shaped and defined the debate on appropriate standards of elephant welfare in the tourism industry. The approach of the animal welfare NGOs examined here is that in the future, all elephants should be wild and they should strongly object to the use of elephants in the tourism industry. As Northern-based NGOs, their approach is at odds with the locally based practices in the South. In particular, they fail to engage with the genuine barriers to move elephants out of tourism and into the wild, which are especially significant in Thailand. Yet, as critically important knowledge brokers of expertise on elephant welfare, they are able to push forward new governance agendas for the use of elephants in the tourism industry. This disconnection between "agents" and potential "subjects" of governance in the South allows us to examine the power dynamics of who governs, at what scale and with what implications. However, we do not suggest that Southern actors are passive subjects of international governance mechanisms. Rather, the variations in practices, living and working conditions of elephants used in the safari industry, and in trekking demonstrate that attempts to standardise the industry will be very challenging. Some of the approaches of Northern-based NGOs are mirrored by Southern partners, including the commitment to good welfare standards. Where they might diverge or clash is over the commitment to end the use of captive trained elephants in the industry and that all elephants should ideally be in the wild. This paper indicates important variations within and between Botswana and Thailand in terms of the history of using elephants as work animals, the relationships between mahouts and elephants, the living and working conditions for elephants, and the training practices used to create working animals. Animal welfare NGOs and tour operators need to take a nuanced view of these variations in any attempt to draw up standards for the industry. They will have to engage with and develop standards that are appropriate to the local contexts, especially in Thailand where there is a long-standing history of working with elephants and where working elephants may be critical to long-term species conservation. This is vital to ensure new regulations that are credible and workable for tour operators, elephant owners, animal welfare NGOs and tourists alike.

Finally, it is important to re-state that, while this paper takes the use of elephants in tourism as its case study, many of the questions raised about global governance and the role of NGOs relate to much wider questions in the evolving governance discussion. NGOs have to ask questions about their legitimacy and their claims to ethical "superiority" and to power. The paper raises emerging issues about the governance of heritage resources and the roles of non-local, non-state stakeholders. These issues are more complex than even this paper reveals. A recent paper by Briassoulis (in press) on the emergence of international e-petitions is a useful parallel.

References

Abu Camp. (n.d.). *Abu camp*. Retrieved February 25, 2010, from http://www.abucamp.com/Abu%20Camp.htm

African Conservation Foundation. (n.d.). *Linking people and conservation*. Retrieved March 5, 2010, from http://www.africanconservation.org/component/option,com_mtree/task,viewlink/link_id,89/Itemid,3/

Anantara. (n.d.). *Golden triangle*. Retrieved March 15, 2010, from http://goldentriangle.anantara.com

Bäckstrand, K. (2006). Democratising global environmental governance. Stakeholder democracy after the world summit on sustainable development. *European Journal of International Relations, 12*, 467–498.

Barrientos, S., & Dolan, C. (Eds.). (2006). *Ethical sourcing in the global food system*. London: Earthscan.

Bentrupperbäumer, J. (2005). Human dimensions of wildlife interactions. In D. Newsome, R. Dowling, & S. Moore (Eds.), *Wildlife tourism* (pp. 82–112). Clevedon: Channel View Publications.

Born Free Foundation. (n.d.a). *About us*. Retrieved March 3, 2010, from http://www.bornfree.org.uk

Born Free Foundation. (n.d.b). *Asian elephants*. Retrieved March 3, 2010, from http://www.bornfree.org.uk/animals/asian-elephants/

Born Free Foundation. (n.d.c). *Circuses and performing animals*. Retrieved March 3, 2010, from http://www.bornfree.org.uk/campaigns/zoo-check/circuses-performing-animals/

Born Free Foundation. (n.d.d). *Corporpate sponsorship–Thomson Airways*. Retrieved March 3, 2010, from http://www.bornfree.org.uk/who-we-work-with/corporate-sponsorship/thomson-airways/

Born Free Foundation. (n.d.e). *Corporate sponsorship Kuoni*. Retrieved March 3, 2010, from http://www.bornfree.org.uk/who-we-work-with/corporate-sponsorship/kuoni/

Briassoulis, H. (in press). Opposition to golf-related tourism development: An interpretivist analysis of an on-line petition. *Journal of Sustainable Tourism*. doi: 10.1080/09669582.2010.548559.

Bulbeck, C. (2004). *Facing the wild: Ecotourism, conservation and animal encounters*. London: Earthscan.

Bulkeley, H. (2005). Reconfiguring environmental governance: Towards a politics of scales and networks. *Political Geography, 24*, 875–902.

Butcher, J. (2007). *Ecotourism, NGOs and development: A critical analysis*. London: Routledge.

Chiang Do. (n.d.). *Chiang Dao*. Retrieved March 5, 2010, from http://www.chiangdao.com/nest

Cohen, E. (2008). *Explorations in Thai tourism: Collected case studies*. Amsterdam: Elsevier Science.

Commission on Global Governance. (1995). *Our global neighbourhood*. Oxford: Oxford University Press.

Demeritt, D. (2006). Science studies, climate change and the prospects for a constructivist critique. *Economy and Society, 35*, 453–479.

Dingwerth, K. (2008). Private transnational governance and the developing world: A comparative perspective. *International Studies Quarterly, 52*, 607–634.

Dingwerth, K., & Pattberg, P. (2009). World politics and organizational fields: The case of transnational sustainability governance. *European Journal of International Relations, 15*, 707–743.

Duffy, R., & Moore, L.M. (2010). Neoliberalising nature: Elephant back safaris in Thailand and Botswana. *Antipode: A Radical Journal of Geography, 42*, 469–484.

EMOA. (n.d.). *Elephant managers and owners association.* Retrieved August 20, 2008, from www.emoa.org.za

Evans, K. (n.d.). *Elephant research.* Retrieved November 9, 2010, from http://www.elephantresearch. co.uk/kate-evans.html

Government of South Africa. (2008). *National norms and standards for the management of elephants in South Africa.* Retrieved November 9, 2010, from http://www.environment.gov.za/ HotIssues/2006/elephant/NSE%20Published%20(Master%20copy)%20(26–02-07).doc

Haas, P.M. (1992). Introduction: Epistemic communities and international policy coordination. *International Organisation, 46*, 1–35.

Hewson, M., & Sinclair, T.J. (1999). The emergence of global governance theory. In M. Hewson & T.J. Sinclair (Eds.), *Approaches to global governance theory* (pp. 5–11). New York: State University of New York Press.

HSUS. (2008, February 28). *The HSUS/HSI applauds new regulations on elephant management in South Africa, warns against culling.* Retrieved March 3, 2009, from http://www.hsus.org/ press_and_publications/press_releases/hsus_hsi_applauds_south_africa_elephant_regulations_warn s_against_culling_022808.html

HSUS. (n.d.a). *About us.* Retrieved March 3, 2009, from http://www.hsus.org/hsi/about_us/

HSUS. (n.d.b). *Accomplishments.* Retrieved March 3, 2010, from http://www.hsus.org/hsi/ about_us/accomplishments/2009_accomplishments.html

IFAW. (2006a, March 10). *Deadly elephant safari tourism under fire.* Retrieved March 3, 2010, from http://www.ifaw.org/ifaw_southern_africa/media_center/press_releases/3_10_2006_47659.php

IFAW. (2006b, November 8). *Elephants taken from the wild in Zimbabwe for tourism trade.* Retrieved March 3, 2010, from http://www.ifaw.org/ifaw_united_kingdom/ media_center/press_releases/11_08_2006_10580.php

IFAW. (2007, May 10). *Elephant-back safaris simply "accidents waiting to happen" warns top tourism insurer.* Retrieved March 3, 2010, from http://www.ifaw.org/ifaw_southern_africa/ media_center/press_releases/5_10_2007_47668.php

IFAW. (2008, February 25). *South Africa slams the door on elephant tourism, NGOs rejoice.* Retrieved March 3, 2010, from http://www.ifaw.org/ifaw_southern_africa/ media_center/press_releases/02_25_2008_47935.php

IFAW. (n.d.a). *Who we are.* Retrieved March 3, 2010, from http://www.ifaw.org/ ifaw_united_kingdom/who_we_are/index.php

IFAW. (n.d.b). *Save the world's remaining elephants.* Retrieved March 3, 2010, from http://www. ifaw.org/ifaw_united_kingdom/join_campaigns/save_the_world's_remaining_elephants/securing_ elephant_habitats/shortcut_of_helping_elephants_in_danger.php

Keitumetse, S.O. (2009). The eco-tourism of cultural heritage management (ECT-CHM): Linking heritage and "environment" in the Okavango delta regions of Botswana. *International Journal of Heritage Studies, 15*, 223–244.

Kontogeorgopoulos, N. (1999). Sustainable tourism or sustainable development? Financial crisis, ecotourism, and the "Amazing Thailand". *Current Issues in Tourism, 2*, 316–332.

Kontogeorgopoulos, N. (2009a). The role of tourism in elephant welfare in Northern Thailand. *Journal of Tourism, 10*, 1–19.

Kontogeorgopoulos, N. (2009b). Wildlife tourism in semi-captive settings: A case study of elephant camps in Northern Thailand. *Current Issues in Tourism, 12*, 429–449.

Lair, R.C. (2004). *Gone astray: The care and management of the Asian elephant in domesticity* (4th ed.). Bangkok: FAO Regional Office for Asia and the Pacific.

Litfin, K. (1994). *Ozone discourses: Science and politics in global environmental co-operation.* New York: Columbia University Press.

Liverman, D. (2004). Who governs, at what scale and at what price? Geography, environmental governance, and the commodification of nature. *Annals of the Association of American Geographers, 94*, 734–738.

LWE. (n.d.a). *Living with elephants.* Retrieved February 25, 2010, from http://www. livingwithelephants.org/index.htm

LWE. (n.d.b). *Living with elephants project*. Retrieved July 15, 2010, from http://www. livingwithelephants.org/project.htm

Mae Sa Elephant Camp. (n.d.). *Mae Sa elephant camp*. Retrieved March 5, 2010, from www.MaeSaelephantcamp.com

Mbaiwa, J. (2008). The realities of ecotourism development in Botswana. In A. Spenceley (Ed.), *Responsible tourism: Critical issues for conservation and development* (pp. 205–223). London: Earthscan.

Millspaugh, J.T., Burke, T., Van Dyk, G., Slotow, R., Washburn, B.E., & Woods, R.J. (2007). Stress response of working African elephants to transportation and safari adventures. *Journal of Wildlife Management, 71*, 1257–1260.

Ministry of Foreign Affairs. (2003, July 8). *Thailand's facts and truths about PETA's video footage and elephants in Thailand, Ministry of Foreign Affairs*. Retrieved March 25, 2010, from http://www.mfa.go.th/web/2370.php?id=3250

Murphy, C. (2000). Global governance: Poorly done and poorly understood. *International Affairs, 76*, 789–804.

Newell, P. (2008). The political economy of global environmental governance. *Review of International Studies, 34*, 507–529.

Pattberg, P. (2006). Private governance and the South: Lessons from global forest politics. *Third World Quarterly, 27*, 579–593.

PETA. (n.d.a). *Animals are not ours to use for entertainment*. Retrieved March 3, 2010, from http://www.peta.org.uk/issues/animals-are-not-ours-to-use-for-entertainment/

PETA. (n.d.b). *Urge Thailand to stop elephant torture*. Retrieved March 25, 2010, from http://action.petaasiapacific.com/ea-campaign/clientcampaign.do?ea.client.id=110& ea.campaign.id=2644

PETA. (n.d.c). *Torture of baby elephants in Thailand*. Retrieved March 25, 2010, from http://www.thepetitionsite.com/1/torture-of-baby-elephants-in-thailand

Rosenau, J.N., & Czempiel, E.O. (1992). *Governance without government: Order and change in world politics*. Cambridge: Cambridge University Press.

Sanctuary Lodges. (n.d.). *Sanctuary lodges*. Retrieved July 13, 2008, from http://www. sanctuarylodges.com

Sanctuary Retreats. (n.d.). *Botswana*. Retrieved March 5, 2010, from http://www. sanctuaryretreats.com/lodges/botswana/index.cfm

TAT. (n.d.a). *Amazing Thailand campaign*. Retrieved March 5, 2010, from http://www.amazing-thailand.com/chiang-mai.html

TAT. (n.d.b). *Tourism Thailand*. Retrieved March 5, 2010, from http://www. tourismthailand.org/activities/

TECC. (n.d.). *Thai Elephant Conservation Center*. Retrieved March 15, 2010, from www.chiangthai.com

The Times. (2002, December 22). *Thais say elephant torture video is false*. Retrieved March 15, 2010, from http://www.timesonline.co.uk/tol/news/world/article804512.ece

Tollefson, C., Gale, F., & Haley, D. (2008). *Setting the standard: Certification, governance, and the forest stewardship council*. Vancouver: University of British Columbia Press.

TUI. (n.d.). *Corporate profile*. Retrieved March 3, 2010, from http://www.tuitravelplc.com/ tui/pages/aboutus/corporateprofile

Weiss, T.G. (2009). What happened to the idea of world government. *International Studies Quarterly, 12*, 253–271.

Wilderness Safaris. (n.d.). *Abu camp*. Retrieved March 5, 2010, from http://www.wilderness-safaris.com/botswana_okavango_delta/abu_camp/

Young, O. (Ed.). (1997). *Global governance: Drawing insights from the environmental experience*. Cambridge, MA: MIT Press.

Adopting and implementing a transactive approach to sustainable tourism planning: translating theory into practice

Meredith Wray

School of Tourism & Hospitality Management, Southern Cross University, Gold Coast, New South Wales, Australia

This paper builds on the developing literature on stakeholder engagement, community participation and transactive planning for sustainable tourism. The attributes and conditions needed to foster effective partnerships in strategic tourism planning are discussed, and links to social learning explained. Practical applications of these concepts are demonstrated through case analyses of two-year-long strategic tourism planning processes undertaken for the Australian destination regions of Daylesford and Hepburn Springs (Victoria) and Byron Shire (New South Wales) during 2007–2008. Both used a comprehensive approach to stakeholder engagement, using a transactive planning approach that sought to establish a participatory and inclusive framework for stakeholders to engage in multi-loop learning and corresponding action to achieve sustainable tourism planning outcomes. A seven-stage stakeholder engagement process was used, bringing together stakeholder consultation workshops, setting up a destination planning website to accept broader community input, as well as creating Stakeholder Reference Groups and citizen's juries. The process continued with consultation reports, workshops, draft plans and the communication and implementation of the final plan. The outcomes of the two planning processes were, however, very different, demonstrating the complexity of working in dynamic socio-political contexts, with greater success for the concept of "enabler" organisations and problems for "provider" organisations.

Introduction

The concept of collaborative and participatory approaches to tourism planning and policy-making has been widely advocated as a means to engage government, corporate and community stakeholders with an interest in tourism planning and decision-making processes (e.g. Bramwell, 2004; Bramwell & Lane, 2000; Bramwell & Sharman, 1999; de Araujo & Bramwell, 2002; Hall, 1999, 2000; Selin, 1999; Tosun, 2000, 2006; Vernon, Essex, Pinder, & Curry, 2005). Public participation and engagement has been supported as a growing part of broader urban and regional planning and decision-making, but has been acknowledged as being problematic in practice (Hansen & Mäenpää, 2008). To achieve effective public participation in tourism planning processes, planners must properly collect and act on evidence, opinions and perspectives from all interested or affected stakeholders, who are fully involved in the decision-making process, from the outset of the planning process (Byrd, 2007). The role of tourism planning in addressing social, economic, environmental and political implications of tourism development has also been increasingly discussed (e.g. Costa, 2001; Mair & Reid, 2007; Okazaki, 2008). Moreover, the concept of sustainable tourism is considered by Lew (2007) to offer the greatest potential of placing tourism planners in the role of social change agents.

This paper begins by discussing concepts, from recent literature, that relate to stake-holder engagement and community participation in strategic tourism planning. Principles derived from social learning theory and transactive planning (Friedmann, 1973, 1987; Healy, 2003; Koutsouris, 2009) are then proposed as a means to better identify community needs and goals, expand the number and kinds of stakeholders engaged in tourism planning processes, combat resistant power structures, and foster learning amongst those involved (Lew, 2007; Mair & Reid, 2007). Practical application of these theories is then demonstrated through case analysis of two-year-long strategic tourism planning processes that were undertaken concurrently by tourism planners from Southern Cross University for the Australian destination regions of Daylesford and Hepburn Springs (located in central Victoria) and Byron Shire (located on the far north coast of New South Wales) during 2007–2008.

An important component of both planning processes was the development and implementation of a comprehensive stakeholder engagement framework to foster learning and effective engagement across government, business and community stakeholders throughout the year-long processes. The attributes and conditions identified by McCool and Guthrie (2001) for effective planning in complex situations are used as a framework to analyse both strategic planning processes. From this, the factors that influenced the outcomes of the planning processes are discussed. The approach and analysis of both planning processes may be relevant to stakeholders in other regional destination contexts that aim to achieve effective sustainable tourism planning outcomes and to foster on-going stakeholder engagement in tourism planning and decision-making.

Stakeholder engagement in tourism planning

The emergence of collaborative policymaking is considered to be part of a broader shift in the role of the state from a neo-liberal role as a "provider" to that of an "enabler" (Vernon et al., 2005, p. 327). Furthermore, the public sector's "top-down" approach has been replaced by a more "bottom-up", decentralised and inclusive form of governance in which local communities and businesses are encouraged to take more responsibility for management decisions (Hall, 2000).

A number of tourism scholars have acknowledged the importance of the community in tourism policy and planning (e.g. Bramwell & Sharman, 1999; Murphy, 1985; Richards & Hall, 2000; Scheyvens, 2003; Simmons, 1994; Telfer, 2003; Tosun, 2000, 2006). Hall (2003) contends that this has become a key tenet of sustainable and socially responsible tourism, and suggests that, when examining the role of the community in tourism, it is impossible to separate the social, economic and political processes that operate within a community. The tourism policy and planning framework that underpins a tourism destination system has, however, been described as "complex institutional framework" through which planning and policymaking are filtered (Brooks, 1979, cited by Hall & Page, 2002, p. 6). Inter-dependence and inter-relationships amongst stakeholders are considered to further complicate the already complex planning issues in tourism destination settings (Jamal & Getz, 1999). According to McCool, "it is this change, complexity and uncertainty that form the backdrop against which planning for tourism is developed, tested and implemented"

(2009, p. 137). This growth in community-based tourism planning represents an important shift away from traditional "top-down" approaches; it has been suggested that tourism planning needs to go much further to meet broader community development goals (Mair & Reid, 2007).

From an urban planning perspective, stakeholder engagement and community participation are considered fundamental to fair and representative decision-making (Lew, 2007; Mahjabeen, Shrestha, & Dee, 2009). The voices of the traditionally voiceless are considered critical if plans are to succeed in achieving equity, efficiency and sustainability (Lew, 2007; Mahjabeen et al., 2009). Mahjabeen et al. explain that "when community groups are actively engaged in planning and implementation processes, plans are likely to be more closely matched with stakeholders' needs, interests and expectations, motivating them to achieve social and ecological benefits" (2009, p. 46). Furthermore, stakeholder engagement and community participation in urban planning can help bring together information, knowledge and skills from various backgrounds; achieve mutual learning and personal growth of participants; create a sense of ownership of outcomes; and generate agreement over solutions and increase support for implementation (Mahjabeen et al., 2009).

High levels of public participation in government planning processes are considered to represent "citizen power" whereby citizens are in control and can veto agency decisions (Hansen & Mäenpää, 2008). This high level of participation should be in combination with a high level of access to information. This is in contrast to "token" opportunities or zero opportunity to participate (non-participation). Furthermore, tourism planners should be aware of the negative consequences of uncontrolled tourism development and minimise these negative impacts by respecting the local community's interests (Oviedo-Garcia, Castellanos-Verdugo, & Martin-Ruiz, 2008). Quaghebeur, Masschelein, and Nguyen have also questioned whether participation is "merely a process of giving opportunities, as it is frequently presented, or whether participation also requires specific imposed engagements from the participants?" (2004, p. 154).

For stakeholder participation to be empowering, "stakeholders must be engaged throughout the process and know that their participation has the potential to influence the decision" (Byrd, 2007, p. 8). The extent of community participation is, however, affected by the available financial resources at local level, the cultural relationship of the host community with tourism businesses, levels of experience of tourism, and expertise and competence in tourism locally (Tosun, 2006). Moreover, developing and undertaking a participatory approach has been criticised for being time-consuming and requiring the ability to overcome barriers, including lack of experience, business inexperience, insufficient financial assistance, conflicting vested interests and high transaction costs in terms of getting the programme started and maintained (Okazaki, 2008). Okazaki (2008), however, claims that despite these implementation barriers, a community-based approach is still the best course of action.

Mediating stakeholder interests in sustainable tourism development

The growing complexity of communities and relationships between them are considered to pose challenges for the sustainable development of tourism. Richins and Pearce (2000) explain that this is because of the divergent priorities of tourists, residents, investors, providers of tourist and leisure experiences, and non-government and government organisations; also, the complex relationships that occur between these groups create enormous challenges in meeting the needs of all concerned. Destinations are, however, recognised as being highly varied, and each faces a unique set of problems and opportunities (Laws, 1995).

Conflict resolution and meditation are, however, considered as an integral component of sustainable tourism development (Hall, 2000). Conflicting goals are the core of arguments about sustainable tourism policies and actions (McCool, 2009). Although many goals are in conflict, there may also be many shared goals and interests, and it is this tension that can create the impetus for creative solutions to pragmatic problems (McCool, 2009). Tourism planners have to mediate the values and interests of stakeholders involved in tourism to deliver planning outcomes that are acceptable. Planning must therefore build the "consensus about appropriate direction and emphasise learning to deal with uncertainty" and create venues that encourage dialogue and learning (McCool, 2009, p. 138).

Mediating public interests and sustainable tourism goals, and determining methods to achieve them, has traditionally been approached through rational-comprehensive planning processes (McCool, 2009). This process uses "neutral" experts to provide a systematic, reproducible process for identifying desired futures and the pathways to them, with the aim of avoiding bias in decisions (McCool, 2009). In terms of managing the tourism planning process, Mair and Reid (2007) suggest that consideration should be given to: what components must be in place for sound community-based tourism planning? What are the roles of the expert and the community? Who is in charge of generating skills necessary for tourism planning and development processes? And who controls these processes? McCool (2009) further explains that tourism planning requires a partnership composed of planners/managers, scientists and various constituencies representing different tourism players. McCool and Guthrie (2001) proposed four major attributes and three conditions to effective partnerships in "messy" tourism planning contexts for protected areas. These attributes and conditions can readily apply to strategic tourism destination planning processes (see Table 1).

Transactive planning and social learning

Building on the need to engage and mediate public and private sector interests in tourism planning, the adoption of a transactive planning approach, which is based on social learning theory and interpersonal interaction with stakeholders, allows the planner to bring process knowledge (theory, methodology, skills and larger societal perspectives) to facilitate a shared understanding about principles of sustainable tourism (Lew, 2007) and the process of strategic tourism planning. In turn, stakeholders bring their personal knowledge (experience and local conditions and needs) to the planning process (Lew, 2007). The goal is to foster engagement amongst diverse stakeholder interests (Wray, 2009) and to build self-learning and intelligent institutions that are able to self-adjust to a changing world (Lew, 2007).

Social learning is described as focusing on overcoming the contradictions between theory and practice, or knowing and acting (Friedmann, 1987). Its theory is derived from John Dewey and his scientific epistemology that emphasised "learning by doing" and that of Marxist philosophy and theory (Friedmann, 1987). The underpinning philosophy of social learning is that "knowledge is derived from experience and validated in practice, and is integrally part of action" (Friedmann, 1987, p. 81). Knowledge therefore emerges from "an on-going dialectical process in which the main emphasis is on new practical undertakings; existing understanding (theory) is enriched with lessons drawn from experience, and the 'new' understanding is then applied in a continual process of change and action" (Friedmann, 1987, p. 81). Friedmann's (1987) social learning typology is widely cited in urban and regional planning literature and is founded on the following meanings and ideologies:

Table 1. Attributes and conditions needed to foster effective partnerships in strategic tourism planning.

	Description
Attributes	
Representativeness	Constructing a carefully engineered, explicitly deliberative and inclusive process that attends to the diversity of values and beliefs of public interests. By being inclusive, the power relationships in a setting are transformed, changing the role and reducing the influence of technocratic expertise and strengthening the authority of experiential knowledge and public preferences.
Ownership	A sense of caring and responsibility not only for the destination but also for the plan and its actions. That is, stakeholders (partners) have an intrinsic interest in the outcome and thus are motivated to ensure the implementation of agreed-upon actions. The resulting plan is developed by the people affected by or who have an interest in the destination.
Learning	Creating opportunities for learning that focus not only on cause–effect relationships but also on understanding the broader tourism system.
Relationships	Mechanisms that build relationships so that partners focus their energies on framing and resolving issues rather than taking positions. Good relationships are characterised by openness, lack of hidden agendas, understanding of beliefs and a focus on authentic communication and mutual respect.
Conditions	
Trust	Includes organisational trust that involves fairness of the process used to develop the plan and people being treated fairly, and interpersonal trust that includes honesty, benevolence and reciprocity.
Power	Raise attention to the existence of power within the tourism system and foster opportunities to renegotiate power relationships that incorporate and empower a wider diversity of knowledge to achieve implementation of planning actions.
Access to knowledge	A strategic willingness to share expertise and communicate technical information to various stakeholders by partners involved in tourism planning processes.

Source: Adapted from McCool (2009); McCool and Guthrie (2001).

- *What is action?* – The purposeful activity undertaken by an actor, individual or collective, within the actor's environment. The actor is engaged in the action autonomously and develops strategy and tactics that will guide the actor through the action. The actor requires useful information that may lead to cumulative learning; each new cycle of actions leads to a new start.
- *Who is the actor?* – Actors may be individual persons, small groups or "human organisations" and communities. The principal focus of the social learning approach is a task-orientated action group that is dynamic, interactive and involves fewer than a dozen participants. Collective actors, such as organisations, communities and social movements, may be disassembled into component action groups.
- *Who learns?* – In social learning, actor and learner are assumed to be one and the same. The action group learns from its own practice. Whether organisation, community or movement also learns will depend on the nature of intergroup relations and the formal structure of authority.
- *What are the principal modes of learning?* – Learning manifests itself as a change in practical activity that is directly woven into social practice. It is rarely systematised or articulated in the formal language of scientific discourse. It is a form of tacit and

informal learning. It may involve change agents that guide and assist an actor in the process of changing reality. They are generally professionals or paraprofessionals (trainers, facilitators, process consultants, organisers) who bring kinds of formal knowledge to the on-going social practice of their client or group. To be effective, change agents must develop a transactive relationship with their client conducive to mutual learning. Single or double-loop learning may also be involved. The former involves a simple change in tactics or strategy of the action to solve a given problem; the latter requires an adjustment of the norms governing the action process and, specifically, change in the actor's theory of reality, values and beliefs.

• *Does social learning require theory?* – In social learning, knowledge of reality and practice exerts a mutual influence on each other. Theory, however, is based not only on an actor's evolving experience but on prior learning as well, reflecting the actor's class position, work experience and formal education (adapted from Friedmann, 1987, pp. 183–187).

These concepts are important for sustainable tourism planning processes that aim to integrate varied stakeholder perspectives and to better engage these stakeholders in the decision-making process. From the planner's perspective, an understanding of the destination context, specific destination conditions and issues, and stakeholder (actor) roles and activities emerge through effective and meaningful engagement with stakeholders involved in the planning process. In turn, a planner's education and practical planning experience in sustainable tourism planning can influence the knowledge passed onto stakeholders engaged in a planning process. An ability to develop a "transactive relationship" with stakeholders and to be open to their varied learning processes and underpinning values is significant.

Application of social learning typologies in sustainable tourism planning is limited. Case study research undertaken by Koutsouris (2009) applied concepts from social learning to sustainable tourism development in the Lake Pastiras area of Greece. This study confirmed that "it is only through interactive (participative), concerted action that stakeholders are able to co-construct an issue and its solution" (Kotsouris, 2009, p. 567). Furthermore, the shift towards sustainable development involves double-loop learning. If networks for interaction and learning are not established, interventions may generate uncertainties, alienation and potential social disintegration, and sustainable tourism development will not be achieved.

A transactive approach to sustainable tourism planning therefore relies on a process that is rigorous, informed and grounded in its engagement with diverse stakeholders and communities of interest (Dredge & Lawrence, 2007); fosters an action cycle of knowledge and learning amongst stakeholders (Friedmann, 1987); and mediates public interests and sustainable tourism goals (McCool, 2009). The major challenge of utilising this approach is, however, the level of time and personal commitment that is required by the planner (Lew, 2007).

Study methodology

A case study methodology was used to trace the tourism planning processes undertaken for the two destinations. This approach is highly suitable for developing in-depth understandings of complex social phenomenon and unfolding processes within contextual situations (Brotherton, 1999; Merriam, 1998; Yin, 2003). Case study discussion and analysis is based upon the personal knowledge and observations of the author who undertook the role of lead planner for both strategic planning processes. Observations were recorded in project diaries and a voice recorder during and following relevant forums and meetings related to both planning processes. Analysis of these observations was supplemented with an analysis of published and unpublished secondary data, including government and non-government documents (e.g. relevant planning documents and reports, media reports), and contrasted to relevant literature. For the purposes of this research, a stakeholder is defined as any individual or group that had actively been involved in tourism policy, planning, destination management and marketing for the destination cases. The following explains the methods that underpinned the approach to both strategic tourism planning processes.

Establishment of a sustainable tourism research team

A research team comprising three senior academics with considerable theoretical and practical knowledge and experience of sustainable tourism planning was established. A consultation expert, with extensive theoretical knowledge and practical experience in community consultation, was also recruited to the destination planning team. Quaghebeur et al. (2004) confirm the usefulness of employing an outside facilitator for the participatory process in which all actors are obliged to take and clarify a position. The team's approach to tourism planning incorporated concepts derived from stakeholder and community engagement, mediation of stakeholder interests, sustainable tourism, social learning theory and transactive approaches to tourism planning as explained earlier. In line with Friedmann's (1973, 1987) principles for social learning, the research team became an "action team", adopting the role of change agents to coordinate and bring formal knowledge and expertise to the planning processes. Furthermore, the team undertook both planning processes as research rather than as consultancy projects. This was important: it meant that considerable time was invested in consideration and application of sustainable tourism planning theories to practice and the development of an action cycle of knowledge and learning amongst the team, clients and stakeholders.

Appointment of a lead planner

A strategic tourism planner/researcher with considerable knowledge of sustainable tourism and tourism planning processes, established socio-political networks within the destination regions and a real interest in working with diverse destination stakeholders was then appointed. As argued by Friedmann (1973), effective planning depends on the planner's skill in managing personal relations. The role of this planner was to coordinate and manage both strategic tourism planning processes, *and* to foster trust and maintain a dialogue amongst government, business and community stakeholders. This helped foster a transactive relationship with clients and stakeholders, to enhance the learning capacity of these relational networks and to create stakeholder ownership of the resulting tourism plans, so that strategies and actions could be implemented over the 10-year life of the plans. It was also considered important that the lead planner should be embedded as much as possible within both destinations to cultivate regular interpersonal interaction and rapport with stakeholders and "learning by doing". Thus, the researcher became one of the actors "so they can understand the subjective experience of the individuals involved and because the participants draw in the researcher in current politics as an informant and as a source of knowledge" (Zahra & Ryan, 2005, p. 7).

Planning time frame

Both year-long planning processes were undertaken almost concurrently. The Destination Daylesford planning process commenced in February; the Byron Shire process commenced in May 2007. This allowed planners to gain and apply knowledge learnt from the Daylesford planning process to the Byron process. The underpinning philosophy of the team's approach to strategic tourism planning was to foster the emergence and adoption of knowledge throughout the planning processes. As explained by Friedmann in "an on-going dialectical process in which the main emphasis was on new practical undertakings; existing understanding (theory) that was enriched with lessons drawn from experience, and the 'new' understanding were then applied in a continual process of change and action" (1987, p. 81).

Background to the cases

Daylesford and Hepburn Springs

The twin towns of Daylesford and Hepburn Springs are located in the local government area of Hepburn Shire, Victoria. The population of Hepburn Shire is 13,732 individuals (ABS, 2006a). The region is c. one hour's drive from Melbourne, adjacent to the cities of Ballarat and Bendigo. This is a "Spa Country", with over 80% of Australia's mineral water reserves. The Hepburn Mineral Springs Bathhouse was Australia's original spa experience, dating from 1895. The area is also renowned for its natural beauty, historic architecture, innovative and quality tourism enterprises, dynamic creative industries and diverse communities. Tourism is an important contributor to the growth and character of the region. Daylesford and Hepburn Springs attracted 234,000 domestic overnight visitors in 2008, with a further 520,000 day visitors. International visitation was relatively low at 4651 visitors (Tourism Research Australia, 2009).

Tourism Victoria has identified Daylesford and Hepburn Springs as a Level-One[1] destination region. Tourism Victoria, along with the Daylesford & Macedon Ranges Campaign Committee, provides considerable marketing and professional support. The Victorian Government has also invested $8.6 million in the redevelopment of the Hepburn Springs Bathhouse (completed in September 2008), with the remaining $10.3 million coming from Hepburn Shire Council. In 2006, Tourism Victoria identified the need for a Strategic Tourism Plan for Daylesford and Hepburn Springs and its surroundings to provide focus and direction for the tourism industry and better utilise opportunities provided by the area's unique Mineral Water Reserves and Bathhouse redevelopment (Lawrence & Buultjens, 2008a).

Byron Shire

Located 180 km south of Brisbane and 800 km north of Sydney, Byron Shire is on the north coast of New South Wales. The region is diverse, with World Heritage-listed rain-forests, an extensive coastal region providing excellent bathing and surf beaches, unspoilt hinterland, tropical agriculture, relaxed and diverse cultural communities, and innovative enterprises. Tourism is important for the Shire's economic development. Byron Bay is a well-established destination attracting 416,000 domestic overnight visitors, 181,400 international overnight visitors and 812,000 day visitors in 2008 (Tourism Research Australia, 2009). The population of Byron Shire is 28,766 individuals (ABS, 2006b).

The popularity of Byron Bay and the broader Shire as a destination coupled with its attractiveness as a sea change locality[2] has placed strains on infrastructure and service facilities, with an increased concern from residents about tourism and residential growth. The Shire's tourism and business sectors have also supported the need for a coordinated and strategic approach to tourism management. And, despite its popularity as a destination, visitor numbers have remained relatively flat since 2002. Although Byron Shire Council (BSC) has developed sustainable development policies in many areas, there had not been a comprehensive tourism strategy formulated since 1988. The need for a Tourism Management Plan and an accompanying Action Plan was identified as part of the Council's commitment to ensure the sustainable development, management and marketing of tourism for Byron Shire over the next 10 years (Lawrence & Buultjens, 2008b).

The strategic tourism planning process

A chronological review integrating the theory and practice of the stages undertaken for both strategic tourism planning processes is presented and discussed below.

Stage 1: appointment of a Destination Steering Committee

Mahjabeen et al. (2009, p. 46) propose that specifically targeted platforms organised under an independent body that is downwardly accountable to stakeholder groups are needed to initiate, institutionalise and sustain effective and fair participation in planning. McCool (2009) explains that such planning requires a partnership composed of planners/managers, scientists (experts) and various constituencies representing different tourism players. Churugsa, McIntosh, and Simmons (2007) also confirm that to ensure better tourism management at a local level, the establishment of a local working group consisting of representatives from public and private sectors and the community is an essential starting point.

The first step was, therefore, to establish a Destination Steering Committee to guide the development of the tourism planning processes. For Daylesford and Hepburn Springs, a Destination Daylesford Steering Committee (DDSC) was considered and appointed by Tourism Victoria, in conjunction with Hepburn Shire Council and the Hepburn Regional Tourism Association (HRTA). The Committee comprised 12 ordinary members representing local tourism and business operations and a member from the local community association. The Steering Committee was guided by an executive team comprising the president of the local tourism association, a representative from Tourism Victoria, the General Manager of Hepburn Shire Council, an elected Councillor and the tourism manager. This executive was led by an independent Chairperson (not involved in the tourism industry), selected for the position on the basis of his professional management skills, community leadership and local knowledge. The DDSC had, therefore, a range of "experts" who were able to make assessment about the immediate and foreseeable future (Treuen & Lane, 2003). The selection of the DDSC was undertaken prior to appointing the tourism planners. However, the research team supported the broad stakeholder representation of the Committee and its executive.

In contrast to this broad committee representing government, business and community interests, the steering committee formed for the Byron Shire tourism planning process comprised a small committee that included three Councillors (including the Mayor), Council's Planning Director and the Community Economic Development Officer (Chair of the Committee). At the outset of the planning process, the tourism planners expressed concern to Council planners that a small and council-centric committee could shape or frustrate the planning process (Treuen & Lane, 2003), alienate other important business and community stakeholder interests, and impact on stakeholder engagement in the planning process. It was explained that this was the usual structure of the Council steering committees and would not be altered. The research team was, however, confident that a good working relationship could be developed with the Council's Planning Director, as he was well experienced in mediating dynamic and contentious Council planning issues, and the Community Economic Development Officer had considerable professional experience and economic development knowledge.

The research team met with the respective steering committees to review their expectations and to discuss the strategic planning process to be adopted over the coming year. From this meeting, the Committee and planners developed objectives to guide the development of the respective tourism plans. The Destination Daylesford planning process had commenced in February 2007; the Byron Shire Tourism Management planning process commenced three months later in May 2007. This allowed the research team to take knowledge learnt from engaging with Daylesford to the Byron planning project. Both committees were convened on a regular basis during the year-long strategic planning processes to discuss progress and provide advice to the planners.

Stage 2: development and communication of a strategic planning approach

A comprehensive literature review was undertaken by the research team to determine best practice in sustainable tourism planning and to explain the significance of adopting a sustainable and collaborative approach that engaged government, business and community stakeholders. In addition, a comprehensive situational analysis was undertaken for each destination region that involved examining the demographic and economic profile; analysing visitation statistics; auditing all accommodation and tourism product facilities, attractions and supporting facilities; and identifying the key issues associated with tourism for each destination region. Lankford (2001) confirms that the data from a community environmental scan become the starting point in developing a citizen involvement process.

The sustainable tourism planning approach and situational analysis findings were documented in separate reports presented to each of the Destination Steering Committees and their Council. This was an important step in the transactive planning process and served as a means for the research team to advocate to politicians and bureaucrats the importance of a collaborative and sustainable approach to tourism planning and to engage bureaucrats and politicians from the outset in the planning journey. This approach is supported by McCool (2009) who confirms that the process of consensus-building can be integrated with collaborative learning processes to facilitate an understanding of multiple interests and a basic scientific understanding of relevant destination conditions.

Stage 3: Regional Expert Panel

Experts with considerable knowledge about regional tourism were invited by the research team to participate in a Regional Expert Panel to provide advice to the planning processes. Experts volunteered their time willingly and included the Chair of Australian Regional Tourism Network, Manager of Regional Tourism Development – Tourism Victoria, Marketing Manager Tourism Noosa, a strategic planner – Tourism New South Wales, a leading tourism professor, and a community and cultural tourism professional. The Panel also provided feedback on the draft plans.

Stage 4: stakeholder engagement

A comprehensive stakeholder engagement process was developed by the research team for each destination region to effectively engage business, government and community stakeholders in the planning processes in order to:

- Understand the interests, values and aspirations of the government, business and community towards tourism;
- Educate local stakeholders about a sustainable tourism approach and the issues facing tourism;
- Develop a transactive relationship with government, business and community stakeholders to establish a shared vision for the future development and management of tourism within the region; and
- Identify important destination development, management and marketing issues to be addressed by the Plan (Lawrence, 2007; Lawrence & Buultjens, 2009).

The stakeholder engagement framework that was developed to inform the strategic tourism planning process is shown in Figure 1. From this, each of the seven phases is explained.

Phase 1: stakeholder consultation workshops

Stakeholder organisations were identified by both steering committees to represent the eight stakeholder groups, with an interest in tourism for the regions, including tourism organisations and key tourism operations; business organisations, Council and their relevant committees, environmental groups; arts and cultural groups, events and festivals, government departments (local, regional and state), and community groups. For Daylesford and Hepburn Springs, 45 organisations accepted the invitation to participate to be represented in the workshop process. For Byron, 63 organisations participated. The research team was pleased with the interest and support of the diverse stakeholder representation. Consultation workshops were facilitated in Daylesford in July 2008 and Byron in September 2008. Each workshop comprised 8–20 participants to allow for effective focus group discussion.

Participants at the workshops were presented with an overview of the strategic planning process and the importance of adopting a collaborative and sustainable approach to tourism planning. As confirmed by McCool (2009), the integration of different forms of knowledge and perspectives leads to an enhanced knowledge of the tourism system and ways to solve the challenges confronting it.

Participants were then asked to:

(1) Identify the values that should underpin the development of a vision statement to guide the development and management of tourism in their destination regions over the next 10 years;
(2) Develop a vision statement from these values; and
(3) Identify and discuss the important issues to be considered in the development of the strategic tourism management plans in a focus group forum (Lawrence, 2007). This part of the workshop process was important as it allowed stakeholders to hear the views of different groups and organisations and debate the key issues and challenges facing the destination.

Stakeholder engagement process

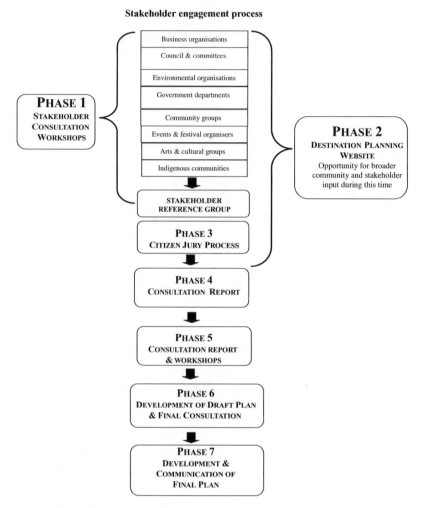

Figure 1. Stakeholder engagement process.

The research team found that workshop participants demonstrated a high level of enthusiasm and interest in contributing to strategic planning process. Planners were pleased and surprised to find that, from the diverse range of stakeholders represented, most had common values and visions for tourism. These values and visions were then shared amongst the various stakeholder workshops, thereby creating an educative forum for information exchange. As confirmed by Hall (2000, p. 188):

> if sustainability is to be treated seriously, then it therefore becomes vital that tourism planning, and public participation as a component of tourism planning, addresses values and people's perception of the "truth" rather than just be geared to short-term interest management which deals with the "facts" as seen by the makers of the rules of the tourism planning game.

To facilitate on-going stakeholder engagement in the strategic planning processes, each of the eight stakeholder groups were then asked to nominate a representative from their group to form a Stakeholder Reference Group for each destination region. The role of this group was to consider and communicate plans, findings and actions as they developed during the life of the planning process back to their various stakeholder organisations. The research team considered that the establishment of the Stakeholder Reference Group would help create a sense of ownership over the planning outcomes, generate agreement over solutions and increase support for the Plan's implementation (Healy, 1997). Moreover, stakeholder organisations were given some power and authority to influence strategic tourism planning decisions in a meaningful way. The Stakeholder Reference Group was invited to further consultation workshops in phases 3 and 4 of the consultation process.

Phase 2: development of a destination planning website

To gain support for tourism planning, planners should be concerned about how to communicate benefits through marketing techniques to gain resident engagement (Oviedo-Garcia et al., 2008). A dedicated planning website for each destination region was developed by the research team, in consultation with a web design professional, as an additional means for interested individuals and stakeholder groups to source information about sustainable tourism, the strategic planning process and to provide input into the consultation process. As with the stakeholder workshops, the community was invited to identify the important values and issues that should be addressed within the Plan. The public were informed about this opportunity through media articles and council notices that appeared in the local newspapers during the stakeholder engagement process. A media consultant was also employed to strategically consider the public relations and media aspects of the planning processes for both destination regions. The research team had expected considerable input from the community through this public forum. However, for Daylesford, only three people contributed to the site, and for Byron, 17 people contributed. The poor response to these planning websites may indicate the relative newness of information and communications technology (ICT) as a means to engage with interested public in planning. It may also demonstrate that although many assumed that the development of ICT would bring a global community of interaction and learning, there may be a "digital divide": some have no access to ICT (first-order effects) and some people lack the ability to use the technology (second-order effects) (Dewan & Riggins, 2005).

The research team was also mindful that an open website forum could allow certain individuals or groups to dominate this consultation forum. However, this was not the case, and analysis of the contributions to the websites showed issues similar to those raised in the workshops.

Phase 3: citizen jury process

An important aspect of managing tourism in a destination is working with and empowering local people who are not directly involved in tourism (Lawrence & Buultjens, 2009). To do this, it is necessary to build their capacity to reflect on tourism decision-making processes and to participate constructively in decisions about tourism. Rather than conducting public meetings or calling for public submissions, a citizen's jury approach was proposed as an appropriate and innovative method to engage the local community in a meaningful way in the tourism planning process (Lawrence & Buultjens, 2009). Citizen's juries are acknowledged as newer methods of consultation designed to focus on the need for informed views in the policy process (Catt & Murphy, 2003). The most widely discussed example is the planning cell initiated in Germany in the 1970s and later adopted in Britain and Australia (Catt & Murphy, 2003). A citizen jury could be considered to be situated on the "partnership" level of the "ladder of citizen participation", as proposed by Arnstein (1969), where citizens are encouraged to share planning and decision-making responsibilities.

To consult the community using a citizens' jury process requires a randomly selected group of citizens reflecting, as far as possible, the profile of the community from which it is drawn (Fisher, 2007). This is important: the community will be affected by decisions that the jury makes on its behalf. As in a legal jury, it is assumed that the jury is made up of people who do not have a vested interest in the outcome and who consider the evidence before them in coming to a consensus decision. Jury selection is thus an important component of making the jury process transparent and assuring the citizens that those making decisions on their behalf reflect as far as possible the views of the broader community (Fisher, 2007). The citizen jury process was developed by an independent and experienced consultant and comprised the following stages:

(1) Random selection of households drawn from the Council database (Hepburn Shire Council) and 350 residents of Byron Shire generated from the 2004 Electoral Roll.
(2) Letters were sent to each selected household, inviting them to put their names forward to be included in a "pool" from which the jury would be selected.
(3) Citizens were asked to send back a consent letter with information about their gender, age group, place of residence, occupation and length of residency in the region.
(4) Each household on the list was then contacted by phone. This was an important part of the process as people needed to ask questions, and in some cases, be reassured that their input would be valuable before making a decision about making themselves available to participate in the jury.
(5) A jury pool was then determined. At Daylesford, 41 people, and at Byron, 45 people put their names forward to be included in the jury pool.
(6) An ideal statistical profile was then developed for each destination region sourced from the 2006 Australian Bureau of Statistics data.
(7) The profile of each of the destination regions was then matched to the jury pool and a jury of 20 members was selected.
(8) Final juries of 15 residents representing the Daylesford and 18 residents representing the Byron Shire were then confirmed. Juries of this nature have varied from between 12 and 25 participants (Fisher, 2007).

Jury members were called to meet over a two and half day period from Friday evening to Sunday (August 2007 – Daylesford and November 2007 – Byron). At the outset of the jury process, members were presented with an overview of the jury deliberation process and asked to consider their role. As explained by Quaghebeur et al. (2004), the project should be clearly positioned as part of the negotiation process, with project personnel expressing their objectives and interests in the negotiation process. Each jury was then first presented with information by a range of experts engaged in tourism across state, regional and local levels. These experts were selected by the research team to present a balanced overview of tourism to the jury. Topics covered included the factors that contribute to the success of regional tourism destinations, concepts about sustainable tourism and government roles in tourism for the region (national, state and local). Experienced tourism practitioners discussed positive and negative issues and impacts of tourism from a local perspective. This approach is supported by Harrill who advocates "on-going resident participation and education must be key components of tourism development processes, with planners reinforcing perceptions of positive economic benefits and effectively addressing what is being done or can be done to mitigate adverse social and environmental impacts" (2004, p. 263).

Each jury was also presented with an overview of the issues that had been raised in the stakeholder workshops, facilitating double-loop learning. McCool (2009) confirms that deliberation that results from the integration of different forms of knowledge and perspectives is considered to enhance understanding of the tourism system and ways to solve the challenges confronting it. The jury was then asked to deliberate on this information and develop a vision for the future of tourism for their destination region and the issues they considered important from a community perspective. The outcome was a presentation to the respective Destination Steering Committees.

Phase 4: consultation report

A consultation report was prepared by the research team and presented to each Destination Steering Committee at the consultation of the stakeholder engagement process. Analysis involved transcription of the data collected from the stakeholder workshops, contributions submitted to the planning websites and the citizen jury process. The important values derived from these processes were organised under common themes. A common vision statement was determined from those developed during the consultation process. Analysis of issues and challenges revealed the need for Daylesford and Hepburn Springs to consider 20, and for Byron Shire 28, principal issues. These were organised under the platforms of destination management, development and marketing.

Phase 5: consultation workshops

An important initiative of the consultation process was to provide an opportunity for stakeholder feedback on the findings of the consultation process. The consultation report was distributed to the Destination Steering Committees and the Stakeholder Reference Groups for consideration prior to a second consultation workshop. The Stakeholder Reference Group for each destination region was instructed to distribute their consultation report to their stakeholder organisations to gather feedback from their constituents for discussion at the workshop. The workshop was scheduled as an important forum for the Steering Committees and the Stakeholder Reference Group members to co-construct the important issues arising in the development of the Plan and help develop goals and objectives cooperatively. Koutsouris confirms that "the creation of spaces of exchange may facilitate a reflexive process and engage new stakeholders in joint action and learning" (2009, p. 575).

For Daylesford and Hepburn Springs, a final consultation workshop was undertaken with the Destination Steering Committee and Stakeholder Reference Group together. The research team considered it important to foster an on-going relationship between stakeholders to ensure effective implementation of the Plan and its strategies. A final version of the Plan was developed from this last stage of feedback. An additional report was also prepared detailing stakeholder feedback and how it had been addressed within each of the final plans, thus ensuring transparency and on-going trust in the planning process.

A consultation workshop was also facilitated with the Byron Shire Destination Steering Committee. However, the Committee decided not to invite the Stakeholder Reference Group and Citizen Jury to this forum. This was a significant decision that could be considered a trigger point in the alienation of business and community stakeholders involved in the Byron Shire tourism planning process. The consultation report was, however, distributed to the Stakeholder Reference Group for distribution and consideration by constituents prior to a workshop that was facilitated separately with this Group. The research team prepared an additional report that detailed the Stakeholder Reference Group's feedback and how it had been addressed within the Plan. However, the momentum for engagement of Council, business and community stakeholder engagement had been lost.

Phase 6: development of a draft plan and final consultation

A draft strategic tourism management plan was developed for each destination. Objectives, strategies and actions were organised under the themes of destination management, development and marketing. Both plans incorporated an annual evaluation and monitoring process to ensure that the strategies and actions were actioned and plans could be adjusted where appropriate to ensure a flexible, adaptive planning approach. For each destination region, the Steering Committee, the Stakeholder Reference Group and the Citizen Jury were invited to review the Draft Plan and provide the final feedback. The Plans were also considered by the Regional Expert Panel. The research team then provided a report for each Destination Steering Committee on how the feedback had been addressed in the final version of the respective Plans. Feedback for the *Destination Daylesford Strategic Tourism Plan* was relatively minor, and the Plan was adopted by the Council.

In contrast, the development and adoption of a final version of the *Byron Shire Tourism Management Plan* was not so straightforward. Following the development and submission of a Draft Plan to the Council in August 2008, the Council determined that the Plan would have to go through a six-week public exhibition process from 11 September to 23 October. This was contrary to what had been determined at the outset of the planning process in May 2007, when the Steering Committee had determined that given the extensive consultation process, a public exhibition process was not necessary. Interestingly, local government elections were scheduled for 30 October 2008. At that time, the research team viewed that the placement of the Plan on public exhibition process was a way to stall the adoption of the Plan by the Council until a new Council was in office.

The Byron Destination Steering Committee determined that the principal strategies and recommendations of the Draft Plan should be presented to stakeholders and the community through public meetings prior to the public exhibition process. Two public meetings were held in September 2008 in two separate parts of the Shire (Byron Bay and Brunswick Heads). Two members of the research team provided participants with an overview of the sustainable tourism planning process, including an overview of the consultation process, a snapshot of tourism in the Shire, key priorities of the plan and important next steps. More significantly, the research team emphasised the ways by which stakeholders and community members could have further input to the final plan.

Results of the public exhibition process were analysed by the Council staff and no feedback was provided to the research team, stakeholders or the community. This was contrary to the objectives of the stakeholder engagement process undertaken during the year-long planning process, that sought to foster transparency had proposed consultation reports clearly explaining how stakeholder input had been addressed in the development of the Plan.

Phase 7: development and communication of the final plan

A final version of the *Destination Daylesford Strategic Tourism Plan* was publically released in August 2008. To communicate the Plan more concisely, a four-page executive summary was produced by Tourism Victoria in consultation with the research team. The Plan was launched at a function for regional and local tourism and business operators, the DDSC and Citizen Jury in August 2008 by the Chief Executive Officer of Tourism Victoria. He stated: "tourism, if it is to work effectively, requires a level of cohesion and commitment . . . this plan will enable Daylesford, Hepburn Springs and the region to become a renowned national and international wellness and mineral water centre that it has the capacity to be" (Greg Hywood, personal communication, 2008). The positive acceptance of a potentially controversial plan was due in large part to the thorough and genuine stakeholder engagement process adopted. As stated by Tourism Victoria's Regional Advisor at the launch, "consultation has been very important – it has been world's best practice" (Smith, personal communication, 2008).

For Byron Shire, a final version of the Plan was amended internally by the Council, and in places was contrary to what the research team, Destination Steering Committee, Stakeholder Reference Group and Citizen Jury had determined through extensive and transparent consultation. The resulting Plan was not adopted by BSC until September 2009, a year after the planning process had been completed. There was no public launch.

Discussion

From a social learning perspective, the adoption of a transactive and sustainable approach to tourism planning sought to facilitate stakeholder engagement and an action cycle of learning with government, business and community stakeholders throughout both planning processes. Important strategies to facilitate this approach included the establishment of:

- a research planning team and a Regional Tourism Expert Panel, with considerable expertise in sustainable tourism planning that provided considerable tourism planning knowledge and expertise;
- appointment of a lead planner who became embedded in both destinations to develop a transactive relationship with clients and stakeholders, and in particular, developed an effective transactive relationship with the Chair of both Destination Steering Committees;
- an extensive stakeholder engagement process that sought to mediate broad represen-tation and trust of stakeholder interests across government, business and community interests across state, regional and local levels; and
- regular feedback mechanisms (workshops, formal and informal meetings, reports) employed throughout the planning processes to nurture dialogue, foster cooperation amongst stakeholders and joint ownership of the resulting plan.

Although both planning processes were similar, the outcomes were different. Dayles-ford and Hepburn Springs had benefited from a supportive state tourism organisation that acted as an "enabler" (Vernon et al., 2005) that helped to establish an effective steering committee structure from the outset and provided expertise throughout the year-long plan-ning process. At a destination level, local government and the local tourism organisation had also recognised from the outset of the benefit of working collaboratively. From a social learning perspective, the DDSC was a core task-orientated action group that was dynamic and interactive with the research team, Stakeholder Reference Group and Citizen Jury. As a result, an active network of actors emerged who were actively engaged in multiple-loop learning that considered strategies to foster long-term sustainable tourism management for the region. Multi-loop learning and innovative planning solutions were developed across the research team, Destination Steering Committee, Stakeholder Reference Group, Citizen Jury and interested stakeholders. As explained by Friedmann (1987, p. 185):

In the social learning tradition, actor and learner are assumed to be one and the same. The action group learns from its own practice. Whether organisation, community, or movement also learns will depend on the nature of intergroup relations and the formal structure of authority.

As a consequence, the final Destination Daylesford Strategic Tourism Plan was well supported and owned by stakeholders.

In contrast, BSC acted in a neo-liberal role as a "provider" rather than as an "enabler" (Vernon et al., 2005) of the Byron Shire Tourism Management planning process. As such, stakeholders were mistrustful of the Council from the outset rather than "supportive, confident and productive" (Eber 1992, cited by Yuksel & Yuksel, 2008). The relationship between the Research Team and the Byron Steering Committee was dogmatic, with local governance and political agendas dominating the planning process. This meant that the Research Team and the BSC Community Economic Development Officer had to work hard to foster stakeholder engagement and double-loop learning. The outcome was a final Plan that did not represent the consensus of stakeholder input determined by the stakeholder engagement process. As a result, the final Plan was not adopted until a year after the planning process had been completed. By this stage, key stakeholders had retreated from the planning process and the momentum for collaboration and further engagement had been lost. This meant that the resulting plan lacked effective and cooperative leadership to drive and initiate the implementation of the Plan. As explained by Byrd, "stakeholders must be engaged throughout the process and know that their participation has the potential to influence the decision" (2007, p. 8). Yuksel and Yuksel (2008) confirm that the lack of community and stakeholder engagement can lead to tourism plan failure. Furthermore, the Byron case highlights that mutual learning cannot be imposed. Planners must respect the socio-political context in which they are situated and the processes and underpinning values by which stakeholders learn.

Using attributes and conditions identified by McCool and Guthrie (2001) for effective planning in complex situations, Table 2 shows the factors that influenced the Destination Daylesford and Byron Shire tourism planning process.

Conclusion

This paper has sought to build on the developing literature related to stakeholder engagement, community participation and transactive planning for sustainable tourism. The practical application of these concepts has been demonstrated through case analysis of year-long strategic tourism planning processes undertaken concurrently for the destination regions of Daylesford and Hepburn Springs, and Byron Shire, during 2007–2008. An important initiative that applied to both destinations was to develop a comprehensive approach to stakeholder engagement. This involved the adoption of a transactive planning approach that sought to establish a participatory and inclusive framework for stakeholders to engage in multi-loop learning and corresponding action to achieve sustainable tourism planning outcomes. Koutsouris (2009) explains that if networks for interaction and learning are not established, interventions may generate uncertainties, alienation and potentially social disintegration, and will not lead to sustainable tourism development.

In addition, an important objective of these planning processes was to provide knowledge and facilitate understanding amongst stakeholders about the principles of sustainable tourism and the process of strategic tourism planning. This involved utilising the expertise of planners with considerable knowledge and practical experience in sustainable tourism planning and stakeholder consultation. An initial planning activity was to undertake a

Table 2. Attributes and conditions of the Destination Daylesford and Byron Shire tourism planning processes.

Criteria*	Destination Daylesford	Byron Shire
Representativeness	• 12-member Steering Committee comprising diverse tourism knowledge and expertise representing tourism, business, community and local government interests • 41 stakeholder groups represented in consultation process • Citizen Jury represented profile of community • Opportunity for broader community representation through planning website	• Small local government-centric Steering Committee comprising 5 members (2 Council staff and 3 Councillors) • 60 stakeholder groups represented in consultation process • Citizen Jury represented profile of community • Opportunity for broader community representation through planning website
Ownership	• From the outset, the planning process was owned by tourism stakeholder groups across state, regional and destination level in partnership with local government. • Establishment of Stakeholder Reference Group and Citizen Jury sought to foster ownership of the planning process across stakeholder groups and community	• Planning process owned by local government • Resistance by local government to broaden stakeholder involvement • Establishment of Stakeholder Reference Group and Citizen Jury sought to foster ownership of the planning process across stakeholder groups and community
Learning	• Multiple-loop learning evident amongst the Steering Committee, Council, Stakeholder Reference Group and Citizen Jury	• Steering Committee, Council and Stakeholder Reference Group were internally divisive; this meant that their commitment to learning and adopting a sustainable tourism planning approach was problematic, and as such, only a level of single-loop learning was achieved. • The Citizen Jury were, however, committed to learning.
Relationships	• Destination Daylesford Steering Committee was consistently cohesive and enthusiastic. • Effective working relationship between Research Team and Steering Committee and Steering Committee Project leader • A good relationship was developed between the Steering Committee and the Stakeholder Reference Group.	• Effective working relationship between Research Team and Council Project leader • Byron Shire Tourism Management Steering Committee was divisive and at times lacked cohesive direction. • No opportunity for the Steering Committee and the Stakeholder Reference Group to form a working relationship
Trust	• Trust mostly evident amongst all groups (Steering Committee, Stakeholder Reference Group, Citizen Jury) • Some mistrust amongst Councillors related to the importance of tourism to the region	• Research team wary of political agendas within the Steering Committee and Council • Traditionally, stakeholder organisations in Byron Shire have mistrust across business and environmental interests.

(Continued on next page)

Table 2.   Attributes and conditions of the Destination Daylesford and Byron Shire tourism planning processes. (*Continued*)

Criteria*	Destination Daylesford	Byron Shire
Power	• Collaborative approach that was fostered by Tourism Victoria and Hepburn Shire Council ensured shared power amongst key stakeholders (*enabler role*).	• Mayor involvement on Steering Committee ensured that the power was retained by the Council of the planning process (*provider role*).
Access to knowledge	• Tourism Victoria provided considerable expertise to assist and inform the tourism planning process. • Breadth and depth of the Steering Committee ensured further access to regional and destination level knowledge and expertise related to tourism.	• No state level contribution to planning process • Limited tourism knowledge of Council and Steering Committee

*Source: Adapted from McCool and Guthrie (2001).

comprehensive literature review to determine best practice in sustainable tourism planning and a comprehensive situational analysis. A Regional Expert Panel was established to provide further expertise.

The role of a lead planner who became embedded in both destinations was to build a "transactive relationship" with client and stakeholder representatives. This involved establishment of a deliberative and inclusive stakeholder engagement framework that sought to bring together information, knowledge and skills from various stakeholder perspectives, achieve mutual leaning and growth of participants, create a sense of ownership of outcomes, and generate agreement over solutions whilst increasing support for their implementation (Mahjabeen et al., 2009). The engagement process comprised stakeholder consultation workshops, development of a destination planning website, establishment of a Stakeholder Reference Group, a citizen jury process and creation of a dedicated planning website to better engage diverse stakeholder interests in the year-long planning processes. A consultation reporting system helped to communicate the varied issues and challenges identified by the participants in the stakeholder engagement process. This helped to establish an "on-going dialectical process that used existing understanding (theory) that was enriched with lessons that was then applied in a continual process of change and action" (Friedmann, 1987, p. 81).

Case analyses confirmed the dynamism and complexity of regional destination environments involving the mediation of varied stakeholder interests and inter-relationships. Both case studies showed that stakeholder engagement and transactive planning is not an easy process. It requires commitment and effort from planners and destination champions to lead and drive the planning process over the long-term. More importantly, transactive planning requires planners to understand diverse stakeholder values and learning processes. The contrast between the Daylesford and Hepburn Springs and the Byron Shire cases has demonstrated that despite efforts to foster learning and dialogue, if principal destination stakeholders are not committed to this approach at the outset, or if governance and socio-political agendas dominate, the transactive process may be ineffectual. The transactive planning approach explained in this paper provides a useful framework that can be applied to other complex destination contexts to facilitate sustainable tourism outcomes. Research is still required, however, to determine stakeholder views of such an approach.

Notes

1. A level-one destination is defined as a destination that attracts a strong mix of international, interstate and intrastate visitors and particularly demonstrates international appeal matched to Victoria's key product strengths.
2. A sea change locality is a place that attracts tourists for holidays and then attracts some of those people to move permanently to that locality for lifestyle reasons.

References

ABS. (Australian Bureau of Statistics). (2006a). *QuickStats: Latest issue – Hepburn (S) local government area*. Retrieved April 6, 2010, from http://www.censusdata.abs.gov.au/ABSNavigation/prenav/ProductSelect?newproducttype=QuickStats&btnSelectProduct=View+QuickStats+%3E&collection=Census&period=2006&areacode=LGA22910&geography=&method=&productlabel=&producttype=&topic=&navmapdisplayed=true&javascript=true&bread

ABS. (2006b). *QuickStats: Latest issue – Byron (A) local government area*. Retrieved April 6, 2010, from http://www.censusdata.abs.gov.au/ABSNavigation/prenav/ProductSelect?newproducttype=QuickStats&btnSelectProduct=View+QuickStats+%3E&collection=Census&period=2006&areacode=LGA11350&geography=&method=&productlabel=&producttype=&topic=&navmapdisplayed=true&javascript=true&bread

Arnstein, S.R. (1969). A ladder of citizen participation. *Journal of American Institute of Planners, 35*, 215–224

Bramwell, B. (2004). Partnerships, participation, and social science research in tourism planning. In A.L. Lew, C.M. Hall, & A.M. Williams (Eds.), *A companion to tourism* (pp. 541–554). Oxford: Blackwell.

Bramwell, B., & Lane, B. (2000). Collaboration and partnerships in tourism planning. In B. Bramwell & B. Lane (Eds.), *Tourism collaboration and partnerships: Politics, practice and sustainability* (pp. 1–19). Clevedon: Channel View Publications.

Bramwell, B., & Sharman, A. (1999). Collaboration in local tourism policymaking. *Annals of Tourism Research, 26*, 392–415.

Brotherton, B. (1999). Case study research. In B. Brotherton (Ed.), *The handbook of contemporary hospitality management research* (pp. 115–142). Chichester: John Wiley.

Byrd, E.T. (2007). Stakeholders in sustainable tourism development and their roles: Applying stakeholder theory to sustainable tourism development. *Tourism Review, 62*(2), 6–13.

Catt, H., & Murphy, M. (2003). What voices for the people? Categorising methods of public consultation. *Australian Journal of Political Science, 38*(3), 407–421.

Churugsa, W., McIntosh, A., & Simmons, D. (2007). Sustainable tourism planning and development: Understanding the capacity of local government. *Leisure/Loisir, 31*(2), 453–473.

Costa, C. (2001). An emerging tourism planning paradigm? A comparative analysis between town and tourism planning. *International Journal of Tourism Research, 3*, 425–441.

de Araujo, L.M., & Bramwell, B. (2002). Partnership and regional tourism in Brazil. *Annals of Tourism Research, 29*(4), 1138–1164.

Dewan, S., & Riggins, F.J. (2005). The digital divide: Current and future research directions. *Journal of the Association for Information Systems, 6*(12), 298–337.

Dredge, D., & Lawrence, M. (2007). Tourism planning and policy processes. In D. Dredge & J. Jenkins (Eds.), *Tourism planning and policy* (pp. 191–224). Milton: John Wiley.

Fisher, K. (2007). Jury selection process. In M. Lawrence (Ed.), *Destination Daylesford consultation report* (pp. 13–14). Lismore: Southern Cross University.

Friedmann, J. (1973). *Retracking America: A theory of transactive planning.* New York: Anchor Press/Double Day.

Friedmann, J. (1987). *Planning in the public domain: From knowledge to action.* Princeton, NJ: Princeton University Press.

Hall, C.M. (1999). Rethinking collaboration and partnership: A public policy perspective. *Journal of Sustainable Tourism, 7*(3&4), 274–289.

Hall, C.M. (2000). *Tourism planning, policies, processes and relationships.* Harlow: Pearson Hall.

Hall, C.M. (2003). Politics and place: An analysis of power in tourism communities. In S. Singh, D.J. Timothy, & R.K. Dowling (Eds.), *Tourism in destination communities* (pp. 99–114). Wallingford: CABI.

Hall, C.M., & Page, S.J. (2002). *The geography of tourism and recreation: Environment, place and space* (2nd ed.). New York: Routledge.

Hansen, H.S., & Mäenpää, M. (2008). An overview of the challenges for public participation in river basin management and planning. *Management of Environmental Quality: An International Journal, 19*(1), 67–84.

Harrill, R. (2004). Residents' attitudes toward tourism development: A literature review with implications for tourism planning. *Journal of Planning Literature, 18*, 251–266.

Healy, P. (1997). *Collaborative planning: Shaping places in fragmented societies.* Basingstoke: MacMillan Press.

Healy, P. (2003). The communicative turn in planning theory and its implications for spatial strategy formulation. In S. Campbell & S.S. Fainstein (Eds.), *Readings in planning theory* (2nd ed., pp. 237–257). London: Blackwell.

Jamal, T., & Getz, D. (1999). Community roundtables for tourism-related conflicts: The dialetics of consensus and process structures. *Journal of Sustainable Tourism, 7*(3&4), 290–313.

Koutsouris, A. (2009). Social learning and sustainable tourism development; local quality conventions in tourism: A Greek study. *Journal of Sustainable Tourism, 17*(5), 567–581.

Lankford, S. (2001). A comment concerning "developing and testing a tourism impact scale". *Journal of Travel Research, 39*, 315–316.

Lawrence, M. (2007). *Draft Byron Shire tourism management plan: Stage 3 consultation report.* Lismore: Southern Cross University.

Lawrence, M., & Buultjens, J. (2008a). *Destination Daylesford strategic tourism plan 2008 to 2018.* Lismore: Australian Regional Tourism Research Centre.

Lawrence, M., & Buultjens, J. (2008b). *Byron Shire tourism management plan 2008 to 2018.* Lismore: Australian Regional Tourism Research Centre.

Lawrence, M., & Buultjens, J. (2009, February 10–13). *Comprehensive community consultation in destination management planning: The destination Daylesford and Hepburn Springs strategic tourism planning process* [CD ROM]. Paper presented at the 18th International Research Conference of the Council for Australian University Tourism and Hospitality Education (CAUTHE), Fremantle, WA.

Laws, E. (1995). *Tourist destination management: Issues, analysis and policies.* New York: Routledge.

Lew, A. (2007). Invited commentary: Tourism planning and traditional urban planning theory – The planner as an agent of social change. *Leisure/Loisir, 31*(2), 383–391.

Mahjabeen, Z., Shresha, K.K., & Dee, J.A. (2009). Rethinking community participation in urban planning: The role of disadvantaged groups in Sydney metropolitan strategy. *Australiasian Journal of Regional Studies, 15*(1), 45–63.

Mair, H., & Reid, D. (2007). Tourism and community development vs. tourism for community development: Conceptualising planning as power, knowledge and control. *Leisure/Loisir, 31*(2), 403–425.

McCool, S. (2009). Constructing partnerships for protected area tourism planning in an era of change and messiness. *Journal of Sustainable Tourism, 17*(2), 133–148.

McCool, S., & Guthrie, K. (2001). Mapping the dimensions of successful participation in messy natural resources management situations. *Society and Natural Resources, 14*, 309–323.

Merriam, S.B. (1998). *Qualitative research and case study applications in education*. San Francisco, CA: Jossey-Bass.

Murphy, P.E. (1985). *Tourism: A community approach*. New York: Methuen.

Okazaki, E. (2008). A community-based tourism model: Its conception and use. *Journal of Sustainable Tourism, 16*(5), 511–529.

Oviedo-Garcia, M., Castellanos-Verdugo, M., & Martin-Ruiz, D. (2008). Gaining residents' support for tourism and planning. *International Journal of Tourism Research, 10*, 95–109.

Quaghebeur, K., Masschelein, J., & Nguyen, H.H. (2004). Paradox of participation: Giving or taking part? *Journal of Community and Applied Social Psychology, 14*, 154–165.

Richards, G., & Hall, D. (2000). *Tourism and sustainable community development*. New York: Routledge.

Richins, H., & Pearce, P. (2000). Influences on tourism development decision making: Coastal local government areas in eastern Australia. *Journal of Sustainable Tourism, 8*(3), 207–225.

Scheyvens, R. (2003). Local involvement in managing tourism. *Tourism in destination communities*. In S. Singh, D.J. Timothy, & R.K. Dowling (Eds.), *Tourism in destination communities* (pp. 229–252). Wallingford: CABI.

Selin, S. (1999). Developing a typology of sustainable tourism partnerships. *Journal of Sustainable Tourism, 7*(3&4), 260–273.

Simmons, D. (1994). Community participation in tourism planning. *Tourism Management, 15*(2), 98–108.

Telfer, D.J. (2003). Development issues in destination communities. In S. Singh, D.J. Timothy, & R.K. Dowling (Eds.), *Tourism in destination communities* (pp. 155–180). Wallingford: CABI.

Tosun, C. (2000). Limits to community participation in the tourism development process in developing countries. *Tourism Management, 21*, 613–633.

Tosun, C. (2006). Expected nature of community participation in tourism development. *Tourism Management, 27*(3), 493–504.

Tourism Research Australia. (2009). *National visitor survey and international visitor survey*. Canberra: Author.

Treuen, G., & Lane, D. (2003). The tourism planning process in the context of organised interests, industry structure, state capacity, accumulation and sustainability. *Current Issues in Tourism, 6*(1), 1–18.

Vernon, J., Essex, S., Pinder, D., & Curry, K. (2005). Collaborative policy-making: Local sustainable projects. *Annals of Tourism Research, 32*(2), 325–345.

Wray, M. (2009). Policy communities, networks and issue cycles in tourism destination systems. *Journal of Sustainable Tourism, 17*(6), 673–690.

Yin, R.K. (2003). *Case study research: Design and methods* (3rd ed.). Thousand Oaks, CA: Sage.

Yuksel, F., & Yuksel, A. (2008). Perceived clientelism: Effects on residents' evaluation of municipal services and their intentions for participation in tourism development projects. *Journal of Hospitality and Tourism Research, 32*(2), 187–208.

Zahra, A., & Ryan, C. (2005). Reflections on the research process: The researcher as actor and audience in the world of regional tourist organisations. *Current Issues in Tourism, 8*(1), 1–21.

Rethinking resort growth: understanding evolving governance strategies in Whistler, British Columbia

Alison M. Gill[a,b] and Peter W. Williams[b]

[a]Department of Geography, Simon Fraser University, 8888 University Drive, Burnaby, British Columbia, Canada; [b]School of Resource and Environmental Management, Simon Fraser University, 8888 University Drive, Burnaby, British Columbia, Canada

This paper examines shifts in governance and management strategies that have occurred in response to endogenous and exogenous pressures on the mountain resort of Whistler, British Columbia. Since its inception in the mid-1970s, Whistler has pursued successive innovative management approaches that have emphasized growth. The most recent approach, integrated comprehensive sustainability planning, reflects a response to reaching the planned limits of resort development and suggests the emergence of a new "corporatist" governance model based on principles of sustainability. However, the complex effects associated with exogenous factors, such as the global economic crisis, hosting the Winter Olympic Games and the increasing political necessity of collaboration with local First Nations (indigenous peoples), raise questions concerning the degree to which Whistler is "locked-in" to the pro-growth model of governance. A path dependency framework is employed to explore and explain Whistler's evolving forms of governance. While briefly reviewing the earlier pro-growth path of Whistler's development, particular attention is paid to factors underlying the implementation and continuing challenges of the comprehensive sustainability governance model. Other issues explored include the viability of no-growth governance, the issues surrounding growth limits and the role of "The Natural Step" framework in tourism governance.

Introduction

The rapid growth of resort destinations in recent decades has created interest in the governance models facilitating such developments and the management strategies shaping their sustainability. As the vulnerabilities of such places to global forces emerge, there are calls to rethink the appropriateness of pro-growth resort development models that are essentially investor-driven. Increasingly, destination stakeholders are rethinking how they "do business", who has the power in decision-making, within what spatial and temporal frames should decisions be made and to whom should decision-makers be accountable? The general sentiment is that innovative governance policies and practices are needed to increase the competitiveness and sustainability of many destinations (Guia, Prats, & Comas, 2006). Dwyer, Edwards, Mistilis, Roman, and Scott observe that, "achieving competitive advantage in times of rapid change requires tourism stakeholders to have a clear understanding of the direction of change and its implications for ... destination management" (2009, p. 63).

This paper provides conceptual insights into the evolving governance approaches employed by the resort community of Whistler, British Columbia (BC) in Canada, to retain its competitive position as a leading mountain tourism destination. These approaches have evolved from an initial focus on objectives and strategies related to a pro-growth model, toward ones that align with a more corporatist[1] (Pierre, 1999), community-driven form of governance that is guided by comprehensive and integrated sustainability principles associated with "The Natural Step"[2] (TNS, 2010). The principles are designed to guide collective community decisions toward actions that minimize or eliminate ongoing build-ups of substances taken from the earth's crust, accumulations of substances produced by society, the degradation of natural environments and decreases in the ability of people to meet their human needs (*Whistler 2020*, 2010). The new model emerged in response to the complex implications of Whistler reaching its prescribed growth limit capacity, the spillover impacts of global financial turbulence, the legacies from co-hosting the 2010 Winter Olympic and Paralympic Games and an increasing necessity to collaborate with local aboriginal communities.

An evolutionary political economy perspective broadly frames the discussion of Whistler's evolving governance system. Path dependency, a key concept within this approach, that in its broadest sense implies "history matters" (David, 1994), is the lens through which the resort community's evolving governance system is examined. This approach highlights the underlying endogenous and exogenous pressures that over time have catalyzed shifts in Whistler's governance features (e.g. policy objectives, processes and values). The central issue that this paper examines is to what extent has Whistler, in its more corporatist approach to comprehensive sustainability, extracted itself from previous "locked-in" strategies that imposed constraints on adopting alternative governance paths.

To contextualize the Whistler case study, a brief review of the pertinent resort evolution and governance literature is presented. This is followed by a discussion of path dependency as a tool for examining evolutionary change in governance systems. The ensuing Whistler case study integrates concepts from theories on urban governance and path dependency into the case analysis. The analysis first summarizes how path dependency was initially embedded into Whistler's pro-growth development model. As much of this history is documented elsewhere (Gill, 2000; Gill & Williams, 2005, 2006; Williams, Gill, & Chura, 2004), the discussion only highlights critical factors affecting Whistler's evolving governance approaches. The subsequent sections identify forces shaping the emergence of Whistler's most recent comprehensive sustainability planning governance model. The paper concludes with conceptual insights into resort governance drawn from the case study.

Resort evolution and governance

Resort evolution

Resorts vary from comprehensively planned, fully integrated places (Stanton & Aislabie, 1992) to catalytic developments (Flagestad & Hope, 2001; Gill, 1998). The degree to which local institutions and residents are engaged with or exercise control over such developments varies, depending on the governance approach employed. These governance options are situated on a continuum ranging from "corporate-directed" to "community-focused" extremes (Flagestad & Hope, 2001; Murphy, 2008). These terms are more or less synonymous with the terms "pro-growth" and "corporatist", respectively, used in this paper. Of the numerous models of resort evolution that exist, Butler's (1980) tourist area lifecycle model is the most discussed and criticized (Butler, 2006a, 2006b). It identifies temporal development stages defined by growth in tourist numbers and infrastructure. It also recognizes limits to growth after which destinations may follow a range of trajectories ranging from decline to rejuvenation. Criticisms of Butler's tourist area life cycle model concern the degree to which the model can be operationalized, as well as conceptual issues about its focus on internal dynamics as opposed to external forces, the degree to which the destination can be conceived as a coherent product that can be reduced to a single curve, and the nature of the rejuvenation phase (Butler, 2006b). However, Butler's paradigm represents only one evolutionary scenario among a range of potential pathways that resort development may take (Prideaux, 2000; Weaver, 2000). For instance, Weaver (2000) suggests a "broad context model" in which different evolutionary sequences may occur depending on the extent to which the destination is engaged in mass or alternative tourism, and the type of regulations in effect. As Ioannides (2009) observes, typically, the management responses to growth challenges are shaped by local cultures and the inherent responsiveness of the resort community's specific sociopolitical and cultural systems. Such approaches better reflect the range of resort destination types and evolutionary pathways available. Although many resort evolution studies exist, few report on the evolving structures of governance and their implications for such places. Nonetheless, there is a growing interest in this dimension of destination management in Europe (Keller & Bieger, 2008; Svensson, Nordin, & Flagestad, 2006), Australia (Dredge, 2006a, 2006b; Ruhanen, Scott, Ritchie, & Tkaczynski, 2010) and North America (Gill & Williams, 2006; Murphy, 2008).

Resort governance

Governance encompasses the values, rules, institutions and processes through which public and private stakeholders seek to achieve common objectives and make decisions (Beritelli, Bieger, & Laesser, 2007; Murphy, 2008). In recent years, neo-liberal agendas and the downsizing of governments have led to merged responsibilities for governance between public and private institutions. Increasingly, governments are playing roles as enablers rather than providers of a wide range of tourism products and services (Dredge, 2006b; Painter, 2000; Vernon, Essex, Pinder, & Curry, 2005). Changes in governance strategies provide useful keys to understanding the dynamics and competitiveness of destinations (Svensson et al., 2006). Generally, governance mode choice depends on the context of the destination's development, which affects a resort's ability to respond to exogenous forces (Beritelli et al., 2007). Some recent studies on destination governance have adopted network approaches especially with respect to understanding the preconditions for innovation (Baggio, Scott, & Cooper, 2010; Beritelli et al., 2007; Erkus-Osturk & Eraydin, 2010; Guia et al., 2006; Lazzeretti & Petrillo, 2006; Pforr, 2002). Dredge (2006a) indicates that this approach provides an effective means of examining the "messy", multidimensional dynamics of public and private sector stakeholder realities operating at different spatial and temporal scales in tourism destinations. Beritelli et al. (2007) conclude that, whereas hierarchical relationships with concentrated power predominate in corporate models of development, "for community-type destinations, the development process involves informal connections, knowledge and trust" (p. 2), thus making the dynamic (and therefore a historical) perspective crucial to the analysis of the network's formation and influence.

Over the past two decades, global increases in the mobility of capital and people have increased demand for vacation and/or permanent residential home ownership in amenity-rich resort destinations (Keller & Bieger, 2008; Williams & Gill, 2006). Consequently, many resort destination governance models are now predicated on the ability of real estate development to finance related infrastructure and community service needs. Dependence on such development models has increasingly challenged the capacity of resort decision-makers to proactively respond to rapid changes in global conditions (Ladurantaye, 2010). Unfortunately, relatively little research has focused on the attendant problems associated with real-estate-driven resort growth models (Keller & Bieger, 2008). Most of what has been published focuses primarily on structural questions and the role of destination management organizations (e.g. Bodega, Cioccarelli, & Denicolai, 2004; Nordin & Svensson, 2005; Pavlovitch, 2003). Specific questions concerning what dimensions of governance theory are especially relevant to destinations, and in what context these conditions produce innovative and sustainable practices, remain largely unanswered.

Models of urban governance

Pierre (1999) proposed four general models of urban governance: welfare, managerial, pro-growth and corporatist. With the exception of the welfare model, found primarily in areas of declining industrial activity in which the main influx of capital into the economy comes from the welfare system, the other three models are, to varying degrees, relevant to tourism destinations. However, Pierre (1999) cautions that these are ideal types that may empirically vary in different locales and indeed even between policy sectors in any one locale. The managerial model, which has gained prominence in recent years in the face of fiscal crises, focuses priority on the efficient production and delivery of services. In this approach, engaging professional management resources in a market-based model that responds to consumer demand blurs the distinction between public and private sector roles. In doing so, the role of democratically elected officials is marginalized (Pierre, 1999). The focus in this paper is on the pro-growth and corporatist models – the two models most closely aligned with the case study. Key defining characteristics of these two models are shown in Table 1.

Whistler has experienced a shift from an investor-driven pro-growth model, with limited public input into decision-making, to a highly democratic community-driven governance approach that can be characterized as a corporatist model. The corporatist model is more ideologically aligned than the other three governance models with the principles of sustainability as it encourages inclusive participation of citizens in decision-making. Although many resorts exhibit pro-growth approaches to governance, an examination of the corporatist model developed in Whistler offers new insights into how this strategy can be utilized to chart a more sustainable path. Elsewhere, recently developed Swiss destinations, which are centrally coordinated, also demonstrate a shift toward more corporatist approaches that help create more focused and integrated responses to global market forces and reduce transaction costs, thus addressing issues of competitiveness (Beritelli et al., 2007).

Table 1. Selected defining characteristics of corporatist and pro-growth urban governance.

	Models of urban governance	
Defining characteristics	Corporatist	Pro-growth
Policy objectives	Distribution	Growth
Policy style	Ideological	Pragmatic
Nature of public – private exchange	Concerted	Interactive
Local state – citizen relationship	Inclusive	Exclusive
Primary constituency	Civic leaders	Business
Key instruments	Deliberations	Partnerships
Key evaluative criterion	Participation	Growth

Source: Adapted from Pierre (1999, p. 388).

A path dependency lens

Evolutionary economics has spawned a growing social science interest in ways of using evolutionary approaches to conceptualize change (e.g. Boschma & Martin, 2007; Essletzbichler & Rigby, 2007; MacKinnon, Cumbers, Pike, Birch, & McMaster, 2009; Mahoney, 2000; Pierson, 2000; Pike, Birch, Cumber, MacKinnon, & McMaster, 2009). Path dependence is a central concept in many evolutionary approaches. It helps explain how the set of decisions faced in any given circumstance is limited by decisions made in the past, even though past circumstances may no longer be relevant. This implies that institutions are self-reinforcing (Pierson, 2000). The original models of path dependency (Arthur, 1989; David, 1985, 1993) emphasize continuity through the core concept of "lock-in". Grabher (1993) identifies three components of lock-in: structural, cognitive and political. An important aspect of structural lock-in is dependency on increasing returns on investments. For example, in the mountain resort context discussed in this paper, the long-term benefits accruing from the high initial cost of investment in mountain lift systems are intricately tied to escalated returns on the sale of real estate developed in close proximity to the slopes. Cognitive lock-in relates to institutional embeddedness and the structure of social relationships that link people to institutional environments, whereas political lock-in has much to do with power relationships. However, recent work by sociologists has led to new perspectives on path dependency and institutional change that emphasize not only change but also continuity (Martin, 2010). Two mechanisms operating at the micro-level that impart slow change to path-dependent institutional evolution are layering and conversion. Layering implies the gradual addition of amendments, new rules and procedures to existing systems. Although the changes are path-dependent, over time, new path creation may occur (Boas, 2007). Conversion, which involves a more radical reorientation of an institution's form or function, may result from either layering or as a result of external pressures or developments (Boas, 2007; Martin, 2010).

Few published applications of path dependence concepts in tourism contexts exist. Notable exceptions include the works of Williams and Baláž (2002) on tourism in some Central European transitioning economies, as well as that of Bramwell and Cox (2009) on tourism partnerships. As Bramwell and Cox observe, "A path dependence approach to a tourism partnership can be used to highlight temporal continuities and changes in its organizational arrangements and its activities ... and ... [i]t can also explore the reasons for these continuities and changes" (2009, p. 194). The approach also has the potential to be applied to studies of changing governance approaches in tourism destinations.

A case study of Whistler's growth and governance

Whistler, located 120 km north of Vancouver, is a comprehensively planned resort community. Since its origin over 35 years ago, it has evolved into an international resort that is regularly acclaimed as North America's premier mountain destination. Annually, it hosts about two million visitors year-round and has a permanent population base of around 11,000 residents. Nonresidents own about half of all residential properties. Whistler has grown rapidly over its short lifetime and has received frequent accolades for its environmental management approaches, and more recently its inclusive and participatory community development practices (Gill & Williams, 2005).

The central objective of this research was to adopt an evolutionary approach to identify the factors that affected Whistler's shift from a pro-growth to a more corporatist governance strategy that embodies sustainability as a key objective. Data were drawn from empirical research extending over a 20-year period. They were collected by employing a

KEY GOVERNANCE STRATEGIES

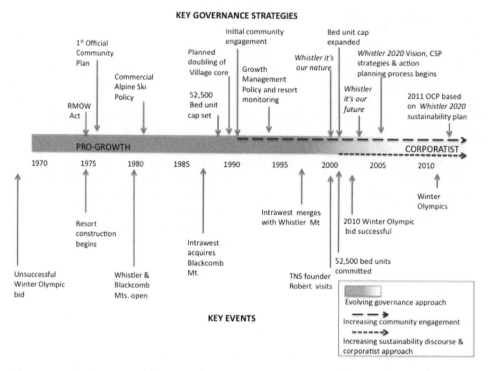

Figure 1.   Influential key events and strategies in Whistler's evolving governance approach.

range of multi-method techniques, including informant interviews, document reviews (e.g. municipal planning documents, community reports and local newspaper articles), resident surveys and public meeting observations. In interpreting the evolution of governance, a path dependency lens was employed to examine the degree to which changes in the features, objectives and strategies of Whistler's governance structure were affected by the historical circumstances. Changes in the core components of "lock-in" – structural, cognitive and political (Grabher, 1993) – were considered together with process elements of layering and conversion (Boas, 2007). The following sections elaborate on the causal factors influencing the ways in which key dimensions of Whistler's governance changed over time and the influence of path dependency on this evolution. Ultimately, this discourse raises the question of whether or not there has been a genuine shift in the governance model of Whistler from pro-growth to corporatist – including both a change in strategy and a change of objectives toward more comprehensive and ambitious sustainability goals – or, is there just a change of strategy and governance features pursuing old pro-growth goals? Figure 1 illustrates the chronological interface between key events and evolving governance strategies.

Pro-growth governance and path dependency

The provincial government's attention was drawn to the potential of the Whistler area as an international ski destination by Vancouver-based businessmen, who (unsuccessfully) lobbied the government to bid for the 1968 Winter Olympic Games. One might consider this to be the "historical accident" (Martin, 2010), the small random or chance event that would have long-run effects on establishing Whistler's path dependence. Coincidentally, BC's provincial government had already embarked on a major regional economic development strategy designed to support resource development (especially forestry and mining). Central to the government's approach was the development of new communities through joint investment with private sector resource firms (Young, 2008). While sharing many similarities with the "instant resource town" strategy, creating a resort community involved recognizing and protecting valued mountain terrain and landscape as a tourism resource, rather than valuing it for extractive uses. This involved adopting new approaches to community planning and design. For these skills, the government drew on the expertise of planners and developers creating and managing new ski resort developments in the United States – in particular Vail, Colorado.

The "Resort Municipality of Whistler" (RMOW) was officially designated by a special act of the provincial government in 1975. The Act granted unique financial and taxation powers to Whistler designed to support and encourage tourism growth, as well as to control and manage development. As a consequence, external private investors, supported by the favorable tenure and investment terms established by the provincial and federal governments, worked in the newly created RMOW to establish a critical mass of development that would make Whistler uniquely competitive in the marketplace. A pro-growth governance model was established to guide the development of Whistler's customized growth machine model (Gill, 2000). An important part of the Whistler Resort Act facilitated the creation of a land development company as a wholly owned subsidiary of the RMOW. Its role was to sell strategic portions of the RMOW land base to developers willing to comply with and contribute to the long-term development and "build out" of Whistler's Official Community Plan (OCP). All members of Whistler's democratically elected council were automatically directors of the Land Company, with the mayor as chair. Thus, the role of local government was integrally bound to land development. Indeed, several elected members of the RMOW council were actively involved in development projects. This was not perceived as a conflict of interest, but rather as an acceptable practice within a growth machine approach.

Several changes to the corporate structures of the two ski lift companies operating on Whistler and Blackcomb mountains occurred during the first decade of the resort's existence (Gill, 2000). As a consequence, a major driving force of growth was the competition between the two ski lift companies who received the long-term leases to operate on Crown (public) land within the town's boundary. Operating under the edicts of the newly crafted provincial Commercial Alpine Ski Policy, these ski lift companies were also granted participation in an innovative "lands for lifts" program that enabled them to acquire development rights on specific Whistler land in return for their investment in mountain infrastructure. This policy proved to be a major and positive influence on the level and rate of corporate real estate development that took place in the ensuing years. In particular, after Intrawest, a Vancouver-based development company, acquired the ski operations on Blackcomb Mountain in 1986, their pro-growth real estate development strategy became a widely emulated model. As Beaudry observes:

> Exploiting the alpine policy in those years was like shooting fish in a barrel. But the government wasn't complaining. After all, the churning stream of tax money coming from Whistler was a new source of revenue that the shekel-counters in Victoria had never even contemplated. So they just closed their eyes and let the flow go . . . . Overnight the B.C. government decided it was in the destination tourism business. (2010, p. 33)

From an RMOW perspective, Whistler's OCP was an important regulatory instrument. It essentially provided the legal framework and policies for regulating land use and real estate development, infrastructure services, and the protection of the natural environment within Whistler's boundaries. Further regulation of the built environment was imposed through by-laws that established zoning regulations and design guidelines (Dorward, 1990). Although the ski companies were major players in the power structure of the resort, they were required under the Act to comply with local land use development requirements and coordinate their marketing strategies with all other commercial enterprises in the RMOW. Such required and collective marketing collaborations were relatively rare in tourism destinations. All of these initial policies and regulations still remain in place, although significant "layering" (Boas, 2007) has occurred through successive OCP updates, by-law amendments and marketing strategy alterations. However, the overall intent of these new strategies still reflects Whistler's path dependency on principles of governance identified at Whistler's inception that embrace growth and competitive advantage.

Growth machine governance challenges

The first challenge to growth machine governance came in 1990 after a period of rapid resort growth. By 1990, the resident population of Whistler had grown from a few hundred to around 4000, and it was becoming a more organized community with ever-increasing numbers of young families. The RMOW's electoral process provided these community members with a growing role in setting priorities for the town's development. In response to rapid growth, they overwhelmingly demanded that Whistler's elected Council addresses their needs for more affordable housing and schools. Emerging community-based non-governmental organizations that credibly voiced resident quality of life concerns associated with the rapid commercial growth in Whistler reinforced their position. In response to these pressures, the RMOW instituted a more community-based and responsive form of governance. It was formalized in 1994 when the RMOW instigated a growth management policy. Gill observed that "[g]rowth management was initially introduced as a buzzword and a compromise that might appeal both to growth and to no-growth factions with business interests focusing on growth and no-growth interests emphasizing management" (2000, p. 1099). It fundamentally embedded local concerns and consensus-building into the heart of the governance process. It acknowledged that Whistler was not just a resort but also a community in which decisions should represent a balance of stakeholder interests. Nevertheless, despite this rhetoric, Whistler continued on a pro-growth path that ultimately enlarged Whistler's core, doubling its commercial business space capacity and greatly expanding its real estate base.

Two components of the growth management approach were critical in securing stakeholder confidence in the RMOW and its growth management governance processes. Most important was the creation of a "bed unit" capacity indicator that tracked the magnitude and mix of residential and visitor accommodation growth in Whistler. Although the concept of bed units was installed in the early stages of Whistler's development, it gained significance in 1989. At that time, a new cap of 52,500 bed units was established as the maximum limit of Whistler's commercial and residential growth. The limit to "build out" was based on arguments that related bed units to environmental limits such as water and sewage capacity. As Gill (2007) has discussed, bed units became important political "currency" tools in leveraging community benefits from agreements negotiated with real estate developers.

The second important component was the RMOW's establishment of a resort and community-monitoring program that measured the performance of specific indicators of environmental, economic and social change within the resort (Waldron & Williams, 2002). Presented in the form of annual state of the community reports, the findings were publicly distributed and used as the basis of discussion concerning Whistler's performance and future management strategies. The monitoring program included a feedback system that gathered community reactions to existing growth patterns via resident surveys, as well as comments expressed at annual town hall meetings. Although Arnstein (1969) observes that such relatively simple information and consultation mechanisms are typically not enough to ensure that stakeholders' concerns and ideas are fully taken into account, they did provide much greater transparency to the governance process than had previously been the case and also generated considerable confidence in the RMOW's ability to represent and protect local interests.

Over the following 15 years or so, the priorities of Whistler's growth management approach have evolved and changed in response to changing circumstances. For instance, during the 1990s, the resort doubled its village core's commercial space and was able to attract significant levels of international capital for its real estate developments. Because of its internationally acclaimed design, investors wanted to "own a part of Whistler". Consequently, the RMOW was able to leverage high levels of social and environmental benefits from these investors in the form of "development bonuses" and related "affordable housing fees" on new commercial real estate projects. From a path dependence perspective, the success of the growth management governance approach reflected the concept of "increasing returns", whereby all stakeholders were benefitting, and in turn producing positive feedback loops that reinforced existing development policy paths (Martin & Sunley, 2006).

Other incidents also occurred that reminded residents of their dependence on preexisting power relationships in the resort community and also the rapidly approaching self-determined limits to growth. For example, the relationship between the community and corporate interests changed in 1997, when Intrawest acquired the Whistler Mountain Skiing Company. The emergence of this single dominant company within the community caused concern among residents who envisaged many of the common problems evident in a "single-industry town". Fortunately, Intrawest recognized the importance of good community relations to their success in Whistler and sought to establish a "social license to operate" (Williams, Gill, & Ponsford, 2007). It deliberately informed and engaged community stakeholders in a variety of its environmental initiatives with the expressed intent of reducing its future development "transaction costs" with local decision-makers. It reflected the forms of public and private sector collaboration envisioned in the original pro-growth model of Whistler's governance.

Another Intrawest example illustrated the role that innovative relations between public and private sector partners played in addressing an impending encroachment on Whistler's bed unit cap limit. In 1999, an individual landowner who possessed a particularly large and environmentally significant property within Whistler's wetlands offered to sell it to the RMOW for C$10 million. The RMOW wanted to preserve the land as part of its future protected areas network. However, it did not have the resources to purchase the property. An alternative solution emerged when Intrawest offered to purchase the land and transfer it to the RMOW in exchange of C$1 million and the right to develop an additional 434 bed units elsewhere in Whistler. The offer effectively obliged the community to extend its long-established 52,500 bed unit cap in exchange for land that achieved other important environmental goals. Although the Intrawest offer was eventually accepted after much public debate, it revealed the challenges inherent in adhering to a fixed growth cap limit. This was particularly the case in a community with a pro-growth dependency path history. At the end of the day, this event placed an unprecedented critical wedge in the previously fixed bed unit cap door. A comment in a letter to the editor of the local newspaper from a resident reveals the degree to which the importance of the 52,500 bed unit cap was entrenched in some people's minds. The letter stated that "I have three beliefs in life: death, taxes and the 52,500 bed unit cap" (*Pique Newsmagazine*, August 27, 1999, p. 8, as cited in Horner, 2000, p. 110). Many other challenges to the cap limit followed.

The shift to a sustainability model for growth

By 2001, Whistler was confronted with unprecedented high levels of tourist traffic, rising real estate prices, escalating infrastructure costs, diminishing levels of affordable resident and employee housing, mounting ecosystem stresses and emerging climate change challenges. Of particular immediate concern to residents was the limited amount of affordable housing available for Whistler residents. For the first time since monitoring began, this issue ranked higher than environmental concerns as most important to residents' quality of life (Gill & Williams, 2008). In addition, many of these pressures were intensified by the rapidly approaching build-out of Whistler's available bed units (Gill, 2007). It was increasingly evident that the growth management strategy was not sufficient as a guiding framework for Whistler's future development (Gill, 2007; Gill & Williams, 2008). Furthermore, an impending no-growth scenario was not attractive, especially in light of the potential negative impact it would have on traditional local government and business revenues generated by new real estate developments. In addition, the bed unit cap was creating an excessive escalation in housing prices that threatened the ability of the resort to house an acceptable proportion of the community's labor force. Seemingly, the RMOW was painted into a corner. The solution lay in changing the discourse regarding growth by diffusing the tight causal relationship that was perceived to exist between bed units and environmental quality. The concept of sustainability served this purpose. Although many sustainability strategies were embedded in the RMOW's growth management rhetoric, translating them into an overriding and workable governance model had been problematic. Fortunately, an unexpected and timely event occurred that significantly affected the path that the resort community took.

Unexpectedly, Karl Henrik Robèrt, the founder of TNS program, came to Whistler on a personal visit and informally spoke with RMOW representatives about their future sustainability plans. He introduced them to a shared mental model, fundamental guiding principles and a common language that made sustainability easier to understand, plan for and implement across a range of stakeholder groups (Robèrt, 2008). The coincidence of Whistler's emergent interest in a sustainability approach to growth with Robèrt's discourse on the TNS principles and approach to planning acted as a "tipping point" in triggering action (Gill & Williams, 2008). Shortly after Robèrt's visit, a small but influential group of local public and private organizations was created to develop and implement a range of TNS-framed sustainability programs within their own institutions. It was composed of "early adopters" from the RMOW, Whistler Blackcomb (Intrawest's ski lift company and major real estate developer), the Fairmont Chateau Whistler hotel, Tourism Whistler (the main marketing organization), One-hour Photo (a small but prominent retail operation) and AWARE (the leading environmental nongovernment organization).

Over a two-year period, the RMOW engaged Whistler stakeholders in what Sailor (2010) (in another setting) has aptly referred to as a "community conditioning" process. This included an awareness campaign entitled *Whistler: It's Our Nature* that promoted understanding and adoption of the TNS framework and engaged the community in the process, and a community consultation program called *Whistler: It's Our Future* that uncovered community stakeholder hopes and priorities for Whistler's future. These initiatives, along with a previously developed *Whistler Environmental Strategy* (Waldron, 2000), provided the impetus and focus for the creation of *Whistler 2020* – a long-term community vision that became the foundation for the RMOW's Comprehensive Sustainability Plan (CSP). The CSP is Whistler's highest-level policy document and provides the destination with an integrated, long-term, community-wide vision and planning framework that is guided by local values and core TNS sustainability principles. It frames all RMOW decisions about future development plans and programs (Vance & Williams, 2005). The overriding intent of the CSP is to operationalize the consensus-based vision expressed in *Whistler 2020* that "Whistler will be the premier mountain resort community – as we move toward sustainability" (*Whistler 2020*, 2010).

The *Whistler 2020* vision and principles emphasize that the traditional "pillars of sustainability" are not distinct "silos" for individual consideration but are interconnected components of the destination system. Framed in this manner, any action undertaken for a specific purpose – referred to in *Whistler 2020* as "Sustainability Program Tasks" – must consider wider upstream and downstream implications. For example, although creating affordable housing is an important sustainability task for both economic and social reasons, these facilities must be accommodated in places readily accessible to the workplace for social purposes, and in environmentally appropriate locations for ecological reasons. This more holistic approach developed around action priorities that include enriching community life, enhancing the resort experience, protecting the environment, ensuring economic viability and partnering for success. The approach forces individual action plans through a structured sustainability filter, as well as requires all Sustainability Program Tasks to seek alignment and fit with others (Vance & Williams, 2005). The RMOW sustainability initiatives are guided by the perspectives of 15 Task Force Working Groups composed of a wide range of stakeholders (including representatives of private and public institutions as well as individual community members) from both within and beyond the community. The Task Force's themes are arts, culture and heritage; built environment; economic; energy; food; learning; materials and solid waste; natural areas; recreation and leisure; transportation; visitor experience; water; resident affordability; health and social; and resident housing.

Each Working Group addresses specific priorities embedded in the *Whistler 2020* vision. Overriding filtering criteria related to TNS principles and Whistler's vision guide all Task Force reviews. Each task force group examines the results of previously recommended actions, evaluates the most current indicator data, strategically assesses local and regional opportunities and then presents a recommended set of actions to specific community stakeholders for action. About half of the action items need municipal approval, and others are dealt with directly by the affected agency or organization. *Whistler 2020*'s interactive and informative website provides on-going progress reports to the broader community on the implementation of recommended Task Force priorities, as well as on-going efforts to engage locals in "owning the plan" (*Whistler 2020*, 2010). Interestingly, on-going discussions among some *Whistler 2020* stakeholders suggest that more targeted growth in "non-commercial" bed units may be needed to ensure that Whistler achieves some of its social service goals (Whistler Centre for Sustainability, personal communication, June 9, 2010).

Whistler in a post-Olympic era

As with its inception, Whistler used the momentum of the Winter Olympic Games to further its development goals beyond 2010. In partnership with the Canadian and British Columbian governments, the City of Vancouver and the four Host First Nations,[3] it eventually became the first official "Host Mountain Resort" for the 2010 Vancouver Winter Olympic and Paralympic Games. Throughout the preparations for the Games, and the delivery of its responsibilities, it used the principles and priorities of the *Whistler 2020* vision to guide its involvement. In initial negotiations with the Vancouver Olympic Organizing Committee, it embedded Whistler's sustainability principles into formal agreements and extracted many different benefits designed to advance the resort community's sustainability mandate.

However, during the seven-year lead up to the Games, it was confronted by rapidly changing fiscal, social-cultural and political realities that partially reconfigured its own Olympic goals and sustainability opportunities. During the Games "run-up", the RMOW was faced with increasingly reduced levels of real estate revenues due to global economic downturns and limited bed unit development options. This meant that previously available financial resources for development bonuses and building permits were less available to support the development of community infrastructure. Most significantly, the RMOW was falling behind on its commitment to provide affordable housing for its resident labor force. From political and social perspectives, Whistler's vision had never addressed the needs of the region's growing aboriginal population, on whose traditional territory the destination had developed and the Games would be delivered. Several Supreme Court rulings over the preceding decade highlighted the need to consult and accommodate their needs in future land use development initiatives, including those related to tourism (Williams & O'Neil, 2007). As a consequence, Whistler needed to find ways of embedding aboriginal rights and opportunities into their Olympic and future planning and development initiatives.

In response, the RMOW used the urgency and momentum of the Olympic Games to help address these "elephant in the closet" issues. Beyond acquiring additional "tagged funding" for specific projects from the federal and provincial governments to cover the cost of its Games-related initiatives, it negotiated a greater on-going proportion of the destination's hotel sales tax from the provincial government for destination-related tourism infrastructure support and marketing. In addition, a C\$50 million Legacy Fund supporting the future management of the sport venues in Whistler was negotiated. Notably, the most significant financial legacy associated with the Games involved Whistler gaining control over additional lands in the region. Specifically, the RMOW used its unique Olympic role to leverage additional space for development and control. For instance, to meet its Games-related athlete's village responsibilities, it obtained additional Crown Land from the BC government for Games-time athlete housing. An important part of this transaction involved designing the housing so that it could be transitioned into an additional 800 bed units of affordable resident housing after the Games. The homes were designed to high-level environmental standards so as to align them with the broader sustainability goals of the community. From a governance perspective, this development also increased Whistler's long-standing bed unit cap beyond past limits and opened discussions about the possibility of further targeted increases in this limit. An emerging community discussion now centers around the extent to which future cap limits should be reviewed in the context of fiscal, social and environmental priorities and not be fixed (Whistler Centre for Sustainability, personal communication, May 3, 2010). In addition, because some Games venues extended into traditionally non-developed Crown lands adjacent to the municipal boundaries (e.g. Callahan Valley), the RMOW negotiated formal jurisdiction and control over those lands. This not only limited intrusions by other non-community stakeholders into Whistler's backcountry "playground" but also provided another land bank for potential future development that might align with Whistler's vision (as well as provide much needed development bonuses) for the future. This land acquisition effectively increased the RMOW's land jurisdiction from 16,500 to 24,300 ha (RMOW, personal communication, May 3, 2010).

From a sociopolitical perspective, and to accommodate the rights of aboriginal people, the RMOW approved and helped guide the development of the Squamish – Lil'wet Cultural

Centre in Whistler. This Olympic-driven and federally funded project provided Whistler with an impressive aboriginal tourism attraction and offered the local aboriginal nations an unprecedented economic and cultural presence in the resort community. In addition, aboriginal groups were allocated additional lands for development within Whistler's boundaries. These lands are anticipated to eventually escalate Whistler's bed unit level well beyond current capacity limits and generate new revenue streams for the RMOW. In strategic terms, both projects provide Whistler with potentially significant streams of new revenues that support its historical growth path and sustainability agenda.

Discussion

It is argued that Whistler's path dependency was determined by the political and regulatory system established at its inception. That system locked the resort community's development into a defined land base that guided varying levels of controlled growth for over three decades. This is not to imply that governance practices remained static over that period. In fact, they evolved toward a more participatory form that included widening stakeholder engagement. As discussed by Boas (2007), path-dependent institutional evolution occurs through processes of layering and conversion. These processes are evident in Whistler's governance system. Nevertheless, power remained with the three key groups of decision-makers: the municipality, the mountain operator(s) and the provincial government, all of whom were committed to continued growth. As economic and social circumstances changed in Whistler, so did the priorities and actions of these stakeholders with respect to managing growth. For instance, a major policy and management crisis occurred when Whistler reached its long-established bed unit limit more quickly than anticipated. The solution to this crisis involved creating a new governance system centered on an integrated, comprehensive and sustainable model. Built on a foundation of readily understandable science-based principles and ongoing stakeholder engagement, it included not only environmental but also social and economic principles and priorities that went beyond traditional growth management bed unit capacity limits. However, do these changes in governance represent the creation of a new path or simply a conversion that reconstitutes growth objectives in a form that is acceptable to the varied constituent stakeholders?

The chance event that led to Whistler's initial development as a new ski resort involved the role of a small but influential group of local businessmen who drew attention to its site for Olympic and related international tourism development. It coincided with timely political recognition that this form of resource development aligned with BC regional economic development programs already in place. These root incidents established a path of development dependence and governance that mirrored the principles employed successfully in other resource sector cases across BC. The guiding principles involved creating governance systems that encouraged close relationships between public and private sector partners for the purposes of stimulating growth.

The pro-growth model of governance, as outlined by Pierre (see Table 1), is clearly apparent in Whistler's early existence and follows a classic growth machine path. High levels of both public and private infrastructural investment needed to make Whistler viable meant that the resort locked into a path of "increasing return effects" (Arthur, 1989) even in the face of economic challenges. The resort reached a critical mass of commercial development in the early 1990s when demand for space and resources accelerated. Until that time, the RMOW maintained tight control on the location and type of new development that happened. However, once the mountain operators commenced exercising their rights to develop real estate under the "lands for lifts policy" and other investors were attracted to the initial success of the destination, growth rates escalated and controlled development became more challenging.

In response to rapid growth in the mid-1990s, Whistler adopted a growth management governance system. This represented a shift toward a more corporatist model (see Table 1), as the views of resident stakeholders, community organizations and local businesses gained some influence in decision-making. However, growth was still the driving force behind most programs. Although pro-growth strategies are typically the least participatory of all forms of governance, with control centralized among public and private elites, Molotch (1976) and Logan and Molotch (1987) observe that pro-growth politics have few opponents and most stakeholders have a vested interest in more development. This appears to be the case in Whistler. Market success gave considerable powers to the RMOW to negotiate with and extract community benefits from developers. These included the creation of a wide range of community infrastructure not normally associated with towns of Whistler's size. Overall, there was relatively little opposition to development proposals during the growth management era. Whistler was generally perceived to have a well-established OCP, appropriate planning regulations and a portfolio of sound environmental programs (Gill, 2000). The tactics employed reflected widely held environmental values held by the community. Whistler's bed unit cap and seemingly transparent approach to governance created confidence in the RMOW's growth management approach.

The original interpretation of "lock-in" in the path dependence model is defined as "the self-reinforcing process of collective behavior by which an economic system [or in this instance governance approach] converges to a history dependent equilibrium state from which it cannot escape" (Martin, 2010, p. 9). Whistler's attainment of its planned development cap suggests that such a state of equilibrium may have occurred (despite the fact that is very uncommon). However, it is theorized (Arthur, 1989; David, 1985) that such a state might exist until some external event occurs that disrupts this equilibrium. Several events in this case support their perspectives.

Although the attainment of the bed unit cap was expected, accelerated development, as the cap limit neared, was not anticipated. This situation created some urgency regarding how to move to a non-growth model. The initial components of the sustainability concept in Whistler's growth management planning systems were primarily environmentally oriented. The move to a more integrated comprehensive sustainability approach with wide-ranging stakeholder input shifted focus from a narrow attention to environmental issues, to a need to also address residents' affordable housing needs. As such, it did not deny the possibilities of growth. Indeed, it can be seen as a further layering of the existing path. However, two events acted as exogenous forces that allowed Whistler to move beyond the equilibrium state toward a potential new path. First, there was the unexpected introduction to TNS through Robèrt's visit. It offered a framework to approach integrated comprehensive sustainability planning in a way that did not relinquish the possibility of future growth. The second event, Whistler's successful bid to host the 2010 Winter Olympic Games, provided the ability to follow this path. As development for the Games unfolded, so did the political will and financial resources needed to foster the development of additional community legacies. This in turn has opened discussions about returning to the successful growth model that Whistler had engineered in past years. The discussions now include additional partners such as First Nations. For instance, aboriginal community interest in tourism-related development has ramped up dramatically in recent years. This is fuelled by opportunities afforded to aboriginal groups by both legal rulings and government policy directives supporting the involvement of indigenous peoples in economic enterprises, particularly in their traditional territories (BC Resort Task Force, 2004). In response, aspiring aboriginals are aggressively seeking opportunities to develop tourism businesses in established tourism regions, including environments in and around Whistler. Learning how to accommodate their specific interests within existing sustainable development guidelines adds potentially unprecedented layers of complexity to the current governance model.

Finally, other powerful circumstances are shaping current discussions about adopting the corporatist model. These circumstances include the lingering effects of the global financial downturn that continue to limit development options. Some residents are beginning to question Whistler's commitment to its sophisticated integrated comprehensive sustainability model. A report in the local paper suggests that:

> [w]ith too many empty beds, too many struggling hotels and a business community desperate to keep the money flow going, the province's diamond in the crown is struggling mightily to reinvent itself for the new century ... Doesn't look all that sustainable at this point does it? (Beaudry, 2010, p. 33)

Conclusion

The authors of this paper contend that the resort's trajectory and outcomes were largely influenced by its historical growth-focused path dependency. It is argued that Whistler's path dependency was determined by a political and regulatory system established at its inception. That system locked the resort community's development into a defined land base and planning strategy that promoted controlled growth. Although the ensuing governance practices did not stay static, power remained with three primary decision-making groups: the municipality, the mountain operator(s) and the provincial government. All of these stakeholders remained committed to continued growth up to an agreed upon limit linked to an ambiguously defined environmental quality standard. However, when Whistler approached this capacity limit faster than anticipated, the stakeholders embarked on an alternative governance model centered on an innovative integrated comprehensive sustainability strategy. This strategy was specifically designed to address environmental, as well as social and economic objectives. Formed through a process of unprecedented levels of community engagement and input, the strategy established the principles and conditions under which development might exceed the previously established growth limit.

This paper's review and assessment of factors affecting Whistler's changing governance approach suggests that the tenets of path dependency theory are very much evident in this community. This raises the question of whether or not the integrated comprehensive sustainability approach to management marks the creation of a new path or simply an adaptation that reconstitutes growth objectives in a form that is acceptable to the varied constituent private and public sector stakeholders. Although its approaches to governance exhibit different nuances over time, they appear to be evolving rather than attaining an equilibrium or even creating a new path. Collectively, they represent a hybrid pro-growth and corporatist model (Pierre, 1999). Even the resort's most recent *Whistler 2020* vision and associated CSP offers opportunities for growth – within specific limits of appropriateness. The Task Force Working Groups that guide the CSP's interpretation and implementation recognize the inherent importance of integrating a combination of economic, social and environmental principles into their decisions. However, there still exists an underlying recognition among most residents that continuing growth (perhaps in innovative forms) is still fundamental to the Whistler governance model. This suggests that Whistler remains locked in by history and is dependent on a pro-growth approach to governance.

Whistler has traditionally been locked in by artificially induced land base restrictions that have shaped its bed-unit limits as well as revenue generation options. If growth stagnates, Whistler loses some of its competitive edge. Unless it gets a new land, it can only "grow" affordable housing developments that generate less tax revenues for community services than do more commercially focused bed units. Although the Olympics provided more developable land, and brought First Nations into Whistler's governance regime, their push for more development creates complicated joint partnerships, as well as possibilities of unfettered growth and loss of control over governance processes.

McCool and Moisey (2001) observe that in tourism contexts, powerful arguments exist that suggest that affected publics should be involved in "helping identify desirable futures and acceptable pathways to achieving them" (p. 11). In tracing the path of stakeholder engagement in Whistler's governance, it is evident that, following the early growth machine era, there has been evolving engagement of community stakeholders that has culminated in the most recent comprehensive sustainability model. Although a general concern about growth's negative effects is apparent throughout that strategy, there is still an underlying and ongoing perspective that more development in Whistler is critical to its sustainability.

Whistler's story is unique, but, as a frequently acknowledged innovative leader in the competitive environment of North American (if not global) mountain resort destinations, many other destinations look to Whistler for direction and expertise in how to be successful. The integrated comprehensive sustainability model of governance that Whistler has developed is innovative. It exhibits a high level of diverse stakeholder engagement through its task forces, supported by a sophisticated, accessible and transparent web-based information system. The uncertainty expressed about whether or not this represents a new model of governance is not related to the actual mechanisms for widespread participatory democracy, but rather to issues such as political agendas, corporate competitive strategies and power relationships that underlie decision-making. Further, the ability of stakeholders to sustain on-going high levels of engagement and the overall cost to the resort of implementing this model of distributive governance are yet to be determined.

In this paper, the focus on aspects of path dependency has proved valuable in untangling the temporal continuity and change in governance approaches. However, as Bramwell and Cox (2009) observe, due to the complexity of interactions, "it may be quite challenging to distinguish between path dependence and path creation" (p. 195). A potential avenue for further research in this area would be through a more focused examination of governance interactions. It could center on providing more detailed and nuanced insights into the alliances and power relations that underlie change in governance systems. Other useful research directions relate to the innovative nature of Whistler's integrated comprehensive sustainability model. Studies of innovation applying network approaches (e.g. Guia et al., 2006) already suggest that this is a useful avenue. Future comparative research into the adoption (or adaptation) of Whistler's initiatives by other resort communities would be helpful in revealing the influence of place and path dependency in adopting innovative approaches. And, there remain the fundamental issues of how to govern with and for growth limits – both for no growth and slow growth.

Acknowledgements

We wish to thank the Social Sciences and Humanities Research Council of Canada who have supported our longitudinal research efforts in Whistler through several grants. We also thank many people in Whistler, especially the Resort Municipality staff, for their collaboration and input into our research projects.

Notes

1. In line with Pierre's (1999) identification of governance models, the term "corporatist" is used in this paper to characterize the recent change in governance approach in Whistler. A corporatist model should not be confused with notions of corporate-directed control. Indeed, it is quite the opposite as it is based on principles of participatory local democracy and high levels of interest participation.
2. The Natural Step is a nonprofit organization founded in Sweden in 1989 by Karl-Henrik Robèrt to promote the principles and adoption of a framework for sustainable development. See www.naturalstep.org. It has branches in 11 countries.
3. The 2010 Olympic and Paralympic Winter Games were held on the shared traditional territories of four First Nations (the Lil'wat, Musqueam, Squamish and Tsleil-Waututh). For the first time, Indigenous peoples were recognized by the International Olympic Committee as full host partners.

References

Arnstein, S.R. (1969). A ladder of citizen participation. *Journal of the American Institute of Planners, 35*(4), 216–224.

Arthur, W.B. (1989). Competing technologies, increasing returns, and "lock-in" by historical events. *Economic Journal, 99*, 116–131.

Baggio, R., Scott, N., & Cooper, C. (2010). Improving tourism destination governance: A complexity science approach. *Tourism Review, 65*(4), 51–60.

BC Resort Task Force. (2004). *Recommendations of the BC resort task force: Report to honourable Sandy Santori, Minister of State for resort development*. Victoria: Government of British Columbia.

Beaudry, M. (2010, June 3). Rethinking Garibaldi at Squamish – A 21st century perspective. *Pique Newsmagazine*, p. 33.

Beritelli, P., Bieger, T., & Laesser, C. (2007). Destination governance: Using corporate governance theories as a foundation for effective destination management. *Journal of Travel Research, 20*, 1–12.

Boas, T.C. (2007). Conceptualizing continuity and change: The composite-standard model of path dependence. *Journal of Theoretical Politics, 19*(1), 33–54.

Bodega, D., Cioccarelli, G., & Denicolai, S. (2004). Evolution of relationship structures in mountain tourism. *Tourism Review, 59*(3), 13–19.

Boschma, R., & Martin, R. (2007). Editorial: Constructing an evolutionary economic geography. *Journal of Economic Geography, 7*, 537–548.

Bramwell, B., & Cox, V. (2009). Stage and path dependency approaches to the evolution of a national park tourism partnership. *Journal of Sustainable Tourism, 17*(2), 191–206.

Butler, R. (1980). The concept of a tourist area cycle of evolution: Implications for management of resources. *The Canadian Geographer, 24*, 5–12.

Butler, R. (2006a). *The tourism area life cycle, vol 1: Applications and modifications*. Clevedon: Channel View Publications.

Butler, R. (2006b). *The tourism area life cycle, vol. 2: Conceptual and theoretical issues*. Clevedon: Channel View Publications.

David, P.A. (1985). Clio and the economics of QWERTY: The necessity of history. *American Economic Review, 75*, 332–337.

David, P.A. (1993). Path dependence and predictability in dynamic systems with local network externalities: A paradigm for historical economics. In D. Foray & C. Freeman (Eds.), *Technology and the wealth of nations* (pp. 187–216). London: Pinter.

David, P.A. (1994). Why are institutions the "carriers of history?" Path dependence and the evolution of conventions, organizations and institutions. *Structural Change and Economic Dynamics, 5*(2), 205–220.

Dorward, S. (1990). *Design for mountain communities: A landscape and architectural guide.* New York: Van Nostrand Reinhold.

Dredge, D. (2006a). Policy networks and the local organization of tourism. *Tourism Management, 27,* 269–280.

Dredge, D. (2006b). Networks, conflict and collaborative communities. *Journal of Sustainable Tourism, 14*(6), 562–581.

Dwyer, L., Edwards, D., Mistilis, N., Roman, C., & Scott, N. (2009). Destination and enterprise management for a tourism future. *Tourism Management, 30,* 63–74.

Erkus-Osturk, H., & Eraydin, A. (2010). Environmental governance for sustainable tourism development: Collaborative networks and organisation building in the Antalya region. *Tourism Management, 31*(1), 113–124.

Essletzbichler, J., & Rigby, D. (2007). Exploring evolutionary economic geographies. *Journal of Economic Geography, 7,* 549–571.

Flagestad, A., & Hope, C. (2001). Strategic success in winter sports destinations: A sustainable value creation perspective. *Tourism Management, 22,* 445–461.

Gill, A.M. (1998). Local and resort development. In R.W. Butler, C.M. Hall, & J. Jenkins (Eds.), *Tourism and recreation in rural areas* (pp. 97–111). Chichester: Wiley.

Gill, A.M. (2000). From growth machine to growth management: The dynamics of resort development in Whistler, British Columbia. *Environment and Planning A, 32,* 1083–1103.

Gill, A.M. (2007). The politics of bed units: The case of Whistler, British Columbia. In T. Coles & A. Church (Eds.), *Tourism, politics and place* (pp. 125–159). London: Routledge.

Gill, A.M., & Williams, P.W. (2005). Corporate-community relations in the tourism sector: A stakeholder perspective. In A. Gilg, R. Yarwood, S. Essex, J. Smithers, & R. Wilson (Eds.), *Rural change and sustainability: Agriculture, the environment and communities* (pp. 309–325). Wallingford: CABI.

Gill, A.M., & Williams, P.W. (2006). Corporate responsibility and place: The case of Whistler, British Columbia. In T. Clark, A.M. Gill, & R. Hartmann (Eds.), *Mountain resort planning and development in an era of globalization* (pp. 26–40). Elmsford, NY: Cognizant Communication.

Gill, A.M., & Williams, P.W. (2008). From "guiding fiction" to action: Applying "The Natural Step" to sustainability planning in the resort of Whistler, British Columbia. In S.F. McCool & R.N. Moisey (Eds.), *Tourism, recreation and sustainability: Linking culture and environment* (2nd ed., pp. 121–130). Wallingford: CABI.

Grabher, G. (1993), The weakness of strong ties: The lock-in of regional development in the Ruhr area. In G. Grabher (Ed.), *The embedded firm: On the socio-economics of industrial networks* (pp. 255–277). London: Routledge.

Guia, J., Prats, L., & Comas, J. (2006). The destination as a local system of innovation: The role of relational networks. In L. Lazzeretti & C. Petrillo (Eds.), *Tourism local systems and networking* (pp. 57–66). Oxford: Elsevier.

Horner, G. (2000). *Mountains of money: The corporate production of Whistler resort* (Unpublished master's thesis). University of British Columbia, Vancouver, British Columbia, Canada.

Ioannides, D. (2009). Hypothesizing the shifting mosaic of attitudes through time: A dynamic framework for sustainable tourism development on a Mediterranean Isle. In S.F. McCool & R.N. Moisey (Eds.), *Tourism, recreation and sustainability: Linking culture and the environment* (pp. 51–75). Wallingford: CABI.

Keller, P., & Bieger, T. (Eds.). (2008). *Real estate and destination development in tourism.* Berlin: Erich Schmidt Verlag.

Ladurantaye, S. (2010, July 13). Bye-bye G8, hello buyers: Deerhurst up for sale [report on business, section b]. *Globe and Mail,* pp. 1, 4. Retrieved March 3, 2011, from http://www.theglobeandmail.com/report-on-business/deerhurst-resort-on-the-block/article1636823/

Lazzeretti, L., & Petrillo, C.L. (Eds.). (2006). *Tourism local systems and networking.* Oxford: Elsevier.

Logan, J.R., & Molotch, H. (1987). *Urban fortunes: The political economy of place*. Berkeley: University of California Press.

MacKinnon, D., Cumbers, A., Pike, A., Birch, K., & McMaster, R. (2009). Evolution in economic geography: Institutions, political economy and adaptation. *Economic Geography, 85*(2), 129–150.

Mahoney, J. (2000). Path dependence in historical sociology. *Theory and Society, 29*, 507–548.

Martin, R. (2010). Roepke lecture in economic geography-rethinking regional path dependence: Beyond lock-in to evolution. *Economic Geography, 86*(1), 1–27.

Martin, R., & Sunley, P. (2006). Path dependence and regional economic evolution. *Journal of Economic Geography, 6*, 395–437.

McCool, S.F., & Moisey, R.N. (2001). Pathways and pitfalls in the search for sustainable tourism. In S.F. McCool & R.N. Moisey (Eds.), *Tourism, recreation and sustainability: Linking culture and the environment* (1st ed., pp. 1–16). Wallingford: CABI.

Molotch, H. (1976). The city as a growth machine. *American Journal of Sociology, 82*, 309–330.

Murphy, P. (2008). *The business of resort management*. Oxford: Elsevier.

Nordin, S., & Svensson, B. (2005). The significance of governance in innovative tourism destinations. In P. Keller & T. Bieger (Eds.), *Innovation in tourism: Creating customer value* (pp. 159–170). St Gallen: AIEST.

Painter, J. (2000). State and governance. In E. Sheppard & T. Barnes (Eds.), *A companion to economic geography* (pp. 359–376). Oxford: Blackwell.

Pavlovitch, K. (2003). The evolution and transformation of a tourism destination network: The Waitomo Caves, New Zealand. *Tourism Management, 24*, 203–216.

Pforr, C. (2002). The makers and shakers of tourism policy in the northern territory of Australia: A policy network analysis of actors and their relational constellations. *Journal of Hospitality and Tourism Management, 9*(2), 134–151.

Pierre, J. (1999). Models of urban governance: The institutional dimension of urban politics. *Urban Affairs Review, 34*(3), 372–396.

Pierson, P. (2000). Increasing returns, path dependence, and the study of politics. *The American Political Science Review, 94*(2), 251–267.

Pike, A., Birch, K., Cumbers, A., MacKinnon, R., & McMaster, R. (2009). A geographical political economy of evolution in economic geography. *Economic Geography, 85*(2), 175–182.

Prideaux, B. (2000). The resort development spectrum – A new approach to modeling resort development. *Tourism Management, 21*, 225–240.

Robèrt, K.-H. (2008). *The natural step story: Seeding a quiet revolution*. Gabriola, BC: New Society Publishers.

Ruhanen, L., Scott, N., Ritchie, B., & Tkaczynski, A. (2010). Governance: A review and synthesis of literature. *Tourism Review, 65*(4), 4–16.

Sailor, L. (2010). *Conditioning community: Power and decision-making in transitioning an industry-based community* (Unpublished doctoral dissertation). University of Waterloo, Ontario, Canada.

Stanton, J., & Aislabie, C. (1992). Up-market integrated resorts in Australia. *Annals of Tourism Research, 19*, 435–449.

Svensson, B., Nordin, S., & Flagestad, A. (2006). Destination governance and contemporary development models. In L. Lazzeretti & C. Petrillo (Eds.), *Tourism local systems and networking* (pp. 83–96). Oxford: Elsevier.

TNS. (2010). *The natural step*. Retrieved December 9, 2010, from http://www.naturalstep.org

Vance, M., & Williams, P.W. (2005). A system based approach to sustainability planning in resort destinations: Whistler 2020. *Integra, 4/5*, 20–23.

Vernon, J., Essex, S., Pinder, D., & Curry, K. (2005). Collaborative policy-making: Local sustainable projects. *Annals of Tourism Research, 32*(2), 325–345.

Waldron, D. (2000). *An environmental sustainability strategy for tourism communities: The case of Whistler, B.C.* (Unpublished Master of Resource Management Report #269). Simon Fraser University, Burnaby, British Columbia, Canada.

Waldron, D., & Williams, P.W. (2002). Steps towards sustainability monitoring: The case of the resort municipality of Whistler. In R. Harris, T. Griffin, & P.W. Williams (Eds.), *Sustainable tourism: A global perspective* (pp. 180–194). New York: Butterworth Heinemann.

Weaver, D. (2000). A broad context model of destination development scenarios. *Tourism Management, 21*, 217–224.

Whistler 2020. (2010). *Whistler 2020: Moving toward a sustainable future.* Retrieved July 29, 2010, from http://www.whistler2020.ca

Williams, A.M., & Baláž, V. (2002). The Czech and Slovak Republics: Conceptual issues in the economic analysis of tourism in transition. *Tourism Management, 23*(1), 37–45.

Williams, P.W., & Gill, A.M. (2006). A research agenda for tourism amenity migration destinations. *Tourism Recreation Research, 31*(1), 92–98.

Williams, P.W., Gill, A.M., & Chura, N. (2004). Branding mountain destinations: The battle for "placefulness". *Tourism Review, 59*(1), 6–15.

William, P.W., Gill, A.M., & Ponsford, I. (2007). Corporate social responsibility at tourism destinations: Towards a social license to operate. *Tourism Review International, 11*(2), 133–144.

Williams, P.W., & O'Neil, B. (2007). Building a triangulated research foundation for Aboriginal tourism in BC, Canada. In R. Butler & T. Hinch (Eds.), *Tourism and indigenous peoples* (pp. 40–57). New York: Elsevier.

Young, N. (2008). Radical neoliberalism in British Columbia: Remaking rural geographies. *Canadian Journal of Sociology, 33*(1), 1–36.

Policy learning and policy failure in sustainable tourism governance: from first- and second-order to third-order change?

C. Michael Hall

Department of Management, University of Canterbury, Christchurch, New Zealand

Sustainable tourism presents a paradox. At one level sustainable tourism is a success given the concept's diffusion among industry, government, academics and policy actors. Yet, it is simultaneously a policy failure given the continued growth in the environmental impacts of tourism in absolute terms. This paper analyses sustainable tourism, and the governance systems for sustainable tourism, via the concepts of policy learning and failure. The tractability of sustainable tourism policy problems is identified. Policy learning is discussed in instrumental, conceptual/paradigmatic and political learning/strategic terms. Although policy failure should encourage learning with respect to sustainable tourism this has only related to first- and second-order change which focus on changes to indicators and settings rather than the dominant policy paradigm. This is despite the dominant paradigm of "balanced" sustainable development that promotes economic growth failing on a number of indicators. A reason for this may be the unwillingness of key actors in tourism policy networks to acknowledge policy failure. The paper concludes that although exogenous factors such as a crisis event may lead to policy paradigmatic change, there is insufficient evidence that such a shift in sustainable tourism policy will necessarily occur given the entrenched dominance of the existing paradigm.

Introduction: the sustainability of sustainable tourism

By some measures, the notion of sustainable tourism must be regarded as one of the great success stories of tourism research and knowledge transfer. It has become incorporated into the fabric of tourism discourse in academic, business and governance terms. In addition to a specific academic journal (*Journal of Sustainable Tourism*), there are a number of dedicated texts (e.g. Gössling, Hall, & Weaver, 2009; Hall & Lew, 1998; Mowforth & Munt, 1998; Swarbrooke, 1999; Weaver, 2006) as well as a steadily increasing number of academic articles. Table 1 illustrates the growing significance of the topic as an area of academic interest as evidenced by a search of the number of times the term "sustainable tourism" has been used in abstracts, keywords or titles in three major databases of academic literature from 1989 to 2010.

At the same time that sustainable tourism has grown as an area of academic interest, the term has been increasingly adopted into tourism policymaking by both the public and private sectors at all levels of governance. For example, the concept of sustainable tourism has been at the forefront of the policy statements of organizations such as the United Nations

Table 1.   Records of the term "sustainable tourism" in major academic databases.

Year	Within Scopus keywords	Scopus abstracts	Within ScienceDirect keywords	Within ScienceDirect abstracts	Within ISI web of knowledge titles
2010	59	80	9	15	24
2009	55	58	9	8	32
2008	40	58	3	4	35
2007	34	46	3	3	16
2006	30	49	2	5	19
2005	20	32	6	10	13
2004	12	30	1	4	14
2003	11	30	2	2	6
2002	19	33	9	6	14
2001	9	25	5	6	11
2000	6	24	1	–	14
1999	2	16	1	3	6
1998	2	9	2	3	6
1997	6	13	–	4	17
1996	8	7	–	2	11
1995	8	7	2	4	8
1994	7	7	2	3	4
1993	–	3	–	2	2
1992	5	8	–	3	2
1991	–	–	–	–	–
1990	–	1	–	1	1
1989	–	2	–	–	–

Note: Searches undertaken 1 June 2010; 6 January 2011.

Environmental Programme (UNEP, 2005a, 2005b, 2005c, 2009), United Nations World Tourism Organization (UNWTO, 2007a, 2010) and the World Travel and Tourism Council (WTTC, 2003, 2009, 2010), as well as joint exercises between them (e.g. International Task Force on Sustainable Tourism Development, 2009; United Nations Environmental Programme and the World Tourism Organization, 2005; World Travel & Tourism Council, International Federation of Tour Operators, International Hotel & Restaurant Association, & International Council of Cruise Lines, 2002). The concept is also mentioned in most national or regional government tourism policies or statements (e.g. Department of Resources, Energy and Tourism, 2008; Industry Canada, 2006; Ministry of Tourism, Tourism New Zealand, and Tourism Industry Association New Zealand, 2007; South Australian Tourism Commission, 2009; USAID, 2007) as well as corporate statements (e.g. Tourism Industry Association of Canada, 2010; TUI Travel PLC, 2010).

Despite the success of the concept of sustainable tourism in academic and policy discourse, tourism's contribution to environmental change, one of the benchmarks of sustainability in terms of the maintenance of "natural" or "ecological" capital (Pearce, Barbier, & Markandya, 1990; World Commission for Environment and Development, 1987), is greater than ever. Gössling (2002) provided the first comprehensive overview of the global environmental consequences of tourism and argued that from a global perspective, tourism contributes to: changes in land cover and land use; energy use; biotic exchange and extinction of wild species; exchange and dispersion of diseases and changes in the perception and understanding of the environment. Gössling's (2002) estimates for 2001 with respect to tourism's contribution to global environmental change, and updated in Gössling and

Table 2.   Tourism's contribution to global environmental change.

Dimension	2001 estimates	2007 estimates
Number of international tourist arrivals	682 million[1]	898 million[1]
Number of domestic tourist arrivals	3,580.5 million[2]	4,714.5 million[2]
Total number of tourist arrivals	4,262.5 million[2]	5,612.5 million[2]
Change of land cover – alteration of biologically productive lands	0.5% contribution[3]	0.6–0.66% contribution[4]
Energy consumption	14,080 PJ[3]	18,585.6 PJ[4]
Emissions	1400 Mt of CO_2-e[3]	1848 Mt of CO_2-e[4] (1461.6 Mt of CO_2)[5]
Biotic exchange	Difficult to assess[3]	Difficult to assess, however rate of exchange is increasing[4]
Extinction of wild species	Difficult to assess[3]	Difficult to assess, particularly because of time between initial tourism effects and extinction events but increasing. One estimate of 3.5–5.5% of species loss with a future higher figure being likely if climate change factors are considered[6]
Health	Difficult to assess[3]	Difficult to assess in host populations, but sickness in tourists in tropical destinations assessed at 50% by WHO[7]
World Population[8]	6,169.8 million	6,632.2 million
Total number of tourist arrivals as% of world population	69.1%	84.6%
Number of international tourist arrivals as% of world population	11.1%	13.5%

[1]UNWTO figures.
[2]Hall and Lew (2009) estimates based on UNWTO data.
[3]Gössling (2002) estimate.
[4]Hall and Lew (2009) extrapolation based on Gössling's estimates and other research.
[5]UNWTO and UNEP (2008) estimate for 2005.
[6]In Hall (2010a).
[7]World Health Organisation (2003).
[8]Mid-year world population estimate by US Census Bureau International Data Base (http://www.census.gov/ipc/www/idb/worldpop.html).

Hall (2006), have been more recently examined in Hall and Lew (2009) and Hall (2009a) and suggest that the contribution of tourism to global change is continuing to grow as a result of increasing numbers of domestic and international tourist trips as well as increases in distance travelled (Table 2). In the case of CO_2 emissions resulting from tourism, for example, the United Nations World Tourism Organization, United Nations Environmental Programme & World Meteorological Organization (UNWTO, UNEP & WMO, 2008) estimate that approximately 40% come from air transport, 32% from car transport and 21% from accommodation, with growth continuing to occur in all areas (Gössling, Hall, Peeters, & Scott, 2010).

Some issues of environmental change are plagued by a lack of tourism-specific data. For example, although the rate of biotic exchange is increasing and tourism is recognised as a major mechanism for biological invasion, the exact contribution of tourism is difficult to determine (Hall, 2010c, 2010d, 2010e, in press). Nevertheless, Vilà and Pujadas (2001) in a study of the socio-economic parameters influencing plant invasions in Europe and North Africa found that the density of naturalised species was positively correlated to the number of tourists that visit a country (r = 0.49), with Mediterranean international tourist destinations also having high densities of naturalised species. Mozumder, Berrens and Bohara (2006) also identified the association of tourism with increasing biodiversity risk when examining the regression results between the log of tourist arrivals and the log of an upgraded national biodiversity risk index for 61 countries (see also Hall, James, & Wilson, 2010). Given the relationship observed by Ehrlich (1994) between energy and emissions as well as energy use and biodiversity loss, Hall (2010a) conservatively estimated that tourism is responsible for approximately 3.5–5.5% of species loss with a future higher figure being likely if climate change scenarios are considered.

Indeed, the estimated growth of future emissions from the tourism industry despite potential technological improvements (UNWTO, UNEP & WMO, 2008; World Economic Forum, 2009a), is one of the most significant contributing factors to tourism being regarded as unsustainable (Gössling et al., 2010). Car travel has a large potential to become more energy efficient in the future, with supply-side approaches including use of biofuels, increased use of gas, new engine concepts, hybridisation and use of hydrogen fuel (Pricewaterhouse-Coopers, 2007), but due to a rapidly increasing number of cars in countries such as India or China, it is anticipated that despite these efficiency gains, overall tourism-related emissions from this transport mode will continue to increase (Gössling et al., 2010). Similarly, in order to meet the emission reduction target of 25–30% for tourism-related aviation by 2020 (WTTC, 2009), efficiency gains in the order of 6% per year would have to be achieved between 2010 and 2020. However, the final report of International Civil Aviation Organization's Group on International Aviation and Climate Change (GIACC, 2009) did not include any emission reduction target for the sector over either the near- or long term. The only commitment was to a fuel efficiency goal of 2% per annum through to 2020, although the rate of aviation growth means that emissions would continue to grow in absolute terms. Even the most optimistic emission reduction scenarios presented by scientists do not expect emission reductions beyond 2% per annum by 2030 (e.g. Lee et al., 2009). Furthermore, the annual gains in fuel efficiency may inevitably decline due to physical and technical limits, with the pace of efficiency reductions showing strong reductions over time from over 6% annually in the 1960s to c.1.5% by 2000 (Peeters & Middel, 2007). As Gössling et al. (2010, p. 124) observe:

> Overall, it would appear that *technologically optimistic* perspectives dominate the discourses of GHG emission reductions in the tourism sector. While observed emission trends from aviation and tourism continue to grow, the technology needed to bring about absolute emission reductions is always in the near future – though never at hand.

The growing contribution of tourism to environmental change while it is simultaneously being promoted as a means of economic growth suggests that sustainable tourism development is a significant policy problem and that policymaking is a significant part of the governance process. That is, "a sub-issue, issue or suite of issues perceived to require resolution in some way" (Dovers, 1995, p. 95), that poses the governance challenge of selecting an optimum set of policy actions and their associated implementation. The difference between the goals of sustainable tourism and the actualities of tourism's impacts at various scales has been referred to as an implementation gap or deficit (Hall, 2009b; Hjalager, 1996; Treuren & Lane, 2003). However, the literature on policy failure, and the subsequent opportunities for policy learning that such failure might bring, may also potentially help explain how policies, and therefore governance, change over time, and therefore provide a better understanding of the differentials between policies, actions and outcomes (Hall, 2010f).

Policy failure can be said to have occurred if policy has failed to achieve an objective or perceived set of outcomes. "Learning is the process in which information becomes knowledge. Governance allows for mutual, interactive learning in image formation" (Kooiman, 2003, p. 33). Nevertheless, notions of policy failure and learning are public policy concepts which, although applied to issues of sustainability and environmental policy (e.g. Brody, 2003; Szarka, 2006), are surprisingly underutilised in studies of tourism (Kerr, 2003; Michael & Plowman, 2002; Mycoo, 2006). The following, therefore, examines the utility of the concepts of policy failure and learning in helping to explain the difficulties encountered in achieving more sustainable forms of tourism. However, before looking at policy learning and failure in detail it may be advantageous to re-examine the policy problem attributes of sustainable tourism which affect its tractability.

The policy problem attributes of sustainable tourism

Sustainability is a meta-policy problem that has led to new institutional arrangements and policy settings at international, national and local scales. Sustainable tourism is a sub-set of this broader policy arena with its own specific set of institutions and policy actors at various scales as well as being a sub-set of tourism policy overall. Sustainability problems may also pose different challenges than other policy problems (e.g. education, taxation and health) because of its attributes including (Butler, 1991; Dovers, 1996; Gössling & Hall, 2006; Hall, 2008; Hall & Lew, 1998, 2009):

- Temporality: Natural systems function over timescales that are often vastly greater than those which determine political and policy cycles.
- Spatiality: Sustainability and environmental problems tend to be cross-boundary in nature and for some types of problems, such as climate change, global in scale. One of the most significant forms of spatial problem in sustainability is the mismatch between government, regulatory space and ecological/environmental boundaries which greatly complicates difficulties in managing watershed and species habitat issues for example.
- Limits: The concept of sustainability suggests that there are limits to exploitation of natural capital because of its limited capacity for renewal
- Cumulative: Most anthropogenic impacts are cumulative rather than discrete.
- Irreversibility: Some natural capital or environmental assets cannot be renewed once they have gone, such as a species, or are not easily substitutable. In some cases (e.g. soil or ozone), the timescale for renewal is well outside the normal parameters of policy cycles.
- Complexity and connectivity: Sustainability problems are interconnected or interlocking (World Commission for Environment and Development [WCED], 1987), meaning that issues such as climate change and biodiversity cannot be easily separated in scientific terms although they often are in policymaking and institutional arrangements. Furthermore, solutions to sustainability problems impact on social and economic policy.
- Ontology: The terms "human impact" or "tourism impact" ontologically position tourism and tourists as "outside" the system under analysis, as outside of nature from a realist material ontology of classical empiricism. This is despite research on

243

global environmental change demonstrating just how deeply entangled tourism is in environmental systems (Gössling & Hall, 2006). The emphasis on the moment(s) of impact also assumes a stable natural, social or economic baseline (Hall & Lew, 2009). Such an approach is inappropriate for understanding complex and dynamic socio-environmental systems (Hall & Lew, 2009; Head, 2008), while putting a significant explanatory divide between humans and nature requires the conflation of bundles of variable processes under such headings as "human", "climate", "environment" and "nature" (Head, 2008).

- Uncertainty: Some aspects of sustainability are characterised by "pervasive uncertainty" making it difficult to judge the efficacy, implications and socio-economic impacts of policy measures (Dovers & Handmer, 1992).
- Ethical issues: Although ethical questions are integral to all policy choices, sustainability is complicated by the centrality of generational and intergenerational equity to the concept, as well as the rights of non-human species.

It has long been recognised that the various elements of sustainability affect the capacity of public policymaking to provide effective sustainable tourism outcomes (e.g. Bramwell & Lane, 1993; Butler, 1991; Hall & Lew, 1998; Wheeller, 1993). Yet, despite the length of time the policy problem attributes of sustainability have been recognised, there appears little advance in making the sustainability of tourism more tractable to solution. Several reasons for this can be advanced. It is possible that policymaking is continually seeking to "catch up" with the issue of sustainability because environmental change, as well as associated economic, social and political change, is occurring faster than corresponding changes in policy systems. The sheer complexity of sustainability issues and sustainable tourism potentially requires a "whole of government" response that lies outside of the usual jurisdiction of tourism-specific governance (Hall, 2008). This may be an issue of spatial scale, in that a government body may have limited or even no jurisdictional authority over a policy problem, or it may be an issue of means with respect to the existence of operational policy processes, technologies and/or institutional arrangements. Or perhaps the policy capacity to respond to issues of sustainable tourism may reflect the political acceptability of any solution, i.e. increases in tax, greater regulation and concern over travel lifestyle change. These issues are illustrated in Table 3.

The typology presented in Table 3 has two qualifications. First, it is heuristic and approximate. Second, it is designed to apply to the problem set faced by a given polity and is therefore scale-dependent (Dovers, 1996). In order to make policy problems more tractable, there has been a tendency to seek to address them via micro-policy means that work within existing policy processes and arrangements. However, the nature of the sustainability problem is such that while policy actions may appear logical or appropriate at the micro-scale, the emergent nature of tourism systems, let alone the inherent complexity of environmental and related change, can mean that such measures may have little effect at the meso- or macro-scales (Dovers, 2005). Indeed, Table 3 suggests that the larger the scale the more the sustainability of tourism is affected by what is occurring *outside* of the tourism policy domain. Such a situation, if correct, therefore poses particular challenges for destination and regional governance and sustainability, which is, by definition, spatially constrained as well as to the position of the tourism industry within broader governance and policy network contexts. It also possibly suggests that if sustainable tourism policy only focuses on micro-scale solutions then it may be inherently doomed to fail. So is this the reason for the failure of sustainable tourism policies?

Table 3. The relative tractability of sustainable tourism policy solutions.

Policy problem	Spatial scale	Problem nature	Policy challenge	Examples
Macro-policy	Spatially and temporally diffuse. International or global in scope	Complex and highly uncertain and often connected to other macro-policy issues as part of the meta-policy problem of sustainability. Ill-structured, "wicked" or "messy" policy problem	Potentially highly disruptive of natural and socio-economic systems and challenges existing patterns of consumption and production, policy processes and institutional arrangements	International biodiversity conservation, emissions reduction and climate change conventions
Meso-policy	Usually addressed within a national or bilateral governance context	Significant problem that is often high on the policy agenda. Moderately structured policy problem	Routine policy management. Does not pose overwhelming threats to existing patterns of production and consumption, policy processes, and/or institutional arrangements	Integrated catchment management, transboundary pollution and resource problems
Micro-policy	Spatially and temporally discrete. Usually local or sectoral scale	Not overly complex or uncertain. Well-structured policy problem	Day-to-day policy management. Does not require large resource commitment. Uses existing technology, policy process and/or institutional arrangements	Environmental impact assessment, tourism development approval, pollution licensing, tourism industry regulation

Source: Dovers, 1995; Hall, 2008.

Policy failure and learning

The failure of policy can provide a significant opportunity for policy learning. Dissatisfaction with policy performance and outcomes can provide a stimulus to consider other policy and implementation alternatives. At a more fundamental level, policy failure can also lead to a reconsideration "of the existing dominant causal reasoning about policy, potentially leading to social learning" (May, 1992, p. 341). Nevertheless, even though dissatisfaction may serve as a strong stimulus for a search for new policy ideas, it does not necessarily mean that they will be forthcoming. Several reasons why this may be the case have been put forward in the policy literature (Freeman, 2006; Grin & Loeber, 2007). First, organizations may limit evaluative efforts because of concerns about the repercussions if they are deemed to have failed to achieve policy goals. Fear of policy failure may be a factor in writing policy goals in such a way that they are "fuzzy" and difficult to assess objectively. Second, governments may be unwilling to acknowledge failure. This may be especially strong in ideologically based administrations in which acknowledgement of the need to learn from failure would entail a fundamental reconsideration of the utility or appropriateness of core ideological values with respect to specific policy problems (May, 1992; Sabatier, 1988). Such a behavioural perspective recognises that the notion of what constitutes a policy fact, or at least how facts will be interpreted, will be shaped by the values of the viewer (Majone, 1989).

Learning is an integral part of the public policy process (Freeman, 2006; Grin & Loeber, 2007). Some scholars have long regarded policymaking as a form of social learning (e.g. Deutsch, 1963, 1966; Freeman, 2006; Klein, 1997; Rose, 1993); Meppem and Gill (1998) also regarded planning for sustainability as a learning concept. Three different types of learning are usually identified in the policy literature with respect to learning within policy domains (Grin & Loeber, 2007; Nilsson, 2005). First, instrumental or technical learning which is concerned with adjusting or modifying existing policy instruments in order to pursue policy goals. Such incremental learning is generally regarded as a normal part of the policy process (Bennett & Howlett, 1992; Hall, 1993). Second, conceptual or social policy learning that is concerned with changes in basic policy beliefs and paradigms (Fiorino, 2001; Hall, 1993; May, 1992). These first two types of learning are broadly comparable to "single-loop" and "double-loop" learning as identified in the organisational learning literature (Busenberg, 2001; Grin & Loeber, 2007), where the former refers to superficial change with respect to goal achievement and the latter to more fundamental changes in organisational goals and norms (Argyris, 1992). For Hall (1993, p. 279) a "policy paradigm" is the "framework of ideas and standards that specifies not only the goals of policy and the kind of instruments used to attain them, but also the very nature of the problems they are meant to be addressing". A third type of learning is that of political learning, proposed by May (1992) which "entails lessons about policy processes and prospects. Policy advocates become more sophisticated in advancing problems and ideas by learning how to enhance the political feasibility of policy proposals" (May, 1992, p. 332). This third type of learning therefore potentially provides for a distinction between strategic behaviour and a genuine shift in policy beliefs.

Hall's (1989, 1993) approach towards policy learning has been extremely influential (Grin & Loeber, 2007). His interest in the field grew out of an attempt to understand long-term changes in British economic policy from the time of Keynes to that of Thatcher (Hall, 1989). Hall (1993, p. 278) regards policy learning as "a deliberate attempt to adjust the goals or techniques of policy in response to past experience or new information. Learning is indicated when policy changes as the result of such a process". According to Hall (1993,

p. 227) there are three central elements of this "prevailing model of social learning as utilised by contemporary theorists of the state". First, previous policy settings or "legacies" are more influential on policy than contemporary economic and social conditions. (And, in the present context, we can add environmental conditions.) As Hall (1993, p. 277) argues, "one of the principal factors affecting policy at time $= 1$ is policy at time -1". Second, policy experts or "entrepreneurs" (Dolowitz & Marsh, 1996; Mintrom & Vergari, 1996; Mintrom, 1997; Rose, 1993) located both within and at the edge of the state act as promoters of policy learning in given policy domains. Third, Hall (1993) argues that policy learning is also affected by the extent to which policy experts (and the instrumental arrangements that they put into place to implement policy) are insulated from external public political pressure, also referred to as societal pressure. Paradigm shifts, such as when the dominant economic paradigm in western liberal democracies shifted from Keynesianism to monetarianism, may occur as a result of public political pressure over perceived policy failures of government (Greener, 2001; Hall, 1989).

Hall (1993) also regards the elements of policy learning as being related to different orders of change that usually involve three core variables: overarching policy goals; the policy instruments, techniques and technologies used to achieve policy goals; and the settings of policy instruments (Greener, 2001). The work of Hall and Taylor (1996) was also extremely influential on Kooiman (2003) who refers to three orders of governance:

> First-order governing involved in day-to-day problem solving and opportunity creation, and second-order governing dealing with institutional governance conditions. . . .third-order governance is of a different type. It folds back on the theory and practise of governing and governance as such. Meta governing is like an imaginary governor, teleported to a point "outside" and holding the whole governance experience against a normative light. (Kooiman, 2003, p. 170).

First-order change is likely to be characterised by incremental, routinised, satisficing behaviour that is based around government officials and policy experts that leads to a change in the "levels (or settings) of the basic instruments of. . . policy" (Hall, 1993, p. 279). Second-order change is characterised by the selection of new policy instruments and techniques and policy settings due to previous policy experience but the overarching policy goals remain the same. Second-order change is therefore more strategic in form although officials and policy experts still remain relatively isolated from external political pressures. According to Greener (2001) this order of change is far more significant for policy learning than what Hall (1993) had suggested. Third-order change, or a policy paradigm shift, takes place when a new goal hierarchy is adopted by policymakers because the coherence of existing policy paradigm(s) has been undermined. This occurs "Where experiment and perceived policy failure has resulted in discrepancies or inconsistencies appearing which cannot be explained within the existing paradigm" (Greener, 2001, p. 135) and its set of institutional norms that support particular kinds of values and goals (Bernstein, 2002). In situations where existing institutions and policies cease to be relevant to policy problems, policy failure may also lead the state to search for policy advice outside of previous internal and external sources, including academia, think tanks and non-government organizations (Pierre & Peters, 2000).

For paradigm shifts to be sustained, the promotion of sympathetic individuals to key positions within government agencies, changes in the composition of advisory bodies and the development of new sets of institutional arrangements are necessary. This is what Hall (1993, p. 280) described as "significant shifts in the locus of authority over policy". This order of change is also similar to what May (1992) described as "social policy learning" in which the policy elites of a specific policy domain undertake the social construction of a policy. According to May (1992, p. 337)

> The foci are the policy problem itself, the scope of policy, or policy goals. . . . The process of social construction is the central component of this definition of social learning. The objects of social construction are beliefs about cause and effect. . . preferences concerning desired policy outcomes, perceptions of policy targets, and beliefs about the policy ideas that undergird policies.

As Greener (2001) observes, the resemblance between May and Peter Hall's approaches is "striking". The social policy learning of May is equivalent to Peter Hall's third-order change, while "political learning" concerns "strategies for advocating policy ideas or drawing attention to policy problems" (May, 1992, p. 339); and "instrumental learning" relates to "new understandings about the viability of policy interventions or implementation designs" (May, 1992, p. 335), and is comparable to first- and second-order change. Furthermore, May (1992), drawing on the advocacy coalition framework of Sabatier (1988), also highlights the way that policymaking is socially constructed within policy networks. Similarly, Hall (1993) comments

> Organised interests, political parties and policy experts do not simply "exert power"; they acquire power in part by trying to influence the political discourse of their day. To the degree that they are able to do so, they may have a major impact on policy without necessarily acquiring the formal trappings of influence. The resultant flow of ideas is an important dimension of the process in which policy is made. (Hall, 1993, p. 290).

Although in re-analysing Hall's (1993) suggestion with respect to the relationships between networks and third-order change, Pemberton (2000, p. 789) argues that policy networks are better understood as "a particularly important intermediate variable". Noting, in a manner similar to Kooiman's (2003) concept of meta- or third-order governance, that although policy change was brought about by learning in policy networks, such networks are also shaped by changes in the policy environment as part of a recursive policy process (Pemberton, 2003).

The relative complexities of policy problems and the required order of change are therefore related to different types of learning. May's understanding of policy learning is significant as it suggests the possibility of policy learning occurring "without a paradigm shift that is, the social construction of a policy changing without its replacement" (Greener, 2001, p. 137). This can occur if political learning does not occur in tandem with conceptual learning. For example, if the proponents of alternative social constructions of a policy problem and its solution are unable to implement their ideas because of insufficient political capital (Bourdieu, 1998), political resources or power within a policy network (Hall, 1999; Pemberton, 2000, 2003), and/or set of governance structures (Papadopoulos, 2007). Power in this sense reflects the definition of Deutsch (1963, p. 111) as "the ability to talk instead of listen. In a sense, it is the ability to afford not to learn".

Sustainable tourism and policy learning

What then does policy learning and the different orders of change potentially suggest with respect to sustainable tourism? Although the concept of sustainable development has been described as "as the central challenge of our times" (Wheeler, 2002, p. 110), its impact on policy and governance has arguably been one of incremental rather than paradigmatic change and has often been associated with an issue-attention cycle (Downs, 1972; Hall,

2002). Indeed, the antecedents of sustainable development extend back well over a hundred years in western economic and environmental thought with respect to the notion of economic conservation (Hall, 1998).

In tourism policy terms, sustainability is primarily seen as being "environmental" and development as "economic" (and to a lesser extent "social") and the concept of sustainable tourism or sustainable tourism development aims to mitigate the paradox between them (Hall, 2008, 2009a; Saarinen, 2006; Swarbrooke, 1999). Baeten (2000) argues that, as portrayed via government and supranational institutions, the sustainable development concept suggests that contemporary economic development paradigms are able to cope with environmental crisis without fundamentally affecting existing economic relationships. This approach is conveyed at various scales of governance (e.g. Czech, 2008; Gössling & Hall, 2008), but is perhaps most widely accessible in the work of extremely influential supranational organizations in international tourism policy networks such as the World Economic Forum (2009a, 2009b), the UNWTO (2002, 2007b) and the WTTC (2003, 2009). For example, the UNEP and the UNWTO (2005) publication *Making Tourism More Sustainable: Guide for Policy Makers* was described by Eugenio Yunis, UNWTO Head of sustainable development of tourism as "applicable world-wide. It is a 'bible' for all decision-makers who are encouraged to be actively involved in the development of an environmentally and socially responsible tourism which creates long term economic benefits for the businesses and destinations" (Yunis, 2006, p. 2). The UNEP and the UNWTO (2005) argue that the concept of sustainable development has evolved since the 1987 Brundtland definition:

Three dimensions or "pillars" of sustainable development are now recognised and underlined. These are:

• Economic sustainability, which means generating prosperity at different levels of society and addressing the cost effectiveness of all economic activity. Crucially, it is about the viability of enterprises and activities and their ability to be maintained in the long term.

• Social sustainability, which means respecting human rights and equal opportunities for all in society. It requires an equitable distribution of benefits, with a focus on alleviating poverty. There is an emphasis on local communities, maintaining and strengthening their life support systems, recognizing and respecting different cultures and avoiding any form of exploitation.

• Environmental sustainability, which means conserving and managing resources, especially those that are not renewable or are precious in terms of life support. It requires action to minimize pollution of air, land and water, and to conserve biological diversity and natural heritage.

It is important to appreciate that these three pillars are in many ways interdependent and can be both mutually reinforcing and in competition. *Delivering sustainable development means striking a balance between them.* (UNEP & UNWTO, 2005, p. 9, author's italics)

The UNEP and the UNWTO (2005, p. 71) identified a number of instruments and indicators "that governments can use to influence the sustainability of tourism". A number of the proposed indicators included information that was potentially already collected such as levels of tourism. However, information with respect to the state of the environment and society may constitute a new set of policy indicators. The introduction of new policy indicators may potentially demonstrate that a change is taking place in the policymakers' worldview, and therefore represent either a first- or second-order change. However, when new policy instruments are not adopted, but alternative measures are instead developed that demonstrate that existing policies are working, or which help policymakers get better feedback on the success or otherwise of their polices even when the old indicators seem to be implying otherwise, then change is only of the first order (Greener, 2001, p.138). Although given that policy indicators are a social construction (Callon, 1998; May, 1992; Peters, 2005), when it occurs alongside political learning, their change may also be a "symptom of possible future paradigm change, or at least present paradigm dissatisfaction" (Greener, 2001, p. 139).

The selection of policy indicators is not a neutral device. "Imposing the rules of the game, that is to say, the rules used to calculate decisions, by imposing the tools in which these rules are incorporated, is the starting point of relationships of domination" (Callon, 1998, p. 46) not only between institutions, but also of one policy paradigm over another. Similarly, Majone (1989, pp. 116 – 117) stressed that "policy instruments are seldom ideologically neutral. . . distributionally neutral. . . [and] . . .cannot be neatly separated from goals" and instead tend to reflect the values of the policy paradigms within which they are selected. "The performance of instruments depends less on their formal properties than on the political and administrative context in which they operate" (Majone, 1989, p. 118). Majone states that

> The choice of policy instruments is not a technical problem that can be safely left to experts. It raises institutional, social, and moral issues that must be clarified. . . . The naive faith of some analysts in the fail-safe properties of certain instruments allegedly capable of lifting the entire regulatory process out of the morass of public debate and compromise can only be explained by the constraining hold on their minds of a model of policymaking in which decisions are, in James Buchanan's words, "handed down from on high by omniscient beings who cannot err" (Majone, 1989, p. 143).

In the case of the UNWTO policy recommendations, as well as those of many other supranational, national and destination governance bodies, one of the cornerstones of the sustainable tourism policy paradigm is that of "balance" (Hall, 1994, 2010a; Hunter, 2002; Mercer, 2000; Wall, 1997). For example, according to the then UNWTO Secretary-General Francesco Frangialli, the UNWTO is "committed to seek balanced and equitable policies to encourage both responsible energy related consumption as well as anti-poverty operational patterns. This can and must lead to truly sustainable growth within the framework of the Millennium Development Goals" (UNWTO, 2007a). Similarly, the Northern Ireland Tourist Board (2009) state that "The term Sustainable Tourism was conceived and adopted at the World Earth Summit in 2002 and has provided a platform for propelling the importance of a balance between the economic, environmental and socio-cultural aspects of tourism".

Yet what does balance mean? Perhaps one of the best statements can be found in an editorial in *The Ecologist* which referred to an inquiry undertaken by the British Independent Television Commission in 1998 with respect to an attack on the environmental movement in a Channel Four television programme "Against Nature", first shown in the United Kingdom in November and December 1997. In the programme's defence, Michael Jackson, Chief Executive of Channel Four, wrote "The small but significant group of people who hold views opposed to the environmental lobby have rarely been seen on British television" (quoted in Edwards, 1998, p. 201). In response *The Ecologist* editorial stated: "Jackson's view is the norm for a culture in which business dominance is so total, so normal, that any challenges to that domination are seen as 'biased' and 'strange', requiring immediate balance" (Edwards, 1998, p. 201). The centrality of continued economic growth in conceptualising sustainable tourism is also a theme in much academic writing on the subject. For example, Edgell (2006, p. 24) states that, "For sustainable tourism to be successful, long-term policies that balance environmental, social, and economic issues must be fashioned" with his book preface noting that it "stresses that positive sustainable tourism development is dependent on forward-looking policies and new management philosophies that seek harmonious relations between local communities, the private sector, not-for-profit organizations, academic institutions, and governments at all levels to develop practices that protect natural, built, and cultural environments *in a way compatible with economic growth*" (2006, p. xiii) (this author's emphasis).

Yet the continuing contribution of a growing tourism industry to environmental change (Table 3) raises a clear question as to whether sustainable tourism can actually be achieved via a so-called "balanced" approach that seeks to continue to promote economic growth. For example, even the highly conservative World Economic Forum (2009a) estimate that CO_2 emissions from tourism (excluding aviation) will grow at 2.5% per year until 2035 with annual increases in carbon emissions from aviation growing at about 2.7%. The International Air Transport Association (2010) forecasts 16 billion air travellers by 2050, although noting "Today's jet fuel cannot sustain air transport in the long-term. We must find a sustainable alternative and our most promising opportunity is bio fuels, which have the potential to reduce our carbon footprint by up to 80%". The notion that you can promote international tourism as a means of alleviating poverty while simultaneously reducing tourism's contribution to climate change is also increasingly criticised (Gössling, Hall, & Scott, 2009; Hall, 2007a, 2010a), given that there is clear evidence that there is not a simple and predictable relationship between pollution and per capita income so that as incomes or GDP rise the level of pollution and biodiversity loss declines (the so-called environmental Kuznets curve) (Czech et al., 2005; Dirtz & Adger, 2003; Mills & Waite, 2009; Mozumder et al., 2006; Stern, 2004).

In economic policy terms Hood (1994, p. 68) observed that social and economic factors cause anomalies with policy until "the conditions which it requires no longer exist" (see also May, 1992). Could the same also be the case with respect to sustainable tourism? For example, even though the UNEP and the UNWTO (2005) promote the voluntary *Guidelines on Biodiversity and Tourism Development* of the *Convention on Biological Diversity* (Secretariat of the Convention on Biological Diversity [CBD], 2004), the reality is that few countries have implemented them (Hall, 2010c). This is despite them being developed "in order to promote sustainable tourism" which "has the potential to reconcile economic and environmental concerns and give a practical meaning to sustainable development", and them being "a tangible tool in keeping with the commitment of Parties to focus on the practical implementation of the Convention and the target to achieve, by 2010, a significant reduction in the current rate of biodiversity loss, which is at the heart of the Convention's strategic plan" (Hamdallah Zedan, Executive Secretary Convention on Biological Diversity, in Secretariat of the CBD, 2004, p. 1). Instead, the Secretariat of the CBD (2010, p. 9) note that the target agreed by the world's Governments "'to achieve by 2010 a significant reduction of the current rate of biodiversity loss at the global, regional and national level as a contribution to poverty alleviation and to the benefit of all life on Earth', has not been met. There are multiple indications of continuing decline in biodiversity in all three of its main components – genes, species and ecosystems". Furthermore, the five principal pressures directly driving biodiversity loss – habitat change, overexploitation, pollution, invasive alien species and climate change – and to which tourism is a significant contributor (Hall, 2010e), "are either constant or increasing in intensity... The ecological footprint of humanity exceeds the biological capacity of the Earth by a wider margin than at the time the 2010 target was agreed" (Secretariat of the CBD, 2010, p. 9).

In such circumstances, Greener (2001, p.140) notes, "policymakers may well realise that existing policy is not working, but be afraid of the political implications of appearing to learn from the error". For example, the fourth UNEP *Global Environment Outlook* report (2007, p. 159) identified that "Biodiversity loss continues because current policies and economic systems do not incorporate the values of biodiversity effectively in either the political or the market systems, and many current policies are not fully implemented". Nevertheless, the voluntary, market-oriented instruments of the dominant paradigm of sustainable tourism and sustainability have remained little affected. May (1992) and Greener (2001) observe that this is because if instruments were substantially changed policymakers could then be accused of making a policy "U-turn" and abandoning their values.

Nevertheless, there is clearly the development of an alternative ecological economic or "degrowth" perspective with respect to sustainability and sustainable tourism that seeks to provide a different paradigm from the so-called "balanced" approach to sustainable development (Gössling, Hall, Lane, & Weaver, 2008; Hall, 2009a, 2010a). Fundamental to this alternative articulation of sustainable development is the centrality of the need to conserve natural capital. Hall (2010a, p. 137) suggests that "much tourism growth, as with much economic growth in general, is already uneconomic at the present margin as we currently measure it given that it is leading to a clear running down of natural capital". As Daly (2008, p. 2) commented in a report to the UK Sustainable Development Commission:

> The growth economy is failing. In other words, the quantitative expansion of the economic subsystem increases environmental and social costs faster than production benefits, making us poorer not richer, at least in high-consumption countries. Given the laws of diminishing marginal utility and increasing marginal costs, this should not have been unexpected.

Hall (2009a) argues that sustainable tourism needs to be understood from a steady-state economic perspective that explicitly recognises the extent to which economic development, including tourism, is dependent on the stock of natural capital. Steady state tourism is a tourism system that encourages qualitative development but not aggregate quantitative growth to the detriment of natural capital (Hall, 2010a). A steady state economy, including at the destination level, can therefore be defined in terms of "a constant flow of throughput at a sustainable (low) level, with population and capital stock free to adjust to whatever size can be maintained by the constant throughput beginning with depletion and ending with pollution" (Daly, 2008, p. 3). Such an approach focuses on economic sufficiency as well as economic efficiency. The sufficiency approach aims to slow the rate and amount of consumption via a mix of market and regulatory mechanisms. The focus on time in much of the sufficiency literature has meant the approach is often related to the notion of "slow" consumption as well as the concept of "décroissance", "degrowth" or "slow tourism" (Flipo & Schneider, 2008; Hall, 2009a; Martínez-Alier, Pascual, Vivien, & Zaccai, 2010). Elements of such an approach in tourism policy terms include (Hall, 2007b, 2010a):

- The development of voluntary and mandated environmental standards at various scales of governance;
- The adoption of cradle-to-cradle lifecycle analysis in determining tourism infrastructure and product life spans;
- Relocalisation schemes that reinforce the potential economic, social and environmental benefits of consuming, producing and travelling locally;
- Ethical consumption measures that focus on living better by consuming less and the satisfaction of non-material needs; and
- Taxation and other measures that reflect the full environmental cost of travel and tourism development.

The necessity of such measures is perhaps also beginning to be recognised in "official" documents of lead organizations involved in sustainability. For example, the Secretariat of the CBD (2010, p. 12) state "The real benefits of biodiversity, and the costs of its loss, need to be reflected within economic systems and markets". The establishment of the Sustainable Development Commission in the United Kingdom in 2000 was also perhaps an indication of the need to articulate alternative expert policy advice. However, when a new hierarchy of policy goals is being adopted, the framework of ideas which becomes dominant is not necessarily the most technically coherent. Instead, with respect to the idea of political learning and its relationship to paradigm change, it will be the one whose supporters are best politically able to implement it despite opposition. As Greener (2001, p. 136) notes, "Politicians have the most influence over the final choice of goals, but they must mobilise popular support within the media and public to carry the electorate with them". One potential driver for change in policy paradigms is the influence of exogenous shocks or "crises" on the wider public of policy (Hall, 1993; Hall, 2010b). Greener, along with May (1992) and Hall (1993), emphasised that, "The oil price and currency shocks of the early 1970s helped create hostile economic conditions which made it possible for advocates of monetarism to question the ability of Keynesians to run the economy" (Greener, 2001, p. 136). In the same way the combined pressures of biodiversity loss, climate change and peak oil as well as other elements of environmental change might contribute to a policy paradigm change with respect to sustainability and sustainable tourism.

Conclusion

This paper has set out to relate the relevance of the concept of policy learning and policy failure to our understanding of the policy domain of sustainable tourism and consequent change. Drawing primarily on the work of May (1992) and Greener (2001), it has highlighted that policy learning within policy domains takes different forms ranging from instrumental learning through to conceptual and political learning. It has also sought to connect the different levels of policy problems to the different orders of policy learning (Hall, 1993).

It has been argued that most sustainable tourism policy learning, as well as academic work on sustainable tourism, is primarily focused on the setting of policy instruments and/or indicators and therefore constitutes only first order change. Or, where there has been change to policy instruments, this has occurred within the existing policy paradigm of "balanced" sustainable development (second-order change). These measures have been evidenced with respect to the work of some of the key institutional actors in tourism policy networks, such as the UNEP, UNWTO, WEF and WTTC. However, such an approach is also to be found at various levels of government (e.g. Department for Culture, Media and Sport Tourism Division [UK], 2005; Hawaii Department of Business, Economic Development and Tourism, 2005). It has also highlighted that there is a developing alternative paradigm of sustainability and sustainable tourism variously described as "de-growth", "slow" or "steady-state" tourism (Hall, 2007b, 2009a) and has posited that environmentally related exogenous pressures on public perceptions of policies may influence policy paradigm change or reorientation towards the alternative paradigm (see also Heinberg, 2007; Zhao, Feng, & Hall, 2009).

Nevertheless, such third-order change is by no means guaranteed. Indeed, the announcement in July 2010 by the UK coalition government that it would withdraw its funding from the Sustainable Development Commission despite Prime Minister Cameron pledging to be the "greenest government ever" (Bevins, 2010) and the Commission having "delivered efficiency savings totalling many times what the organisation has cost the Government, and contributed towards much greater sustainability in Government – both in the way it runs itself, and the decisions it makes about our wellbeing and our future" (Sustainable

Development Commission, 2010), only reinforces the difficulties of achieving fundamental change. As discussed above, May's (1992) notion of policy learning is significant as it highlights the possibility of policy learning occurring without a paradigm shift as a result of political rather than conceptual learning. This is particularly likely to happen when the holders of the alternative policy paradigm do not have sufficient political capital, political resources or power within a policy network. Arguably this has already happened with respect to the articulation of an alternative development paradigm. In the late 1960s and early 1970s as a result of oil and other environmental shocks substantial concerns were expressed with respect to an overconcentration in government policies on economic growth without consideration of the limits of natural resources (e.g. Daly, 1974; Meadows, Meadow, Randers, & Behrens, 1972; Mishan, 1967). These were also discussed with respect to the implications of tourism and travel. For example, Mishan (1970) in concluding his evaluation of the Commission on the Third London Airport commented

> ... equity is wholly ignored. If indeed, the business tycoons and the Mallorca holiday-makers are shown to benefit, after paying their fares, to such an extent that they could more than compensate the victims of aircraft spillover, the cost-benefit criterion is met. But compensation is not paid. The former continue to enjoy the profit and the pleasure; the latter continue to suffer the disamenities (Mishan, 1970, p. 234).

Similarly, in an article entitled "slow is beautiful" Gleditsch (1975) noted, "the severe environmental problems involved in an unlimited or uncontrolled further growth in aviation" (1975, p. 91) as well as the uneven structure of personal mobility. In a prescient observation of what would now be described as the "hypermobile" (Gössling, Ceron, Dubios, & Hall, 2009), Gleditsch (1975, p. 91) "hypothesized ... that topdogs will secure a disproportionately high share of the advantages and a disproportionately low share of the disadvantages of any new transportation system. ... With resources such as education and income, topdogs are in a position to make use of new transportation technology – and avoid its cost".

The above comments suggest that the alternative policy paradigm for sustainable tourism is a continuation of previous critiques of a public policy focus on economic growth at the expense of environmental and social concerns. However they also suggest that, some 40 years on, an alternative policy paradigm has failed to make significant policy headway. The degree of policy failure with respect to conservation of natural capital is considerable but it has not yet been matched by an accompanying conceptual policy change that removes the focus on economic growth and the market.

Significant issues also remain with respect to the relationship between orders of change and scales of governance. As Dovers (2005, p. 167) notes, "the issue of spatial scale is deeply recurrent in sustainability and deserves closer attention". This paper has tended to concentrate on examples of the dominance of the "balanced growth" paradigm of sustainable tourism and sustainable development at the international/supranational scale but it is something that permeates all levels of governance in tourism. Within the public policy and governance of sustainable development literature the notion of subsidiarity has become quite significant (e.g. Kemp, Parto, & Gibson, 2005), whereby "responsibility should be located at the lowest level of government in terms of effectiveness and appropriateness for the function in question" (Dovers, 2005, p. 167). This has often been interpreted as the region being the optimal scale for sustainable management (Roberts, 2006), particularly in terms of the capacity to develop greater policy integration; common objectives, criteria, trade-off rules and indicators; information and incentives for practical implementation and system innovation (Kemp et al., 2005).

However, while regions are the ideal basis for sustainable adaptive management and innovation (Hall & Williams, 2008), or even being "islands of sustainability" that "can be seen as 'trouble makers' which infiltrate the whole unsustainable system and act as cells of development" (Wallner, Narodoslawsky, & Moser, 1996, p. 1763), they remain framed by national and supranational institutions and regulation. This means that while the old adage to "think globally, act locally" is undoubtedly integral to sustainability, the macro-policy global nature of many environmental and economic problems (see Table 3) also necessitates the development of a global institutional and regulatory superstructure. Yet while this superstructure remains wedded to assumptions based on the compatibility between the environment and economic growth and acceptance of market forces the development of steady-state perspective on sustainability remains all the more problematic (Demerritt, 2006; Gareau, 2008; Igoe, Neves, & Brockington, 2010; MacDonald, 2010). As Bernstein (2002, p. 2) notes, "the institutions that have developed in response to global environmental problems support particular kinds of values and goals, with important implications for the constraints and opportunities to combat the world's most serious environmental problems".

Undoubtedly, from a steady-state perspective paradigm change is something that is required at all levels. However, in order to achieve change the norms that are central to all governance structures need to undergo a substantial shift. Far too much attention has been given to the assumption that a well-designed institution is "good" because it facilitates cooperation and network development rather than a focus on norms and institutionalisation as first and necessary steps in the assessment of what kind of changes institutional arrangements are promoting and their potential outcomes. As this paper has suggested, such an approach has only reinforced first- and second-order change rather than conceptual policy learning.

> ...the consequence is that liberal environmentalism has resulted in enabling certain kinds of responses to global environmental problems consistent with it, such as possibilities for the privatization of environmental governance in some areas or the increasing use of market mechanisms. But at the same time it has made trade offs much more difficult because it denies that they may be necessary among values of efficiency, economic growth, corporate freedom, and environmental protection (Bernstein, 2002, p. 14).

Nevertheless, it is the growing awareness of the contradictions in, and policy failure of, liberal environmentalism that may also offer an opportunity for third-order change.

The role of policy failure and learning with respect to sustainable tourism policy and governance issues in relation to first- and second-order change is important and clearly warrants further study. However, any understanding of the potential for third-order change needs to be grounded in research of the interrelationships between power, values, norms and interests and how they influence the selection of policy instruments, indicators and settings within broader frames of governance and change.

Acknowledgements

With acknowledgements to the Fijian Ministry of Provincial Development and Multi-ethnic Affairs, National Disaster Management and Sugar and the Fiji Police Force for permission to present a public lecture based on this paper at the University of the South Pacific; and to the helpful comments of the reviewers.

References

Argyris, C. (1992). *On organizational learning*. Oxford: Blackwell.
Baeten, G. (2000). The tragedy of the highway: Empowerment, disempowerment and the politics of sustainability discourses and practices. *European Planning Studies, 8*, 69–86.
Bennett, C.J., & Howlett, M. (1992). The lessons of learning: Reconciling theories of policy learning and policy change. *Policy Sciences, 25*, 275–294.
Bernstein, S. (2002). Liberal environmentalism and global environmental governance. *Global Environmental Politics, 2*(3), 1–16.
Bevins, V. (2010, May 14). Cameron promises "greenest government ever". Lib Dem climate secretary Chris Huhne will oversee 10% central government emissions reductions this year. *Guardian.co.uk*, Retrieved 14 May, 2010, from http://www.guardian.co.uk/sustainable-business/5
Bourdieu, P. (1998). *Practical reason: On the theory of action*. Cambridge: Polity.
Bramwell, B., & Lane, B. (1993). Sustainable tourism: An evolving global approach. *Journal of Sustainable Tourism, 1*, 1–5.
Brody, S.D. (2003). Are we learning to make better plans? A longitudinal analysis of plan quality associated with natural hazards. *Journal of Planning Education and Research, 23*, 191–201.
Busenberg, G.J. (2001). Learning in organizations and public policy. *Journal of Public Policy, 21*, 173–189.
Butler, R.W. (1991). Tourism, environment and sustainable development. *Environmental Conservation, 18*, 201–209.
Callon, M. (1998). Introduction: The embeddedness of economic markets in economics. In M. Callon (Ed.), *The laws of the markets* (pp. 1–57). Oxford: Blackwell.
Czech, B. (2008). Prospects for reconciling the conflict between economic growth and biodiversity conservation with technological progress. *Conservation Biology, 22*, 1389–1398.
Czech, B., Trauger, D.L., Farley, J., Costanza, R., Daly, H., Hall, C.S., et al. (2005). Establishing indicators for biodiversity. *Science, 308*(6), 791–792.
Daly, H.E. (1974). The economics of the steady state. *American Economic Review, 64*(2), 15–21.
Daly, H.E. (2008). *A steady-state economy*. London: Sustainable Development Commission.
Demeritt, D. (2006). Science studies, climate change and the prospects for constructivist critique. *Economy and Society, 35*, 453–479.
Department for Culture, Media and Sport Tourism Division. (2005). *National sustainable tourism indicators. Getting it right: Monitoring progress towards sustainable tourism in England*. London: Author.
Department of Resources, Energy and Tourism. (2008). *National long term tourism strategy*. Canberra: Author.
Deutsch, K. (1963). *The nerves of government: Models of political communication and control*. New York: Free Press.
Dirtz, S., & Adger, W.N. (2003). Economic growth, biodiversity loss and conservation effort. *Journal of Environmental Management, 68*, 23–35.
Dolowitz, D., & Marsh, D. (1996). Who learns what from whom: A review of the policy transfer literature. *Political Studies, 44*, 343–357.
Dovers, S. (1995). A framework for scaling and framing policy problems in sustainability. *Ecological Economics, 12*, 93–106.
Dovers, S. (1996). Sustainability: Demands on policy. *Journal of Public Policy, 16*, 303–318.
Dovers, S. (2005). *Environment and sustainability policy: Creation, implementation, evaluation*. Sydney: Federation Press.
Dovers, S.R., & Handmer, J.W. (1992). Uncertainty, sustainability and change. *Global Environmental Change, 2*, 262–276.
Downs, A. (1972). Up and down with ecology: The issue attention cycle. *The Public Interest, 28*, 38–50.
Edgell, D.L., Sr. (2006). *Managing sustainable tourism: A legacy for the future*. Binghamption: Haworth Press.

Edwards, D. (1998). Learning to think the right thoughts: "Channel One". *The Ecologist, 28*, 201–203.

Ehrlich, P.R. (1994). Energy use and biodiversity loss. *Philosophical Transactions: Biological Sciences, 344*(1307), 99–104.

Fiorino, D. (2001). Environmental policy as learning: A new view of an old landscape. *Public Administration Review, 61*, 322–334.

Flipo, F., & Schneider, F. (Eds.). (2008). *Proceedings of the first international conference on economic de-growth for ecological sustainability and social equity*, Paris, 18–19 April 2008. Paris.

Freeman, R. (2006). Learning in public policy. In M. Moran, M. Rein, & R.E. Goodin (Eds.), *The Oxford handbook of public policy* (pp. 367–388). Oxford: Oxford University Press.

Gareau, B.J. (2008). Dangerous holes in global environmental governance: The roles of neoliberal discourse, science, and California agriculture in the Montreal Protocol. *Antipode, 40*, 120–130.

Gleditsch, N.P. (1975). Slow is beautiful. The stratification of personal mobility, with special reference to international aviation. *Acta Sociologica, 18*(1), 76–94.

Gössling, S. (2002). Global environmental consequences of tourism. *Global Environmental Change, 12*, 283–302.

Gössling, S., Ceron, J-P., Dubois, G., & Hall, C.M. (2009). Hypermobile travellers. In S. Gössling & P. Upham (Eds.), *Climate change and aviation* (pp. 131–149). London: Earthscan.

Gössling, S., & Hall, C.M. (Eds.). (2006). *Tourism and global environmental change*. London: Routledge.

Gössling, S., & Hall, C.M. (2008). Swedish tourism and climate change mitigation: An emerging conflict? *Scandinavian Journal of Hospitality and Tourism, 8*(2), 141–158.

Gössling, S., Hall, C.M., Lane, B., & Weaver, D. (2008). The Helsingborg Statement on sustainable tourism. *Journal of Sustainable Tourism, 16*, 122–124.

Gössling, S., Hall, C.M., Peeters, P., & Scott, D. (2010). The future of tourism: Can tourism growth and climate policy be reconciled? A climate change mitigation perspective. *Tourism Recreation Research, 35*(2), 119–130.

Gössling, S., Hall, C.M., & Scott, D. (2009). The challenges of tourism as a development strategy in an era of global climate change. In E. Palosou (Ed.), *Rethinking development in a carbon-constrained world. Development cooperation and climate change* (pp. 100–119). Helsinki: Ministry of Foreign Affairs.

Gössling, S., Hall, C.M., & Weaver, D. (2009). *Sustainable tourism futures: Perspectives on systems, restructuring and innovations*. New York: Routledge.

Greener, I. (2001). Social learning and macroeconomic policy in Britain. *Journal of Public Policy, 21*, 133–152.

Grin, J., & Loeber, A. (2007). Theories of policy learning: Agency, structure and change. In F. Fischer, G.J. Miller, & M.S. Sidney (Eds.), *Handbook of public policy analysis: Theory, politics, and methods* (pp. 201–219). Boca Raton: CRC Press.

Hall, C.M. (1994). *The politics of tourism*. Chichester: John Wiley.

Hall, C.M. (1998). Historical antecedents of sustainable development and ecotourism: New labels on old bottles? In C.M. Hall & A. Lew (Eds.), *Sustainable tourism development: Geographical perspectives* (pp. 13–24). London: Addison-Wesley Longman.

Hall, C.M. (1999). Rethinking collaboration and partnership: A public policy perspective. *Journal of Sustainable Tourism, 7*, 274–289.

Hall, C.M. (2002). Travel safety, terrorism and the media: The significance of the issue-attention cycle. *Current Issues in Tourism, 5*, 458–466.

Hall, C.M. (2007a). Pro-poor tourism: Do "tourism exchanges benefit primarily the countries of the South"? *Current Issues in Tourism, 10*, 111–118.

Hall, C.M. (2007b, September 11–14). *The possibilities of slow tourism: Can the slow movement help develop sustainable forms of tourism consumption?* Paper presented at Achieving Sustainable Tourism, Helsingborg, Sweden. Retrieved from http://canterbury-nz.academia.edu/CMichaelHall/attachment/509730/full/The-Possibilities-of-Slow-Tourism-Can-the-Slow-Movement-Help-Develop-Sustainable-Forms-of-Consumption-

Hall, C.M. (2008). *Tourism planning* (2nd ed.). London: Prentice-Hall.

Hall, C.M. (2009a). Degrowing tourism: Décroissance, sustainable consumption and steady-state tourism. *Anatolia: An International Journal of Tourism and Hospitality Research, 20*(1), 46–61.

Hall, C.M. (2009b). Archetypal approaches to implementation and their implications for tourism policy. *Tourism Recreation Research, 34*, 235–245.

Hall, C.M. (2010a). Changing paradigms and global change: From sustainable to steady-state tourism. *Tourism Recreation Research, 35*(2), 131–145.

Hall, C.M. (2010b). Crisis events in tourism: Subjects of crisis in tourism. *Current Issues in Tourism, 13*, 401–417.

Hall, C.M. (2010c). Implementation of the convention on biological diversity guidelines on biodiversity and tourism development. *Journal of Heritage Tourism, 5*(4), 267–284.

Hall, C.M. (2010d). An island biogeographical approach to island tourism and biodiversity: An exploratory study of the Caribbean and Pacific Islands. *Asia Pacific Journal of Tourism Research, 15*(3), 383–399.

Hall, C.M. (2010e). Tourism and biodiversity: More significant than climate change? *Journal of Heritage Tourism, 5*(4), 253–266.

Hall, C.M. (2010f). Politics and tourism: Interdependency and implications in understanding change. In R. Butler & W. Suntikul (Eds.), *Tourism and political change* (pp. 7–18). Oxford: Goodfellow Publishers.

Hall, C.M., James, M., & Wilson, S. (2010). Biodiversity, biosecurity, and cruising in the Arctic and sub-Arctic. *Journal of Heritage Tourism, 5*(4), 351–364.

Hall, C.M., & Lew, A.A. (Eds.). (1998). *Sustainable tourism. A geographical perspective*. London: Addison Wesley Longman.

Hall, C.M., & Lew, A.A. (2009). *Understanding and managing tourism impacts: An integrated approach*. London: Routledge.

Hall, C.M., & Williams, A. (2008). *Tourism and innovation*. London: Routledge.

Hall, C.M. (in press). Biosecurity, tourism and mobility: Institutional arrangements for managing biological invasions. *Journal of Policy Research in Tourism, Leisure and Events*.

Hall, P.A. (1989). Conclusion: The political power of economic ideas. In P.A. Hall (Ed.), *The political power of economic ideas: Keynesianism across nations* (pp. 361–392). Princeton: Princeton University Press.

Hall, P.A. (1993). Policy paradigms, social learning, and the state: The case of economic policymaking in Britain. *Comparative Politics, 25*, 275–296.

Hall, P.A., & Taylor, R.C.R. (1996). Political science and the three new institutionalisms. *Political Studies, 44*, 936–957.

Hawaii Department of Business, Economic Development and Tourism. (2005). *Planning for sustainable tourism*. Honolulu: Author.

Head, L. (2008). Is the concept of human impacts past its use-by date? *The Holocene, 18*, 373–377.

Heinberg, R. (2007). *Peak everything: Waking up to the century of decline in Earth's resources*. Forest Row: Clairview.

Hjalager, A. (1996). Tourism and the environment: The innovation connection. *Journal of Sustainable Tourism, 4*, 201–218.

Hood, C. (1994). *Explaining economic policy reversals*. Buckingham: Open University Press.

Hunter, C. (2002). Aspects of the sustainable tourism debate from a natural resources perspective. In R. Harris, T. Griffin, & P. Williams (Eds.), *Sustainable tourism: A global perspective* (pp. 3–23). Oxford: Butterworth-Heinemann.

Igoe, J., Neves, K., & Brockington, D. (2010). A spectacular eco-tour around the historic bloc: Theorising the convergence of biodiversity conservation and capitalist expansion. *Antipode, 42*, 486–512.

Industry Canada. (2006). *Building a national tourism strategy*. Ottawa: Industry Canada. Retrieved April 1, 2010, from http://www.ic.gc.ca/eic/site/dsib-tour.nsf/eng/h_qq00141.html

International Air Transport Association. (2010, June 7). *Four cornerstones of change–IATA launches vision 2050*. IATA Press Release No. 24. Retrieved from http://www.iata.org/pressroom/pr/Pages/2010-06-07-02.aspx

International Civil Aviation Organization (ICAO). (2009). *Fourth meeting of the Group on International Aviation and Climate Change* (GIACC/4), ICAO Headquarters, Montréal, Canada 25 to 27 May 2009. Retrieved 1 April, 2010, from http://www.icao.int/env/meetings/2009/GIACC_4/GIACC_4.html

International Task Force on Sustainable Tourism Development. (2009). *A three-year journey for sustainable tourism*. Paris: French Ministries of Ecology, Energy, Sustainable Development and the Oceans, UNEP, Sustainable Consumption and Production Marrakech Process.

Kemp, R., Parto, S., & Gibson, R.B. (2005). Governance for sustainable development: Moving from theory to practice. *International Journal of Sustainable Development, 8*, 12–30.

Kerr, W. (2003). *Tourism public policy and the strategic management of failure*. Amsterdam: Pergamon.

Klein, R. (1997). Learning from others: Shall the last be the first? *Journal of Health Politics, Policy and Law, 22*, 1267–1278.

Kooiman, J. (2003). *Governing as governance*. London: Sage.

Lee, D.S., Fahey, D.W., Forster, P.M., Newton, P.J., Wit, R.C.N., Lim, L.L., et al. (2009). Aviation and global climate change in the 21st century. *Atmospheric Environment, 43*, 3520–3537.

MacDonald, K.I. (2010). The devil is in the (bio)diversity: Private sector "engagement" and the restructuring of biodiversity conservation. *Antipode, 42*, 513–550.

Majone, G. (1989). *Evidence, argument and persuasion in the policy process*. New Haven: Yale University Press.

Martínez-Alier, J., Pascual, U., Vivien, F.-D., & Zaccai, E. (2010). Sustainable de-growth: Mapping the context, criticisms and future prospects of an emergent paradigm. *Ecological Economics, 69*, 1741–1747.

May, P.J. (1992). Policy learning and failure. *Journal of Public Policy, 12*, 331–354.

Meadows, D.H., Meadow, D.L., Randers, J., & Behrens, W.W. (1972). *The limits to growth. Report to the Club of Rome*. New York: Universe Books.

Meppem, T., & Gill, R. (1998). Planning for sustainability as a learning concept. *Ecological Economics, 26*, 121–137.

Mercer, D.C. (2000). *A question of balance: Natural resources conflict issues in Australia* (3rd ed.). Leichhardt: The Federation Press.

Michael, E., & Plowman, G. (2002). Mount Stirling: The politics of process failure. *Journal of Sustainable Tourism, 10*, 154–169.

Mills, J.H., & Waite, T.A. (2009). Economic prosperity, biodiversity conservation, and the environmental Kuznets curve. *Ecological Economics, 68*, 2087–2095.

Ministry of Tourism, Tourism New Zealand, and Tourism Industry Association New Zealand. (2007). *New Zealand tourism strategy 2015*. Wellington: Author.

Mintrom, M. (1997). Policy entrepreneurs and the diffusion of innovation. *American Journal of Political Science, 41*, 738–770.

Mintrom, M., & Vergari, S. (1996). Advocacy coalitions, policy entrepreneurs, and policy change. *Policy Studies Journal, 24*, 420–434.

Mishan, E.J. (1967). *The costs of economic growth*. New York: Frederick A. Praeger.

Mishan, E.J. (1970). What is wrong with Roskill? *Journal of Transport Economics and Policy, 4*, 221–234.

Mowforth, M., & Munt, I. (1998). *Tourism and sustainability: Development and new tourism in the Third World*. London: Routledge.

Mozumder, P., Berrens, R.P., & Bohara, A.K. (2006). Is there an environmental Kuznets curve for the risk of biodiversity loss? *The Journal of Developing Areas, 39*(2), 175–190.

Mycoo, M. (2006). Sustainable tourism using regulations, market mechanisms and green certification: A case study of Barbados. *Journal of Sustainable Tourism, 14*, 489–511.

Nilsson, M. (2005). Learning, frames, and environmental policy integration: The case of Swedish energy policy. *Environment and Planning C: Government & Policy, 23*, 207–226.

Northern Ireland Tourist Board. (2009). *Sustainable tourism*. Retrieved April 1, 2010, from http://www.nitb.com/DocumentPage.aspx?path=aedbda88-d741-4bec-b324-36204c735653,b352140e-dc92-4907-b532-7b41573422e5,3aa0946a-3857-4585-a4b3-b97c25823697

Papadopoulos, Y. (2007). Problems of democratic accountability in network and multilevel governance. *European Law Journal, 13*, 469–486.

Pearce, D., Barbier, E., & Markandya, A. (1990). *Sustainable development: Economics and environment in the Third World*. London: Earthscan.

Peeters, P.M., & Middel, J. (2007). Historical and future development of air transport fuel efficiency. In R. Sausen, A. Blum, D.S. Lee, & C. Brüning (Eds.), *Proceedings of an international conference on transport, atmosphere and climate* (pp. 42–47). Luxembourg: Office for Official Publications of the European Communities.

Pemberton, H. (2000). Policy networks and policy learning. UK economic policy in the 1960s and 1970s. *Public Administration, 78*, 771–792.

Pemberton, H. (2003). Learning, governance and economic policy. *British Journal of Politics and International Relations, 5*, 500–524.

Peters, G.B. (2005). The problem of policy problems. *Journal of Comparative Policy Analysis: Research and Practice, 7*, 349–370.

Pierre, J., & Peters, G.B. (2000). *Governance, politics and the state*. London: Palgrave Macmillan.

PricewaterhouseCoopers. (2007). *The automotive industry and climate change: Framework and dynamics of the CO_2 (r)evolution*. Stuttgart: PricewaterhouseCoopers AG.

Roberts, P. (2006). Evaluating regional sustainable development: Approaches, methods and the politics of analysis. *Journal of Environmental Planning and Management, 49*, 515–532.

Rose, R. (1993). *Lesson-drawing in public policy: A guide to learning across time and space*. New Jersey: Chatham House.

Saarinen, J. (2006). Traditions of sustainability in tourism studies. *Annals of Tourism Research, 33*, 1121–1140.

Sabatier, Paul A. (1988). An advocacy coalition framework of policy change and the role of policy-oriented learning therein. *Policy Sciences, 21*, 129–168.

Secretariat of the Convention on Biological Diversity (CBD). (2004). *Guidelines on biodiversity and tourism development*. Montreal: Author.

Secretariat of the Convention on Biological Diversity (CBD). (2010). *Global biodiversity outlook 3*. Montreal: Author.

South Australian Tourism Commission. (2009). *Sustainable tourism package*. Retrieved April 1, 2010, from http://www.tourism.sa.gov.au/tourism/SustainableTourismPackage.asp

Stern, D.I. (2004). The rise and fall of the environmental Kuznets curve. *World Development, 32*, 1419–1439.

Sustainable Development Commission. (2010, July 22). *SDC responds to Defra funding decision*. Retrieved July 22, 2010, from http://www.sd-commission.org.uk/news.php?id=365

Swarbrooke, J. (1999). *Sustinable tourism management*. Wallingford: CABI.

Szarka, J. (2006). Wind power, policy learning and paradigm change. *Energy Policy, 34*, 3041–3048.

Tourism Industry Association of Canada. (2010). *Fast facts on TIAC's advocacy issues: Sustainability*. Retrieved April 1, 2010, from http://www.tiac-aitc.ca/english/advocacy_sustainabletourism.asp

Treuren, G., & Lane, D. (2003). The tourism planning process in the context of organized interests, industry structure, state capacity, accumulation and sustainability. *Current Issues in Tourism, 6*(1), 1–22.

TUI Travel PLC. (2010). *Group sustainable development policy*. Retrieved April 1, 2010, from http://www.tuitravelplc.com/tui/pages/sustainabledevelopment/strategysd/policy

United Nations Environmental Programme (UNEP). (2005a). *Marketing sustainable tourism products*. Paris: United Nations Environment Programme and Region Toscana.

United Nations Environmental Programme (UNEP). (2005b). *Integrating sustainability into business: an implementation guide for responsible tourism coordinators*. Paris: Author.

United Nations Environmental Programme (UNEP). (2005c). *Integrating sustainability into business: management guide for responsible tourism coordinators*. Paris: Author.

United Nations Environmental Programme (UNEP). (2007). *Global environment outlook (GEO-4): Environment for development*. Paris: Author.

United Nations Environmental Programme (UNEP). (2009). *Sustainable coastal tourism. An integrated planning and management approach*. Paris: Author.

United Nations Environmental Programme and the World Tourism Organization (UNEP and UNWTO). (2005). *Making tourism more sustainable: A guide for policy makers*. Paris: United Nations Environmental Programme.

United Nations World Tourism Organization (UNWTO). (2007a). *Tourism will contribute to solutions for global climate change and poverty challenges*, Press release, UNWTO Press and Communications Department, March 8, Berlin/Madrid.

United Nations World Tourism Organization (UNWTO). (2007b). *From Davos to Bali – A tourism contribution to the challenge of climate change, policy document*. Madrid: World Tourism Organization.

United Nations World Tourism Organization (UNWTO). (2010). *Sustainable development of tourism, mission statement*. Retrieved from http://www.world-tourism.org/sdt/mission/en/mission.php

United Nations World Tourism Organization, United Nations Environmental Programme, & World Meteorological Organization (UNWTO, UNEP & WMO). (2008). *Climate change and tourism: Responding to global challenges*. Madrid: Author.

USAID. (2007). *Dominica sustainable tourism policy and marketing strategy. Prepared for the Discover Dominica Authority by Chenmonics International*. Washington, DC: Author.

Vilà, M., & Pujadas, J. (2001). Socio-economic parameters influencing plant invasions in Europe and North Africa. In J.A. McNeely (Ed.), *The great reshuffling: Human dimensions of invasive alien species* (pp. 75–79). Gland: IUCN Biodiversity Policy Coordination Division.

Wall, G. (1997). Sustainable tourism – Unsustainable development. In S. Wahab & J. Pigram (Eds.), *Tourism, development and growth* (pp. 33–49). London: Routledge.

Wallner, H.P., Narodoslawsky, M., & Moser, F. (1996). Islands of sustainability: A bottom-up approach towards sustainable development. *Environment and Planning A, 28,* 1763–1778.

Weaver, D.B. (2006). *Sustainable tourism: Theory and practice.* Oxford: Butterworth-Heinemann.

Wheeller, B. (1993). Sustaining the ego. *Journal of Sustainable Tourism, 1,* 121–129.

Wheeler, S.M. (2002). Constructing sustainable development/safeguarding our common future: Rethinking sustainable development. *Journal of the American Planning Association, 68*(1), 110–111.

World Commission for Environment and Development (WCED). (1987). *Our common future. The Brundtland report.* Oxford: Oxford University Press.

World Economic Forum. (2009a). *Towards a low carbon travel & tourism sector.* Davos: Author.

World Economic Forum. (2009b). *The travel & tourism competitiveness report 2009: Managing in a time of turbulence.* Davos: Author.

World Health Organization (WHO). (2003). *International travel and health.* Geneva: Information Resource Centre Communicable Diseases.

World Travel and Tourism Council (WTTC). (2003). *Blueprint for new tourism.* London: Author.

World Travel and Tourism Council (WTTC). (2009). *Leading the challenge on climate change.* London: Author.

World Travel and Tourism Council (WTTC). (2010, April 21). *Travel and tourism demands 21st century thinking for future sustainability.* Press Release. London: Author.

World Travel & Tourism Council, International Federation of Tour Operators, International Hotel & Restaurant Association, & International Council of Cruise Lines. (2002). *Industry as a partner for sustainable development. Developed through a multi-stakeholder process facilitated by UNEP.* London: World Travel & Tourism Council, International Hotel & Restaurant Association, International Federation of Tour Operators, International Council of Cruise Lines and United Nations Environment Programme.

World Travel & Tourism Council, & International Hotel & Restaurant Association. (1999, April 19–30). *Tourism and sustainable development. The global importance of tourism.* Background Paper #1. Commission on Sustainable Development, Seventh Session. Department of Economic and Social Affairs, New York.

World Tourism Organization (UNWTO). (2002). *Tourism and poverty alleviation.* Madrid: Author.

Yunis, E. (2006, February 3). *12 aims of a sustainable tourism.* Presentation at EcoTrans European network for sustainable tourism development. Making Tourism More Sustainable – helpful instruments and examples of good practice in Europe, Reisepavillon fairgrounds, Hanover, Germany. Retrieved from www.ecotrans.org/docs/1_hamele_Yunis_intro_aims.pdf

Zhao, L., Feng, L., & Hall, C.A.S. (2009). Is peakoilism coming? *Energy Policy, 37,* 2136–2138.

Index

Page numbers in *Italics* represent tables.
Page numbers in **Bold** represent figures.